Gamefowl Breeders Manual
And Cockers Guide

Understanding the Principles of Breeding
and the Laws of Inheritance

Chronicles of Kenny Troiano

Volume Two

GAMEFOWL BREEDERS MANUAL AND COCKERS GUIDE

UNDERSTANDING THE PRINCIPLES OF BREEDING AND THE LAWS OF INHERITANCE

Chronicles of Kenny Troiano

Volume Two

This book is a collection of articles written for the following magazines; "The Gamecock," "The Grit and Steel," and "The Poultry Press." These consist of five years of work covering the basics of breeding American and Old English Games.

The American Gamecock is to the chicken world what the Thoroughbred is to the horse world, a national treasure of great magnificence and a true representative of a high standard of excellence, they give class and elegance to everything they touch.

Written By
Kenny Troiano

With Illustrations and Artwork By
Diane Jacky, Ramon A. Vargas, and Kenny Troiano

Edited By
Nancy Troiano and Megan Troiano

Published by

MAXIMUS TROY PUBLICATIONS

GAMEFOWL BREEDERS MANUAL AND COCKERS GUIDE

UNDERSTANDING THE PRINCIPLES OF BREEDING
AND THE LAWS OF INHERITANCE

Chronicles of Kenny Troiano

Volume Two

*Our Mission is to serve our customers by publishing practical
information that encourages personal growth and independence.*

For additional information please contact

MAXIMUS TROY PUBLICATIONS
P.O. Box 2727,
Ramona, California 92065.
Or visit
www.maximustroypublications.com

Order this book online at www.trafford.com
or email orders@trafford.com

Most Trafford titles are also available at major online book retailers.

Printed in the United States of America.

ISBN: 978-1-4269-6024-6 (sc)

Trafford rev. 03/03/2011

Trafford PUBLISHING® www.trafford.com

North America & international
toll-free: 1 888 232 4444 (USA & Canada)
phone: 250 383 6864 ♦ fax: 812 355 4082

The following is my personal mission statement, which I read and live by every day. It is what motivates me to continue my writing and to produce better articles and books.

My Personal Mission Statement

I have dedicated my life to the preservation and perpetuation of American Games, and to the edification of Cockers and gamefowl enthusiast throughout the world.

Knowledge and skill is the key to success, but only when it is put to good use, that knowledge must be acted upon. Therefore, it is my goal to help advance the lives of my fellow cockers by motivating and improving the overall understanding and ability of the breeding and raising of American Games. By improving the lives of my fellow cockers, American Games will endure these trying times, and survive for future generations.

My promise to you, my fellow cockers, is that I will always strive to provide useful information at every opportunity through my magazine articles, books, seminars and internet interactions, as well as phone calls and letters.

It is my goal that the modern cocker will find peace in a world that only shows them contempt and distain, and that American Gamefowl will earn its proper place in American History and will continue to survive and thrive for future generations.

This book is dedicated to:

My loving wife, Nancy, you are my soul mate. Thank you for walking this amazing path with me and for standing by my side every day. And for teaching me that "Believing is truly Seeing."

This book is also dedicated to my beautiful daughters:
Megan, Samantha, and little Tawny.

As Charles Darwin once said:
"How paramount the future is to the present when one is surrounded by children." Amen!

I want to thank you all for showing me how to be the husband and father I always dreamt of being, you mean everything to me.

I love you all!

ACKNOWLEDGMENTS

I have written a lot of articles, which I hope someday will become books, and lately it seems like I am always writing something or other hoping my work will make a difference in the world. I spend much of my time putting together notes, collecting information, and writing down ideas before I even start writing. Then there's the actual writing. Once I finish writing the individual articles, which become separate chapters of my book, I begin the editing process, and prepare illustrations. The whole endeavor of creating a finished manuscript takes a lot of time, patience, and persistence, but when I see the first printed copies come off the press I feel a wave of satisfaction at a job well done. Although most readers know that books do not just appear out of nowhere, they never see all the sweat and hard work that goes into producing a book.

While I was in the process of writing this book, I suddenly realized all the people who helped make this one a reality. A project such as this is the result of a huge team effort, one that that is equally shared by all. I extend my deepest gratitude and thanks to these very special people in my life:

My wife Nancy, who sustained me with an abundance of encouragement and support, as I embarked on what is now turning out to be a career, writing about American Games and the art of "Selective Breeding." You are my rock and I am deeply grateful for your devotion and help in the editing process.

My daughter Megan, thank you for your devotion to this passion and dream. We share a love for knowledge and I cherish the many moments we spend passing ideas around. Thank you for your help through the editing process.

Anthony and Frances Seville, I couldn't have done it without you. Tony! You are my mentor and friend. You have my sincere thanks and appreciation. You are the first to share with me your knowledge and your love of American and Old English Games. You have been a wonderful inspiration for me and for all who have gained an appreciation or passion for this great hobby.

My good friend, Frank Torres, you are a mentor to me in more ways than

Frank Torres, Anthony (Tony) Saville, and Kenny Troiano.

you know. It is clear that we share the same passion for American Games, and I value our conversations. I highly appreciate all that you have done for me, my family, and for the hobby. I wish we had more cockers like you. I am blessed to have your support and look forward to a long friendship.

Doug Huggins has a wonderful insight in genetics and the inheritance of traits, who is one of my mentors and one of the best breeders I know, a true Master Breeder. He has been a great influence, not only for me, but for many who have read his articles. Thanks for all your help; you have opened my eyes to new and greater possibilities.

J.C. Griffiths and the entire staff at the Gamecock Magazine, for printing and distributing a fine magazine with the usual efficiency that has made your outfit our most important publisher of American Games that we have today. You have printed my articles in a professional manner for all to read. You have also been very accommodating of my ideas, which cater to a highly specialized audience. You gave me a place to express myself and a chance to help others, for that I am grateful.

The Poultry Press, thanks for giving me the opportunity to reach readers outside our hobby. It has always been my hope that American Games would grow in popularity, receive respect, and gain interest throughout the chicken world. You are helping to accomplish just that.

Most of the illustrations in this book are the work of Diane Jacky, whose artistry was made possible by her keen observation, accurate eye, and remarkable knowledge of the structure and conformation of these magnificent birds. Therefore, I wish to acknowledge my deepest gratitude to Diane Jacky, my artist/illustrator. Thank you for the wonderful drawings and illustrations. Your work gives my book imagery and life, and has made this book truly unique and original.

Ramon Vargas, thank you for wanting to be a part of something grand, and providing the great drawings.

My good friend John Cogorno, thank you for your hard work and dedication to the supporters of American Games; cockers and gamefowl enthusiast everywhere. You are another reason why we are able to continue breeding and raising these magnificent birds. Your work has, and always will be instrumental and extremely valuable, not to mention, appreciated in the preservation of American Games. We are lucky that you are one of us!

And last but not least, to all my readers who love American Games everywhere. My ultimate debt is to you. The readers of my articles have encouraged me to write this book. Thank you to my customers who have bought my books, which has allowed me to work full time on a project that has become my life's work, one that I believe is important for the survival of American Games and our way of life.

I would like to thank all of you for supporting my work. Without you there would be no reason for a book such as this. May it be a stepping stone in this great and growing hobby.

John Cogorno and Tony Saville.

FOREWORD
By J.C. Griffiths

This book is the work of a very dedicated person who has spent many, many hours in trying to continue a breed of fowl that was developed and treasured by our forefathers. Included are many color drawings of gamefowl that are as good as any produced in the history of gamefowl. Many of the articles herein are the results of trying to produce a solid and well maintained family of gamecocks to be carried into the future and perhaps save the gamecocks from extinction. Each and every article, if followed will save the breeders of gamecocks many trial and error experiments. Any breeder of gamefowl will find something of interest to help him along with his breeding program. Breeders of gamefowl today are very fortunate to have the works of Kenny Troiano to guide them in the continuing care and breeding selection of their gamefowl.

J.C. Griffiths
(Editor of Gamecock Magazine 2010)

FOREWORD

By Megan Troiano

Megan Troiano

I have to share this short story with you because it expresses my father's nature. This story displays who he is, not only as a father of all girls, but as a person. Not long ago my sister, Tawny, walked into my father's office where he and I often meet to have our discussions. Her little voice interrupted us in mid sentence as she turned to me and asked, "Megan, is dad teaching you about life?" I smile every time I think about that young voice speaking such true words.

"Be like water and find your own version of happiness." These simple words stick with me every day as I strive to follow them within each challenge, each word and each step. These words are among many that my father has taught me. As my father he is always open to provide valuable advice and wisdoms that I have learned to follow, but above all else I consider him my mentor.

I would not call it luck that I was blessed with a good family, rather I would refer to my good fortune as a gift that I cherish and hold dear. My family is strong and passionate and we owe these qualities to the man who instilled belief in himself and taught us to do the same. As he leads by example we have all become like him and found happiness in living our lives full.

His wisdoms were greatly missed when I left the nest and joined the U.S. Air Force. It may be for that reason that most of my father's readers know little of his oldest daughter, but I desired nothing more than to walk at my father's side. That desire brought me just that. When I left the military, my father and mother were eagerly waiting with open arms to welcome my return. Sense then I have been learning and working with my father which is a true honor.

My father has reached new boundaries by creating proven broodfowl through careful selection and breeding. His secret rests within this book where he provides a collection of articles that take you beyond the limits of any other poultry book written prior to. I am confident when I say that this book is for all who desire to open the door to becoming experts within the field. My father believes in knowledge and desires nothing more than to share his experiences and knowledge with others so that our beloved gamefowl will continue to live on and thrive.

My father has devoted much of his life to effectively raising and improving Gamefowl. With that said, he is always open to discuss his life work with others who seek the same knowledge or experiences. I highly recommend that you set time aside to ask questions or speak to him; he is always open for conversation. After speaking with him, I'm sure you will walk away feeling a sense of "wow" just as I do.

Megan Troiano

PREFACE

*"Doing what little one can to increase the general stock of knowledge is
as respectable an object of life, as one can in any likelihood pursue"*
Charles Darwin

This may be the first time in the history of our hobby that a book such as this has been made available to the average cocker and backyard breeder. Prior to this, information was not passed or given freely. In order to gain information on this subject you had to develop a trusting relationship with others; even then such knowledge was not easily obtained.

This book is a collection of articles that I have written for the <u>Gamecock Magazine</u>, the <u>Grit and Steel Magazine</u>, and the <u>Poultry Press News Paper</u>. All cover five years of work that is combined into one collection. To benefit those who did not get a chance to read these articles in the magazines, or read the entire versions, this book covers the complete contents of those articles which were written from January 2006 to December 2010.

<u>I underestimated the expectations of my readers</u>: Back in January of 2002 when I wrote my first article concerning American Games, the four part series of the "Selection Process," I did not expect the enthusiastic response that I received from my readers.

Many readers called or wrote to thank me for writing the articles. They asked for advice on subjects that I have yet covered. The calls and letters started soon after the articles were published and continue to this day. Needless to say, what started out as a monthly editorial (something to help the beginner get started on the right foot) turned into a full scale project. My main purpose became simple, to educate, inform and preserve these birds for future generations. I wanted to help the modern cocker and backyard breeder in perpetuating a specific breed of fowl, a breed that was developed and treasured by our forefathers and is now a bird of historical importance.

The inspiration for this book was the result of a positive response to my articles. With that said I was encouraged to publish more information on this great subject and help preserve American Games for future generations.

I soon realized that many beginners in this hobby were hungry for information. I thought, if I could help others minimize their mistakes, they may begin to breed and perpetuate exceptional gamefowl. However, this made me realize that the articles were only the beginning. The demand for this information between the cockers and backyard breeders is great.

To meet this demand, I have compiled many books in the works. Books on the breeding and selection process, health care, incubation and chick care, not to mention, stag and pullet development. Every few years I plan to have a new book to offer that will help our struggling beginners; not to exclude our veteran cockers.

<u>My approach to this project</u>: Throughout this book you will find the pronoun "I" used frequently. It is merely a style of writing I have chosen to use, to display a casual conversation. My hope is to make it easier for you to read and clearly understand. It is not my intention to sound like a "know it all" or have an attitude that depicts a power of authority. Rather, it represents an honest expression of opinion based upon my own experiences.

My main concern is to provide you (the reader) something to work with. American Games are a lot of work and it takes a lot of dedication to learn how to breed them properly. Therefore, the basis of my work is to produce something that will help the beginner and veteran understand what it takes to select, breed, and perpetuate high quality American Games and stay on the right path, sort of speak.

<u>Who will get something from this book</u>? If the burden of teaching is upon the person who wants to teach, with whom does the burden of learning lie? The burden of learning is on the person who wants to learn, not on the person who wants to teach.

If you happen to be the kind of person who believes that an idea is not good for you unless you are the creator of that idea, your success will be limited. I believe in emulating the actions of successful people. Everything I have learned and everything I have accomplished, I have acquired from other people.

I am fortunate to have great mentors in my life. I have always showed respect and listened to those who have experience. The knowledge found in an experienced man is what I seek. You must seek knowledge out, and emulate from success, that is why I associate with older, more successful men than myself; to improve and expand my knowledge. I take the knowledge and experiences they have, with the exception of their weaknesses and apply it to my actions. As a result, I benefit greatly.

To learn, one must pay the price; I was willing to pay that price. I have always said that I was not taught, I learned, and it took hanging around the best to achieve what I have achieved in my life. You can begin by asking yourself some questions: "Am I willing to pay the price?" "Am I willing to apply both the knowledge and experiences from others (men who have done this longer than me) and learn from their weaknesses?" Although this may appear to be a simple question, in reality, there is nothing more difficult than to honestly evaluate oneself? To <u>know yourself</u> is probably the most difficult advice given to man. I advise you to take some time and evaluate your desires in raising the best gamefowl. Consolidate a list of questions that you seek answers to, so that you can honestly say that you are managing your fowl within high standards. I had to do the same, which was the start of a journey through my learning process. This book is a compilation of everything I have learned, and I would like to pass it onto you.

To get the most from this book I suggest you read it more than once. Repetition is key to learning. Every time you read this book, you will learn something new. If you do this you will be successful. That is my promise to you.

<u>My intention</u>: It is not my intention to discuss the fighting qualities of this noble breed. I prefer to give my readers some practical and helpful knowledge concerning the selection, breeding, perpetuation of American Games, and ways to improve the overall quality of exhibition birds. My hope is that this book helps you improve your understand of the American Gamefowl while gaining knowledge necessary to correctly breed, raise and show your birds.

It occurred to me that beginners could only benefit through encouragement delivered within a book that discusses the challenges of raising, breeding and exhibiting fine purebred American Games.

Within these challenges rests the understanding of how to care and manage our fowl so that we could increase our possibilities of becoming grand champion at the shows.

Most books published on this subject lack adequate pictures and illustrations necessary to better understand the material. For this reason, I wanted to further your understanding by providing examples in areas that would best fit, to ensure your comprehension of the subject. All in all, I strive to effectively communicate this information in an interesting and informative manner, which is displayed in this book.

In the event I have forgotten some important or valuable information, I would appreciate it if you would contact me and bring it to my attention so that I can improve on future editions.

I know that this book fulfills a long waiting period among American Gamefowl breeders. For many years an efficient system of breeding (a system that worked for our forefathers) was desired. To fulfill this desire I have fulfilled my dream in delivering the second book that covers the subject of American Gamefowl; a publication that for the first time has been put into book form for the benefit of the breed.

I know this book holds the promise of becoming a standard publication for this breed. For those that have gained admiration and love for American Games, this book is for you. For those that hold the desire to further perpetuate these beautiful birds, this book is for you. This book has been written in order to help those who desire or are eager to keep American Games true in form, function and beauty. It was also written to fulfill the demand to promote an intellectual understanding of the structural requirements of these birds.

The breeding of American Games is an international activity, practiced by all classes of people, workmen and businessmen alike. There are no social barriers in this pastime, so rest assured that everyone may share equally in its pleasure.

As you dig into this book, no matter if you're a veteran or a beginner; you will be able to identify the finer points within this great bird. Through the battles displayed daily in raising gamefowl, I have learned and gained experiences. By seeking knowledge in all we do, we inspire ourselves and those around us. This book is the result of my desire to educate all on what inspires me.

TABLE OF CONTENTS

INTRODUCTION

"I am dedicated to preserving our heritage, our culture, and all its traditions for the next generation" - Kenny Troiano

Breeding poultry and gamefowl was practice within the United States centuries ago and has continued to this day. Though a longtime practice, issues have risen that require our attention due to the overall level of importance. Not only is breeding a very important part of raising poultry and gamefowl, it requires skill with specialized knowledge. Because it is identified as a comprehensive subject, improved methods are steadily evolving; you must make up your mind, right now, to be part of that evolutionary process.

As expected, due to new laws, such as proposition 2, there is an abundance of information which is being published. Some of this information is based on sound experimental data, to include, conflicting information, often purely hypothetical, while some information is widely off the mark. The problem is that many of these books are written by those who fail to have the proper experience. The purpose of this book is to deliver practical and factual information on the subject of selection, breeding, and perpetuation of American Games and Old English Games. This information can also be applied to most poultry breeds. My intention is to communicate to you and others some ideas of the fundamental principles involved in the breeding practices of American Games, not to mention various up to date information concerning these methods.

This book is a collection of chronicles that I have put together in effort to help you and others improve your understanding of the principles and laws that govern the breeding of high quality American Games. I have written this book with the vision of teaching the reader how to breed and manage his fowl in such a way that they shall prove to be a source of pleasure to him as they have always been to me.

My ultimate goal has been to write a structured book for the benefit of all cockers. These articles are just a means to an end. This material will be provided in a more generalized book on Selective Breeding. These articles are displayed in their full versions, the way I intended them, and originally wanted them to be read.

The greater part of my life has been devoted solely to this subject. Through specializing and practicing, I have experienced the phases as a whole beginning with small backyard breeding to breeding highly competitive gamefowl. This book is a collaboration of my efforts to better understand this subject through personal experiences in breeding and managing American Games. All information comes from reliable sources with exception of the portions of the book that I have quoted.

Either through working along large or small lines, cockers and backyard breeders will find a worthy project through examination and study of the material and by practicing the principles. Therefore, those who seek to breed and raise American Games as a hobby, part time occupation or full time occupation should seek out valuable information to assist them.

The information in this book is tried, tested and proven: The information presented in the book is a compilation of many years of trial and error. By reading a great amount of material, surrounding myself and listening to wisdoms from great cockers and applying tested methods and discarding failed attempts, I was able to develop methods that were flawless.

By studying great men such as Charles Darwin and Gregor Mendel, I began to apply their work to breeding chickens and gamefowl. Through the study of Natural Selection, I was able to better understand how birds evolve. As I studied the principles of genetics, I developed a better understanding of how traits are inherited. When I combined Natural Selection and the laws of inheritance, I was able to develop a set of principles that, when used in unison, would comprise the practice known as Selective Breeding. This enabled me to create the family of fowl that I desired. In other words, through Selective Breeding I was able to create the fowl of my dreams. This book will teach you these principles. And by taking these principles and applying them to the breeding of your fowl, you too, can have the kind of fowl that you desire most.

Every breeder should know the principles of inheritance to be successful: In many respects, what cockers and backyard breeders need most are better-bred fowl. Improvement in methods of rearing, feeding, and general management would accomplish much, but beyond a certain point, further progress is impossible without improvement in the method and system of breeding, to include understanding how traits are passed from parents to offspring.

Since numerous characteristics and traits, which American Games possesses are inherited, including conformation of body and color of plumage, and since many of the heritable characteristics are of functional importance (pit performance), cockers and backyard breeders everywhere should be as well informed as possible concerning the principles and practices of breeding, in order that their work may be both interesting and rewarding.

It is a significant fact that the chicken was one of the first organisms used by early geneticists to establish the laws of inheritance worked with animals as they did with plants. Poultry are domestic animals that are commonly used to establish some of the basic knowledge regarding inheritance. A considerable amount of information has been collected on the genetics of the fowl. Much of this knowledge has been of little use to the average cocker and backyard breeder since they are usually more interested in functional traits which, by nature, are of relatively complicated inheritance.

The purpose of this book is to convey to the readers some concepts of various characteristics possessed by American Games that are inherited. The discussion of fundamental principles involved should stimulate further research concerning the problems raised.

Be aware of controversial subjects: Considerable change has taken place in the past few years. This shift has been so recent that some disagreement persists. What are these disagreements? It's the use of family breeding, such as inbreeding, line-breeding and outcrossing. The early cocker and backyard breeder gave major emphasis to individual value in the selection of his broodfowl. The use of family breeding, which includes family selection and progeny testing, was only used by the more progressive breeders.

This change may (at times) leave the average cocker and backyard breeder in a somewhat confused state of mind. It is displayed through the progress shown in the science of breeding, which should lead to more effective efforts. Today, there is considerable emphasis on breeding techniques, which are designed to take advantage of hybrid vigor, such as crossbreeding. What the overall effects of this will have on the future of American Games remains problematical at best, but there is one thing I know for sure, and that is there will be strong repercussions.

As you can see from the previous paragraphs and for the benefit of the readers, a certain amount of this controversial matter has been included. As a result, my own views may seem to be overly stressed. Please take this as a warning. I only have your best interest in mind. For the same reason that I have written this book, I only want you to succeed.

The following discussions concerning breeding practices should be valuable to anyone who is interested in breeding high quality American Games. Furthermore, since the most successful practices in breeding are based upon the fundamental principles of inheritance, it is obvious that every breeder should know something of these principles in order to make his family or strain most successful from a practical standpoint. The value of progeny testing is made clear, for it is only by progeny testing that a breeder can expect to make the greatest progress.

<u>One last thought</u>: Success in raising and breeding American Games depends largely upon your knowledge of the breed and their overall form and function, and your ability to reproduce offspring that are better than their parents each year.

Fundamental principles must be understood to some extent before you can practice these methods intelligently. For this reason the major aspects of breeding American Games, in respect to principles involved, are discussed in great detail.

This book has been published primarily for the modern cocker and backyard breeder who find the breeding of American Games fascinating and rewarding. The research of this book has been inspired in the spirit of rendering the greatest possible service to my fellow cocker and backyard breeders throughout the world.

A bibliography and list of recommended books is provided at the end of this book. They are typical of the references used as sources of information in this book and may be used for additional information.

INSTRUCTIONS
"HOW TO READ THIS BOOK"

In the following pages I have provided instructions on how to read and gain the most from this book. As a "how-to-book" it must be read and studied differently than a novel or a magazine article. Each part of the book builds on the next, until you have read through to the end, where it all comes together in one tight comprehensible package. Follow these instructions to the letter, and I promise that you will gain a better understanding of the breeding and raising of American Games.

HOW TO GET THE MOST FROM THIS BOOK

Although this collection of chronicles is best used as a "step-by-step" or "how-to-book," it can also be used as a reference manual, especially after you have read through it a few times and have taken the proper notes. If you have a particular question, chances are the answers are in this book. This book is written and organized from known factors, which govern the laws of "Selective Breeding." This is the foundation for which all master breeders have used, and must always be used for the successful breeding of American and Old English Games, not to mention poultry of all kinds.

Some of the principles described in this book may be familiar to all whom will read it. Others principles are described for the first time. Keep in mind (from the first chapter to the last) that the value of these principles rests entirely in the thought process of the reader and his willingness to use the information given, and not merely in the principles themselves. Stated in another way, this book is intended as a way to get you to look at breeding, and the preservation of American Games in a more hopeful and productive manner, one in which it will cause you to rethink the way you are breeding your fowl. Are you breeding to a definite end, or are you breeding haphazardly? By using the information provided in this book, you will harness the stupendous power of Mother Nature, and create the fowl that you want.

You will do yourself a great injustice if you read this book with even the slightest feeling that you do not need more knowledge than you now possess. In truth, no man knows enough about any worthwhile subject to entitle him to feel that he has the last word on that subject. As I was once told, by a very smart man, "Humility is a forerunner of success!" Until we become humble we are not going to advance greatly by the experiences and thoughts of others.

THE ACCEPTANCE OF NEW IDEAS

New ideas, if accepted at all, are taken with the proverbial grain of salt. It is for this reason that the Introduction of this book, and the principle for which it covers, discusses subjects intended to pave the way for new ideas and methods, so it will not be too much of a shock to the mind of the reader.

"The road of the teacher has always been rocky." Socrates sipping the hemlock, Christ crucified, Galileo terrified into retraction of his starry truths, one could easily follow the bloody trail through the pages of history. "Something in human nature makes us resent the impact of new ideas."

We hate to be bothered with beliefs that have been handed down with the family furniture. At adulthood, too many of us go into hibernation and live off the fat of ancient obsessions. If a new idea invades our den we rise up snarling from our winter sleep. In other words, we rely on "old wives tales" and not on facts and proven principles.

There is no reason why the average man should ever close his mind to fresh "perspectives." He does, just the same. Nothing is more tragic, or more common than mental inaction. For every ten men who are physically lazy there are ten thousand with stagnant minds. And stagnant minds are the breeding places of fear.

There was once a farmer that would always end his prayers with this plea: "Oh, God, give me an open mind!" If more people followed his example we might escape the constraints of closed mindedness. And wouldn't it be a pleasant place to live in.

Every person should make it his business to gather new ideas from sources other than the environment in which he lives and works, otherwise the mind becomes withered, stagnant, narrow, and closed. The farmer that often walks among the strange faces and tall buildings of the city will return to his farm with a refreshed mind, accompanied by more courage and an abundance of enthusiasm. The city man that takes a trip to the country, every so often, refreshes his mind with sights, new and different from those of his daily existence.

Everyone needs a change. A frequent change in our mental environment is necessary for all of us, just as a change and variety of food are essential. The mind becomes more alert, more elastic and more ready to work with speed and accuracy after it has been bathed in new ideas outside of one's own habitual and mundane life.

As you read this book you will temporarily set aside ideas that you currently operate and enter a field of entirely new ideas. You will come out, at the other end of this book, with a new supply of knowledge and ideas, which will bring you more success. Do not be afraid of new ideas! They may mean to you the difference between success and failure.

HAVING A DEFINITENESS OF PURPOSE IS ESSENTIAL FOR SUCCESS

No matter what may be your idea of the perfect bird, you must have a definiteness of purpose. Without it nothing in this book will help you. You must know what it is that you want and you must be willing to do what it takes to get it. Master breeders are always clear of their objective, you must be too.

Some of the ideas introduced in this book will not require further explanation or proof of their soundness because they are familiar to practically everyone. Other ideas that are introduced aren't so much new, but are not practiced as they should be and for that reason those who read these principles may hesitate to accept them as sound.

All the principles that have been described in this book are thoroughly tested by myself, and the majority of the principles covered have been tested by scores of breeders who were quite capable of distinguishing between the merely theoretic and the practical.

For these reasons, all principles which I have covered are proven and verified. However, as a reader of this book you will not be asked to accept any statement made in these principles without, first, gaining satisfaction by tests, experiments and analysis providing that the information is sound.

The greatest evil the reader is requested to avoid is the urge to form opinions without definite facts that are formed by biases.

HOW TO READ THIS BOOK

This book was written in such a way that literary style was place as a secondary importance for the sake of explaining the principles and laws that are discussed within this book. These laws are discussed in such a manner that they may be quickly and easily understood by all whom read this book.

It will not take long for you to observe that the principles discussed in the book will encourage thoughts that will cover a wide range of subjects. For this reason you should read this book with a notebook and pencil at hand, and follow the practice of recording these "ideas" as they come into your mind. By following this suggestion you will establish a collection of ideas that by the time the book has been read two or three times, you will have a sufficient amount of information to transform your entire plan of action.

There is an art to reading a reference book such as this. When you read, concentrate. Read as if the author were a close personal friend and were writing to you and you alone.

Abraham Lincoln was known to take time for reflection when he read, by doing this he was able to relate and assimilate the principles into his own experience. It would be wise for you to follow his good example.

Determine what you are looking for before you read this book. If you know what you are looking for you are more apt to find it than if you don't have a specific purpose. If you really want to recognize, relate, assimilate, and apply these principles you must work at it. A book such as this is not meant to be skimmed through the same way that you might read a novel. I urge you to follow a definite pattern. Here's one that has worked well for me:

1. Read for general content: This takes place within the first reading. It should be a fast reading to grasp the sweeping flow of information that the book contains. But take the time to underline the important words and phrases. Write notes in the margins and write down briefly the ideas that flash into your mind as you read. Now this obviously may only be done with a book that you own. But the notations and markings make your book more valuable to you.

2. Read for a particular emphasis: A second reading is for the purpose of assimilating specific details. You should pay particular attention to see that you understand and really grasp any new ideas or information the book presents.

<u>3. Read for the future</u>: This third reading is more for memory than anything else. Memorize passages that mean something to you. Find ways these passages can relate to problems you are currently facing. Test new ideas and information; try them; discard the useless, and imprint the useful permanently into your everyday operations.

<u>4. Read later to refresh your memory, and to rekindle your inspiration</u>: There is a famous story about the apprentice who asked his mentor to give him that old talk again. When the mentor asked why, the apprentices simply said - "I'm starting to forget and getting kinda discouraged." All of us may forget and become discouraged from time to time. We should reread the best of our books at such times to rekindle the fires that got us going in the first place.

UNDERSTANDING
THE DYNAMICS OF BREEDING

To understand the dynamics of breeding American Gamefowl, you must first understand the many parts which make up the whole in a process we call "The Principles of Breeding." These consist of proper selection and culling, understanding the principles of genetics, and the practices of proper methods of mating and using proven breeding techniques. Leaving just one piece of the puzzle out can ruin the entire breeding process.

I fully understand that the subject of genetics can seem like a mind boggling study of useless information and mundane words. Hell, who hasn't fallen asleep during a biology class? But trust me, genetics plays an important role in the principles of Selective Breeding; more than you might think. Without a basic understanding of genetics, breeding is nothing more than a guessing game. You could waste valuable time, effort and money, trying to create or perpetuate something that may never end with flourishing results.

Breeding is a lot more than just putting a cock with a hen. You'll produce chickens all right, but they won't be the top notch, high quality gamefowl you hoped for. Here is a step by step program for learning what it actually takes to breed American Gamefowl properly. These lessons will span numerous months, covering various subjects, throughout many issues of the "Gamecock Magazine." I hope you enjoy them, and hopefully learn something new from them as well.

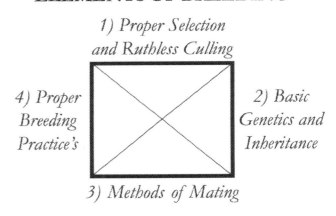

THE FOUR MOST IMPORTANT ELEMENTS OF BREEDING

1) Proper Selection and Ruthless Culling

4) Proper Breeding Practice's

2) Basic Genetics and Inheritance

3) Methods of Mating

PRODUCING SUPERIOR OFFSPRING IS NO ACCIDENT

<u>**UNDERSTANDING THE DEDICATION AND COMMITMENT**</u>: For the man or woman who desires an activity that takes up a few hours of their time and gives a great deal of satisfaction, breeding gamefowl is ideal, whether for the pit or for the purpose of exhibition. Though a personal understanding of the laws and principles of breeding and their function is necessary for success, breeding gamefowl is a livelihood which demands deep, selective thought of complex problems, which are challenges within themselves. It stimulates the intelligence of the breeder as well as supplies a fascinating interest for all.

Furthermore, it's the gamefowl breeder that will have the opportunity to express his artistic instincts in molding the perfect form and function of his birds, and perfecting the color or combination of colors to meet his idea of the ultimate gamecock. In addition, gratification is associated with the sporting instinct of the gamecock, the excitement of competition at the pits and at the shows, and the satisfaction which comes from a "Win" with the realization that the breeder has surpassed the efforts of his competitors and produced a bird that is superior to theirs.

With all the challenges this entails, whoever is interested in the breeding and raising of gamefowl should never hesitate to engage in it. Especially on the grounds that he has neither the room nor the facilities to enable him to compete, no matter how good others are situated. With only a backyard and the crudest of equipment, it is possible to produce gamefowl of the highest excellence. There are many breeders who have birds that lead in competition on a regular basis, and are produced on small farms and a limited budget. They do with what they have available at the time, and they do it very well.

Here is a proven Troiano Red cock, owned and bred by Kenny Troiano. A fine product of good selection from a solid and well maintained family of Gamefowl.

Competing with gamefowl can play an important role in the improvement of the different breeds and varieties that are available to us. Not only do they serve to promote competition and create rivalry, thereby increasing more interest in the department of breeding and creating better gamefowl, but they also make it possible to compare their results with others in their field. This way the breeders have the opportunity to see what other breeders have accomplished and to observe where their birds are strong or weak in comparison with theirs. Therefore, they learn where they must seek to improve if they expect to work their way to the top, or if they expect to stay there once they have arrived.

In this book I will attempt to present the main principles of breeding American Games. These are beliefs and ideologies that have been proven by scientific facts and practical experiences. I would like to point out that in recent years a great deal has been discovered about the laws of heredity, which have motivated and even inspired these principles.

THE PRINCIPLES OF BREEDING GAMEFOWL: This book deals with the principles of breeding in order to produce American Games of the highest degree of excellence, and to obtain a great proportion of fowl of good quality.

Breeding American Games with this objective in mind is not a new idea, but in actuality a very old quest that has always attracted the attention and interest of a great number of individuals. It was motivated by cockers and backyard breeders who simply wanted the best, and they were always looking for ways to maintain the best. Some were successful and some were not. For the unsuccessful ones, no matter what they did, the results were not what they expected. So what problems of mating plagued their efforts? Was it simply that of selecting individuals that possessed the desired characteristics, with the certainty that the offspring would be identical in character to their parents? If this was true it would be a comparatively simple one to fix. As a matter of fact, breeding American Games is not a simple question of "like producing like", and for this reason the successful breeding of American Games of high quality is a difficult problem requiring the most painstaking care and study. And good results that are obtained with a reasonable degree of certainty, which is a result of long time practice and lots of experience.

Before I describe the practices that most of the experienced breeders have used, and have shown the best results, it is a good idea to consider certain laws or principles of breeding. These are more or less commonly used. It's a system for which the experienced breeders are familiar with, the results of which are very successful.

ELEMENTARY GENETICS
And the Mendelian Factor

In order to understand the complexities of breeding, you need to know a little bit about genetics and how it works. Your successes as well as your failures will all be determined by your ability to select and match broodfowl properly, and that's all determined by your knowledge, good or bad, of genetics. This part of the book, which is the study of Mendelism, will help you better comprehend the other parts of breeding, such as inbreeding, line-breeding and crossbreeding, not to mention dominate vs. recessive, and sex-linked traits. These are all important subjects to learn if you plan to become a serious breeder. But before I get to those subjects I want to talk a little bit about basic genetics and how it relates to the breeding of gamefowl.

Gregor Mendel, the unexpected founder of the principles of heredity.

To appreciate genetics you must first know a little bit about Gregor Mendel, an unexpected founder of the principles of heredity, but is now considered the father of modern day genetics. Gregor Mendel was an abbot of an Austrian monastery from 1860 to his death in 1884. His Lam of Independent Segregation of Factors has attracted its share of criticism, but it still stands as the fundamental guide used by all serious breeders.

What Gregor Mendel established by experimenting with plants, can also be applied to birds, and indeed to all living organisms. This is the example by which parents pass individual features onto their offspring, and the way in which certain parts of these features from one parent will give way to more dominant features from the other.

HOW INHERITANCE WORKS: The fundamental nature of inheritance is the passing of particles or units called genes; and these genes are present in pairs; one member of each pair coming from each parent, and each gene maintaining its identity generation after generation. But how does it work? Well, with the fusion of a sperm cell from the cock, called the "gamete" and an egg or ovum from the hen also called the "gamete," a fertilized cell known as a "zygote" is formed. Each gamete brings with it a package of chromosomes, which represents only a sampling of half of the parent's inheritance. These chromosomes are microscopic strings of genes which carries a detailed blueprint for the make-up of a new individual. The chromosomes have their specific roles in controlling future development and those from one parent will pair off with those from the other, creating in the zygote a nucleus of paired chromosomes; therefore paired genes. Multiplication is marked by the chromosomes splitting lengthwise; the two halves drawing to opposite sides of the zygote, which then divides into two cells, each with its own nucleus of carbon-copy chromosomes. Then the process continues, two cells becoming four and four cells becoming eight and so on, but always carrying the same mixture of genetic information from each of the parents.

<u>What Mendel established</u>: Gregor Mendel was able to show us how certain characteristics are interpreted and can be inherited. He established the basis for two of the general laws of inheritance: the "Law of Segregation" and the "Independent Assortment of Genes." Later genetic principles were added, yet all the phenomena of inheritance based upon the reaction of genes is due to the work done by Gregor Mendel. "Mendel's Law" is now considered the general law for all heredity, and is generally known under the collective term, "Mendelism."

Mendel's research showed us (with the use of his plants) how certain characteristics of garden peas are not only inherited but influenced by dominant and recessive factors. For example: a smooth seed vs. a wrinkled seed. In each of the seven pairs of characters, Mendel found that one of each contrasting pair was dominant, while the other was recessive. When he crossed a smooth seeded pea with a wrinkled one all of the progeny came out smooth. In this case the smooth pea is dominant over the wrinkled one, and this was true for all of the seven qualities that Mendel studied.

But when the smooth seed progeny were bred together as in a brother-sister type mating, both smooth and wrinkled seeded plants were produced. Mendel observed that there are other factors called genes that come in different, but distinct pairs in the germ cells of the pea. An individual germ cell can have one copy each of the smooth and wrinkled gene, or two copies of either the smooth or the wrinkle gene. Since the smooth gene is dominant, any seed that has one or two copies of the smooth gene will be smooth. However, the smooth gene is dominant only if a seed has two copies of the wrinkled gene and no copies of the smooth gene; in this case a wrinkled seed is produce, because the wrinkled gene is recessive. Since the original parent peas are pure for either smooth or wrinkled seed, all of the first crosses will have one smooth and one wrinkled gene because each parent contributes one copy each to the progeny. They will all be smooth because smooth is dominant and wrinkled is recessive. But in the second generation, since each parent will have one copy each of the smooth and wrinkled genes, the progeny will carry a combination of smooth or wrinkled. Some will have two wrinkled genes, some will have two smooth genes and some will have one copy of each. Since the arrangement of genes is random, we can calculate, on an average, how many of each kind there will be. For instance, fifty percent will be smooth-wrinkled, twenty-five percent will be smooth-smooth, and twenty-five percent will be wrinkled-wrinkled. Since all seeds having one or two copies of the smooth gene will be smooth, we can see that there will be seventy-five percent smooth and twenty-five percent wrinkled progeny from mating brother and sister. All characteristics that have this simple structure of inheritance are considered Mendelian Factors.

AMERICAN GAMES AND THE MENDELIAN FACTOR OF INHERITANCE: By evaluating the principle of Mendel's experiments with peas and applying them to the inheritance of comb types, I will show you how they are transmitted from parents to offspring.

If a pea-combed bird that is pure for the pea-comb characteristic is mated to any straight (*single*) comb bird, all of the offspring will have pea-combs in the first (F_1) generation. When these offspring mate among themselves, their chicks will consist of both pea-comb and straight (*single*) comb types. This generation is called the F_2 generation. There will be about 75 percent with pea-comb and 25 percent with straight (*single*) comb.

As you can plainly see, pea-comb is dominant and straight (*single*) comb is recessive. All F_2 generation progeny with straight (*single*) comb will breed true for straight (*single*) comb. Only one-third of the F_2 generation pea-comb progeny will breed true for pea-comb. The other two-thirds will give both pea-comb and straight (*single*) comb offspring in the ratio of 3 to 1.

The Inheritance of One Pair of Characters

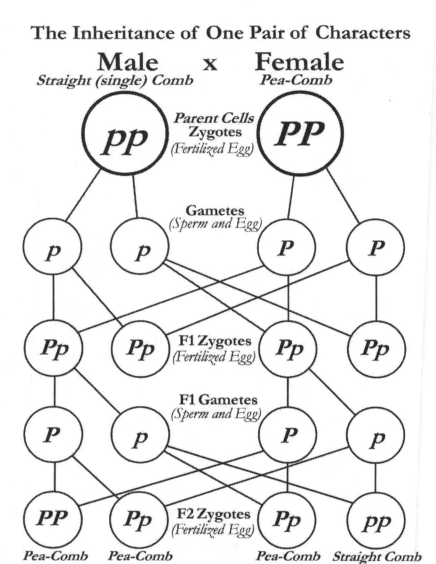

Diagram of a cross between pea-comb and straight (single) comb, the inheritance of a pair of characters: When a pea-comb (P) female is crossed with a straight (single) comb (p) male, the first generation birds have pea-comb (dominant character). When the F_1 birds are mated among themselves, about 75 percent of the F_2 generation will have pea-combs and the remainder will have straight (single) combs. While all the straight (single) combs will be pure for straight (single) combs, only one-third of the F_2 generation will be pure for pea-combs.

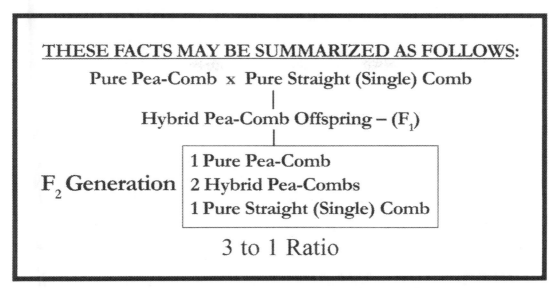

Results of the F_2 Generation is a 3 to 1 Ratio.

The explanation of inheritance is quite simple. The pure pea-comb original parent, known as the (P_1), carried two genes for pea-comb, (PP). The original straight (*single*) comb parent, also (P_1), carried two genes for straight (*single*) comb, (pp). In the production of germ cells, or gametes, (sperms in the male, ova in the female) there is but a single gene in each. The process is as follows:

Inheritance of Two Pairs of Characters

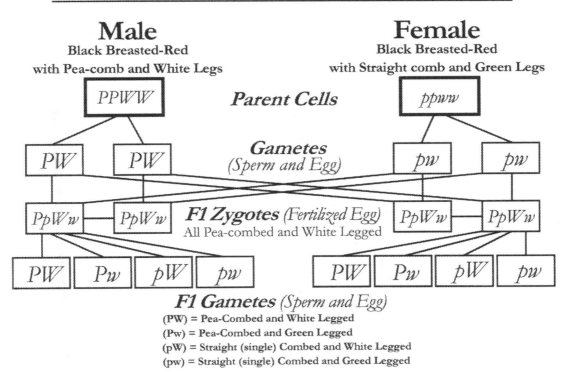

(PW) = Pea-Combed and White Legged
(Pw) = Pea-Combed and Green Legged
(pW) = Straight (single) Combed and White Legged
(pw) = Straight (single) Combed and Greed Legged

Here is a diagram showing the inheritance of two characters.

The genes that produce the characteristics segregate, or separate, to produce the germ cells. The first generation is (Pp), and is heterozygous for dominant gene (P). One-quarter of the second or F_2 generation is homozygous for (P), so they represent or are identified as (PP). One-half of the second or F_2 generation is heterozygous for (P), that is they are (Pp), and one-quarter of the second generation is homozygous recessives. They are (pp).

<u>What happens when we are dealing with two pairs of genes?</u> Instead of only one pair, as in the example above, let's discuss a situation where there are four phenotypes in the F_2 generation in the ratio of 9-3-3-1. Described in useful terms, means that if we mated two birds, one of which carried pea-comb and green legs and the other straight (*single*) comb and white legs, and then mated the F_1 individuals, 9 of the offspring would have pea-comb and white legs, 3 would have pea-comb and green legs, 3 would have straight (*single*) comb and white legs, and 1 would have straight (*single*) comb and green legs.

If there are three pairs of characteristics then the situation becomes far more complicated. There will then be eight different phenotypes in the ratio of 27-9-9-9-3-3-3-1.

<u>Sex-linked inheritance</u>: In this case, the cock carries two chromosomes for sex, while the hen carries a single sex chromosome. Any gene located on the cock's sex chromosome will be transmitted to both his sons and daughters. A gene on the sex chromosome of the hen will go to her sons only. This type of inheritance is called sex-linked inheritance.

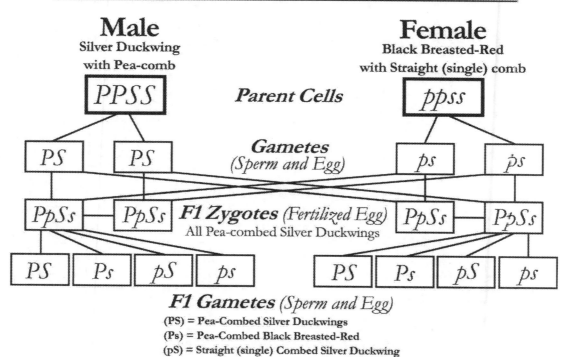

Inheritance of Two Pairs of Characters

Male
Silver Duckwing with Pea-comb

Female
Black Breasted-Red with Straight (single) comb

Parent Cells

Gametes (*Sperm and Egg*)

F1 Zygotes (*Fertilized Egg*)
All Pea-combed Silver Duckwings

F1 Gametes (*Sperm and Egg*)

(PS) = Pea-Combed Silver Duckwings
(Ps) = Pea-Combed Black Breasted-Red
(pS) = Straight (single) Combed Silver Duckwing
(ps) = Straight (single) Combed Black Breasted-Red

In principle, the inheritance of two pairs of characters is exactly the same as for one pair. Here is a diagram showing the inheritance of two characters.

Although this can apply to many characteristics and traits, Silver Duckwing in American Games is a good example of sex-linked inheritance. For example; Silver Duckwing American Game cocks (dominant), when mated to Black-Breasted Red hens (recessive), give all Silver Duckwing offspring. On the other hand, Silver Duckwing hens (dominant), if mated to Black-Breasted Red cocks (recessive), give Silver Duckwing sons only, and red daughters.

Each chromosome carries a series of genes that are usually inherited together. Each group of genes on a single chromosome is called a linkage group. Occasionally the chromosomes break so that one or more genes may separate from their linkage group. All genes except those on the sex chromosome are called autosomal genes.

When a Silver Duckwing male is mated to a non-silver colored female, such as a Black Breasted-Red, the daughters as well as the sons are silver. The dominant sex-linked gene (S), for silver, is transmitted from the sire to the daughters and to the sons, as shown in the illustration above.

BREEDING MENDELIAN TYPE CHARACTERISTICS IN GAMEFOWL: According to earlier views, heredity was looked upon as fluid in nature. For example, we still use words, such as, quarter blood, half blood, three quarter blood, etc., which highly suggest this idea. Nevertheless, the hereditary material composed of units or genes are transmitted almost indefinitely without change. Their behavior may be compared more so to that of little solid marbles contained in a glass jar (germ cell) than to that of fluids. Each marble is a characteristic or trait, and of a different color depending on the trait.

When it comes to gamefowl, the variations of most characteristics, especially after crossing, depend on so many of these units that the mode of inheritance can still be compared roughly to the blending of fluids. However, when explaining the effects of inbreeding and the nature of prepotency, the comparison to that of a pile of marbles for the basis of hereditary of characteristics is much better.

A few characteristics depend on such a small number of units that the effects of the different ones are easily followed in crosses. Mendel's law of heredity was originally discovered in these types of situations.

AMERICAN GAMES AND THE EFFECTS OF GENETIC EROSION: The incredible genetic diversity available within the average chicken is fast becoming a thing of the past. Today gamefowl are still raised primarily in backyards, where very specialized breeders have more time for experimentation and improvement. However, the trend towards diversity is being reversed every day. With the advent of the industrial farmer, which concentrates its genetic resources on a few strains that lay eggs, or grow meat really well, they are abandoning variety for uniformity of function, not type. However, there are some cockers who are following this trend as well, but not for eggs and meat rather in producing a large amount of gamefowl in order to sell. Whether they are functional, as in performance and ability does not matter. They are happy as long as they can sell a large amount of birds at high prices.

If you ask me, they hang on the edge of commercialism. They concentrate on the most popular breeds, which happens to be the Sweaters and the Greys, or otherwise known as Black-Breasted Light Reds and Duckwing, because they sell, and for no other reason. The other varieties such as the old Black-Reds, Furnesses, Brassy Backs, Birchen's, Hennies, Muffs and Tassels, Gingers or Red-Quills, Dom's or Dominique's, are disappearing every day. In the shuffle to make money these varieties are losing out.

This illustrates the inheritance of a sex-linked dominant character. The gene for silver in Silver Duckwings is contained in the sex chromosome and when a Silver Duckwing female is mated to a non-silver colored male, such as a Black Breasted-Red, the gene for silver is transmitted to the sons only. The daughters are non-silver because each one received its sex chromosome from the non-silver sire.

As interests in breeding of the very specialized varieties of gamefowl shifts in other directions, or we lack successors willing to carry on with these old varieties, they are gradually slipping away. In a process called "genetic erosion," the gene pool is becoming less diverse and more uniform as time passes. And if we are not careful, red fowl will be the norm and the other varieties of American Games will be a thing of the past.

Genetic erosion is not just happening among domestic chicken breeds but among all types of poultry including American Games. Although genetic erosion in general is accelerating at an alarming rate, if you ask me, losses of the classic gamefowl breeds are far worse than losses among other domestic fowl. Only a handful of cockers (most of which lack long-term goals) are willing to maintain their gene pools, but only a limited number. They may be well selected birds but they are secretly guarded strains that are not readily available to others; an action which fuels this concept of genetic

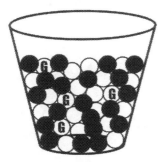

CROSSBREEDING IS LIKE MIXING MARBLES IN A BUCKET

Black Marbles Represent Family (A)
White Marbles Represent Family (B)
Grey Marbles Represent Random Traits and Mutations

When crossbreeding fowl, the method is similar to the mixing of marbles. Black marbles representing traits from family (A), White marbles representing traits from family (B). Some are dominant and some are recessive. Some are sex-linked and some are quantitative. The black and white marbles represent ancestral traits, while the grey marbles represent random traits or mutations.

erosion by preventing genetic diversity. This is nothing more than a selfish act of hording.

The greater the genetic diversity, the better the odds are of finding individuals with the potential to improve characteristics and traits, and in turn reduce the chance for diseases, which change with our ever so growing environment.

I've had plenty of conversations with expert poultrymen and professional specialist, such as ornithologist and geneticist, who see gamefowl as a sort of insurance policy. They feel that traits from gamefowl may prove genetically useful in the future. Unlike valuable livestock, poultry sperm and embryos cannot be easily preserved by freezing. The only way to perpetuate poultry genetics is through living fowl currently kept by cockers and backyard breeders.

Some day the commercial poultry farmer may come to us cockers for help. It may be the gamecock that saves the commercial poultry industry. If, in the future they turn to us for help, it won't be the first time. In the 1940's the meat industry required a bird with a broader breast to integrate into their strains of meat producers. Eventually they found what they needed in the exhibition type Cornish bird, bred and raised by the backyard breeders who specialized in this breed. And it was just in time too, because as luck would have it, the Cornish had become nearly extinct. During the rush toward industrial egg production, the Cornish along with many other breeds were almost forgotten. Today the Cornish are bred with the Plymouth Rock for the production of meat birds, which is called the "Cornish/Rock Cross."

There are pessimists who say it's too late to save some of our rare varieties of American Games, believing the numbers have already dropped off well below practical breeding populations. However, I'm an optimist and as long as there's one pair left to breed, any variety can still be saved and preserved for future generations.

White Plymouth Rocks.

34

THE FUTURE OF DNA AND THE REPRODUCTION OF GAMEFOWL

THE FUTURE OF DNA AND THE REPRODUCTION OF GAMEFOWL: In recent years DNA (the molecular basis of heredity) has become better understood. The most important genetic material in the nucleus of the cell is DNA (deoxyribonucleic acid), which is a long thin molecule that serves as the genetic source of information.

The DNA in a human cell is estimated to consist of six billion pairs of nucleotides. To visualize the enormity of six billion pairs of nucleotides, imagine increasing a cell nucleus to the size of a basketball. Then imagine taking the DNA out of the basketball-sized nucleus and stretching it into a straight line. That line of DNA would stretch for 40 miles.

White Cornish Fowl.

DNA is composed of nucleotide: containing: *A's (adenine), G's (guanine), C's (cytosine),* and *T's (thymine)*. The sequence of these four bases in DNA acts as a code in which messages can be transferred from one cell to another during the process of cell division. The code can be translated by cells to make proteins and enzymes of specific structure that determine the basic morphology and function of a cell. And to control differentiation, which is the process by which a group of cells become an organ, or to control whether an embryo will become a human, ape, or a gamecock.

But DNA is far more than a genetic information center, or master molecule. The recent development of the recombination of DNA techniques introduce a new era of genetic engineering with all its promise and possible dangers.

Recombination of DNA techniques are an enormous help to scientists in mapping the positions of genes and learning their fundamental nature. It may lead to new scientific horizons of allowing introduction of new genetic material directly into the cells of an individual to repair specific genetic defects or to transfer genes from one species to another.

On the other hand, its opponents, who are against the tinkering of DNA, raise the level of vision with questions of re-engineered creatures. They express that they are dangerous and will destroy the earth. There is also the moral responsibility, which examines the question, are we removing nature's evolutionary barrier between different species? Nevertheless, molecular biologists are relentlessly working towards the recombination of DNA. Therefore, it would be wise if poultry specialist, such as geneticist, to keep an eye on new developments in this exciting field and maybe someday the average cocker and backyard breeder can take advantage of this technology as well. Can you imagine the possibilities?

PRINCIPLES OF INHERITANCE
The need for knowledge, and the function of the basic principles of inheritance

<u>**Subject Matter**</u>:
- Introduction into - The Principles of Inheritance
- Simple Definitions of Terms
- Principles of Reproductive Cells, Chromosomes and Genes
- Principles of Sex Determination
- Principles of Sex-Linked Inheritance
- Principles of Variation
- Principles of Dominant and Recessive Characters
- Principles of Incomplete Dominance and Co-Dominance
- Principles of Genotype and Phenotype
- Principles of Zygosity
- Principles of Hybridization
- The Law of Chromosome Segregation
- The Law of Independent Assortment
- Principles of Acquired Characters
- Principles of Quantitative Characteristics
- Inheritance of Important Characteristics in American Games

INTRODUCTION

"The whole subject of inheritance is wonderful. When a new character arises, whatever its nature may be, it generally tends to be inherited, at least in a temporary and sometimes in a most persistent manner."

Charles Darwin

Successful breeders find it necessary to become familiar with the working principles of Mendelism, which is the foundation of modern genetics. Genetics involves the study of inheritance in a manner in which traits are passed down from parent to offspring. There are certain basic laws or rules which govern inheritance. Although these laws are important (enough to justify the need for you to familiarizing yourself with them) it is not necessary for success in breeding American Games to have an exact and extensive knowledge of the subject of genetics. However, knowledge of the relatively simple basics of genetics (which I have presented here for you) helps to give you a better understanding and appreciation of the laws of inheritance. It also aids you in the selection and in the successful breeding of American Games.

Three Fundamental Principles of Mendelian Inheritance: The discussion in this chapter clearly illustrates the three fundamental principles of inheritance which was first established by Gregor Mendel.

- The first is the "Principle of the Dominance." This is where one characteristic is dominant over another of a given pair. When a bird is heterozygous or different, for both characteristics only the dominant one is visible.

- The second is the "Principle of Segregation," whereby a gene for a dominant characteristic from one parent, and a gene for a recessive characteristic from another parent, come together in the F_1 generation and segregate or separate in the F_2 generation.

- Which brings us to the third principle, the "Principle of Independent Assortment," whereby the inheritance of genes in the F_2 generation possesses characteristics in different combinations from those of either of the parents in the original cross.

The fundamental principles of Mendelian inheritance have contributed greatly to the science of breeding. They have enabled breeders of every type, and especially that of American Games, to produce results with increasing rapidity and precision. Among the many breeds and varieties of domestic fowl that exist today, all which have originated from the Wild Junglefowl, we have seen great diversity of conformation of body and color of plumage patterns, not to mention, many other important characteristics and traits. We are beginning to understand, as breeders, that we are able to look upon the whole natural world as a warehouse of potentialities that may be realized in whatsoever permutations and combinations we may desire.

Knowledge of the fundamental principles of Mendelian inheritance enables us to predict the results of many matings. By performing suitable matings of carefully selected individuals, we may introduce good features and eliminate bad ones. As a result we can literally create new breeds and varieties that best meet our needs. But that's not all; in fact, it is not the most important contribution that Mendel's work has done for the science of breeding. Mendel's greatest achievement was when he established the principle that *"the contents of the germ-cells, and not the outward characteristics of the individual, must be our standard in breeding."*

For many cockers and backyard breeders, the practice has been to select broodfowl based upon its performance ability, appearance, or its pedigree. Mendelism demonstrates that this is not good enough. The progressive breeder must consider the kind of offspring produced to determine the worthiness of any bird as a breeder. Instead of looking to the ancestry only, you should also consider the offspring. In fact, in many cases, the kind of offspring produced is the only reliable standard in determining the breeding value of any individual. Therefore, it is through the "Progeny Test" that is of vital importance in the successful breeding of American Games. I will discuss "Progeny Testing" later in the book.

Genetics and Evolution go hand in hand: As you will see, you cannot discuss genetics without including theories of Evolution. And you cannot discuss Evolution without discussing Natural Selection. It is impossible to discuss one without the other. Genetics explains what makes Evolution work and Evolution explains how inheritance occurs, and inheritance explains the process of Natural Selection.

The good news is that the process of Natural Selection is not that far off from the process of Artificial Selection. They both lead to the same outcome, Evolution. The only difference is that one is performed by Mother Nature and the other is manmade. Since the process of Evolution by means of Natural Selection is mirrored by that of Selective Breeding, I will use references to Evolution and Natural Selection to illustrate my point, and to show their close relationship to Artificial Selection and Selective Breeding. Remember, the foundation of Selective Breeding is rooted in Biology, Ornithology, Genetics, and Evolution, which includes Natural and Artificial Selection. Therefore it is imperative that you educate yourself in all areas.

HOW TO READ THIS SECTION: I suggest that you read this chapter from beginning to end before skipping around, for it is set up in such a way that it builds your knowledge as you go on. Every part leads you to the next. It may seem repetitious or redundant at times, but this is a good thing; the more you see and hear the same thing, the more chance you will gain knowledge and remember it. Granted, you may have to read some portions of this book a number of times to fully understand and absorb the material, but trust me, it will all work out in the end. When you are finished studying this chapter, you will have a great understanding of the breeding of American Games, and have the tools to accomplish great things with your fowl.

I know for some, genetics can be a very boring subject and for others, can be confusing. But I promise that the information is this chapter is important, and beneficial to your success as a breeder of high quality American Games.

SIMPLE DEFINITIONS OF TERMS
Definition and Terminology of genetic words and phrases:

Before you go any further, it would be a good idea for you to familiarize yourself with these terms and their meanings. I don't expect you to fully understand them at this point; their meaning will become clearer in time. Just look them over for now:

Genetics: **Genetics** was founded through biology and is the science of heredity and variation of all living organisms. The fact that living things inherit traits from their parents has been used since prehistoric times to improve crop plants and animals through Selective Breeding.

Genome: In modern molecular biology, the **genome** is the genetic material of an organism, its entire hereditary information, encoded in DNA or in RNA. Today, we are able to sequence the **genome** of any living thing and read it as if we were reading a book. **Genomes** are documents, written in billions of letters. They are letters used after the removal of earlier letters, endlessly augmented, erased, and rewritten by the hand of the selective breeder.

DNA - Deoxyribonucleic Acid: DNA is a nucleic acid that contains the genetic instructions used in the development and functioning of all known living organisms. The main role of DNA molecules is the long-term storage of information. DNA is often compared to a set of blueprints since it contains the instructions needed to construct other components of cells, such as proteins and RNA molecules. The DNA segments that carry this genetic information are called genes.

Chromosome: A **chromosome** is an organized structure of DNA and protein that is found in cells. It is a single piece of coiled DNA containing many genes, regulatory elements and other nucleotide sequences. **Chromosomes** also contain DNA-bound proteins, which serve to package the DNA and control its functions.

Autosomes: An **autosome** is a chromosome that is not a sex chromosome — that is to say, there are an equal number of copies of the chromosome in males and females. For example, in chickens, there are 38

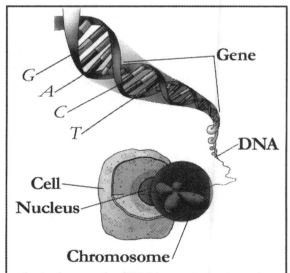

A single strand of DNA consists of a series of nucleotides joined together in a long chain. These are made up of four types - Adenine (A), Thymine (T), Guanine (G), and Cytosine (C). The sequence of the four chemical building blocks of DNA determines the traits of all living things. Each generation passes on this chemical text to its offspring. Occasional mistakes in copying, mutations, can result in new traits.

pairs of **autosomes** and in addition there are (Z) and (W) chromosomes which are sex chromosomes.

Haploid: The **haploid** is the number of chromosomes in a gamete (sperm and egg) of an individual. Gametes are **haploid** cells. Chicken **haploid** gametes have 39 chromosomes.

Diploid (Two Copies of Each Chromosome): Cells have two homologous copies of each chromosome, usually one from the mother and one from the father. Nearly all mammals are **diploid** organisms. Chickens **diploid** cells have 78 chromosomes.

Gene: Also known as a "Factor," a **gene** is the basic unit of heredity in a living organism. The field of genetics predates modern molecular biology, but it is now known that all living things depend on DNA to pass on their traits to offspring. Loosely speaking, a **gene** is a segment of genomic information that, taken as a whole, identifies a trait. The informal usage of the term **gene** often refers to the scientific concept of an allele.

Alleles: Not all copies of a gene are identical. The alternative forms of a gene, leading to alternative forms of a character, are called **alleles**. Two **alleles** make up the individual's genotype. For example, if a gene determines the color of the birds legs, one **allele** of that gene may produce green legs and the other **allele** may produce yellow legs. In diploid organisms there are usually two **alleles** of any one gene (one from each parent).

Dominant and Recessive Alleles: When two gametes containing exactly the same **allele** of a gene fuse during fertilization to form a zygote, the offspring that develops from that zygote is said to be homozygous; when the two gametes contain different **alleles**, the individual offspring is heterozygous.

In many cases, genotypic interactions between the two **alleles** at a locus can be described as **dominant** or **recessive**. An **allele** (A) is **dominant** if the phenotype of the heterozygote (Aa) is the same as the homozygote (AA). The **allele** (a) does not influence the heterozygote's phenotype and is called **recessive**.

Locus: In the fields of genetics, a **locus** (plural for loci) is the specific location of a gene on a chromosome. A variant of the DNA sequence at a given **locus** is called an allele. The ordered list of **loci** known for a particular genome is called a genetic map. Gene mapping is the process of determining the **locus** for a particular biological trait. Diploid cells whose chromosomes have the same allele of a given gene at some **locus** are called homozygous with respect to that gene, while those that have different alleles of a given gene at a **locus**, heterozygous with respect to that gene.

Gamete: The name **gamete** was introduced by the Austrian biologist Gregor Mendel. A **gamete** is a cell that fuses with another **gamete** during fertilization (conception). In species that produce two morphologically distinct types of **gametes**, and in which each individual produces only one type, a female is any individual that produces the larger type of **gamete**—called an ovum (or egg)—and a male produces the smaller tadpole-like type—called a sperm. **Gametes** carry half the genetic information of an individual.

Zygote: (from Ancient Greek zygôtos meaning "joined"). A **Zygote** is the initial cell formed when a new organism is produced by means of sexual reproduction. A **zygote** is produced from the union of two gametes, and constitutes the first stage in an organism's development. **Zygotes** are usually produced by a fertilization event between two haploid cells (an ovum from a female and a sperm cell from a male), which combine to form the single diploid cell. For chickens and American

Games, the fertilized egg is the "zygote." **Zygotes** contain DNA derived from both the mother and the father, and this provides all the genetic information necessary to form a new individual.

Mitosis: (Not to be confused with meiosis) **Mitosis** is the process by which a eukaryotic cell separates the chromosomes in its cell nucleus into two identical sets in two nuclei. It is generally followed immediately by cytokinesis, which divides the nuclei, cytoplasm, organelles and cell membrane into two cells containing roughly equal shares of these cellular components.

Meiosis: In biology, **meiosis** is a process of reductional division in which the number of chromosomes per cell is cut in half. In animals, **meiosis** always results in the formation of gametes. As with mitosis, before **meiosis** begins, the DNA in the original cell is replicated during S-phase of the cell cycle. Two cell divisions separate the replicated chromosomes into four haploid gametes. **Meiosis** is essential for sexual reproduction.

During **meiosis**, the genome of a diploid germ cell, which is composed of long segments of DNA packaged into chromosomes, undergoes DNA replication followed by two rounds of division, resulting in four haploid cells. Each of these cells contains one complete set of chromosomes, or half of the genetic content of the original cell. If **meiosis** produces gametes, these cells must fuse during fertilization to create a new zygote before any new growth can occur. Thus, the division mechanism of **meiosis** is a reciprocal process to the joining of two genomes that occurs at fertilization. Because the chromosomes of each parent undergo homologous recombination during **meiosis**, each gamete, and thus each zygote, will have a unique genetic blueprint encoded in its DNA. Together, **meiosis** and fertilization constitute sexuality in the eukaryotes, and generate genetically distinct individuals in populations.

F1 and F2 Generation: Also known as the F_1 **hybrid** and F_2 **hybrid**, these are terms used in genetics and Selective Breeding, which stands for Filial 1, the first filial generation, and Filial 2, the second filial generation.

F_1 **hybrid** are seeds/plants or animal offspring resulting from a cross mating of distinctly different parental types. The offspring of distinctly different breeds or varieties produce new a variety with specific characteristics from either or both parents.

Gregor Mendel's groundbreaking work in the 19th century focused on patterns of inheritance and the genetic basis for variation. In his cross-pollination experiments involving two true-breeding or homozygous parents, Mendel found that the resulting F_1 **generation** was heterozygous. The offspring showed a combination of those phenotypes from each of the parents that were genetically dominant. Mendel's discoveries involving the F_1 and F_2 **generation** laid the foundation for modern genetics.

Mendel also noticed that, while an F_2 **hybrid**, the result of cross pollination of an F_1, does not have the consistency of the F_1 **hybrid**, it may retain some desirable traits.

Zygosity: The term **zygosity** refers to the similarity of genes for a trait (inherited characteristic) in an organism. If both genes are the same, the organism is "**homozygous**" for the trait. If both genes are different, the organism is "**heterozygous**" for that trait. If one gene is missing, it is "**hemizygous**," and if both genes are missing, it is "**nullizygous**."

Dominance: In genetics, **dominance** is the relationship between different forms of a gene (alleles) at a particular physical location (locus) on a chromosome.

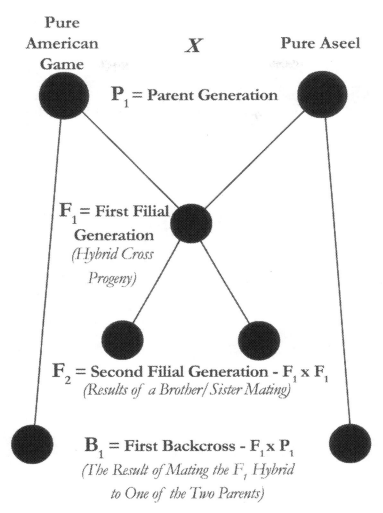

This illustration shows the relationship of the P_1 (parent generation) to the F_1 (first filial generation), F_2 (second filial generation), and B_1 (first backcross).

Heterosis: Also known as "**hybrid vigor**," it is a term used in genetics, and the practice of Selective Breeding, for the purpose of outbreeding enhancement. **Heterosis** increases function of any biological quality in a hybrid offspring. It is the occurrence of a genetically superior offspring from mixing the genes of its parents.

Heterosis is the opposite of "inbreeding depression," which occurs with increasing homozygosity. The term often causes controversy, particularly in terms of the Selective Breeding of domestic animals, because it is sometimes believed that all crossbred plants or animals are genetically superior to their parents. However, this is true only in certain circumstances, such as when a hybrid is seen to be superior to its parents. This is known as "**hybrid vigor**." When the opposite happens, and a hybrid inherits traits from its parents that makes it unfit for survival, or for the purpose for which it is bred, the result is referred to as "outbreeding depression."

Homologues: Each chromosome of a matching pair are called "**homologues**." They are not quite identical. Each chromosome of a homologous pair has the same genes in the same location as the corresponding **homologue**. However, the genes on **homologues**, may be different alleles or the same alleles.

In Mendel's pea plants, for example, on the homologous chromosomes containing the gene for pea plant height, each **homologue** may have a gene identical to the other (like "tall gene" and "tall gene") or it may have the "same" gene but a "different version" of the gene, like "tall gene" and "short gene." The same gene but of a different version is called alleles. Both alleles affect the height, but one version of the gene makes pea plants short and the other makes pea plants tall.

<u>Other important terms</u>:

- **Nucleus**: in eukaryotic cells, the membranous organelle that houses the chromosomal DNA.

- **Somatic Cell**: any of the cells of a multi-cellular organism except those that are destined to form gametes (germ-line cells).

- **Somatic Mutation**: a change in genetic information (mutation) occurring in one of the somatic cells of a multi-cellular organism, not passed from one generation to the next.

- **Incomplete Dominance**: this is an inheritance relationship that occurs when both alleles influence the phenotype.

- **Germ Cells**: Germ cells are the cells that give rise to the gametes (this is a sperm from the cock and an ovum or egg from the hen).

- **Homozygosity**: this is the state of being homozygous.

- **Hemizygous**: characterized by one or more genes (as in a genetic deficiency or in an (Z) chromosome paired with a (W) chromosome) that have no allelic counterparts.

- **Genetic Drift**: is a mechanism of evolution due to random changes in the allelic frequencies of a population; more likely to occur in small populations or when only a few individuals of a large population reproduce.

- **Evolution**: Darwin defined this term as "Descent with Modification." It is the change in a lineage from generation to generation. In general terms, as used in Artificial Selection and Selective Breeding, evolution is the process of change by which new breeds develop from preexisting breeds over time.

PRINCIPLES OF REPRODUCTIVE CELLS, CHROMOSOMES, AND GENES
They are the chief modes of transmission of characteristics
From the parents to the offspring

"Some writers, who have not attended to natural history, have attempted
to show that the force of inheritance has been much exaggerated. The breeders
of animals would smile at such simplicity…"

Charles Darwin

It is not my intention to discuss the entire, but diverse, field of genetics in this section of the book. However, in order to understand the results of your breeding efforts and make any necessary changes or adjustments, you must know a little about genetics and the laws of inheritance; to include, reproductive cells, chromosomes and genes, and how they function. They are the hereditary units that transmit characteristics from the parents to the offspring, and when it comes to breeding American Games this is very important. Chromosomes and genes determine all the hereditary characteristics a game bird will ever have; from the body type to the color of their feathers. They are truly the fundamental unit of genetics.

Molecular genetics is the study of the structure and function of chromosomes and genes. Most of Mendel's findings on this subject are of the same opinion with what biologists now know about molecular genetics. What were their findings? Let's discuss them now.

REPRODUCTIVE CELLS
All birds are the result of the union of two cells, it's described as fertilization

<u>Fertilization and the joining of the reproductive cells</u>: From the standpoint of reproduction and the inheritance of characteristics and traits, the modern cocker and backyard breeder are well aware that the basis for heredity is found in the reproductive cells. It's through the mating of a cock and a hen that allows the reproductive cells to unite; this is the only way in which a chicken can be produced, that's not the whole story.

The job of transmitting qualities from one generation to the next is performed by the germ cells. In many animals, the germ cells originate near the gut and migrate to the developing gonads (testes and ovary). There, they undergo cell division of two types; mitosis and meiosis (see definition of terms).

Germ cells are the cells that give rise to the reproductive cells, otherwise known as gametes. This is known as cellular differentiation. The egg (ovum or ova) is the hen gamete and the sperm (spermatozoon or spermatozoa) is the cock gamete.

At the time of copulation (the engagement of sexual intercourse) the copulatory organ of the cock ejects semen containing sperm into the cloaca of the hen, this is known as a "cloaca kiss," and the sperm then traverse the length of the oviduct. Apparently each ovum is fertilized shortly after it enters the oviduct. However, only one sperm fertilizes the ovum, even though several sperms may be present in the semen surrounding the ovum. The fertilization of the hen gamete by the cock gamete produces the fertilized egg; in other words, they unite to form a single cell, which is called the "zygote," a term meaning joined together. It is the zygote that develops into the chick.

All birds are the result of this union of two such tiny cells, we call this fertilization, but in reality, it is a biological wonder, for these two gametes contain all the anatomical, physiological, and psychological characters that the offspring will inherit.

In the body cells of a bird, each of the chromosomes are duplicated, while in the formation of the sex cells, or "gametes" (sperm and egg), a reduction division occurs and only one chromosome and one gene of each pair goes into a gamete. This means that only half the number of chromosomes and genes present in the body cells of the bird goes into each egg and sperm, but each egg or sperm cell has genes for every characteristic of its breed, variety and strain, not to mention all of its ancestors.

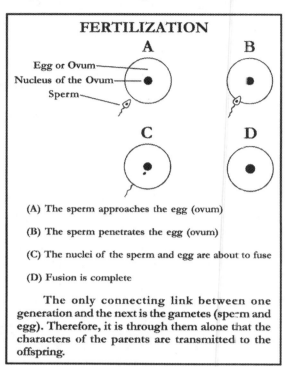

FERTILIZATION

Egg or Ovum
Nucleus of the Ovum
Sperm

A **B**

C **D**

(A) The sperm approaches the egg (ovum)

(B) The sperm penetrates the egg (ovum)

(C) The nuclei of the sperm and egg are about to fuse

(D) Fusion is complete

The only connecting link between one generation and the next is the gametes (sperm and egg). Therefore, it is through them alone that the characters of the parents are transmitted to the offspring.

When fertilization occurs each chick acquires two sets of genes, one from its father and one from its mother, duplicating in the body cells of the embryo, the single chromosomes from the germ cell of each parent unite to form new pairs of like function.

CHROMOSOMES AND GENES

Each gamete contains little threadlike bodies called "chromosomes," which are transmitted from parent to offspring. In this part of the chapter we will discuss chromosomes, as well as genes. However, the real question is what are chromosomes and genes?

The bodies of all animals are made up of millions or even billions of tiny cells; microscopic in size. Each cell contains a nucleus where there are a number of pairs of bodies known as chromosomes. A chromosome is a threadlike structure made up of DNA. Each chromosome is a single DNA molecule associated with proteins. The chromosome consists of two identical halves. Each half of the chromosome is called a chromatid. The chromosomes carry thousands of pairs of minute particles called genes, which are lined up on the chromosomes. A gene is the segment of DNA on a chromosome that controls a particular hereditary trait. Therefore, the genes are the basic hereditary material, which determines the characteristics that will be found in the individual.

Genes Determine:

- The conformation of their body.
- The color of their plumage.
- The color of their legs and feet.
- The color of their eyes.
- Type of comb.
- The color of their skin and face.
- Additional details which together make up the form and function of the bird.

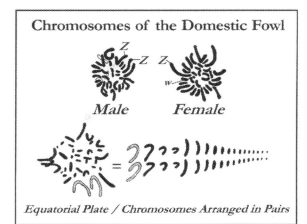

Chromosomes of the Domestic Fowl

Male   *Female*

Equatorial Plate / Chromosomes Arranged in Pairs

The arrangement of genes on the chromosomes is often likened to that of beads on a string, thus giving the impression that each gene is a separate unit and that all of the units are arranged in a linear array. Since the chromosomes are paired and the genes are lined up on the chromosomes, the genes also come in pairs. The genes are too small to be seen, but their existence has been determined by carefully executed breeding experiments.

Each of several alternative forms of a gene is called an allele. During meiosis, gametes (the sperm and ovum or egg) receive one chromosome from each homologous pair of chromosomes. This means that when the gametes (sperm and egg) combine in fertilization the offspring receives one allele for a given trait from each parent. For example, if a gene determines the color of the birds legs, one **allele** of that gene may produce green legs and the other **allele** may produce yellow legs. Depending on which allele is dominant will determine which allele is expressed.

The sex chromosomes are indicated by stippling. The illustration above is the male and female chromosome groups of the domestic fowl. Both are the actual appearance of the chromosomes as they lie in equatorial plane of a mitotic spindle just before the beginning of the metaphase splitting. The chromosomes are contained in the nucleus of the reproductive cell and are always in pairs, except for the single sex chromosome in the female. Each chromosome is made up of a large number of tiny bodies called genes, which are the units that give rise to the numerous hereditary characters of our fowl. Alongside the equatorial plate is a diagram, shown at the same scale, of how the chromosomes may be arranged in pairs, the members of which are similar to each other in size and shape.

DIPLOID AND HAPLOID CELLS: Before we go any further I feel the need to discuss the terms diploid and haploid, for they will be used throughout this section of the chapter.

Most plants, animals, and humans have "paired," or two sets of chromosomes. Organisms with paired chromosomes are considered "diploid." In paired chromosomes, one chromosome of each pair is contributed by a single parent.

For example, in chickens, the mother gives one chromosome in her ova (egg), and the father contributes the rest of the chromosomes in his sperm. For all 39 pairs of chromosomes, one chromosome of each pair came from the mother and the other chromosome from each pair came from the father.

Making organisms from two "half" (haploid) cells requires a special cell division process called meiosis. Meiosis produces egg/ova and sperm in preparation for fertilization (to be precise, in joining of haploid cells). This careful orchestration makes sure that each daughter cell gets exactly one of each matching pair of chromosomes.

The other kind of nucleus replication (mitosis) simply makes two identical copies of nuclei with the same number of chromosomes as the starting cell.

THE NUMBER OF CHROMOSOMES AND GENES: The cells of an organism can be divided into somatic cells and germ cells. The former contains two sets of chromosomes (diploid), known as homologous chromosomes; one of paternal (father) origin and one of maternal (mother) origin.

Each species has a characteristic number of chromosomes in each cell. This is of fundamental importance, for the number of chromosomes in any given species of animal is constant. It never changes! Chickens have 78 chromosomes, no more, no less. Some are dominant and some are recessive, some are homozygous, while some are heterozygous, but there are always 78 chromosomes.

The fruit-fly, which has 4 pairs of chromosomes in each somatic cell, is known to have over 5,000 genes, whereas man has 23 pairs of chromosomes, which are estimated to have a total of 23,000 genes. Recent counts indicate that within the chicken's body, all the cells (except the germ cells) have 78 chromosomes, 39 of paternal and 39 of maternal origin. In other words, there are 39 pairs of chromosomes in the chicken. One of the pairs of chromosomes has to do with sex inheritance. Genes which are carried on the sex chromosomes are called sex-linked genes. Although chickens have twice as many chromosomes as man, they have the same number of genes as man. It is said that chickens have around 23,000 genes.

Also, there are two distinct sizes of chromosomes. As a result, chickens have five pairs of large chromosomes. Additionally, each species has micro-chromosomes, which are very small and without distinguishable features. It is not known whether they carry genetic information or not.

GENES GIVE RISE TO CHARACTERS: The chromosomes are the bearers of the determiners of the hereditary characteristics and traits, but, since there are hundreds of characteristics and only 38 pairs of autosomes, and 1 or 2 sex chromosomes according to the sex, it is obvious that each chromosome must be responsible for the development of many characteristics and traits. Each chromosome is made up of smaller units called "factors" or "genes." It is the genes that give rise to the abundance of hereditary characteristics and traits. This includes the development of such characters as plumage-color [lacing, penciling, spangling, barring], comb type [rose-comb, pea-comb, straight (*single*) comb] feathered shanks, shank color (white, blue, black, yellow, or green shanks), and hatchability, performance ability, and gameness.

SOME PAIRED GENES ARE IDENTICAL TO EACH OTHER WHILE SOME ARE DIFFERENT: For those that are identical, they are considered to be "homozygous." For those that are different, they are considered to be "heterozygous." The word "homo" comes from the Greek word meaning "same," the word "hetero" comes from the Greek word meaning "different," and the word "zygous" comes from the Greek word meaning "pair")

When a bird has a large number of paired genes that are identical, it is a bird that is homozygous in its traits. The more closely birds are related, or inbred, the more homozygous they will become, and the more predictable their offspring will be. This is important when creating or maintaining a strain. Uniformity is only achieved when the traits of the individual are the same as the traits of the entire family.

On the other hand, when a bird has a large number of paired genes that are dissimilar, it is a bird that is heterozygous in its traits. This occurs when two birds, which are not related, are crossbred. When this occurs the genes of the offspring can pair off in many different directions producing many different combinations or results, causing the offspring to be extremely unpredictable in their overall form and function.

<u>LETHAL GENES</u>: Lethal genes are normally recessive traits which are concentrated by inbreeding. Lethal Genes are traits which cause an abnormality in inheritance, which results in death, either at birth or later in their development.

Other defects can occur due to lethal genes, which don't always cause death, but can cause enough harm that it weakens the bird to the point that it becomes totally worthless.

The embryological development, which is the development of the young (from the time that the egg and the sperm unite until the chick is hatched) is a very complicated process. It's amazing how many chicks actually develop normally, as opposed to the few that develop abnormally. A chick that acquires the same lethal gene from both parents usually dies early; often in the embryo stage. When you breed two birds that are carrying the same lethal recessive gene, twenty-five percent of their offspring will display the lethal gene.

Many abnormalities are hereditary, which are caused by certain bad genes, in this case, "Lethal's." However, the majority of lethal genes is recessive and may therefore, remain hidden for many generations. The prevention of such genetic abnormalities requires that the germ plasm be purged of the "bad" genes. This means that where recessive lethal genes are involved, the breeder must be aware of the fact that both parents carry the gene. He must avoid breeding these fowl in the future.

More than thirty-five lethal genes have been identified in chickens. They are easily recognized because they are usually accompanied by such idiosyncrasies as winglessness, twisted legs, missing or twisted beaks, extra toes, and the list goes on and on. Fortunately for the breeder, these lethal genes are relatively rare. Nevertheless, they do contribute to the "genetic pool" of most strains of American Games.

PRINCIPLES OF SEX DETERMINATION
Sex chromosomes and autosomes,
And the establishment of chromosome pairs

Sex determination can be an enormous obstacle when it comes to genetics, for the simple reason that this is the very point where the pairing of chromosomes, as I have described earlier, has been modified. To understand this point it is necessary to look again at the way in which the chromosome pairs are established.

SEX CHROMOSOMES AND AUTOSOMES: All the genetic information that's transmitted from a chicken to its offspring is the result of the "gamete" (sperm and ovum/egg), which carries a half-set of chromosomes from both the father and the mother respectively. Chromosomes are categorized as either sex chromosomes or autosomes. Sex chromosomes are chromosomes that determine the sex of an organism and they may also carry genes for other characteristics

The difference between the number of chromosomes in the cock and the hen is due to the fact that the cock has one more "sex chromosome" than the hen. The chromosomes are contained in the nucleus of the reproductive cell and are always in pairs, except for the single sex chromosome in the hen. The sex chromosomes in any species are always associated with sex and are a factor in its determination, hence their name.

THE NUMBER OF CHROMOSOMES IN A COCK AND HEN: A cock has 39 pairs of chromosomes, 1 pair called the "sex chromosomes," which are alike, and contains information that determines their gender. The other 38 pairs are called "autosomal chromosomes" or "ordinary chromosomes." Like a cock, a hen has 38 pairs of autosomals, but unlike a cock, she has only 1 sex chromosome. Two of the 78 chicken chromosomes are sex chromosomes, while the remaining 76 chromosomes are autosomes.

Every cell of an organism has two copies of each autosome. The organism receives one copy of each autosome from each parent. The two copies of each autosome are called homologous chromosomes, or homologues. Homologous chromosomes are the same size and shape and carry genes for the same traits. For example, if one chromosome in a pair of homologous chromosomes contains a gene for eye color, so will the other chromosome in the homologous pair.

When fertilization takes place and the zygote is formed and the chromosomes come together in order to make the full set necessary for the making of the new individual, only 1 chromosome of each pair is included in the germ cell. The male germ cell, or gamete, will contain 38 autosomes and 1 sex chromosome. The female cell will contain an equal number of autosomes but may or may not contain a sex chromosome. If the female gamete contains a sex chromosome, and is fertilized, the resulting chick will be a male. If it does not contain the sex chromosome, the chick will be a female.

Its actual "sex" is laid down by the presence or absence of a chromosome from the mother. As you can see, the female germ cell determines sex. Every egg that is fertilized contains a sex chromosome from the cock, but a hen transmits her sex chromosome to only fifty percent of the eggs she lays.

SEX DETERMINATION: In humans, an ovum can carry only an (X) chromosome [of the (X) and (Y) chromosomes], whereas a sperm may carry either an (X) or a (Y). Males have the control of the sex of any resulting zygote, as the genotype of the sex-determining chromosomes of a male is (XY), and a female's is (XX). In other words, because the (Y) chromosome can only be present in the sperm, it is that gamete alone which can determine whether an offspring will be a male or female.

The sex chromosomes in chickens are designated (Z) and (W), which correspond respectively to (X) and (Y) in mammals. The (ZW) sex-determination system is a system that determines the sex of offspring, which is found in birds, reptiles, fish, and some insects.

In mammals, the male is the heterogametic sex (XY) and the female the homogametic sex (XX). In avian species, such as chickens, and more specifically American Games, this condition of the (ZW) sex-determination system is reversed compared to the (XY) system of mammals.

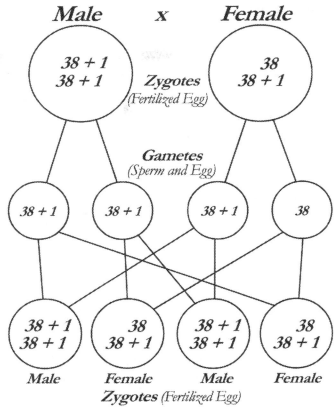

Male x *Female*

Zygotes (Fertilized Egg)

Gametes (Sperm and Egg)

Zygotes (Fertilized Egg)

The male fowl has 38 pairs of autosomes plus 1 pair of sex chromosomes, whereas the female fowl has 38 pairs of autosomes but only 1 sex chromosome. The male produces but one kind of gametes (sperm), each of which contains 38 autosomes plus 1 sex chromosome. The female produces two kinds of gametes (egg), one kind containing 38 autosomes plus 1 sex chromosome and the other containing 38 autosomes but no sex chromosome. A male gamete (sperm) uniting with a female gamete (egg) containing 38 autosomes plus 1 sex chromosome produces a zygote (fertilized egg) containing 38 pairs of autosomes plus 1 pair of sex chromosomes; such a zygote (fertilized egg) develops into a male. A male gamete (sperm) upon uniting with a female gamete (egg) containing 38 autosomes but no sex chromosome produces a zygote (fertilized egg) containing 38 pairs of autosomes but only 1 sex chromosome; such a zygote (fertilized egg) develops into a female.

Females have two different kinds of chromosomes (ZW), and males have two of the same kind of chromosomes (ZZ). In this case, the female has the unlike pair and the male has the like pair. Males are the homogametic sex (ZZ), while females are heterogametic (ZW).

In chickens, a sperm can carry only a (Z) chromosome, whereas an ovum may carry either an (Z) or a (W). In the case of chickens, the hens have the control of the sex of any resulting zygote, as the genotype of the sex-determining chromosomes of a hen (ZW), and a cock is (ZZ). In other words, because the (W) chromosome can only be present in the ovum, it is that gamete alone which can determine whether an offspring will be a male or female. In the (ZW) system it is the ovum that determines the sex of the offspring, in contrast to the (XY) sex-determination system, where it is the sperm which determines the sex.

Let me explain this in simpler terms: If a fertilized egg contains chromosomes from both the cock and the hen, it will not only have a full complement of paired chromosomes, but will contain two chromosomes known

Sex Chromosomes

Sex chromosomes. Birds and mammals differ in the bases of sex determination. In birds, sex chromosomes are of different origins and therefore are given the letters (Z) and (W), rather than (X) and (Y) as in mammals. Male birds are the sex with two of the same sex chromosomes (ZZ), and female birds are the sex with one of each (ZW), the opposite of mammals.

as (ZZ), which would result in the offspring becoming a stag. If the chromosome from the mother happens to be missing, or possibly replaced by a dissimilar chromosome, the fertilized egg will have the sex chromosomes (ZW), and will hatch into a pullet. As you can see, and as I have mentioned earlier, the determination of sex really depends on the hen. So don't blame the cock if your offspring hatch out all pullets.

Since each egg has a fifty-fifty chance of containing two chromosomes, the balance between stags and pullets is usually very close. They hatch at approximately a fifty-fifty stag to pullet ratio. Significant variations from this ratio may be due either to random deaths of embryos and chicks or to sex-linked lethal genes.

Sex-chromosomes are not just for determining the sex: The (Z) chromosome seems to be especially important in chickens. In fact, the (Z) chromosome is larger and has more genes, like the (X) chromosome in the (XY) system. The (Z) chromosome is the fifth largest of the chromosomes and comprises nearly ten percent of the total DNA material. Since a number of genes are carried on the (Z) chromosome, they are "sex-linked," and their effects may show up as dominant or recessive traits. Of the six known linkage groups, the sex-linked group has the most known segregating loci. I will discuss sex-linkage and dominant and recessive traits later in the chapter.

The relation of chickens to humans: No genes are shared between the avian (ZW) and mammal (XY) chromosomes. From a comparison between chickens and humans, the (Z) chromosome appeared similar to the autosomal chromosome 9 in human, rather than (X) or (Y). This leads researchers to believe the (ZW) and (XY) sex determination systems do not share an origin, but that the sex chromosomes are derived from autosomal chromosomes of the common ancestor.

PRINCIPLES OF SEX-LINKED INHERITANCE

In order to understand Sex-Linkage and Sex-Linked Traits, you have to know a little about genes and how they work. We talked about genes earlier in the chapter. However, I would like to revisit this subject once more so that you will have a better understanding of how sex-linkage operates.

SO, WHAT EXACTLY IS A GENE? A gene is the hereditary unit that transmits characteristics from parents to offspring. Each chick receives two genes, one from its mother and one from its father. These two genes match up into pairs of like function.

For example: controlling the type of comb (pea or straight) and color, whether it is the feathers or the legs. If the paired genes are identical, they are considered to be homozygous. This comes from the Greek language, which means "same pair." The closer they're related, and the more inbred the birds are, the more homozygous they will be, and the more predictable their offspring will be as well. When genes are paired differently they are considered to be heterozygous, this also comes from the Greek language, which means "different pair." When heterozygous chickens are bred, in the case of crossing or outcrossed, the results of their offspring become unpredictable. The genes of heterozygous birds can pair off in all different directions as well as many combinations, and the evidence is realized in their offspring.

Since many characteristics are represented by genes on each chromosome, those characters which are carried on the sex chromosome are called sex-linked traits.

WHO CONTROLS SEX-LINKAGE, THE COCK OR THE HEN? Whether it's with American Games or in other domestic type fowl, many characteristics (which chickens possess) are inherited equally from father and mother. The genes which give rise to such characteristics are borne on the 38 pairs of autosomes. They are common to both sexes, half of the chromosomes being of maternal (mother) and half are of paternal (father) origin.

On the other hand, while the cock only produces one kind of germ cell, the hen produces two kinds of eggs, those that develop into stags and those that develop into pullets. Certain hereditary factors are linked with sex in such a way that the hen cannot transmit them in the eggs, which are to develop into pullets. The theory is that the eggs determined to be pullets are such because they lack a certain material body, which is present in the eggs that are determined to be stags.

There are certain characteristics, however, that are transmitted from mother to son, but not from mother to daughter, although they are transmitted from father to both son and daughter. Only characteristics transmitted from mother to son are characteristics that are controlled by genes on a hen's sex chromosome called "sex-linked," while all others are "autosomal." They are called "sex-linked" characteristics because it is reasonably certain that the genes that give rise to such characteristics are borne on the sex chromosomes.

52

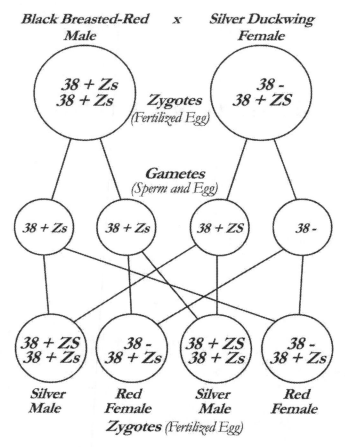

Black Breasted-Red Male x **Silver Duckwing Female**

38 + Zs
38 + Zs

Zygotes
(Fertilized Egg)

38 -
38 + ZS

Gametes
(Sperm and Egg)

38 + Zs   38 + Zs   38 + ZS   38 -

38 + ZS
38 + Zs

38 -
38 + Zs

38 + ZS
38 + Zs

38 -
38 + Zs

Silver Male   **Red Female**   **Silver Male**   **Red Female**

Zygotes *(Fertilized Egg)*

Here is a diagram illustrating the inheritance of sex and the sex-linked character for silver. Now we show the manner in which the gene for silver in a Silver Duckwing female is transmitted to her sons only. The gene for silver is indicated by (S) and the gene for red by (s), each being contained in the sex chromosomes, indicated by (Z). The Black Breasted-Red male has 38 pairs of autosomes and 2 sex chromosomes, designated (Z), associated with each of which is the gene (s) for non-silver (or red). The Silver Duckwing female has 38 pairs of autosomes but only one sex chromosome (Z), associated with which is the sex-linked gene (S) for silver, which is dominant to red. The male progeny are silver colored, whereas the female progeny are red colored.

When a hen with a certain sex-linked trait is mated to a cock without it, the trait is acquired by all the resulting stags, but not the pullets. A pullet does not acquire her mother's sex chromosome, which means she cannot acquire any genetic information it contains. A stag, on the other hand, always acquires genetic information contained on its mother's sex chromosome.

There is an old saying in the chicken world that goes something like this - "*like mother like son,*' and "*like father like daughter,*" which is practically true.

I have always known that if you want to see the attributes of the hen, look to her stags, and if you want to see the attributes of the cock, look to his daughters. This is just one of the reasons that line-breeding works so well.

CHROMOSOMES VERSUS SEX-LINKED DOMINANCE: The fact that certain characteristics are inherited on a sex-linked basis is easy to understand when you keep in mind the difference between the cock and hen in respect to the number of sex chromosomes each possess.

As I have mentioned many times in this chapter, when it comes to chickens, sex is determined by "two sex chromosomes," called the (Z) chromosome and the (W) chromosome. The cock has two sex chromosomes, typically (ZZ), whereas the hen is typically (ZW), and has only one. The remaining pairs of chromosome are found in both sexes and are called "autosomes," and may be dominant or recessive.

The difference between the (ZW) and (XY) inheritance: The (ZW) type of sex inheritance is common to birds, fish, reptiles, and insects, but in many other animals another type of sex inheritance occurs. It is called the (XY) type of sex inheritance, in which the male is heterozygous for sex

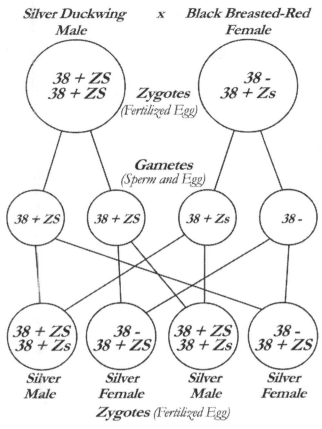

Silver Duckwing Male x Black Breasted-Red Female

Zygotes (Fertilized Egg)

Gametes (Sperm and Egg)

Silver Male · Silver Female · Silver Male · Silver Female

Zygotes (Fertilized Egg)

Showing the manner in which the dominant sex-linked gene, (S) for silver is transmitted to the daughters as well as the sons in a mating of Silver Duckwing male x Black Breasted-Red female.

because he has only 1 sex chromosome (X) and the female is homozygous for sex because she has two similar sex chromosomes, known as (X) and (X). As far as sex is concerned, the female zygote contains (X) and (X) chromosomes and produces gametes each having an (X) chromosome, whereas the male zygote, which contains but 1 (X) chromosome, produces two kinds of gametes in approximate equality; one gamete containing an (X) chromosome for every one without it. The latter being known as the (Y) gamete.

The difference between the (ZW) and (XY) types of sex inheritance is that in the (ZW) type, the male is homozygous for sex chromosomes, and consequently for sex-linked genes; whereas, in the (XY) type, the female is homozygous for sex chromosomes, and consequently for sex-linked genes.

<u>The inheritance of sex in chickens</u>: Genetic traits on the (Z) and (W) chromosomes are called "sex-linked," because they tend to be characteristic of one sex or the other.

The inheritance of sex is commonly referred to as the (ZW) type, because the symbol (Z) is used to indicate the presence and the absence of one of the pair of sex chromosomes, which is the (W).

Every male zygote has 2 sex chromosomes (ZZ) [two copies of every gene locus found on the (Z) chromosome], so that among all male gametes produced, each contains one (Z) chromosome, just as the autosomes; the same dominance relationships apply.

Female zygotes however, have only 1 sex chromosome (Z) [only one copy of each (Z) chromosome gene locus], and it produces gametes in approximate equality with and without the (Z) chromosome, a gamete with the (Z) chromosome being called a (Z) gamete and one without the (Z) chromosome being called a (W) gamete.

Sex-linked genes, being borne on the sex chromosome only, are contained in the (Z) gametes only, the (W) gamete having no sex chromosome and, therefore, containing no sex-linked genes.

Dominance for a sex-linked gene is determined by the behavior in the cock, because the hen has only one allele. That allele is always expressed regardless of whether it is dominant or recessive.

The hen is heterozygous (from heteros, meaning different), referring to the condition of the zygote, (ZW) for sex because she has only 1 sex chromosome, whereas the cock is homozygous (from homo meaning alike), referring to the condition of the zygote, (ZZ) because he has 2 sex chromosomes.

A good example of this would be the gene for "red plumage" in a Grey colored family, or "green legs," in a yellow legged family. The red plumage or green legs (being sex-linked), is borne on the sex chromosome (Z).

SEX-LINKED INHERITANCE AND COLOR OF PLUMAGE: One of the most important sex-linked traits in poultry breeding is color of plumage. Before the genetic background of chickens was completely understood, cockers of the past had already noticed that in the breeding of certain lines, cocks and hens had different feather coloring, which helped them to pick out the stags from the pullets at an early age, sometimes even when they were a day-old. Nowadays the reason is well known, it's the function of genes, which affects their feather coloring.

Sex-linkage and the inheritance of Grey and Red plumage color: Although this book covers the breeding of American Games, all chickens carry the gene for silver or for gold on the sex chromosome. This is a genetic classification that also takes into account the many variations that are in between. For instance, the silver gene gives the plumage a white or silver background on which feather patterns can be superimposed. This is expressed in varieties of American Games, known as "Silver and Gold Duckwings," also known as "Greys." The gold gene causes the red, brown, or buff background, as seen in other varieties, such as "Black-Breasted Black-Reds, Brown-Breasted Brown-Reds, Black-Breasted Reds, Black-Breasted Light-Reds and Gingers." The presence of either gene may be hidden by solid black, or by the presence of genes which inhibit color that takes into account all the different varieties of American Games that exist today.

For American Games, they come into one of two categories, either "Red" or "Silver" coloration. A typical "Red" variety is the Black-Breasted Reds, and a typical "Silver" variety is the Black-Breasted-Silver Duckwing, or "Grey" as we know them today. The order of dominance of these colors is "Grey" and then "Red." However, there are other genes called dilution factors, which can lead to the creation of Blue fowl, and there is a dominant gene for Spangling, which interacts in complex ways to produce Spangled gamefowl with various degrees of Spangling.

Illustrating the inheritance of a sex-linked dominant factor: When a Grey colored cock, such as an American Game Silver Duckwing, is mated to a Red colored hen, such as an American Game Black-Breasted Red (Partridge bred), all the resulting offspring, both the stags and pullets, will be Silver or Grey. The dominant sex-linked gene, for "Grey" is transmitted from the father to the daughters,

Parents

Silver Duckwing   Black Breasted-Red

Progeny

Silver Duckwing Colors

This illustrates what occurs when a pure Silver-Duckwing cock is bred with a pure Black-Breasted Red hen.

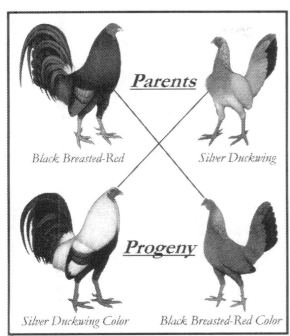

Parents

Black Breasted-Red   *Silver Duckwing*

Progeny

Silver Duckwing Color   *Black Breasted-Red Color*

This illustrates what occurs when a pure Black-Breasted Red cock is bred with a pure Silver-Duckwing hen.

and to the sons. Since the Inheritance of Silver could not come from the hens, it must have been inherited by both sexes from their father. Therefore, it is obvious that the hen can only transmit her color to her stag offspring and not to the pullets, and when the cock is the one who carries the dominant color, such as Silver (Grey) over Red, the hen's traits become nonexistent. This proves that the gene for Silver (Grey) in American Game Silver Duckwings is contained in the sex chromosome.

If a Black-Breasted Red cock with two recessive genes for Red coloring, such as an American Game Black-Breasted Red, is bred to a Black-Breasted Silver Duckwing hen with a dominant Silver gene, it might be thought that the dominant gene would come through and make all the offspring Silver, and indeed it does, but for the stags/sons only! The gene for Silver (Grey) is transmitted to the sons only, while the daughters are all red. The stags/sons alone receive the dominant gene from their mother and will appear as "Greys." The daughters are not Silver (Grey) because each one received its sex chromosome only from the Red father. Since the pullets received no gene from their mother, the recessive red gene that came from the father will determine the pullets color. And because they hatch out as Red (Partridge) chicks, while their brothers hatch out Silver (Grey), it makes it very easy to tell the pullets from the stags.

The practicality of this is that it is possible, by using the Silver (Grey) hens and Red cocks, to produce chicks that can be sexed by sight at hatching time.

As you have learned, in the mating of Black-Breasted Reds and Silver Duckwings, a "Silver" (Grey) hen when mated to a "Red" cock will produce stags which are Silver (Grey) and pullets which are Red. If a "Red" hen is mated to a "Silver" (Grey) cock, the dominant Grey of the cock would cause all chicks, stags and pullets to be Grey.

As you can plainly see, different results are produced in these two matings, depending upon whether the hen used was Silver Duckwing or not. The results secured in the reciprocal matings between Black-Breasted Red and Silver Duckwing demonstrate that the gene that produces Grey/Silver is sex-linked, inasmuch as the Silver Duckwing female transmits Grey/Silver to her sons but not to her daughters.

<u>Using sex-linked traits as a tool for selection</u>: Since all the pullets are like their father and all the stags are like their mother, this so-called crisscross inheritance allows the sex-linked categorization of the stags and pullets according to such things as their feather color and leg color. Have you ever noticed how some strains that are yellow legged will produce yellow legged stags, but all the pullets are green legged? This is sex-linkage at work.

Since color sexing takes advantage of the sex-linked gene that controls feather color, numerous variations are possible. For instance, just as we have discussed in the preceding paragraphs, if you breed a Silver (Grey) hen with a Red cock, the resulting stags will have the Silver (Grey) color pattern while the pullets will be Red.

Hereditary units, which are transmitted may or may not be present in the germ cells of the cock, or in the egg determined to be a stag, in all of which the material body is present, but they can never be transmitted in the eggs that are determined to be pullets where material body is completely absent.

Testing for sex-linkage using Silver Duckwings and Black-Breasted Reds: The difficulty comes when a heterozygous Silver-Duckwing cock (normally a cross) is bred to a recessive Black-Breasted Red hen, which leads to a mixture of chicks that are Grey and Red, both being in the stags as well as in the pullets. This is not noticeable when

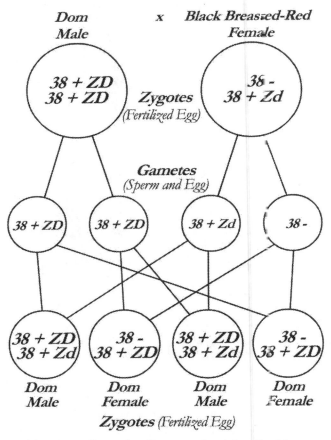

The breeding of a Dom cock with a Red hen.

a homozygous or pure Silver-Duckwing or Grey cock and hen are bred together, for the offspring of both sexes inherit silver from their father. However, when the Grey is bred with a non-Grey variety, such as a Red, like mentioned before, the affects of this becomes very obvious.

A true test of the sex-linkage of the gene for Grey/Silver is a mating of a Black-Breasted Red male and the Grey/Silver females, which were produced from a cross between a Black-Breasted Red male and Silver Duckwing females. The progeny of the Black-Breasted Red male mated to the Grey/Silver female produces females that are non-Grey, showing that the Grey/Silver females did not possess the gene for Grey/Silver. However, since the Black-Breasted Red male, when mated to Silver Duckwing females, produces Grey/Silver sons and red daughters, it is obvious that the gene for Grey/Silver is sex-linked and is transmitted from the Grey/Silver female parent to her sons only.

Sex-linkage and the breeding of Doms: Another example is the effect of barring. This is the characteristic of light and dark "cuckoo" feathers, a bluish-grey barring pattern that's commonly found in both the American and Old English Game Doms, otherwise known as Dominique, Creel or Cuckoo. Barring is actually influenced by another sex-linked gene.

The Dom cock can transmit his barred or bluish-grey plumage to both his stag and pullet offspring, while the Dom hen is limited. She can only transmit her barring to her stag offspring. This is, of course, not noticeable when a Dom cock and hen are bred together, for the offspring of both sexes inherit barring from their father. However, when the Dom is bred with a non-barred variety of gamefowl, its affects becomes very noticeable, almost immediately. If a Dom cock is bred with a

The breeding of a Dom cock
with a Red hen.

The breeding of a Red cock
with a Dom hen.

Black-Breasted Red (partridge type) hen, all the resulting offspring, both the stags and pullets, will be barred. Since this barring could not come from the hens, it is inherited by both sexes from their father.

If, on the other hand, a Dom hen is bred with a Black-Breasted Red cock, only the male offspring will be barred. The Dom hen can only transmit barring to her stag offspring and not to the pullets. Also, if you were to breed a Dom hen with an unbarred stag, such as a Black American Game, she'll pass her barring to the sons only, the daughters will all end up being Black like the father.

<u>Sex-linkage and the effects of Autosomal Genes</u>: Even after everything I have said, it would be wrong to think that feather coloring is always determined by sex-linked genes. "Autosomal Genes," which are genes that is located on the sex chromosomes which can also play a part, and sometimes a quite powerful one. The

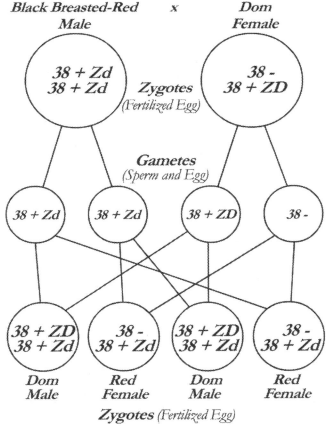

The breeding of a Red cock with a Dom hen.

dominant White feathering of, let's say, the White American and Old English Gamefowl, for instance, result from an Autosomal gene, and can override the effects of the sex-linked genes. There are other breeds, such as the Barred Plymouth Rocks, that also have barring, but in their case it is determined by an Autosomal gene, and therefore has no value as a sexing method.

THE RATE OF FEATHERING IN CHICKS CAN BE SEX-LINKED: For example, when cocks of the American Game class are mated to hens of the Asiatic classes, the female chicks will show well developed wing feathers. The male chicks will have no wing feathers or very short ones.

SEX-LINKAGE AND THE COLOR OF LEG: There are many other examples of Sex-linked Inheritance that I could give you, for it is not limited to their color of plumage only, but for many other attributes such as leg color. Leg color is another way of sex-linking gamefowl. By crossing a white legged hen with a yellow legged cock gives you stags with white legs and pullets with yellow legs, but this is not always an easy thing to pick out especially when the chicks are only one day old. By crossing a yellow legged hen with a green legged cock, this gives you stags with yellow legs and pullets with green legs, a method of sex-linking that is much easier to detect in the young offspring.

PRINCIPLES OF VARIATION

"I have called this principle, by which each slight variation, if useful, is preserved, by the term of Natural Selection."

Charles Darwin

As we know the domestic chicken possesses numerous characteristics and traits, this point must be emphasized. For instance, I have a family of American Games that are Black-Breasted Reds, known as Troiano Hatch, which possess a pea-comb; black breast and tail, with red hackles and saddle feathers; they have red earlobes; and green shanks and feet; four toes, a dark ring around their eyes, as well as many other characteristics and traits.

I also have another family of American Games that are Black-Breasted Black-Red, known as the Troiano Black Pearls. They are pea-combed, black-breasted and very dark-red in the hackle and saddle feathers, and they are crow-winged. They have a gypsy face, dark eyes and beak, and have black shanks and feet, with a slightly different build from that of the Troiano Hatch family.

Maximus, a Troiano Red cock.

However, not all American Games, of these plumage colors are exactly alike. There is always some difference, however minute, that distinguishes two individuals that are otherwise much alike, and this is as true among men as among domestic chickens.

Black Pearl cock.

Since it is true that there are no duplicates among American Games and domestic chickens in general, it is obvious that the old saying "like begets like" cannot be entirely true, for the simple reason that there is no exact likeness between parent and offspring or among brothers and sisters. It is true, of course, that all American Games do resemble each other to a noticeable degree, especially when compared with their closest cousin, the Old English Games. The fact that there is great variation among American Games is of particular significance in inheritance. Why is variation so important? Without variation, progress in breeding work would be impossible. Without variation, the selection of superior individuals would be impossible. Without

American Games.

produced, except for the occasional white "sport." The Black-Breasted Red color is regarded as a stable character that is transmitted regularly from generation to generation, although the quality of Red in any two individuals always differs somewhat.

The characteristic black-red plumage in Black-Breasted Black-Reds, and other crow-wing varieties is regarded as a stable characteristic transmitted regularly, except for the occasional brown-red, which appears from time to time when birds of the same variety are mated among themselves.

Creating the ideal bird. Due to variants in characteristics in the gene pool, birds can be sculpted into whatever the breeder wishes. As long as he is aware of beneficial variations, selects properly, improvement is assured. In time he can create the ideal fowl.

selection, improvement is impossible. In short, variation makes selection possible, and selection makes improvement possible.

The fact that there is great variation among birds has made the science of breeding possible. Although it is true that there are no two Black-Breasted Red American Games that are exactly alike, it is also true that as long as Black-Breasted Red American Games are mated among themselves nothing but Black-Breasted Red American Games are

Old English Games.

White American Games and other white varieties breed true when bred among themselves so that the characteristic white plumage is regarded as stable.

THE BREEDING OF UNLIKE CHARACTERS: When birds possessing unlike characteristics are mated together, some very interesting and sometimes very surprising results are obtained.

In presenting the results, it is easier to designate the different generation of families by symbols. The parental generation, meaning the parents used in the first cross, is designated by the symbol P_1. The family or progeny obtained from the original cross or mating is known as the first filial generation, and is designated by the symbol F_1. When members of the first filial generation are mated among themselves they produce the second filial generation, which is designated by the symbol F_2 (P_1 produces F_1, and F_1 produces F_2 and F_2 produces F_3).

Let's use pea-comb and straight (*single*) comb to illustrate the breeding of unlike characters: The manner in which pea-comb and straight (*single*) comb is inherited in a cross between pea-comb and straight (*single*) comb helps to illustrate the kind of results obtained in the inheritance of most pairs of characteristics. In this case, the pea-comb is one character and the straight (*single*) comb is the other.

The manner in which the character pea-comb and straight (*single*) comb is inherited in a cross between pea-comb and straight (*single*) comb serves to illustrate the mechanism involved in the inheritance of most pairs of characters.

When a pea-combed cock is bred to another pea-combed hen of another strain (P_1) all the offspring in the F_1 generation will come out pea-combed. And when a straight (*single*) combed cock is bred to another straight (*single*) combed hen of another strain (P_1), all the offspring of the F_1 generation will come out straight (*single*) combed.

But when a pea-combed cock is bred to a straight (*single*) combed hen (P_1), the offspring of the F_1 generation will come out all pea-combed.

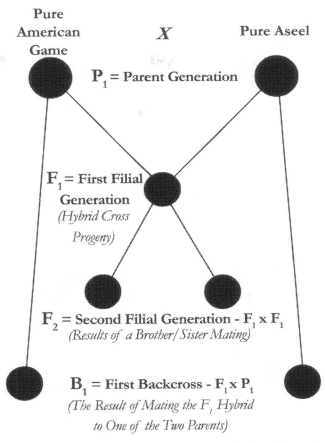

Pure American Game X Pure Aseel

P_1 = Parent Generation

F_1 = First Filial Generation
(Hybrid Cross Progeny)

F_2 = Second Filial Generation - F_1 x F_1
(Results of a Brother/Sister Mating)

B_1 = First Backcross - F_1 x P_1
(The Result of Mating the F_1 Hybrid to One of the Two Parents)

This illustration shows the relationship of the P_1 (parent generation) to the F_1 (first filial generation), F_2 (second filial generation), and B_1 (first backcross).

When the pea-combed stags, of the F_1 generation, are bred to their full sibs, the outcome in the F_2 generation is quite different. They produced a phenotype ratio of 3:1 but the genotype ratio is 1:2:1. One is homozygous for pea-comb (*phenotype and genotype for pea-comb*), two are heterozygous for both characters (*phenotype for pea-comb/genotype for both pea and straight*), and one is homozygous for straight (*single*) combs (*phenotype and genotype for straight [single] comb*).

The interesting thing however, is that when some of the pea-combs (the twenty-five percent of the offspring that are pure for pea-combs) are bred to sibs that are also pure for pea-combs, all the subsequent offspring of the F₃ generation will come pure pea-combed. They continue to be homozygous for pea-comb. Just as interesting, maybe even more so, when the straight (*single*) combs, of the F_2 generation, are bred to sibs that are also straight (*single*) combed, all the subsequent offspring of the F_3 generation will come out pure straight (*single*) combed. The pea-comb characteristic completely disappears. From that point on they will breed true for straight (*single*) combs. They went from being homozygous for pea-comb to homozygous for straight (*single*) comb in just three generations.

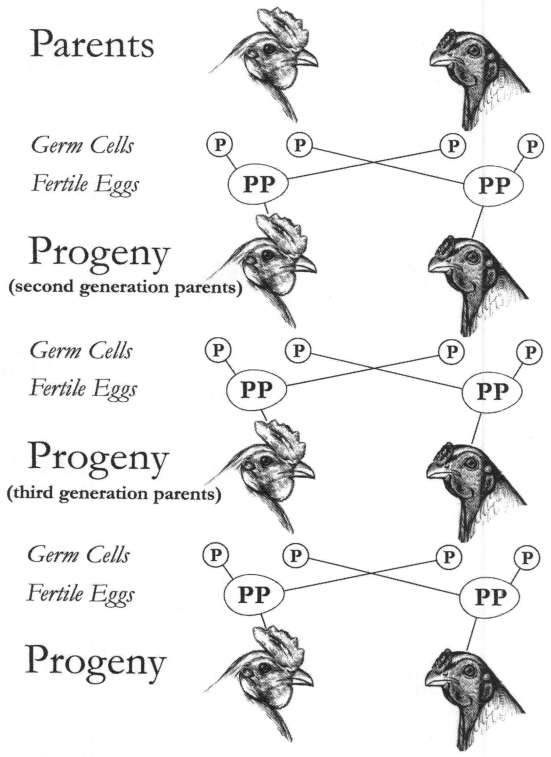

Parents

Germ Cells

Fertile Eggs

Progeny
(second generation parents)

Germ Cells

Fertile Eggs

Progeny
(third generation parents)

Germ Cells

Fertile Eggs

Progeny

This illustration shows how pea-comb, when pure, is transmitted from generation to generation.

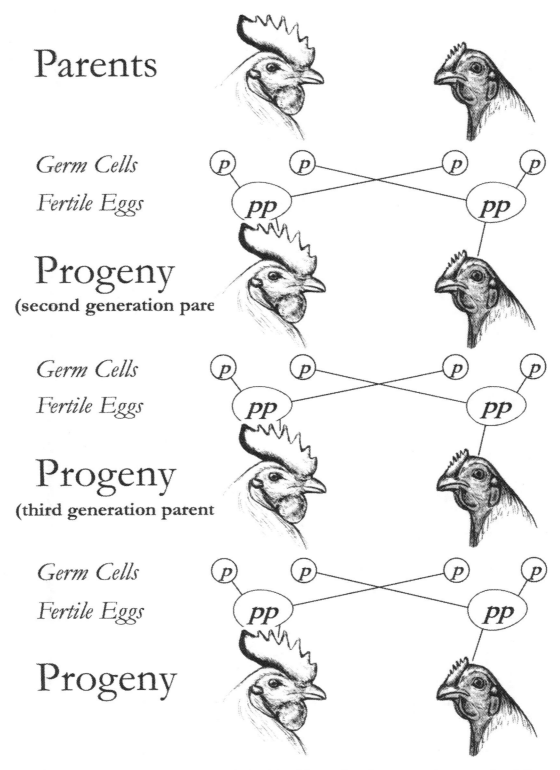

Parents

Germ Cells

Fertile Eggs

Progeny
(second generation pare

Germ Cells

Fertile Eggs

Progeny
(third generation parent

Germ Cells

Fertile Eggs

Progeny

This illustration shows how straight (*single*) comb, when pure, is transmitted from generation to generation.

64

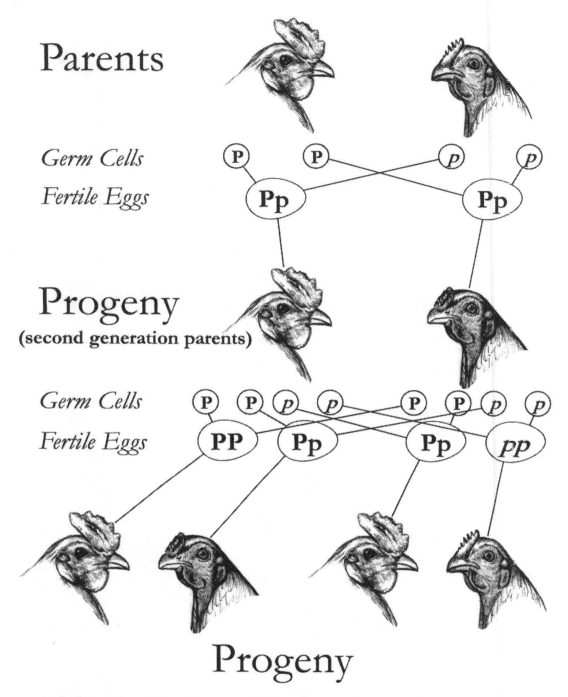

Parents

Germ Cells

Fertile Eggs

Progeny
(second generation parents)

Germ Cells

Fertile Eggs

Progeny

This illustration shows the transmission of genes for pea and straight (*single*) comb after mating an individual pure for pea-comb with one pure for straight (*single*) comb. Only four individuals are shown in the second generation, but it should be understood that straight (single) comb males and females would appear in equal numbers.

The results obtained in this simple experiment involving one pair of characters demonstrate two important features. The first important feature is the demonstration of the fact that in this particular cross, the first filial generation is all pea-combed, in spite of the fact that one of the parents is straight (*single*) combed. The second important feature is the fact that in the second filial generation, the two characters pea-comb and straight (*single*) comb appear in the proportion of approximately 3 pea-combs to 1 straight (*single*) comb.

Let's use Blue plumage to illustrate the breeding of unlike characters: Here is another example of Mendelian Inheritance, in the breeding of Blues. As my good friend and mentor has always told me, "*If you want to learn about the inheritance of American Games just breed Blues. Blues will teach you everything you need to know about genetics.*"

A pea-comb cock, dubbed.

For American Games, the most popular Blues are those known as Miner Blues. These were fowl that were bred by Lloyd and Rex Miner in the middle 1900's, and made quite a name for them. A strain known as Mugs is also Blue-bred.

The manner in which Blue American Games are expressed is by crossing Black fowl with that of White fowl. This type of breeding helps to illustrate the kind of results obtained in the inheritance of other factors known as "dilutions." In this case, black is one character and white the other. however, in the case of the offspring, Blue is not expressed due to dominant and recessive characters or due to sex-linkage, it is due to a dilution factor; a blending of a sort of the two characters.

When a black cock is bred to another black hen of another strain (P_1) all the offspring in the F_1 generation will come out black. And when a white cock is bred to another white hen of another strain (P_1), all the offspring of the F_1 generation will come out white. As expected, they breed true.

But when a black cock is bred to a white hen (P_1), the offspring of the F_1 generation will come out a mixture of black, blue, and splash/white. In order to produce Blues, the chick must receive a factor for black from one parent and white from the other, this is imperative.

The breeding of Blue fowl resembles that of crossbred pea-combs in that it produces two kinds of germ cells in equal numbers. A chick in the F_2 generation, produced by the union of like germ cells from a pair of Blue fowls, as in the case of a Blue stag of the F_1 generation being bred to his Blue sisters, is either splashed, white or black. This may or may not be mixed with red or other colors, dependent on other hereditary factors.

But when the splash stags of the F_1 generation are bred to their splash sibs, all the offspring of the F_2 generation will come out blue.

The interesting thing however, is that when the black offspring from the F_2 generation are bred to other black sibs, all the offspring in the F_3 generation will come out black. And when the white offspring from the F_2 generation are bred to other white sibs, all the offspring in the F_3 generation will come out white. The blacks and whites, when bred back to their similar colored sibs breed true and they will breed true from that point on. Nevertheless, you can never breed 100 percent blue offspring. Due to the laws of genetics it is impossible!

These two examples constitute the basic principles of Mendelian inheritance; the theory of inheritance first discovered by Gregor Mendel.

Mendel carried on breeding experiments with peas and other plants, and the results he obtained became the foundation of most of the modern work on inheritance of characters in plants and animals. Mendel's results were published

Variation is the Key to Improvement.

in 1866 but attracted little attention at the time and remained practically unknown for 35 years until brought to light in 1900 by three investigators. In 1902, Mr. Bateson, while working with the domestic fowl, was the first to demonstrate that the Mendelian principles of inheritance apply to animals.

During recent years, the results obtained from many matings demonstrate that numerous characters of the domestic fowl are inherited in typical Mendelian manner. Most of these characters are simple ones that involve, for the most part, color and structural characters, but can apply to more complicated characters as well.

PRINCIPLES OF DOMINANCE
Dominant and Recessive Characteristics and Traits
(This is the first basic principle of inheritance that Mendel discovered, but
it is better known as Gregor Mendel's Third Law of Inheritance)

In one of Gregor Mendel's experiments, he crossed a plant pure for green pods with one pure for yellow pods. The resulting seeds produced an F_1 generation with only green-podded plants. No yellow pods developed, even though one parent had been pure for yellow pods. Only one of the two traits found in the P_1 generation appeared in the F_1 generation.

Next Mendel allowed the F_1 plants to self-pollinate and planted the resulting seeds. When the F_2 generation plants grew, he observed that about three-fourths of the F_2 plants had green pods and about one-fourth had yellow pods.

Mendel's observations and his careful records led him to hypothesize that something within the pea plants controlled the characteristics he observed. He called these controls "factors." Mendel hypothesized that each trait was inherited by means of a separate factor. Because the characteristics he studied had two alternative forms, he reasoned that there must be a pair of factors controlling each trait. These factors come in the form of dominant and recessive traits, as well as, in the separation of cells during reproduction, and the distribution of characteristics through independent assortment.

In the following paragraphs we will discuss dominant and recessive factors, and how they affect the way in which our fowl transmit characteristics to their offspring. In the next section we will discuss Gregor Mendel's first law of inheritance, Chromosome Segregation, and his second law of inheritance, Independent Assortment.

<u>DOMINANT AND RECESSIVE TRAITS</u>: Whenever Mendel crossed strains, one of the P_1 traits failed to appear in the F_1 plants. In every case, that trait reappeared in a ratio of about 3:1 in the F_2 generation. This pattern emerged in thousands of crosses and led Mendel to conclude that one factor in a pair may prevent the other from having an effect. Mendel hypothesized that the trait appearing in the F_1 generation was controlled by a dominant factor because it masked, or dominated, the other factor for a specific characteristic. The trait that did not appear in the F_1 generation but reappeared in the F_2 generation was thought to be controlled by a recessive factor.

Therefore, a trait controlled by a recessive factor had no observable effect on an organism's appearance when it was paired with a trait controlled by a dominant factor.

As you can see from Mendel's experiment, some genes have the ability to prevent or mask the expression of other genes, where the genetic makeup of a bird cannot be recognized with any kind of exactness. This ability to cover-up or mask the existence of one gene is called "Dominance."

Every bird carries within its gene pool a combination of genes, some are dominant and some are recessive. The gene which masks the one is the dominant gene; the one which is masked is the recessive gene. If a dominant gene pairs up with a recessive gene, for a particular trait, the dominant gene will cover-up or modify the recessive gene and it's the dominant trait that will show up in the offspring. As long as the bird is pure for that dominant trait, that trait will be expressed every time.

IDENTIFYING WHICH TRAITS ARE DOMINANT: In American Games, it is quite easy to pick out body characteristics that are dominant. For instance, the tendency to come pea-comb is possible because pea-comb is dominant to straight (*single*) comb. When a bird with pea-comb mates with a straight (*single*) comb bird, the progeny will all be pea-comb if the parent is pure for this characteristic, because a pea-comb is dominant to a straight (*single*) comb. The straight (*single*) comb in this case is recessive. When a bird with white legs (dominant) is mated with a bird with yellow legs (recessive), the progeny (the F_1 generation) will all be white legged, once again, if the parent is pure for this characteristic.

When dominant and recessive characteristics are brought together, progeny will possess the dominant characteristics, but will produce in the next generation (the F_2 generation) some birds that possess dominant characteristics and others that possess recessive characteristics.

Can you tell just by looking at a bird whether he will breed pure or not? Strangely enough you can if the bird shows recessive features. A bird with a straight (*single*) comb can only be homozygous if matched with similar genes that produce straight (*single*) comb, because if it had the dominant pea-comb gene it would have to show it. It's more difficult to figure out a bird which shows a dominant feature since (as we have seen before) there is no guarantee of its genetic makeup. He may have a recessive feature that's just under the surface.

A recessive trait will show up in the offspring when both the cock and the hen carry the same recessive traits, such as straight (*single*) comb to straight (*single*) comb, or green leg to green leg. Therefore, it is clear to see how the dominant character will cover up a recessive one. That's why a bird's breeding performance cannot be recognized by its phenotype (how it looks), a fact which is of great significance in the breeding of American Games.

As long as you work with birds that are heterozygous, recessive genes can remain hidden. However, these recessive genes are capable of appearing at any time, depending on who they are bred with. I'm sure you have heard the term "throwback." This is a word that describes a bird that happens to exhibit traits that are

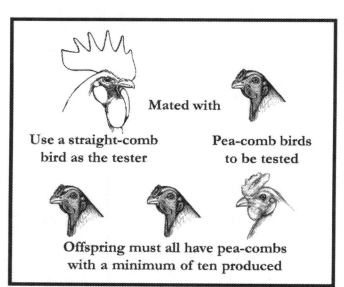

Mated with

Use a straight-comb bird as the tester

Pea-comb birds to be tested

Offspring must all have pea-combs with a minimum of ten produced

This illustration shows how to test for undesirable recessive traits and how to eliminate them. Used in the illustration is the trait straight (*single*) comb. If any straight (*single*) comb appears in the above mating, the pea-comb parent must be discarded, as the test proves that he or she is a carrier of the undesired trait. If pea-comb individuals only are produced from this mating, and continue in the future, no further problem with straight (single) combs will be experienced. This test can be used for any recessive trait.

unrecognizable, most likely traits that have been hidden for numerous generations.

As you can see, dominant factors often makes the task of identifying and discarding birds carrying an undesirable recessive factor a difficult one. Recessive genes can be passed on from generation to generation, appearing only when two birds, both of which carrying a recessive factor happens to breed. A recessive trait only shows up when both genes in a pair control the same recessive trait. Since a homozygous bird is more likely than a heterozygous bird to have a large number of matched pairs, the more inbred a bird is, the more likely it will display certain recessive traits, and the more likely it will show traits (throwbacks) that are hidden within the family. Even then, only one out of four offspring produced will, on the average, be homozygous for the recessive factor and show it.

Following are examples of dominant and recessive characters in chickens:
- Rose-comb is dominant to pea-comb and it is not sex-linked.
- Pea-comb is dominant to straight (single) comb and it is not sex-linked.
- Side sprigs are dominant to normal comb and it is not sex-linked.
- White skin color is dominant to yellow skin color and it is not sex-linked.
- White shank color is dominant to yellow shank color and is sex-linked.
- Yellow shank color is dominant to green shank color and is sex-linked.
- Feathered shanks are dominant to non-feathered shanks and it is not sex-linked.
- Grey (Silver) plumage is dominant to red and is sex-linked.
- Black plumage is dominant to white and it is not sex-linked.
- Tight feathering is dominant to loose feathering and it is not sex-linked.
- Slow feathering is dominant to fast feathering and is sex-linked.
- Broodiness is dominant to nonbroodiness and is sex-linked.
- Early sexual maturity is dominant to late sexual maturity and is sex-linked.

Special Note: when rose-combs are crossed with pea-combs, the comb becomes somewhat intermediate; it becomes a walnut-comb. The same is true when pea-combs are crossed with straight (*single*) combs; the comb becomes a rudimentary crest.

DOMINANT AND RECESSIVE CHARACTERISTICS IN ACTION: The principle of dominance was the first basic principle of inheritance that Mendel discovered. Cases of Mendelian, or simple dominant and recessive inheritance, are frequently seen with cockers who tend to make a lot of crosses, where the mixing of genetic content causes wide variations in the offspring compared to their parents.

The following sections have good examples of how dominance of characteristics actually works. I am using silver and red plumage as well as pea-combs and straight (*single*) combs as the examples. However, this occurs in every trait where dominant characters are paired with recessive characters.

If you are interested in a particular trait, all you have to do is to exchange the silver and red plumage, or pea-comb and straight combs with, for example, white leg and green leg, etc.

Silver Duckwings vs. Black-Breasted Reds: In American Games, there are several examples of Mendelian factors. One example is the breeding of "Silver" and "Red" plumages. As I have mentioned before, in the cross between Silver Duckwing and Black-Breasted Red American Games, all the F_1 progeny are Silver Duckwing. The gene for "Red" was transmitted in exactly the same manner as the gene for "Silver," but none of the F_1 birds show any "Red" in its plumage. Each zygote giving rise to an F₁ bird contains a gene for "Silver" and a gene for "Red," but a "Silver" bird is the result. Due to this illustration it is obvious that the Silver Duckwing color is dominant to Black-Breasted Red.

The symbols (*S*) and (*s*): These are genetic designations used for the sake of simplicity in illustrating the principle of dominance of one character over another and the principle of the segregation of characteristics.

Due to the dominance of the Silver Duckwing over Black-Breasted Red, the character "Silver" is represented by the capital letter (*S*), and the recessive character "Red" is represented by the small letter (*s*), meaning the absence of "Silver." Furthermore, since genes are responsible for the development of the hereditary characters "Silver" and "Red," the genes are represented by the letters (*S*) and (*s*), respectively. The zygote of the purebred Silver Duckwing American Game contains the genes (*SS*), and the zygote of the purebred Black-Breasted Red American Game contains the genes (*ss*).

Note: It should be pointed out at this time that the symbols (*S*) for "Silver" and (*s*) for "Red" are used here purely as a matter of convenience.

Pea-comb vs. Straight-comb: Another good example of dominant and recessive traits in action is the relationship of pea-comb vs. straight (*single*) comb. In this situation, pea-comb is dominant and straight (*single*) comb is recessive. For instance, let's consider what happens when a cocker, who breeds a family of fowl that is pure for pea-comb to a straight (*single*) comb bird, which, as most cockers know, breeds true. The result, the first or F₁ generation offspring, or crossbred progeny, will all have pea-combs. Why, because pea-comb is dominant over straight (*single*) comb.

A chicken that has two copies of the pea-comb gene is pure or homozygous for pea-comb. If he has two copies of the straight (*single*) comb gene, then he is pure or homozygous for straight (*single*) comb. If a chicken has one copy each of the pea-comb and straight (*single*) comb genes, then he is mixed or heterozygous for pea-comb. We could also say that he is heterozygous for straight (*single*) comb as well. However you wish to say it, it doesn't change the fact that any chicken carrying either one or two copies of the gene for pea-comb will be pea-comb! Even if he also has the straight (*single*) comb gene. Why, because pea-comb is dominant. In order to be straight (*single*) comb, the chicken must lack the pea-comb gene and carry two copies of the straight (*single*) comb gene. All straight (*single*) combed individuals must have two copies of the straight (*single*) comb gene. Pea-comb individuals may have one or two copies of the pea-comb gene. They could carry one copy each of the genes for pea-comb and straight (*single*) comb and they will still be pea-comb.

So what have we figured out? Well, a pea-comb cock bred to a straight (*single*) comb hen will result in pea-combed offspring, but only in the first F₁ generation. If breeding is continued, such as in the case of inbreeding (brother to sister) or line-breeding, using the pea-comb offspring bred back to their parents, would give you in the second generation a mixture of pea-comb and straight (*single*) combed offspring. They breed as if three-quarter of their germ cells (spermatozoa in the male/eggs in the females) transmit pea-combs, while the other one-quarter transmit straight (*single*) comb. This is easily seen while crossing pea-combs with straight (*single*) combs, in which case they produce 75 percent pea-combs and 25 percent straight (*single*) combs.

The pea-combs of this generation, when crossed with straight (*single*) combs again produce 75 percent pea-combs and 25 percent straight (*single*) combs. However, the chicks are seven-eighths of the straight (*single*) comb blood. This system of breeding can be carried on indefinitely, the pea-comb chicks always producing 75 percent pea-combs and 25 percent straight (*single*) combs, regardless of the amount of blood from a straight (*single*) combed strain.

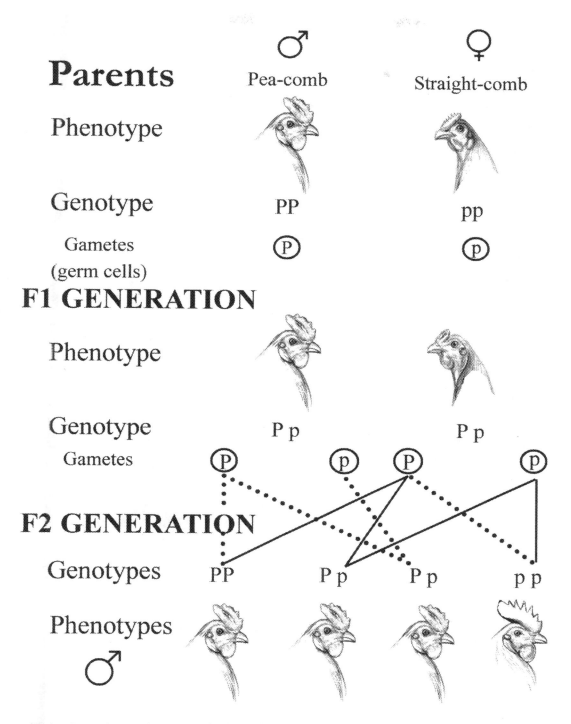

This chart shows the transmission of pea-comb and straight (*single*) comb over two generations. As you can see, pea-comb is dominant to straight (*single*) comb. Only the cocks are illustrated in the F_2 generation.

72

When two of these crossbred pea-combs, of any generation, are bred together, 25 percent of the chicks will have straight (*single*) combs. And they will breed true as straight (*single*) combs when bred to other straight (*single*) combed birds.

As you can see, one-quarter of the eggs transmit straight (*single*) comb and three-quarters of these eggs transmit pea-comb. The result being that 25 percent of the chicks will fail to get the pea-comb from either one of their parents, and will come out straight (*single*) combed.

On the other hand, there will be another 25 percent of the chicks, which get pea-comb from both parents and will breed like pure pea-combs, although, in blood they may be almost entirely of a straight (*single*) comb strain.

The remaining 50 percent of the chicks that get pea-comb from one parent straight (*single*) comb from the other, will breed like the original crossbred offspring's, that is, three-quarter of their germ cells will transmit pea-comb and one-quarter straight (*single*) comb.

This is a good example of dominant and recessive traits. In this case, one of the opposed characteristics (pea-comb) was dominant over the other (straight (*single*) comb).

The symbols (P) and (p): These are genetic designations used for the sake of simplicity in illustrating the principle of dominance of one character over another and the principle of the segregation of characteristics.

Since Pea-comb is dominant to Straight (*single*) comb, the character "Pea-comb" is represented by the capital letter (P) and the recessive character "Straight (*single*) comb" is represented by the small letter (p), meaning the absence of "Pea-comb." Furthermore, since genes are responsible for the development of the hereditary characters "Pea-comb" and "Straight (*single*) comb," the genes are represented by the letters (P) and (p), respectively. The zygote of the purebred Pea-comb contains the genes (PP), and the zygote of the purebred Straight (*single*) comb contains the genes (pp).

Establishing a true straight (*single*) comb strain: It's easy to establish a strain of American Games that will breed true to the straight (*single*) comb trait. All we have to do is choose broodfowl that are both straight (*single*) combed. Since straight (*single*) comb fowl do not carry the gene for pea-comb, all the offspring from straight (*single*) comb fowl will be straight (*single*) comb, and so will all succeeding generations.

Establishing a true pea-comb strain: To establish a true breeding strain of fowl that are pea-comb is somewhat more difficult because a pea-

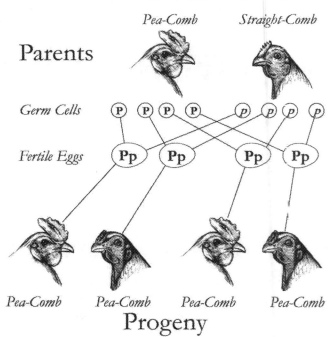

This illustration shows the test for purity of a simple character. The male indicated here is pure for pea-comb. (Compare with the next illustration).

comb chicken may carry two copies of the gene for pea-comb and therefore be pure or homozygous for pea-comb or he may carry one copy each of the pea-comb and straight (*single*) comb genes and therefore be heterozygous or mixed for the pea-comb trait.

There is another set of terms commonly used by geneticists to describe the difference between pure and mixed, they call the body that one can see the "phenotype" and the invisible genetic potential of a parent, its "genotype," this means that an individual who has a pea-comb does not necessarily have a genotype for pea-comb only. All chickens that carry the gene for pea-comb are pea-combed, but their genetics can be different because a pea-comb individual may or may not be pure for pea-comb. We say that the phenotype is pea-comb but the genotype is either homozygous (pure) or heterozygous (mixed), which means, they will carry the hidden straight (*single*) comb gene only to show up in later generations.

In order to establish a strain of gamefowl that will breed true for the pea-comb trait, we need to start with broodfowl, all of whose ancestors are homozygous or pure for the pea-comb trait. This is why it is a bit more difficult to establish a true pea-comb strain, especially if we continue to select pea-comb breeders in the hope of eventually breeding out the straight (*single*) comb gene. The straight (*single*) comb gene can remain hidden only to reappear somewhere down the line. The best thing to do is to test the original pea-comb broodfowl to make sure they are pure for the pea-comb trait.

<u>Testing the genetic integrity of the pea-comb trait</u>: To do this simply breed the pea-comb cock or hen to a straight (*single*) comb bird and hatch the eggs. If all the chicks are pea-comb, then the cock or hen is most likely pure for pea-comb. If any straight (*single*) comb chicks show up, then the pea-comb parent is mixed (heterozygous) for the pea-comb gene and, therefore, should not be used. In fact, breeding a heterozygous pea-comb to a straight (*single*) comb bird will produce chicks that are 25 percent straight (*single*) comb and 75 percent pea-comb. Once you have found pure pea-comb broodfowl, you will never see a straight (*single*) comb again. If you wish to add new pea-comb blood, be sure to test the new breeders to make sure that they are pure pea-comb or you will introduce the straight (*single*) comb gene in to your family, which will be hidden in the first generation but will pop up in later generations.

<u>Note</u>: This test works for all traits that are dominant, not just pea-combs and straight (*single*) combs.

<u>So what have we learned</u>? Let's sum things up a bit. Breeding a pea-comb cock to a straight (*single*) combed hen will result in pea-combed offspring, but only in the first generation. If breeding is continued using the pea-comb offspring and

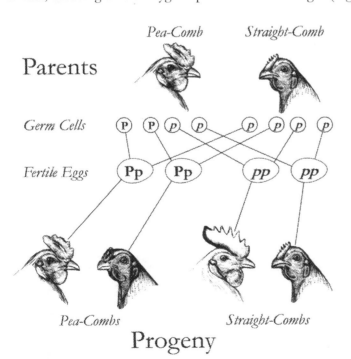

This illustration shows the test for purity of a simple character. The male indicated here is not pure for pea-comb. (Compare with the previous illustration).

bred back to their parents, would give you a mixture of pea-comb and straight (*single*) combed offspring in the second generation.

In their cell structure they inherited a pair of chromosomes, one from each parent, which contains genes that will eventually decide their build. These genes may both be for pea-comb, in which case the individual is pure-bred (homozygous) for pea-comb and will pass on that characteristic onto the next generation. But suppose the individual receives a gene for straight (*single*) comb from one of the parents? Because it has a dominant gene for pea-comb it will be pea-combed, but it will pass on a mixed inheritance of pea and straight (*single*) comb characteristics in the form of a "recessive" gene to the next generation. When this happens it is considered to be impure or heterozygous.

PRINCIPLES OF INCOMPLETE DOMINANCE
And Co-Dominance

A great deal of deviations from Mendel's laws has been discovered. In this section of the chapter we will discuss two of them, "Incomplete Dominance" and "Co-Dominance." "Incomplete Dominance" occurs in quite a number of areas in American Games. These include the genes for crests (tassels/topknots), hen feathering (as in Henny's), muffs and beards, not to mention birds with blue colored plumage. Many of the American Game Blues we see today were bred and perpetuated by Lloyd and Rex Miner. Nowadays they are referred to as Miner Blues. Understanding this concept of "Incomplete Dominance" is very important, especially if you are interested in the breeding and perpetuating American Game Blues. I will explain this concept by using the blue feather color of American Games. As we know, black fowl bred to white fowl produce blue fowl, but why does this occur? It is my intention to help you to fully understand how this works.

The terms "dominant" and "recessive" suggest the two extremes; one in which a gene is fully expressed and the other in which it is not expressed, as in the case of pea-combs bred to straight (*single*) combs, or Silver Duckwings bred to Black-Breasted Reds or white legged fowl bred to yellow legged fowl. However, not all alternative alleles are fully dominant or fully recessive. Instead, there are different degrees to which the pairs of alleles in a heterozygote influence the form of the phenotype. Some pairs of alleles produce a heterozygous phenotype that is either intermediate between those of the parents (incomplete dominance) or representative of both parental phenotypes (co-dominance). In fact they can be measured in sequential order from over-dominance, full-dominance, co-dominance, and incomplete dominance, to recessive.

Before we get started I would like to briefly discuss over-dominance and full-dominance; over-dominance is a rare phenomenon in which the dominant allele has a greater effect in the heterozygote than it does in the dominant homozygote. Full dominance occurs when the phenotype of the heterozygote and the dominant homozygote (genotype) are the same.

American Game Self-Blues.

<u>INCOMPLETE DOMINANCE - A DEVIATION FROM MENDEL'S LAWS</u>: Now that you have a good understanding of dominant and recessive traits, as explained earlier in the chapter, let me throw a wrench in the works by discussing the effects of incomplete dominance.

Mendel's laws are surprisingly simple and fundamental. So it shouldn't come as a surprise that, with the rediscovery of the Austrian monk's work in the early twentieth century, scientists wanted to test how universal these laws actually were. It soon became obvious that there were numerous situations in which his laws no longer seemed to apply. All of a sudden Mendel's idea of dominant and recessive traits became somewhat complicated. Why? Mainly due to the fact that dominance is not always complete. Some of these deviations are caused by variations in the dominance relations between alleles of the same gene. These varying degrees of dominance range from complete dominance to an entire lack of dominance. To add to this complication, there are times when dominance is neither complete nor absent, but simply incomplete. As a result we call these variations "Incomplete Dominance" (or Semi-Dominance).

With complete dominance, which was the case in Mendel's experiments, the heterozygote (Aa) has the same phenotype as the homozygote (AA). In that case, (A) is called dominant. When the alleles are subject to incomplete dominance, the heterozygote (Aa) has an intermediary phenotype in relation to the homozygotes (AA) and (aa). Incomplete dominance is thus defined as the inability of an allele to fully express the homozygote phenotype, such as black plumage or white plumage, in heterozygote individuals (their crossbred progeny), which results in an intermediary phenotype, such as a blue plumage. In other words, when dealing with "incomplete dominance" the expression of the single dominant allele gives rise to a phenotype (for the heterozygote) intermediate between the two homozygotes. For example, although some traits are clear-cut, such as black plumage and white plumage, they are either dominant or they are recessive. However, some traits may exhibit "incomplete dominance," such as a blue plumage, this makes it possible to distinguish some or all of the heterozygous individuals with respect to that trait.

This intermediary expression of a certain inheritable trait can lean towards one of the two possible homozygote phenotypes as a result of the relative proportion that each of the two alleles contributes to the eventual phenotype. Say, for example, that the relative contribution of alleles (A) and (B) is 60/40. In this case, the heterozygote (AB) phenotype will look more like the (AA) homozygote than like the (BB) individual. If both alleles provide an equal contribution 50/50, then the heterozygote phenotype will be an exact intermediary between the two homozygote phenotypes. In each case, the result of incomplete dominance is that a monohybrid cross between two homozygotes will give rise to a heterozygote F_1 generation with a phenotype that differs from both parents. Once again, a good example of this would be the breeding of black fowl to white fowl, which in turn produces offspring that are blue. In this case, blue is the intermediary between the two homozygote phenotypes (black and white).

<u>Incomplete dominance further explained</u>: It is my intention to make sure this is fully understood by my readers. There are so many who are trying to breed American Game Blues who do not understand the difficulty of this process. Understand this; the perfection of blues is impossible! This is all due to the "Incomplete Dominance" of the genes.

In Mendel's pea-plant crosses, one allele was completely dominant over another, a relationship called "Complete Dominance." In "Complete Dominance," heterozygous plants and dominant homozygous plants are indistinguishable, or identical in phenotype. For example, both pea plants (PP) and (Pp) for flower color have purple flowers. Sometimes, however, the F_1 offspring will have a phenotype in between that of the parents. In other words, the heterozygote is intermediate in appearance between the two homozygotes, a relationship called "Incomplete Dominance." "Incomplete Dominance" occurs when two or more alleles influence the phenotype, resulting in a phenotype intermediate between the dominant trait and the recessive trait. For example: there are flowers that are homozygous red and others that are homozygous white, but when crossed they produce heterozygous offspring flowers that are pink.

Here is a good example of "Incomplete Dominance" in action, one that applies very well to American Games. In a cross between black birds and white birds, both the allele for black feathering

(B) and the allele for white feathering (b) influence the phenotype. Neither allele is completely dominant over the other allele. When black feathered birds are bred to black feathered birds, they produce only black feathered offspring. When white feathered birds are bred to white feathered birds they produce only white feathered offspring. The black color of the feathers in black individuals is caused by melanin (white feathered animals do not produce melanin). However, when black feathered birds (homozygote BB) are crossed with white feathered birds (bb) (a monohybrid cross), leads to an F_1 generation exclusively consisting of heterozygote 'blues' (Bb). Stated in another way, one hundred percent of the offspring of this cross have the (Bb) genotype, which results in a blue bird, indicating that neither the allele for black feathering (B) nor the allele for white feathering (b) is completely dominant.

- P1: BB x bb
- F1: 100% Bb

What would be the result of crossing two blue feathered birds (Bb)? Looking only at the F_1 generation, we might conclude that this is a case of blending inheritance. But when two of the F_1 blue birds are crossed, the probable genotypic ratio in the F_2 generation is 1:2:1 [1 (BB): 2 (Bb): 1 (bb)], in which they will be made up of birds that are one quarter black (BB); a half of them will be blue (Bb); and the remaining quarter will have a white feather color (bb)(with a few blue feathers, known as blue-splashed white).

- F1: Bb x Bb
- F2: 25% BB, 50% Bb, 25% bb

The reason for this plumage color is that the blue plumage is that of the heterozygote; the homozygotes are the black and the blue-splashed white. Therefore, in cases of "Incomplete Dominance," such as this, the heterozygote has a phenotype distinct from both homozygotes, and a 1:2:1 ratio occurs instead of the 1:3 ratio.

Hybrids, such as blues never breed true due to the interaction of the two genes that display the colors (black and white), but they can transmit only one gene or the other (black or white) to each offspring.

A further example of "Incomplete Dominance" is the form of crest, known as tassels or topies, or topknots, seen in some varieties of American Games. If birds homozygous for crest are crossed with non-crested birds, the F_1 generation all have small sized crests. If these are self-crossed then the 1:2:1 ratio occurs in the F_2 generation.

Also, it's well known that dominance is not the result of single factor pairs, but the degree of dominance depends upon the bird's entire genetic makeup together with the environment to which it is raised

F1 - Female Gametes

	B	b
B	**BB** *(Black)*	**Bb** *(Blue)*
b	**Bb** *(Blue)*	**bb** *(White/Splash)*

F1 - Male Gametes

This illustration shows the F_2 results produced by a mating of an F_1 male x F_1 female, each of the F_1 birds being blue. The F_2 generation consists of the proportion of 1 black, 2 blues, and 1 white, a 1:2:1 ratio.

in. It's the various interactions between genetics and the environment that influence their degree of dominance.

Note of interest: Sometimes it's the heterozygote trait that is preferred, and on occasion has led to the creation and identification of another breed or variety.

Not too long ago, this concept of "Incomplete Dominance" was considered to be evidence for the "mixing theory" which states that the descendants of two different homozygotes would have a phenotype that is a "mix" of both homozygote phenotypes. However, the segregation in the F_2 generation proves that this is not the case because, if the 'mixing theory' were correct, all F_2 individuals should be "blue."

CO-DOMINANCE: Most genes in a population possess several different alleles, and often no single allele is dominant. "Co-Dominance" occurs when both pairs of alleles for a gene are equally expressed in a heterozygous offspring. For instance, you may breed a red bird and a white bird, yet the offspring in the F_2 generation may be both red and white in their plumage color.

In "Co-Dominance," neither allele is dominant or recessive, nor do the alleles blend in the phenotype. Instead, each allele has its own effect, and the heterozygote shows some aspect of the phenotype of both homozygotes.

"Co-Dominance" can be distinguished from "Incomplete Dominance" by the appearance of the heterozygote. In "Incomplete Dominance," the heterozygote is intermediate between the two homozygotes, whereas in "Co-Dominance," some aspect of both alleles is seen in the heterozygote.

PRINCIPLES OF GENOTYPE AND PHENOTYPE

We discussed this earlier in the chapter. However, I feel it requires further discussion to understand its true worth in breeding American Games.

The terms "genotype" and "phenotype" were first used by Danish geneticist, Wilhelm Johannsen in 1911 to describe the entire genetic or hereditary constitution of an organism. It was studies by, such men as, Johannsen that changed the way in which we breed domestic animals. The genotype-phenotype distinction has become an important factor in genetics and the practice of Selective Breeding. In fact, the distinction between genotype and phenotype is fundamental to the understanding of heredity and development of American Games.

- "Genotype" is an organism's full hereditary blueprint. It is the actual set (complement) of genes that it carries, even if it is not expressed.

- "Phenotype" is an organism's actual observable expression of characters and traits, which are influenced both by its genotype and by the environment. This includes its morphological (form and structure), functional (purpose), developmental, as well as its behavioral characteristics.

This distinction is fundamental in the study of inheritance of traits and their evolution. So in defining the evolution of a family, what we are really concerned with are the changes in the genotypes that make up a population from generation to generation. However, since an organism's genotype generally affects its phenotype, the phenotypes that make up the population are also likely to change. In other words, differences in the genotypes can produce different phenotypes.

It is the organism's physical properties that directly determine its chances of survival, while the inheritance of physical properties occurs only as a secondary consequence of the inheritance of genes. Therefore, to properly understand Artificial Selection and that of Selective Breeding, one must understand the genotype-phenotype distinction.

Genotype and phenotype represent very real differences between genetic composition and expressed form. Let's discuss these differences now.

Genotype: The genotype represents the sum of all genes (alleles) present on the chromosomes. These genes represent the entire range of characteristics and traits possible, whether expressed or not. In other words, the genotype is the bird's exact genetic makeup that was passed to the bird by its parents at the exact moment of its conception. It also describes all the forms or variations of genes (alleles) carried by an individual for which that bird belongs, as determined by the description of the actual physical material made up of DNA, which was contributed to the fertilized egg through gametes from both of its parent's.

The transmission of genes from parents to offspring is under the control of precise molecular mechanisms. As a result, two organisms whose genes differ at even one locus (position in their genome) are said to have different genotypes.

Phenotype: In contrast to the possibilities contained within the genotype, the phenotype is the appearance of the traits, a visual expression of the genotype. It reflects the individual's observable outward manifestation of its genetic makeup, thus the obvious expression of those possibilities or potentialities. The phenotype is the result of the functioning of the enzymes and proteins encoded by the genes it carries. In other words, the genotype is the blueprint, and the phenotype is the visible outcome.

Phenotypic traits are manifested and expressed by the physical properties of the bird, its physiological, morphological and behavioral characteristics. For example, this would include noticeable traits such as the individual's color of eye, comb type, conformation of body, color of plumage, color of leg, size and shape of the spur, and any other specific physiological trait, etc., as well as the individual's potential to be afflicted with a particular disease, and any defects which it may carry within its genetic pool. Therefore, the presence or absence of a defect or disease, or symptoms related to a particular disease state, is also a phenotypic trait.

Genotype + Development = Phenotype: To consider these in the context of Selective Breeding, we want to know how these three are related. In a "genetic" sense, the genotype defines the phenotype. But how does the phenotype "determine" the genotype? Selection acts on phenotypes because differential reproduction and survivorship depend on phenotype. If the phenotype affecting reproduction or survivorship is genetically based, then selection can weed out genotypes indirectly by getting rid of certain phenotypes. In other words, by selecting some traits, while culling others, you can change the genetic makeup of a family of fowl, and therefore change the way in which they look, act and perform.

Genotype is also used to refer to the pair of alleles present at a single locus. With alleles (A) and (a) there are three possible genotypes (AA, Aa and aa). First we must appreciate that genes do not act in isolation. The genome, in which a genotype is found, can affect the expression of that genotype, and the environment can affect the phenotype. In other words, even though the genetic makeup is the largest influence on which characteristics and traits will be expressed, the environment can change the way in which they look, act and perform, giving you, the breeder, a false indication of their true phenotype.

Not all pairs of alleles will have the same phenotype: Dominance when (AA) = (Aa) in phenotype, (A) is dominant, (a) is recessive. An allele can be dominant over one allele but recessive to another allele. Single genes do not always work as simply as indicated by a dominant and recessive relationship. Other genes can affect the phenotypic expression of a given gene.

The concept of "phenotypic plasticity": This describes the degree to which an organism's phenotype is determined by its genotype or by environmental factors. A high level of plasticity, or flexibility, means that environmental factors have a strong influence on the particular phenotype that develops. Although phenotypes are based upon the content of the underlying genes comprising the genotype, the expression of those genes in observable traits (phenotypic expression) is also, to varying degrees, influenced by environmental factors. What this means is that a change in the environment can easily affect the phenotype. For instance, although we often think of flamingos as being pink, pinkness is not encoded into their genotype. The food they eat makes their feathers (phenotype) white or pink.

If there is little plasticity or flexibility (environmental influences), the phenotype of an organism can be reliably and consistently predicted from the knowledge known of the genotype, regardless of environmental peculiarities during development.

The relationship between genotype and phenotype, and dominant and recessive traits: A clear example of the relationship between genotype and phenotype exists in cases where there are dominant and recessive alleles for a particular trait. Using a simplified monogenetic (one gene, one trait) example, a capital (*L*) might be used to represent a dominant allele at a particular locus coding for "high station of leg" in a particular breed of fowl, and the lowercase (*l*) used to represent the recessive allele coding for "shorter station of leg" in fowl. Using this notation, a bird will possess one of three genotypes: (*LL, Ll, or ll*). Although there are three different genotypes, because of the laws governing dominance, the birds will be either "high stationed" or "short stationed" (two phenotypes). Those birds with a (*LL*) or (*Ll*) genotype are observed to be "high stationed" (phenotypically tall). Only those birds that carry the (*ll*) genotype will be observed to be "short stationed" (phenotypically short).

The relationship between genotype and disease: This is an area of intense interest to geneticists, and should be an interest to us (cockers and backyard breeders) as well. In the breeding of American Games, we should focus some of our attention on the relationship between the effects of genetic changes, which are usually caused by mutations and the disease processes. I have always felt that disease prevention and good health are controlled by three factors; proper management; proper nutrition; and proven principles and practices of breeding, not the indiscriminate use of drugs and medicines. Most diseases can be prevented through the practice of Selective Breeding. Simply select the best and healthiest individuals, and breed only to them, and cull the rest. This will give you a family of fowl with a strong constitutional vigor.

PRINCIPLES OF ZYGOSITY

We hear the words "homozygous" and "heterozygous" but do you really know what they mean, and how they affect the breeding of our fowl? We will discuss these terms now. However there are two others as well, "hemizygous" and "nullizygous," which nobody discusses, but are very important as well.

Zygosity refers to the similarity of genes for a trait (inherited characteristic) in an organism. If both genes are the same, the organism is "homozygous" for the trait. If both genes are different, the organism is "heterozygous" for that trait. If one gene is missing, it is "hemizygous," and if both genes are missing, it is "nullizygous."

Most organisms have two sets of chromosomes, that is, they are diploid. Diploid organisms have one copy of each gene on each chromosome.

The DNA sequence of a gene usually varies from one individual to another. Those variations are called "alleles." Some genes have only one allele. Any variation from the DNA sequence of that allele will be fatal in the embryo, and the organism will never survive long enough to be born. But most genes have two or more alleles. The frequency of different alleles varies throughout the population of any group. Some genes may have two alleles with equal distribution. For other genes, one allele may be common, and another allele may be rare. Sometimes, one allele is a disease causing variation while the other allele is healthy. Sometimes, the different variations in the alleles make no difference at all in the function of the organism. In diploid organisms, one allele is inherited from the male parent and one from the female parent. Zygosity is a description of whether those two alleles have identical or different DNA sequences.

THE DIFFERENT TYPES OF ZYGOSITY: The words "homozygous," "heterozygous," and "hemizygous" are used to describe the genotype of a diploid organism at a single locus on the DNA. "Homozygous" describes a genotype consisting of two identical alleles at a given locus. "Heterozygous" describes a genotype consisting of two different alleles at a locus. "Hemizygous" describes a genotype consisting of only a single copy of a particular gene in an otherwise diploid organism. And "nullizygous" refers to an otherwise diploid organism in which both copies of the gene are missing. Here is a further discussion of these forms of zygosity.

Homozygous: A cell is said to be homozygous for a particular gene when identical alleles of the gene are present on both homologous chromosomes. The cell or organism in question is called a homozygote. True breeding organisms are always homozygous for the traits that are to be held constant.

An individual that is homozygous dominant for a particular trait carries two copies of the allele that codes for the dominant trait. This allele, often called the "dominant allele," is normally represented by a capital letter (such as P for the dominant allele producing pea-combs). When an organism is homozygous dominant for a particular trait, the genotype is represented by a doubling of the symbol for that trait, such as (*PP*).

An individual that is homozygous recessive for a particular trait carries two copies of the allele that codes for the recessive trait. This allele, often called the "recessive allele," is usually represented by the lowercase form of the letter used for the corresponding dominant trait [such as, with reference to the example above, (*p*) for the recessive allele producing straight (*single*) combs]. The genotype of an organism that is homozygous recessive for a particular trait is represented by a doubling of the appropriate letter, such as (*pp*).

Heterozygous: Heterozygous is an organism whose cells contain different genes for a characteristic. Heterozygous genotypes are represented by a capital letter (representing the dominant allele) and a lowercase letter (representing the recessive allele), such as (*Pp*) or (*Ss*). The capital letter is usually written first.

If the trait in question is determined by simple (complete) dominance, a heterozygote will express only the trait coded by the dominant allele and the trait coded by the recessive allele will not be present. In more complex dominance schemes the results of heterozygosity can be more complex.

Hemizygous: A diploid organism is hemizygous for a particular gene when only one allele for the gene is present. The cell or organism is called a hemizygote. Hemizygosity is observed when one copy of a gene is deleted, or in the heterogametic sex when a gene is located on a sex chromosome. For organisms in which the male is heterogametic, such as in chickens, almost all (*Z*) linked genes are hemizygous in hens with normal chromosomes because they have only one (*Z*) chromosome and few of the same genes are on the (*W*) chromosome.

In a more extreme example, male honeybees (known as drones) are completely hemizygous organisms. They develop from unfertilized eggs and their entire genome is haploid, unlike female honeybees, which are diploid.

Nullizygous: A nullizygous organism carries two mutant alleles for the same gene. The mutant alleles are both complete loss-of-function and "null" alleles, so homozygous null and nullizygous are synonymous. The mutant cell or organism is called a nullizygote. Researchers sometimes breed organisms to be nullizygous in a particular trait so that they can study how the organism is affected by the loss of the trait. Natural nullizygosity is very rare and can be fatal or extremely harmful to the individual since it prevents an entire trait from being expressed.

HOMOZYGOUS, HETEROZYGOUS AND DOMINANCE: If two alleles, contained in the zygote, or mature bird, are "identical," the organism is called a "homozygote" and is said to be "homozygous." For example, the foundation of the zygote of the pure pea-combed parent (*PP*) is "homozygous" for the pea-comb trait. Likewise, the foundation of the zygote of the straight (*single*) comb parent (*pp*) is also in the homozygous condition.

If instead, the two alleles; that are contained in the zygote or mature bird are different, the organism is a "heterozygote" and is said to be "heterozygous." For example, the foundation of the zygote of each of the first filial generation birds is (*Pp*), as in the case where the offspring are pea-combed, but they carry the straight (*single*) comb trait. This indicates a bird that is "heterozygous" for the pea-comb trait.

The genetic makeup of an organism, either at a single locus or collectively over all its genes, is called the genotype. The genotype of an organism directly or indirectly affects its molecular, physical, behavioral, and other traits, which individually or collectively are called the phenotype. At heterozygous gene loci, the two alleles interact to produce the phenotype. The simplest form of allele interaction is the one described by Mendel, now called Mendelian, in which the appearance/phenotype, caused by one allele is apparent, called dominant, and the appearance/phenotype, caused by the other allele is not apparent, called recessive.

In the simplest case, the phenotypic effect of one allele completely masks the other in heterozygous combination. That is, the phenotype produced by the two alleles in heterozygous combination is identical to that produced by one of the two homozygous genotypes. The allele that masks the other is said to be dominant to the latter, and the alternative allele is said to be recessive to the former.

THE CONCEPT OF DOMINANCE: This was first explained by the "father of genetics," Gregor Mendel, who recognized the principle based on his work with the common garden pea. For example, the edible pea seeds occur in two distinct phenotypes, "round" and "wrinkled." The "shape" phenotype is known to be influenced by a single gene that occurs in two allelic forms, (A) and (B). Pea plants that are homozygous (AA) have round seeds, and those that are homozygous (BB) have wrinkled seeds. Plants that are heterozygous (AB) have round seeds that are indistinguishable in shape from (AA) seeds: the (A) allele "dominates" the (B) allele to produce the round phenotype. That is, the (A) allele is said to be dominant to the (B) allele, and the (B) allele is recessive to the (A) allele. The principle of dominance is known as "Mendel's Third Law of Inheritance."

Which one is dominant? A dominant trait does not mean "more powerful," and recessive does not mean "weaker." Rather, the terms simply refer to the visible trait, the phenotype, seen in a heterozygote. If only two phenotypes are possible, and a heterozygote exhibits one phenotype, by definition the phenotype exhibited by the heterozygote is called "dominant" and the "hidden" phenotype is considered recessive.

The key concept of dominance is that the heterozygote is phenotypically identical to one of the two homozygotes. The homozygous trait seen also in the heterozygous individual is called the "dominant" trait.

It is critical to understand that dominance is a genotypic relationship between alleles, as manifested in the phenotype (form and function of the bird). It is unrelated to the nature of the phenotype itself, whether it is regarded as "normal or abnormal," "standard or nonstandard," "healthy or diseased," "stronger or weaker," or "more or less" extreme. It is also important to distinguish between the "round" gene locus, the "round" allele at that locus, and the "round" phenotype it produces. It is inaccurate to say that "the round gene dominates the wrinkled gene" or that "round peas dominate wrinkled peas."

PRINCIPLES OF HYBRIDIZATION
Improving characteristics and creating diversity
Through the mating of different breeds

<u>INTRODUCTION</u>: The mere mention of the word "hybridization" tends to bring out a very negative reaction from many breeders. Consequently, some breeders view the word "transmutation" as a more agreeable alternative. These opinions could seem similar to those who respond to "inbreeding," using terms, such as, "closed flock" breeding. Regardless of the definition, for many people hybridization is thought to be a horrific practice. For those people there is little point in encouraging or discussing something that "contaminates" the gene pool of a desirable (pure) species, or results in a nest full of offspring that can vary significantly in physical appearance and genetic composition.

I thought hybridization was worth discussing, to determine the role hybridizing has played in different varieties of American Games. The results of my research were quite interesting. Hybridization seems to be a matter of importance and definition, but in the end, the objective is to generate a new breed, variety, or line of bird that excels in some feature or features (traits) that makes it extremely valuable or aesthetically pleasing. That value may be based on a variety of expectations, such as: improved conformation of body and color of plumage; better performance ability and style; and adaptability and survivability to their environment, especially in harsh climates.

The application of hybridization in animals (dairy; beef; poultry; sheep; goats, etc...) and in plants, is well documented in history and has generated a tremendous volume of subjective information, scientific reports and myths. If you ask me, this is completely absurd. When it came to American Games, hybridization occurred a long time ago. It happened when breeders crossed one Junglefowl with another. This led to a variety of forms. When hybridization occurs you get a blurring or blending of species. This blending, in the case of the Wild Junglefowl, resulted in the development of many breeds of chickens. Just look at gamefowl in general, and the efforts that went into developing new variations (breeds/varieties/strains/lines), some for fighting, some for exhibition, and some... because people could. This was no accident, it happened because of hybridization and the art of Selective Breeding for a specific form and function.

<u>WHAT IS HYBRIDIZATION</u>? When a plant or animal is bred with a plant or animal from a different class, breed, variety, strain, or line, the process is known as hybridization.

Hybridization is frequently practiced in the growing of crops, to make stronger, healthier plants with desirable characteristics. Animal breeders also use hybridization to create new breeds, or to make a breed stronger. Or in some families of American Games, breeders use hybridization to try to breed out unwanted traits, such as "low station of leg."

The most common type of hybridization involves crossing two organisms of different breeds within the same species, such as the breeding of American Games with Aseels. This is also called crossbreeding. In the breeding of American Games, crossbreeding is used to create battlefowl. These are fowl that are generally faster, stronger and more powerful than the average game bird, or have an exceptional performance ability or style.

Hybridization can bring about sterility: In another type of hybridization, two animals of different species within the same genus are bred to each other. This is not always possible, but when achieved, the resulting animal or crop is sometimes sterile. Most animals hybridized in this way are, in fact, usually sterile. A good example of this is the mule, using a mare and a jack donkey. The mule has the courage, stamina and surefootedness of the donkey with the strength of a horse, and has been a very useful pack animal that played an important part in history. However, due to the issues of fertility, valuable genes may be lost by breeding dissimilar species together. Thus the mule cannot reproduce.

Aseel.

Nevertheless, hybrids under domestication do not generally give rise to new breeds, usually due to the fact that hybrid males are mostly infertile. In this case, female hybrids are mated back to purebred animals. In only a few generations, the "alien genes" are absorbed into the gene pool of the breed she is bred back to. Theoretically, a new sub-breed may arise if the population is isolated, but they will only have subtle differences. So the question is, why are they bred? The answer, many are bred out of curiosity.

Hybridization also occurs in nature: Evolutionary processes such as recombination and Natural Selection usually develop over extended periods of time. Nevertheless, they are often accelerated in cases of hybridization. Hybrids exhibit new genomes, which are open to Natural Selection. Hybridization does occur naturally, but it is uncommon because animals prefer to breed with their own species. However, when it does occur, it can bring out favorable traits from two different gene pools. Hybridization allows animals to adapt to changing environments and if the hybrids thrive, a new species may emerge.

THE BENEFITS OF HYBRIDIZATION: Hybridization, in the breeding of American Games, is highly important for some families because it has the power to maintain a certain amount of genetic diversity. This improves the health and longevity of the family itself.

Many purebred families are inbred, sometimes due to a limited genetic pool. These are breeders who practice, what I like to call, "mono-inbreeding." This is the breeding and raising of only one line of fowl within a family structure, which is extremely detrimental for the future of the family. There must be some diversity within the family. Inbreeding in this way tends to bring out serious genetic defects. I recommend keeping four or more separate lines of the same family. This way you can maintain a certain amount of genetic diversity (by outcrossing from time to time) and simultaneously continue to preserve the purity of the blood.

HYBRIDIZED FOWL TEND TO BE MORE RESISTANT TO DISEASE: Should the family be susceptible to a particular disease or a damaging defect, the whole family will be lost. By hybridizing in the manner that I have just described, which is known as outcrossing, breeders are able to bring in fresh genes into the mix without adding unknown factors into the family structure. Outcrossing to one of the other lines refreshes and strengthens the inbred line and avoids the harmful effects of inbreeding depression.

WHAT IS A HYBRID? Hybrids are produced by crossing of two species or two breeds. Hybrid chickens are artificial creations. They are unlikely to occur in the wild except in unnatural situations. For example, in very isolated populations where there is no mate of the appropriate species available.

There are numerous reasons to create hybrids, including increasing genetic diversity and breeding for specific traits. In some cases, a crossbred bird can be bred to purebreds to bring the next generation more in alignment with the breed standard. It can also be used in creating fowl that can gain weight incredibly fast, as in the production of commercial poultry meat, or in creating battlefowl for the pit. This is known as hybrid-vigor. Depending on the fowl, this may or may not matter.

All American Games were created by using a certain amount of hybridization.

A bird is considered to be hybrid for a specific characteristic when it possesses one dominant and one recessive gene. For instance, when you cross a pea-combed Silver Duckwing (Grey) with a straight (*single*) combed Black-Breasted Red; the progeny resulting from the crossing will have pea-combs, since pea-combs are dominant over straight (*single*) combs. In the reproductive cell of the progeny there will be one gene (P) carrying the pea-combs characteristic, and one gene (p) carrying the straight (*single*) comb characteristic.

Since Silver (Grey) plumage color is dominant over the Red plumage color, the progeny will be hybrid for plumage color as well. The progeny will have one gene in the reproductive cell for the dominant Silver (Grey) (S) color and one gene for the recessive Red (s) color.

When a hybrid is mated with another hybrid, about 75 percent of the progeny will show the characteristics of the dominant, and 25 percent will show recessive characteristics. Of the 75 percent of the progeny that show dominance, only one-third is pure dominant for the one character. The other two-thirds have the appearance of the dominant but are hybrid. Those which show recessive characteristics are pure recessive.

HYBRIDIZATION OF AMERICAN GAMES, AND THE SPANGLED GENE: Here is a good example of how hybridization operates. As far as I am aware, the Spangled color gene has occurred only among the Black-Breasted Dark-Red and Light-Red varieties. The process of breeding pure Spangled can take anywhere from three to ten years to set the color. Some suggest that statistically it might only take 4 generations to get pure Spangled birds. Either way, it can be a lengthy process.

If you plan to pursue this path, a substantive quantity and quality of American Games that are Spangled should be available to ensure that the best hybrids are mated back to the best (standard) of the recipient strain. Conformation of body, size, and color of plumage are very important at this point in time.

At the end of the road, and under an experienced breeder, the hybrid will come to resemble the recipient strain. The hybrid, no matter how good it looks or how closely it resembles the color of the recipient strain, may sometimes produce an offspring (throwback) that looks more like the progenitor or original strain. This is particularly true if inexperienced cockers and backyard breeders breed "new color variety" birds to each other. The "throwback" is simply the expression of the heterogeneity (sometimes hidden) of the crossbred.

Successful hybrid expression and acceptability is based on the hybrid bird's genome, comprising a greater percentage of the recipient strains genome and only a relatively small percentage of the donor strains genes. The color impact is easily assessed, but the impact of associated genes are neither well-known nor well documented. It is not possible as yet, as far as I am aware, to remove or isolate the complete chromosomal segment (associated genes and loci) transferred with the new hybrid color gene after hybridization has occurred. It is because of these associated genes and the apparent inabilities to remove them from the hybrid genome that people believe there is no reversal in the hybridization process, and that the potential for cockers and backyard breeders to breed these birds indiscriminately with other breeds is high. The result of this indiscriminate breeding is that the pure gene pool becomes rapidly "contaminated" by the presence of the "hybrid gene," and progeny are produced with a mixed color of plumage.

An American Game Spangled-Red Cock.

The offspring, except for a rare occasion, would probably not be shown or exhibited at competitive events because of the demand for the proper structure and color. Not to mention an unspoken expectation that the bird will not be able to pass on certain "pure" and "desirable" traits.

So, what do you do with these poor representatives (hybrid) of the strain? It is important to remember that for every successful hybrid, there is a long trail of birds that did not make the grade. However, this is true in almost every type of domestic fowl, whether they are chickens; pigeons; turkeys; or American Games.

The following points are meant to get people thinking about hybridization concepts and the implications or trickle down effects from hybrids:

- A hybrid may be defined as the offspring from two different breeds, varieties, strains, or species.

- Hybridization, in essence, is the crossing of birds or animals that may or may not differ noticeably in general, physical appearance, and may or may not have significant differences in their genome. This may be only one chromosome that has been subject to a physical alteration, or a substantive change in the genome brought about through Selective Breeding, or natural events.

What do we know about hybridization?

- Someone who mates their birds indiscriminately and gives them away or sells them as something special is usually passing them into the hands of a "beginner." If that beginner receives them in their second or third year and the birds produce offspring, or are mated with other birds, who is to tell the beginner that they have polluted their "gene pool," and stand a good chance of polluting more if they sell those birds as pure American Games?

- A prepotent cock (or hen) in a line or strain of birds carrying homozygous factors for a number of desirable (selected) characteristics can pass on his genome with great expression in the progeny, even if the hen is only average for a few traits. The progeny, or first filial generation F_1, would be very similar in appearance to the cock, but the problem occurs when the F_2 or second filial generation is crossed among itself. In this instance, a number of hybrid or undesirable offspring may be generated.

- Two highly inbred lines of birds may be developed from several pairs of progenitor parents. Persistent inbreeding would lead to birds with a highly select genome, and one that might not occur naturally, or not for a very long time. The progeny resulting from a crossing of two such inbred lines (where the intent was to generate a third line) would be referred to as a recombinant inbred line and again, the F_1 cross would appear very good phenotypically, despite being heterozygous for different traits. The F_1 is a hybrid cross; the F_2 is also a hybrid cross (mono and di-hybrid crosses) but would have greater variety in phenotypes and genotypes.

People seem relatively comfortable with terms like - line, strain, variety and breed. A fixed strain or breed may be the result of ten to fifteen generations of intensive culling, selection and family breeding. The process identifies and attempts to remove many of the more "undesirable traits" so that a relatively homozygous line of birds is created. Their genome would eventually be significantly different to the common American Game that is bred by the average cocker and backyard breeder. Crossing birds with unknown fowl may result in the benefits of Heterosis (hybrid-vigor), and decent looking birds in the F_1 generation, but a mating between the F_2 generations could generate hybrid offspring with significant phenotypic and genotypic variation.

Given the points above, it becomes clear that:

- In nature, the development of a new species might occur through gradual pressure, selection or isolation; or very rapidly through a physical chromosomal alteration.
- In Selective Breeding activities, the genome can be filtered relatively quickly with an aggressive methodology and a close breeding plan.
- A selected strain (line or variety of American Games), at some point can become quite genotypically different from the "parent population."
- In the dog, pigeon, chicken and other species, a number of breeds have been generated (isolated) through selection. New breeds are generated by crossing (hybridizing) these existing breeds and selecting desired traits from the F_1 or more infrequently the F_2. Through further selection a new breed is then developed.
- Breeds and strains can and do disappear without continued work and maintenance by breeders.

- Selection within a family can help to generate and identify mutations, lethal genes, autosomal recessives, structural inheritance and their correlation with other traits.
- Hybrids can result within a family, without the necessity for breeding with another family.
- If certain mutations were not maintained or desired by breeders, they too, would soon disappear, as they are recessive in nature.
- The 1st generation will exhibit some variation among themselves and consequently, birds are selected for their appearance and bred together in an effort to establish a new line. The 1st generation in this case would need to be similar in form and color for the trait being sought by the breeder. After that, it is a matter of Selective Breeding to build up the line.
- Sometimes a line or strain of birds may experience a reduction in size, or a failing in one or more of the desired traits. This is not due to inbreeding depression but to improper selection.
- To improve the family, due to a loss of vitality (usually due to inbreeding depression), the beginner breeder will often go outside the family to breed in a bird of a known pedigree that shows great constitution vigor. The breeder may also look for a bird that has no pedigree but is also strong in that area. However, this may inadvertently lead to a reintroduction of genes that had previously been extracted from the line or strain.
- The conscientious breeder will pair up birds of separate lines but of the same family (outcross) and hope for a strong showing of young with the desired trait. Heterosis should provide the desired increase in fertility and vigor. Having identified the 1st generation stock with the desired conformation of body and color of plumage, not to mention other valuable traits, the breeder will pair the second generation birds back to other birds of their line, in a quarantined area, to ensure that undesirable autosomal recessives or other hidden problems are identified and caught, before introducing the new birds, now strong in desired trait and form, to others of his flock.
- An experienced breeder will always base their success or championship lines on birds that have won on a regular basis (progeny test). From this approach the expected outcome is that hen and cock champions will breed a line of winning progeny.
- The experienced breeder is always on the lookout for "sports" (one-offs) that are without the homozygous potential to reliably pass on their gene composition. The hen too, may be a rather good bird, but lack the prepotency to pass on her characteristics. The offspring in this case may be heterozygous for a number of traits and none may display the desired characteristics.
- As long as there is a demand for birds with a different appearance and form, breeders will continue to hybridize or cross their birds in the hope of having something special to advertise and sell. People look for the rare or different in many of the things that they seek. Different colored birds are some of those rare and wonderful things. If you have ever been to a poultry show and seen the wonderful variation of form and color of the birds present, it would not take long to start thinking how a bird might look really eye-catching if it had a different color of plumage or was bigger or smaller.
- One thing we know is that change is the common denominator and that it will continue, whether it is through a mutation or a conversion. The number of birds being bred and the efforts of a few dedicated enthusiasts ensure this.

LAW OF CHROMOSOME SEGREGATION
(Gregor Mendel's First Law of Inheritance)

Gregor Mendel, who is known as the "father of modern genetics," studied variations in pea plants. Between 1856 and 1863, Mendel cultivated and tested some 29,000 pea plants. His studies showed that one in four pea plants had purebred recessive alleles, two out of four were hybrid, and one out of four was purebred dominant. His experiments led him to the discovery of two laws, the "Law of Segregation" and the "Law of Independent Assortment," which later became known as "Mendel's Laws of Inheritance."

When Mendel's paper was published in 1866, it had little impact. In fact, Charles Darwin was unaware of Mendel's paper, which would have made a huge impact on his theory of "Evolution by means of Natural Selection."

We will start out in this section of the book by discussing Mendel's first law of inheritance, the "Law of Segregation," also known as "Chromosome Segregation" or the "Segregation of Characteristics." And in the next section we will discuss Mendel's second law of inheritance, the "Law of Independent Assortment."

Gregor Mendel concluded that the paired factors separate during the formation of reproductive cells, or gametes (sperm and egg). This means that each reproductive cell, or gamete, receives only one factor of each pair. When two gametes (sperm and egg) combine during fertilization, the offspring have two factors controlling a specific trait. The law of segregation states that a pair of factors is segregated, or separated, during the formation of gametes. In other words, when an individual produces a gamete (a sperm or an egg), the copies of a gene separate so that each gamete receives only one copy. A gamete will receive one allele or the other.

The normal reproductive cell, or gamete (sperm and egg), in chickens contains 39 pairs of chromosomes, yet when two cells are brought together there are still only 39 pairs of chromosomes. A reduction takes place in the process of germ-cell/gamete production, which reduces the number of chromosomes by one-half. Only one chromosome of each pair is included in the germ cell/gamete. As a result, only one gene in each pair of genes is included in the germ cell/gamete. The bringing together of two germ cells/gamete, through fertilization restores the normal number of chromosomes and genes.

The fact that many characters segregate in inheritance according to definite principles has been thoroughly proven, both with plants and animals.

Have you ever noticed that whenever you breed a pea-comb bird to a straight (*single*) comb bird, all the offspring are pea-combed? But when you took these pea-combed offspring and breed them to each other, their offspring showed both pea and straight (*single*) combs? And if you were very observant, you might have notice that the proportion of pea to straight was about 3 to 1. That's one straight (*single*) comb for every three pea-combs produced. Well this is the essence of the "Law of Segregation." Let's discuss this in greater detail.

92

THE PRINCIPLE OF SEGREGATION:

As I mentioned earlier, characters exist in alternative pairs, such as Silver and Red plumage color. Straight (*single*) comb and the pea-comb represent another pair of alternate characters. No matter the characteristic, there is always one character that is an alternative to the other.

The most important fact to be kept in mind, is when there is a crossing of two alternative characters, what results is a separation of characteristics in the second hybrid generation, otherwise known as "segregation." For example: In the cross between two contrasting characters, such as Silver Duckwing and Black-Breasted Red, in the first generation one character will dominate the other (silver over red), but in the second generation there is a segregation of the characters so that the two contrasting color characteristics appear in the proportion of three Silver to one Red. Two contrasted characters brought together in the F_1 generation become separated from each other in the F_2 generation.

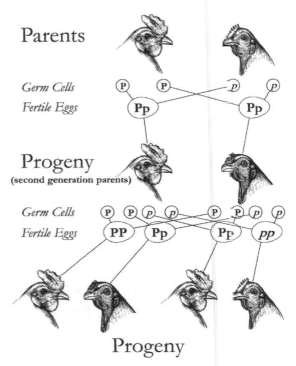

The breeding of a pea-comb cock with a straight (single) comb hen.

Furthermore, in the F_2 generation there will be Silvers that breed true, producing nothing but Silvers, as well as, Reds that breed true, producing nothing but Reds. There are also Silvers that do not breed true, for when they are mated among themselves they produce progeny in the ratio of three Silvers to one Red. Although the F_2 generation is comprised of three Silvers to one Red, the Silvers differ in respect to the results they produce when they are bred. Among every three Silvers one is homozygous, whereas the other two are heterozygous for the Silver color.

From the standpoint of the genetic constitution of the individuals of the second hybrid generation, the F_2 ratio is really 1:2:1, that is, one homozygous for Silver, two heterozygous for both characters (Silver and Red), and one homozygous for Red.

These ratios hold true for other varieties as well, such as the American Games Doms (or Creels) crossed with Black Breasted-Reds.

ANOTHER EXAMPLE OF "SEGREGATION OF CHARACTERISTICS" WOULD BE THAT OF COMB TYPES:

If we were to mate individuals, which are selected from the offspring resulting from a cross of pure pea-combed fowl and those that are straight (*single*) combs (all of which exhibit pea-combs), we would find both pea-combed and straight (*single*) combed specimens among the offspring in the proportion of approximately 3:1. That is one straight (*single*) combed specimen to each three exhibiting pea-combs. Here is a formulated explanation: *PPss(pea-comb) x PPss(pea-comb) = PP(homozygous pea-comb) Ps(heterozygous pea-comb) Ps(heterozygous pea-comb) ss(homozygous straight (single) comb).*

P1 - Parents

Silver Duckwing   Black Breasted-Red

F1 - First Generation

All of offspring are Silver Duckwing in color

F2 - Second Generation

3 to 1 Ratio - all cocks are silver; one-half of hens are silver; one-half of hens are red

A Silver-Duckwing male crossed with a Black Breasted-Red female produces F_1 Silver-Duckwing males and females. An F_1 male crossed to a F_1 female produces an F_2 generation in which the males are silver and one-half of the females are silver but the other half are non-silver (or red).

P1 - Parents

Black Breasted-Red   Silver Duckwing

F1 - First Generation

All cocks are silver; all hens are red

F2 - Second Generation

One-half of the cocks are silver and one-half are red
One-half of the hens are silver and one-half are red

A Black Breasted-Red male crossed to a Silver-Duckwing female produces F_1 silver males but non-silver (or red) females, the sex-linked gene for "Silver" being transmitted from the dam to her sons only. An F_1 male crossed to a F_1 female produces an F_2 generation in which one-half of each sex is silver and one-half is non-silver (or red).

THESE FACTS MAY BE SUMMARIZED AS FOLLOWS:

Pure Silver Duckwing x Pure Black Breasted-Red
|
Hybrid Silver Duckwing Offspring – (F₁)
|

F₂ Generation

| 1 Pure Silver Duckwing |
| 2 Hybrid Silver Duckwings |
| 1 Pure Black Breasted-Red |

3 to 1 Ratio

If we were to continue our breeding operations and mate the straight (*single*) combed specimens with other straight (*single*) combed specimens, we would find that they breed true and all the offspring would exhibit straight (*single*) combs like their parents. Here is a formulated explanation: *ss(homozygous straight (single) comb) X ss(homozygous straight (single) comb) = ss(homozygous straight (single) comb) ss(homozygous straight (single) comb)*.

If, on the other hand, we were to mate some of the pea-comb birds together we would get quite a different result. One-third of these would be pure for the pea-comb factor and, if we happen to get only these types of individuals in our mating, all individuals in the offspring would exhibit a pea-comb. Here is a formulated explanation: *PP(homozygous pea-comb) X PP(homozygous pea-comb) = PP(homozygous pea-comb) PP(homozygous pea-comb)*.

The balance, the other two-thirds of the pea-combed birds from the pea and straight (*single*) comb cross, would be impure for the factor that causes a pea-comb to develop and, when mated together, these would produce offspring in the proportion of one straight (*single*) combed specimen to each three of the individuals exhibiting pea-combs. Here is a formulated explanation: *PPss(pea-comb) X PPss(pea-comb) = PP(homozygous pea-comb) Ps(heterozygous pea-comb) Ps(heterozygous pea-comb) ss(homozygous straight (single) comb)*.

Therefore, we would see that in a cross of a pure pea-combed bird on a straight (*single*) combed one, we would get offspring (in the second generation) in the proportion of one bird exhibiting a straight (*single*) comb, one pure pea-combed specimen, and two exhibiting pea-combs, but carrying the straight (*single*) comb factor in their cells.

If we were to mate one of the pure pea-combed specimens to an impure bird for pea-comb, we would get (on an average, of course), offspring all of which would exhibit pea-combs, but one-half of which are pure for the pea-comb factor and one-half impure from a breeding standpoint, as they would contain the straight (*single*) comb factor in addition to the factor that causes a pea-comb. Here is a formulated explanation: *PP(homozygous pea-comb) X Ps(heterozygous pea-comb) = PP(homozygous pea-comb) Ps(heterozygous pea-comb)*.

If we were to mate a bird having a straight (*single*) comb with one of the impure pea-combed specimens, one-half of the offspring would have straight (*single*) combs and breed pure for this

P1 - Parents

Dom or Creel   Black Breasted-Red

F1 - First Generation
All of offspring are Dom or Creel in color

F2 - Second Generation
3 to 1 Ratio - all cocks are Dom; one-half of
hens are Dom; one-half of hens are red

A Dom male crossed with a Black Breasted-Red female produces F_1 Dom males and females. An F_1 male crossed to a F_1 female produces an F_2 generation in which the males are barred and one-half of the females are barred but the other half are non-barred (or red).

P1 - Parents

Black Breasted-Red   Dom or Creel

F1 - First Generation
All cocks are silver; all hens are red

F2 - Second Generation
One-half of the cocks are silver and one-half are red
One-half of the hens are silver and one-half are red

A Black Breasted-Red male crossed to a Dom female produces F_1 barred males but non-barred (or red) females, the sex-linked gene for "Barring" being transmitted from the dam to her sons only. An F_1 male crossed to a F_1 female produces an F_2 generation in which one-half of each sex is barred and one-half is non-barred (or red).

factor. The other half would exhibit pea-combs, but be impure from a breeding standpoint. Here is a formulated explanation: *Ps(heterozygous pea-comb) X ss(homozygous straight (single) comb) = Ps(heterozygous pea-comb) ss(homozygous straight (single) comb)*.

It is important to remember that in every set of chromosomes there is one copy of each gene in the organism's genome. The chicken, like a pea plant, has two sets of chromosomes in most cells (which are therefore called diploid cells) and therefore two copies of the gene. These two copies may be identical or different.

Segregation occurs during meiosis I, when a diploid cell divides into two haploid cells. Fertilization restores the diploid number.

THE CONTRIBUTIONS OF GREGOR MENDEL: The explanation given of the segregation of character in the F_2 generation, and the explanation given of the segregation of the genes as separate units, is the first of two major contributions Gregor Mendel made to the science of breeding. The establishment of the "Principle of Segregation" gave birth to a new conception concerning the manner in which characters are inherited from generation to generation, and led to remarkable discoveries concerning the mechanism of inheritance. We would be wise to study these mechanisms and apply them in the breeding of American Games.

LAW OF INDEPENDENT ASSORTMENT
(Gregor Mendel's Second Law of Inheritance)

Developed by Gregor Mendel, "The Law of Independent Assortment," also known as "Inheritance Law," is the second of two major contributions Mendel gave to the science of breeding, and has become a basic principle of all genetics. Mendel formulated this principle after discovering another principle now known as "The Law of Segregation," which we have just discussed in the previous pages of this chapter.

THE INDEPENDENT ASSORTMENT OF THE GENES: This principle states that the alleles of different genes assort independently of one another during gamete formation. In other words, these traits separate when gametes are formed. These allele pairs are then randomly united at fertilization. Mendel arrived at this conclusion by performing monohybrid crosses. These were crosspollination experiments with pea plants that differed in one trait, for example pod color.

Mendel began to wonder what would happen if he studied plants that differed in two traits, such as in pod color and seed color. Would both traits be transmitted to the offspring together or would one trait be transmitted independently of the other?

Mendel performed dihybrid crosses in plants that were true-breeding for two traits. For example, a plant that had a green pod color and yellow seed color was cross-pollinated with a plant that had a yellow pod color and green seeds. In this cross, the traits for green pod color (GG) and yellow seed color (YY) are dominant. Yellow pod color (gg) and green seed color (yy) are recessive. The resulting offspring, or F_1 generation were all heterozygous for green pod color and yellow seeds ($GgYy$).

After observing the results of the dihybrid cross, Mendel allowed all of the F_1 plants to self-pollinate. He referred to these offspring as the F_2 generation. Mendel noticed a 9:3:3:1 ratio. About nine of the F_2 plants had green pods and yellow seeds, three had green pods and green seeds, three had yellow pods and yellow seeds, and one had a yellow pod and green seeds.

The data from these more-complex crosses showed that traits produced by dominant factors do not necessarily appear together. Mendel concluded that the factors for different characteristics and traits are not connected. They are inherited independently of each other, so that there is no relation. A good example of this would be the relation of a chicken's color of plumage and the length of their tail or station of leg, or better yet, the color of their plumage and performance ability or gameness. There is no connection between the different characteristics and traits. Therefore, one trait has no effect on the other. This is actually only true for genes that are not linked to each other.

Mendel performed similar experiments focusing on several other traits like seed color and seed shape, pod color and pod shape, and flower position and stem length. He noticed the same ratios in each case. From these experiments Mendel formulated the principle that is now known as Mendel's "Law of Independent Assortment." This law states that factors for different characteristics are distributed to gametes independently. Another way of saying this is that allele pairs separate independently during the formation of gametes. Therefore, traits are transmitted to offspring independently of one another, and therefore have no effect on the other.

So, for any of you who might believe that just because your fowl throw a Light-Red from time to time, in a family that is predominantly dark-red in color; the Light-Reds will be different in performance ability or style, not to mention, gameness, perish the thought! These traits are independent of each other. There is no connection or link between color of plumage and performance ability. Even gameness is independent of the other characteristics.

THE ENORMOUS POSSIBILITIES OF GENETIC COMBINATIONS: Independent assortment occurs during meiosis, to produce a gamete (sperm and egg) with a mixture of the organism's maternal (mother) and paternal (father) chromosomes. Along with chromosomal crossover, this process aids in increasing genetic diversity by producing original genetic combinations.

Of the 78 chromosomes in a normal diploid chicken cell, half are maternally-derived (from the mother's egg) and half are paternally-derived (from the father's sperm). This occurs as sexual reproduction involves the fusion of two haploid gametes (the sperm and egg) to produce a new organism having the full complement of chromosomes. During gametogenesis (the production of new gametes) the normal complement of 78 chromosomes needs to be halved to 39 to ensure that the resulting haploid gamete can join with another gamete to produce a diploid organism.

In "Independent Assortment," the chromosomes that end up in a newly-formed gamete (sperm and egg) are randomly sorted from all possible combinations of maternal and paternal chromosomes. Because gametes end up with a random mix instead of a predefined "set" from either parent, gametes are therefore considered assorted independently. As such, the gamete (sperm or egg) can end up with any combination of paternal or maternal chromosomes. Any of the possible combinations of gametes formed from maternal and paternal chromosomes will occur with equal frequency. For chicken gametes (sperm and egg), with 39 pairs of chromosomes, the number of possible combinations is enormous. The gametes will normally end up with 39 chromosomes, but the origin of any particular one will be randomly selected from paternal or maternal chromosomes. The importance of this fact is that it contributes, to a high degree, the genetic variability of the progeny.

IN THE CASE OF THE INHERITANCE OF TWO PAIRS OF CHARACTERISTICS: The inheritance of two pairs of characteristics is exactly the same, in principle, as the inheritance of one pair. Since two pairs of characteristics are involved, the F_1 hybrids are able to produce four kinds of gametes instead of only two, as in the case of the inheritance of one pair of characteristics. Since four kinds of gametes are produced by each sex, the possibilities for the segregation and recombination of the genes is four times as great as in the case when only two kinds of gametes are formed.

Here is a good example of what I am referring to. The "pea-comb" is the standard type for most American Game families and strains, but occasionally a bird with a "straight (*single*) comb" appears. As we now know, pea-comb is dominant to straight (*single*) comb. Therefore, if Silver Duckwing American Games, with pea-combs are crossed with Black-Breasted Red American Games, with straight (*single*) combs, two pairs of characters are involved in the cross:

- Silver plumage and Red plumage as one pair.
- Pea-comb and straight (*single*) comb as the other pair.

By using proper symbols to designate the genes carried in the chromosomes, the mode of inheritance of the two pairs of characteristics is easily demonstrated. Capital letters are used for the dominant characteristics and small letters (lowercase) for the recessive characteristics:

- (P) represents pea-comb characteristic and the gene that produces it.
- (p) represents straight (*single*) comb characteristic and the gene that produces it.
- (S) represents Silver plumage characteristic and the gene that produces it.
- (s) represents the Red plumage characteristic and the gene that produces it.

Since the genes are borne in pairs, the zygote of the Pea-combed Silver Duckwing contains the genes (*PPSS*), and the zygote of the Straight (*single*) combed Black-Breasted Red contains the genes (*ppss*), the Pea-combed Silver Duckwing, being homozygous for both pea-comb and Silver plumage, and the Straight (*single*) combed Black-Breasted Red, being homozygous for both straight (*single*) comb and Red plumage.

The Pea-combed Silver Duckwing parent produces (*PS*) gametes, and the Straight (*single*) combed Black-Breasted Red parent produces (*ps*) gametes. These unite to form the F_1 zygote (*PpSs*). Such zygotes are heterozygous for both pairs of characteristics, but the presence of (P) and (S) makes the F_1 birds Pea-combed Silver Duckwings. The F_1 male zygote produces four kinds of gametes (sperm) (*PS, Ps, pS, ps*); and, likewise, the F_1 female zygote produces the same four kinds of gametes (eggs): (*PS, Ps, pS, ps*). Each male gamete may mate with each female gamete, so that there are 16 possible combinations.

F1 - Female Gametes

		PS	Ps	pS	ps
		PPSS *(Pea-Comb and Silver)*	**PPSs** *(Pea-Comb and Silver)*	**PpSS** *(Pea-Comb and Silver)*	**PpSs** *(Pea-Comb and Silver)*
	Ps	**PPSs** *(Pea-Comb and Silver)*	**PPss** *(Pea-Comb and Red)*	**PpSs** *(Pea-Comb and Silver)*	**Ppss** *(Pea-Comb and Red)*
F1 – Male Gametes	**pS**	**PpSS** *(Pea-Comb and Silver)*	**PpSs** *(Pea-Comb and Silver)*	**ppSS** *(Single-Comb and Silver)*	**ppSs** *(Single-Comb and Silver)*
	ps	**PpSs** *(Pea-Comb and Silver)*	**Ppss** *(Pea-Comb and Red)*	**ppSs** *(Single-Comb and Silver)*	**ppss** *(Single-Comb and Red)*

The checkerboard plan of showing the kind of zygotes formed by mating two pairs of characters. (P) = pea-comb; (p) = straight (*single*) comb; (S) = silver plumage; (s) = red plumage.

The type of comb and the color of plumage of the bird arise from each of the 16 zygotes formed. Of the 16 zygotes formed, they give rise to 9 pea-combed/Silvers; 3 pea-combed/Reds; 3 straight (*single*) comb/Silvers; and 1 straight (*single*) comb/Red. A 9:3:3:1 ratio.

However, if comb alone is considered, it is apparent that there are 12 pea-combs and 4 straight (*single*) combs. A 3:1 ratio. Also, if color alone is considered, there are 12 Silvers and 4 Reds. A 3:1 ratio.

Of the 16 F_2 birds, 12 are Silver, of which 9 are pea-combs and 3 are straight (*single*) combs. A 3:1 ratio. Of the 16 F_2 birds, 4 are Red, of which 3 are pea-combed and 1 is a straight (*single*) combed. A 3:1 ratio. That is, for either pair of characteristics considered separately, a 3:1 ratio results.

Are you confused yet? I know this is all very complicated but I assure you, it is well worth it to learn this subject. By using a "Punnett's Square" you can see, on average, how many of the offspring will be pea-combed and Silver Duckwing, how many will be straight (*single*) combed and Black-Breasted Red, as well as, the number of possible combinations of all four traits.

F1 - Female Gametes

	P	p
P	**PP** (*Pea-Comb*)	**Pp** (*Pea-Comb*)
p	**Pp** (*Pea-Comb*)	**pp** (*Straight-Comb*)

F1 - Male Gametes

This illustration shows the 3 to 1 ratio that results when breeding a straight (*single*) comb bird into a pea-combed family.

F1 - Female Gametes

	S	s
S	**SS** (*Silver*)	**Ss** (*Silver*)
s	**Ss** (*Silver*)	**ss** (*Red*)

F1 - Male Gametes

This illustration shows the 3 to 1 ratio that results when breeding a Black Breasted-Red bird into a Silver Duckwing family.

DOMINANCE AND INDEPENDENT ASSORTMENT: Four traits in chickens have been identified as having the Mendelian factor of absolute dominance and independent assortment:

1. <u>Feather color</u>: in this case, white is always dominant to color (any color) and Silver (Grey) is always dominant to Red.
2. <u>Leg colors</u>: in this case, white legs are always dominant to yellow legs and yellow legs are always dominant to green legs.
3. <u>Comb type</u>: in this case, rose-combs are always dominant to pea-combs and pea-combs are always dominant to straight (*single*) combs.
4. <u>Shank feathering</u>: in this case, feathered shanks are always dominant to clean shanks.

THE PRINCIPLE OF LINKAGE: If we are going to discuss independent assortment then we will have to discuss linkage, at least briefly. Linkage simply means that genes giving rise to certain characteristics tend to remain together instead of assorting themselves independently of each other when the gametes from the two sexes unite. For instance, if genes (A) and (B) are completely linked so that they never separate, different results are produced in the F_2 generation from those which would be obtained if (A) and (B) separated freely. A good example of this is characters such as rose-comb and creeper legs.

PRINCIPLES OF ACQUIRED CHARACTERS
Are changes, produced by the environment, inherited?

There has been quite a bit of discussion these days about acquired characteristics - "Are changes produced by the environment inherited?" A few breeders have claimed that a characteristic or trait acquired during the lifetime of the bird may be inherited, but the great majority has claimed that such is not possible. It is my hope that I can shed new light on this controversial subject.

THE HISTORY OF ACQUIRED CHARACTERISTICS: Acquired characteristics originated from earlier beliefs of evolution. Actually, early opinions as to whether or not characteristics are acquired reach further back into history than Charles Darwin. In fact, he was not the first to propose a theory of evolution. Rather, he followed a long line of earlier philosophers and naturalists who reasoned that many of the organisms around us were produced by a process of evolution.

Darwin's theory: Unlike his predecessors, Darwin proposed that Natural Selection on variations within populations lead to evolutionary change. Therefore Natural Selection becomes the mechanism for all of evolution. Natural Selection produces evolutionary change when some individuals in a population possess certain inherited characteristics and produce more surviving offspring than individuals lacking these characteristics. As a result, the population gradually produces and comprises more and more individuals with the beneficial and advantageous characteristics. Therefore, the population evolves and becomes better adapted to its environment.

The great naturalist, Charles Darwin

Natural Selection was by no means the only evolutionary mechanism proposed: A rival theory, proposed by the prominent biologist, Jean-Baptiste Lamarck, was that evolution occurred by the inheritance of acquired characteristics. According to Lamarck, individuals passed on to their offspring "body and behavior" changes, which they acquired during their lives. Consequently, Lamarck proposed that ancestral giraffes, with short necks tended to stretch their necks to feed on tree leaves, and this extension of the neck was passed on to subsequent generations, leading to the long-necked giraffe.

By contrast, in Darwin's theory, the variation is not created by experience, but is the result of preexisting genetic differences among individuals.

ARE ENVIRONMENTALLY PRODUCED CHARACTERS INHERITABLE OR TRANSMISSIBLE?

There is definite evidence that changes of environment may greatly affect the character of animals or plants. Nobody can deny that! Nevertheless, this fact raises the old question as to whether or not characteristics, which are caused by environmental reasons, are inheritable or transmissible to the offspring.

For example, is the size of the bird, which is usually due to climatic conditions, as seen in late hatch chicks, passed on to the offspring? While considering this question you must remember that in many cases the modification that has been modified by the environment is probably due to the fact that individuals, who have not shown acceptable characteristics for that particular environment, were therefore, gradually eliminated by the process of Natural Selection. All the while, the individuals who have properly adjusted were especially well adapted physically to their environment. Under these conditions the modification is due to the process of Natural Selection, rather than to the inheritance of acquired characters.

Unless the environment has a modifying effect upon the bird as an individual, the acquired characteristic cannot be inherited. The truth is, the genetic makeup of an individual or specie is very difficult to change or influence in any way. So if you ask me, with the evidence we currently have, the idea whether or not acquired characteristics are inherited is false. Although some conditions of environment have been known to increase the rate of variation, and a significant number of these variations live on, the environment often produces an effect on a character without affecting its inheritance. It may be said, therefore, that environmental changes may increase the number of heritable variations, but that they are much more likely to change the appearance of the bird without affecting its breeding powers.

A good example of this would be the effects of size on late-hatched chicks. Late-hatched chicks tend to be smaller in size due to climatic conditions. The heat of summer tends to slow nutritional intake, not to mention there is less to eat (foraging) than in the spring. Bugs and parasites tend to be a factor as well, especially that of Coccidiosis. However, this reduction is size is not inherited. If you were to breed this bird, the offspring would most likely be of normal size. This is proof positive that notions of acquired characteristics are false.

<u>The inheritance of mutilations or deformities</u>: You may be asking yourself, what about mutilations or deformities, are they inherited? Deformities due to faulty development, either embryonic or later in life, or mutilations which may occur are never inherited. For example: a cock that has lost its upper beak, due to fighting through the wire with another cock, is not likely to produce offspring missing a beak. A good illustration of an acquired character, in the case of American Games, is the practice of dubbing our cocks. This is the cutting or trimming of the combs, wattles and earlobes. For thousands of years, we as cockers have trimmed our fowl and there has never been a single case where

Ancestry and good selection is the key to success.

offspring showed a noticeable tendency to come without combs or wattles. Subsequently, there is no reason to believe that the dubbed comb would be transmitted through inheritance.

I think it's safe to say that breeders of gamefowl should not be concerned over the possibility of mutilations and deformities being inherited, except ones that are in the bloodline of the fowls, as evidenced by their frequent occurrence throughout various generations.

<u>Change can be caused by other processes</u>: Although the value of Natural Selection is now widely accepted, it is not the only process that can lead to changes in the genetic makeup of a family. Allele frequencies can also change when mutations occur repeatedly from one allele to another, and when breeders cross or infuse new alleles into an established family of fowl. In addition, when families or populations of birds are small, the frequencies of alleles can change randomly as the result of chanced events.

In breeding American Games, it would seem advisable to keep the environment as constant as possible and make use of the very best methods of feeding, care and management.

PRINCIPLES OF
QUANTITATIVE CHARACTERISTICS

In the gamefowl journals, we often read of two different ways to breed. One is called Crossbreeding; the other is called Inbreeding.

Crossbreeding is where the breeder simply attempts to find the best performing fowl that he can in order to breed them to his fowl for the production of battlecocks. This usually happens without any regard whatsoever to their genetic background. They can come from the best performers found within his own family of fowl or by obtaining and breeding individual fowl from other breeders that are doing particularly well. These types of breeders are ones who will do everything in their power in order to get what they are looking for.

This type of breeder doesn't have a specific breeding plan, per say, but he knows that by continually breeding the best to the best, he will accumulate the best genes into his fowl. No doubt he will accumulate the good genes to some extent, but since he's often breeding from hybrids, he will not have cocks with any sort of uniformity. He'll spend many years and never reach the level of uniformity that a meticulous or methodical breeder that inbreeds and line-breeds his fowl will have.

Inbreeding, which also includes line-breeding, is used for establishing uniformity of the strain. It makes the family more predictable, and helps the breeder, whether he uses them straight, or cross's them for the production of battlecocks, to obtain the best birds possible. The ultimate goal for the modern cocker is to establish two good strains that "nick." These breeders mostly select fowl from their own yard of birds. If the breeder does develop two families that "nick," then he should be able to produce uniformly good performers year after year for a good long time.

Regardless of what method the breeder uses to improve performance, he is in an area of genetics that is extremely complex and problematic at best. The word genetic, which means "determined by their origins," comes from the word "gene." A gene is a specific sequence of nucleotides in DNA or RNA that is located in the germ plasm, usually on a chromosome. A chromosome is the functional unit of inheritance controlling the transmission and expression of one or more traits by specifying the structure of a particular polypeptide and protein, controlling the function of other genetic material. They are the key factors that carry hereditary qualities from one generation to the next.

<u>CREATING A STRAIN THAT IS WORTHY OF MY NAME</u>: Obviously, we are all trying to locate, concentrate and perpetuate the best genes in our gamefowl, hoping to create a strain that is worthy of our name, but how is it done?

For a gamecock to be exceptional, he must have all the qualities of a Boxer, an Olympic Athlete, and a Mathematician all wrapped up into one neat package. Let's begin with gameness. He must be game to the core. Gameness is the most important trait a gamecock can have. He must also have good performance ability, accompanied by cutting ability, power, speed, strength and endurance, good temperament, intelligence (which is the ability to evaluate the proper angle of attack, as well as, the right time to attack) and who knows how many other characteristics. But the problem is that these are all "Quantitative Characteristics." A Quantitative Character is an inherited character that is expressed by the influence of multiple factors, which means there's no distinct gene for any of these qualities. This is done in such a way that there is a continuous intergradation between the extremes of its expression. A multifactorial character, other examples of this is fertility, productiveness, conformation of body and their overall size and weight.

THE IMPORTANCE OF QUANTITATIVE TRAITS: Unlike characteristics, such as pea-comb vs. straight-comb, or Red plumage vs. Grey (Silver) plumage, which the breeder can easily control by manipulating one or two genetic factors, a quality like gameness is controlled by a huge number of individual genes all working together in unity for one definite purpose. These are called "Multiple-Factor Characteristics" or "Multiple-Gene Characteristics." Because these characteristics show all types of progressions from high to low, they are sometimes referred to as "Quantitative Traits." These traits are not only determined by a large number of genes, they are also less heritable than simple physical features, which means they can be influenced by the environment.

Quantitative Traits are of particular interest to breeders of American Games, because in order to be successful in their breeding programs, they must devise a breeding system that will improve the average performance of their fowl in several characteristics and traits at the same time.

Physical features such as color and type of plumage, the color of the legs, and comb types are determined by relatively fewer genes. You only have to determine whether they are dominant or recessive. However, traits such as fighting qualities are much more complex. A gamecock's fighting qualities are determined by a much greater number of pairs of genes than its looks are. For example, a cock's fighting ability is based on a combination of traits, such as its conformation of body, power and speed, balance and coordination, ability to fly, shuffling and cutting ability, intelligence, aggressiveness, and gameness. Therefore, dozens, perhaps hundreds of paired genes in a cock's body can determine its ability to fight. And this ability can only be obtained, on a consistent level, through close bred families of fowl, and only from birds that carry these traits in abundance.

THE ESTABLISHMENT OF QUANTITATIVE TRAITS: The establishment of Quantitative Traits in your fowl or strain, such as certain fighting qualities, can only be achieved over many generations, and by consistently selecting breeders on both the cock and the hen sides, which possess these qualities to a noticeable degree.

Proper care of broodfowl and their chicks is also important for fowl to be able to express certain Quantitative Traits that have been bred into them, such as fighting qualities.

Haphazard selection of broodfowl in terms of Quantitative Traits is usually unsuccessful because of the nature of the hereditary transmission of these qualities. To breed for consistent fighting ability in a family or line of American Games, it is necessary to select broodfowl that possess this ability to a noticeable degree, and over many generations. Since they are complex qualities, determined by many genes that are bred into a family of fowl over time, most members of the family will possess this ability due to the steady accumulation of the right genes of each bird in the family. It does not matter what the broodfowl are called, what is important is that they are all excellent performers in the pit. After several generations of Selective Breeding, genes for performance ability in a family are multiplied and the opposite genes, such as those that use single-strokes and bill-holding, are eventually eliminated.

However, although it takes many generations and years to develop a quantitative trait, it only takes one breeding or infusion of the wrong bird to wipe it out completely. Gameness is one of those traits. Bred to the wrong bird, it could very well eliminate the trait, and if not noticed, could in time eliminate the trait forever throughout the family or strain.

<u>Note</u>: I should mention though that hatchability is poorly heritable. For this reason, they are sensitive to environmental influences and resistant to change by selection. On the other hand, body size is highly heritable and easily improved by selection.

BREED FOR ONLY A FEW QUALITIES AT A TIME: It should be noted that the complexity of poultry genetics only allows gamefowl breeders to concentrate on a very few traits at the same time. Therefore, it is better to breed for only a few qualities that you think are most important, rather than to randomly breed a series of many good fowl with entirely different characteristics and traits, such as gamefowl that have entirely different performance styles. Breeding for too many "different" qualities greatly lessens the chances that any of them will be established in your family of fowl.

THE LONG WAY AND THE SHORT WAY

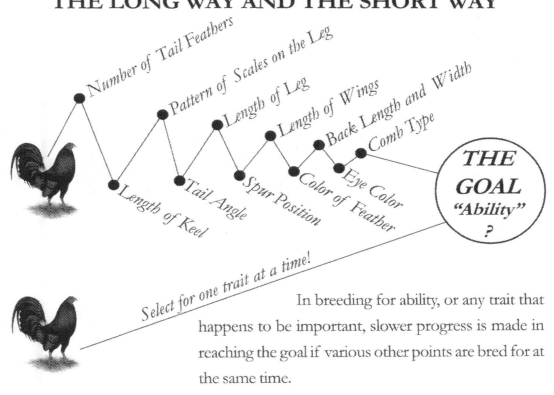

In breeding for ability, or any trait that happens to be important, slower progress is made in reaching the goal if various other points are bred for at the same time.

To achieve the best results, select for one trait at a time.

EXPERIMENT, BUT BE CLEAR OF YOUR OBJECTIVE: While breeding American Games is experimental in nature, it is not the circumstance of hitting or missing the mark that everyone thinks it is. The best breeders of American Games have very clear ideas about the kind of strain they wish to develop. They experiment patiently with different broodfowl and various breeding methods to accomplish their goals and they make many changes in their broodpens along the way. However, their actions are always guided by clear objectives in their breeding. This is how the great laying strains of commercial poultry and the cattle of the modern day dairy strains have been bred. Incidentally, it is also how the most successful American Game strains have been bred.

SELECTION IS THE KEY: Even though we don't know which genes they are (Quantitative Traits), much less how to control them individually, we can improve them by selecting broodfowl that come as close to our idea of the superior gamecock as possible, and create one or two strains through the powers of selection. Continually breeding the best offspring possible, generation to generation, in search for the perfect gamecock, we may never find him but maybe we can, in time, come close.

FINAL THOUGHT: If you doubt or question the information provided, GOOD! I have done my job. Please do some of your own research on the breeding of American Games and then question the reliability and validity of information placed here, in order that you might derive a better understanding of American Games and their true potential.

However, don't dismiss this book based on preconceived notions or because someone has told you something is not possible. Question the facts and the theory, but not the possibility.

Knowledge and acceptance is only gained by educating people and providing examples and descriptions of possible phenotypes and their consequences, not by trying to prevent the production of them.

Finally, don't believe everything you read or what someone says. Always question what you are reading and listening to and determine your opinion based on the evidence and your own research. Nobody has all of the answers. However, the "American Gamefowl Society" (AGS) is probably the most intune and long term overseer and manager of American Games information and knowledge that I am aware of. Write to them, ask them what they think.

Well, I hope this part of the book has helped you out, at least a little bit. Breeding can be a difficult and confusing venture, but with a little understanding and a lot of patience, progress can be made. A lot of people claim to be breeders, but don't even

Selection is significant in preserving characteristics.

know the first thing about it. They breed for one characteristic only to dismiss the others.

The ones that crack me up the most are the ones that say "the level of performance is the only factor they look for." This only shows how ignorant they actually are, and I feel sorry for them, for they will never have high quality fowl, and if they do, they will never be able to maintain that level for very long. Within a few years they will realize that what they have, and what they actually know, is really very little. And they will scratch their heads in wonder, to what actually happened. They then blame the person they got their birds from, never taking the blame themselves. They spend all their days looking for new blood and never committing to one family for very long, and spending a lot of money along the way.

This is the type of attitude that can only hurt the creditability and longevity of our sport. Be sure this doesn't happen to you.

It's the total package that you want to look for. Such as their gameness, ability, performance record, conformation of body, temperament, and yes, even the color of their feather plumage! This shows the consistency and the uniformity of their strain. They must be a well rounded bird produced from a reliable family. One thing is connected to the other, lose just one of these most important factors and your birds are ruined! Let's take responsibility and control of our own birds by becoming breeders again, and we just might save our hobby.

VARIATION
And the laws which govern Selective Breeding

"The power of Selection, whether exercised by man, or brought into play under nature through the struggle for existence and the consequent survival of the fittest, absolutely depends on the variability of organic beings. Without variability nothing can be effected; slight individual differences, however, suffice for the work, and are probably the chief or sole means in the production of new species."

Charles Darwin

INTRODUCTION

WHAT SELECTIVE BREEDING IS ALL ABOUT? Breeding, in the case of domestic fowl, refers to the reproduction and inherent improvement of breeds, varieties and strains. Breeding is the continued progress, through successive generations, toward a desired objective. It is the selection and perpetuation of specific characters and traits to achieve a high level of quality and performance. Although breeding American Games may never be a function of mathematical certainties, it is still thought of as a science. However, the final result must rest largely on the skill and imagination of the breeder himself. In other words, breeding is more of an art form than a science.

It not only involves the replacing of older individuals with younger ones, but the exchanging of the poor, or even the good, for the inherently better. Proper breeding eliminates the mere act of maintaining a family simply by increasing the number of fowl. For most breeders, progress is generally a hit or miss proposition. Trust me, it doesn't have to be that way!

THE IMPORTANCE OF THESE LAWS: Selective Breeding is the science of selection and inheritance, and is used to improve a family or strain, which calls into play all the skill that the modern cocker and backyard breeder is capable of applying. The transmission of qualities or characteristics from parent to offspring is controlled by specific laws. A good breeder understands these laws and uses these laws to his advantage, and it is for this reason that he knows the breeding tendencies of every bird on his farm.

The successful breeder, however, follows, consciously or unconsciously, certain laws or principles that have been established or proved

Variation is the foundation of progress. Here is a good example of how variation has achieved great success.

by science. Explanations of these laws are given in the following pages.

Here is a list of these laws:
- The Law of Variation
- The Law of Mutation or Sport
- The Law of Form and Function
- The Law of Like Begets Like
- The Law of Throwbacks
- The Law of Progression and Regression
- The Law of Correlation
- The Law of Contamination
- The Law of Ancestral Influences
- The Law of Prepotency
- The Law of Mother Nature

Within these laws you have the ability of advancing the breed. By using all these laws, you will have the ability to make great strides in the creation and maintaining of pure lines and families. Although on first sight they may seem overly simplistic. To those who question how and why these laws work; they work because they follow the law of nature. As with Natural Selection, Selective Breeding does not function without the cooperation of these laws.

As Napoleon Hill once put it, - *"A law of nature is determined when a certain stimulus produces the same result time after time, until it is accepted that it is its nature to produce that result every time, all the time."* *"Water always has two atoms of hydrogen, never one; apple seeds never grow into orange trees; and nobody ever falls off the earth for lack of gravity."* You will find that these laws are precise. It is the benefit of every breeder to study them and use them whenever improvement and refinement of the breed is the main objective.

A testament of these laws: For more than thirty-five years, I have studied the most successful breeders and analyzed the relationship between what they believed, when it came to breeding, and the success they achieved. The connection between these laws and their great success happened so consistently, it convinced me that the way they bred their fowl was no accident, but was in fact, in accordance with a predictable law of nature.

To understand the breeding tendencies of American Games, we must first understand the basic laws of breeding. These laws determine how characteristics and traits are transmitted from parents to offspring, and to what frequency. These laws help the breeder in making an educated guess, rather than one that is based on old wives tales, superstition, and hearsay, not to mention, misguided speculation.

> *"If we assume that each particular variation was from the beginning of all time preordained, then that plasticity of organisation, which leads to many injurious deviations of structure, as well as the redundant power of reproduction which inevitably leads to a struggle for existence, and, as a consequence, to the Natural Selection or survival of the fittest, must appear to us superfluous laws of nature. On the other hand, an omnipotent and omniscient Creator ordains everything and foresees everything. Thus we are brought face to face with a difficulty as insoluble as is that of free will and predestination."*
>
> *Charles Darwin*

114

THE NEED FOR KNOWLEDGE OF THESE LAWS: The practice of Selective Breeding necessitates an extensive range of knowledge, experience and skill. The information in this chapter (with my promise) will advance your awareness and understanding of what it takes to breed and raise high quality American Games.

The information in this chapter explains how traits are passed down from parent to offspring and explains how certain basic laws or rules, which govern inheritance of all animals, plants, and even humans, can be used to create and improve a family or strain.

Although it is not necessary for success in the breeding of American Games to have an exact and extensive knowledge of the subject of genetics, it is important to familiarize yourself with the laws that are in this chapter. A knowledge of the relatively simple basic laws of inheritance helps to give a better appreciation of the reasons for procedures connected with successful breeding.

THE LAW OF VARIATION
Probably the most important of all the laws of breeding

"Man does not attempt to cause variability; though he unintentionally effects this by exposing organisms to new conditions of life, and by crossing breeds already formed. But variability being granted, he works wonders."
Charles Darwin

"Improvement doesn't always come from good inheritance, sometimes it's from good management, and other times it's merely from a favorable accident." I have heard this so many times from one of my mentors that I have never forgotten it. What he didn't tell me was that, although inheritance and variation are equally important factors, they both are the effects of opposing forces. I will explain this in just a minute. First of all, let me help you understand how variation works and its importance in the process of Selective Breeding.

VARIATIONS OF THE STRAIN: While the individuals of the offspring, which come from a closely bred family or strain, and one that is the result of single mating, may be uniform and resemble the parents quite closely, they are almost never exactly or absolutely alike, even though in appearances they look and act the same. A group of offspring from the same parents will differ among themselves, and some, or all of them may differ from their parents. Most of the time, these are simply small deviations from the norm. These differences, or small deviations, are usually referred and called "Variations of the Strain."

In a broader sense, variation is the deviation in form or function of the offspring from that of their parents. Although these variations look very random, they are often due to the distribution of traits among the offspring according to a definite method of inheritance.

THE SIGNIFICANCE OF VARIATION: The fact that there is great variation among gamefowl strains is of particular significance when it comes to inheritance. Without variation, progress in breeding would be impossible. Without variation, the selection of superior individuals would be impossible. Without the proper selection, improvement is impossible. Simply put, variation makes selection possible and selection makes improvement possible.

Variation is the raw material on which the breeder works his magic. In almost any flock of birds there is always a sufficient amount of variation, so that the least desirable individuals can be separated from the most desirable ones. But the breeder must always keep in mind that, except for most of the color characteristics that exist with gamefowl and certain traits of the morphological characters, the actual differences between two individuals are caused partly by environmental influences as well as by heredity.

116

"Although every variation is either directly or indirectly caused by some change in the surrounding conditions, we must never forget that the nature of the organisation which is acted on, is by far the more important factor in the result."

Charles Darwin

MANY VARIATIONS ARE DUE TO ENVIRONMENTAL INFLUENCES: All variations are influenced to a greater or less degree by two groups of causes. These causes are internal and external. Accurate knowledge pertaining to this first group of influences is so limited, and the subject so complex, that it is of little value to the average cocker and backyard breeder. However, you cannot fail to notice the great variation in American Games, due to diverse conditions of their environment. By this, what I mean is, all the external conditions of their life, such as diet, climate, shelter, predation, and especially with young growing birds, the freedom to range and forage (exercise and nutrition).

All internal processes of development are dependent upon external influences for their natural expression; hence the breeder has every incentive to create external conditions which will contribute to the growth and highest development of the individual. These conditions will in themselves contribute to the development of the particular type or variation which is desired.

Hereditary influences and their environmental: It has been my observation that environmental influences not only exist but they exercise their effects on such characters as hatchability, rate of growth, and proper development. This makes the problem of selecting birds for breeding purposes more difficult because the breeder may mistake the effects of the environment for the effects of the genes, thus saving some birds for breeding that may actually prove to be poor broodfowl.

As you can see, differences such as heat, light, moisture, and food, as well as many other environmental factors, are serious contributors to their development. Therefore, variations are of many kinds and are due to many causes. In conclusion, individuals in its definitive form are the result of both hereditary and environmental influences.

TWO LAWS – THE LAW OF VARIATION AND THE LAW OF INHERITANCE: The principles of breeding, being based on one universal law; the law of inheritance, is the transmission of qualities from one generation to the next generation. A correct appreciation of this law is essential to a right understanding of Selective Breeding.

In its operation, the law of inheritance shows, always, two phases, which appear to result from conflicting laws. As a result, while fowls of the same pure breed produce offspring unmistakably like themselves, the offspring are never exactly like either parent, or like each other. It is for this reason that it is commonly believed that there are two laws:

1. The law of heredity – which controls uniformity of breed, variety, strain, and family likeness from one individual to the next.
2. The law of variation - which controls diversity from one individual to the next.

The truth of the matter is that "heredity" and "variation" are visible effects of opposing forces, the first working to preserve (breed, variety, and strain), as it has existed, the second to produce change. These forces, especially that which controls variation, work in some mysterious, unpredictable ways, which the breeder cannot fathom.

<u>There are not two laws, there is but one - the law of inheritance</u>: "Heredity" is the inheritance of like qualities, while "variation" is the inheritance of unlike qualities. It is strictly in agreement with the law of inheritance that the unlike characteristics, the individual differences, should pass from generation to generation with a changing kaleidoscopic of effects, as that of the like qualities which should also be transmitted practically unchanged.

> *"No doubt it is difficult to realise that slight changes added up during long centuries can produce such great results; but he who wishes to understand the origin of domestic breeds or of natural species must overcome this difficulty."*
>
> *Charles Darwin*

THE IMPORTANCE OF VARIATION: Variation gives the breeder the opportunity to change or improve his family or strain by selecting the characters best adapted to his needs, and then fixing them by a careful plan of breeding.

Variation is the differences in conformation of body, color of plumage, leg color, and temperament, and many other characteristics, which exist between each of the offspring and even their parents. This can range from a somewhat slight degree to those which are quite mutant. For example, in the case of color, let's say you have a Black-Breasted Dark-Red broodcock and hen, both parents are of fairly good color and they are free from unwanted under color. In this type of mating you may get offspring that range from Dark-Red to a poorly colored Light-Red, looking more like a Black-Breasted Light-Red than a good colored Dark-Red. The offspring may therefore not only differ noticeably from one another, but may also differ greatly from their parents. Some will be much poorer than the original broodfowl, while others will be much better than the original broodfowl.

I have used color to demonstrate this point, but this is also true for other traits and characteristics, such as leg color, conformation of body, size, and temperament. It may also include the elements of detail in the head, face, and beak, etc.

Don't be afraid to take advantage of these variations when the opportunity arises, for variations, in the right direction, can improve your fowl quicker than the normal selection process.

The rapidity and certainty with which characters are more or less fixed varies greatly. Extensive changes may take place at once, or only prove to be a flash in the pan. There is no certainty that every high quality American Gamecock that wins impressively, for example, will exert an influence on his offspring. Although the chances of securing these traits are far better if he is bred to a hen that carries the same attributes, or ones that are better, within her gene pool. There is no hard and fast rule that will tell in advance whether a cock or a hen will breed true or not. The only sure way is to test them in the broodpen.

I have written about the subject of variation before, and it is a subject that I like very much. It is one of the most important factors in the process of Selective Breeding. The theory is actually quite simple and it goes something like this: Variation makes Selection possible, and Selection makes Improvement possible. Nothing more and nothing less!

It is the selection of those individuals showing variation in the desired direction that will constitute most of your efforts in breeding. It is by the use of these individuals that the breeder expects to make much of his progress, and is what dictates his breeding program for the future.

118

*"The degree of distinctness between the various domestic breeds depends
on the amount of modification which they have undergone, and more especially
on the neglect and final extinction of intermediate and less-valued forms."*
Charles Darwin

VARIATION IS THE BASIS OF ALL IMPROVEMENT: Variation is of extreme importance to the modern cocker and backyard breeder. In fact, it is the basis of all improvement. If all the individuals in a flock of birds were exactly alike with reference to their reproductive cells, further selection would be useless as no improvement could be expected. It is for this reason that the true breeder looks for and welcomes variation in his fowl. For he knows without variation improvement cannot be made. It's a matter of "breeding-variation-selection-and-culling." He breeds the best to the best. He looks for variation in desired characteristics. He selects the most superior of individuals or specimens, then culls the inferior, deformed, or defective fowl. Without these four fundamental modes of selection and breeding, progress cannot be made. Leave out just one of these equations from the mix and the whole thing falls apart. In the long run, this is usually the most successful means in obtaining improvement in your strain.

It is easy to see, therefore, that to make the most of this matter of variation, the progressive breeder must be a keen observer, a deep thinker, and must exercise careful judgment at all times.

No part of the organisation escapes the tendency to vary...
Charles Darwin

CAUSES OF VARIATION: A better supply of food undoubtedly accounts for many of the differences seen between the Wild Jungle Fowl and the modern gamefowl, such as American Games. The Wild Jungle Fowl, through time, has differed very little. It breeds true century after century. But under domestication it rapidly evolves and develops new characteristics. The effects of domestication have increased the bird's size, weights, and level of gameness. It has also changed the bird's conformation of body and color. The Wild Jungle Fowl was known to lay a dozen or possibly two dozen eggs in a year, under domestication the same fowl now lays ten times as many.

All gamefowl breeds are created and established by means of variation. However, variation may be encouraged by other conditions or factors. For example: a change from one climate to another is a large cause for variation. A change of climate and soil encourages not only variation but increased vigor and fertility as well. These changes have been powerful factors in the improvement of gamefowl. Even the Wild Jungle Fowl under confinement produces twice the number of eggs that she would have produced in the wild state. Therefore, it's the change to friendlier, more favorable surroundings or environment that gives way to evolution.

This is also true for plants as well as animals. Changes in climate as well as food have undoubtedly had a great deal to do with the evolution of gamefowl. Transplanted to a cooler climate, we find the jungle type of three pounds has evolved into the five to six pound gamefowl. This is because the fleshier type fowl is better adapted to withstand the cold. On the contrary, the southern climates are not conducive to the heavier type of gamefowl, with heavy feathering. As a consequence they gradually evolved to a tighter feathered bird with higher station, and a more athletic looking conformation of body.

Again, better feeds that are plentiful along with domestication, has undoubtedly exercised a strong influence in determining the size, strength, and characteristics of the American Games that we have today. Plenty of food tends to increase the size, while inadequate nutrition results in small lines of fowl.

119

Variation and the benefits of crossing: Probably the most productive source of variation, and therefore evolution, is the crossing of different breeds or varieties. I am not a big proponent of crossing, since I prefer to create and maintain pure lines. However, if the truth be told, crossing is probably the most powerful means of variation there is. Crossing different breeds or varieties opens the door to variation, and in some cases, further improvement of some strains. It has also contributed to new breeds, varieties and strains. Crossing adds to size and vigor, produces variations and abnormalities, restores lost or hidden characteristics and increases fertility. American Games were undoubtedly evolved in part from crossing, even of the different strains of Jungle Fowl from which they originated.

Before methodical selection was practiced, little consideration was given to keeping pure breeds and varieties; therefore, crossing was a common

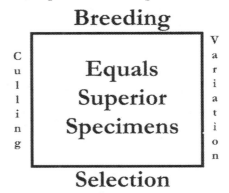

The Value of Variation

The true breeder looks for and welcomes variation in his fowl, for he knows that without variation, improvement is impossible.

Breeding

Culling — Equals Superior Specimens — Variation

Selection

Breeding, Variation, Selection, and Culling
- Breeding - use proven breeding methods
- Variation - look for variations in desired areas
- Selection - select superior specimens
- Culling - cull all inferior or defective fowl

Without these four primary fundamentals, progress cannot be made. Just leave out one part of the equation and the whole formula fails.

place. Although it was from the crossing of different breeds and varieties of gamefowl that American Games came into existence, however, today there is a greater interest in creating and maintaining pure lines, and I think that's great. A revolution such as this is very important to the preservation of American Games.

TYPES OF VARIATION: The unit of variability is not the individual, but the breed. The real measure of variation is the breed character. There are four distinct types of variation.

These types consist of:
1. Morphological Variation
2. Substantive Variation
3. Meristic Variation
4. Functional Variation

Morphological variation: Has to do with differences in conformation of body and size, which are quantitative in character. This type of variation is very common. A simple example of morphological variation being two stags, which are exactly alike except that one is larger than the other. In this instance, there is no difference in the characteristics of the two individuals, but merely the fact that in one, growth had been more rapid and proceeded farther than in the other.

Substantive variation: Also known as the substance or essence or the bird, substantive variation is shown by differences in the quality of different individuals as distinct from mere conformation of body and size. Such variations are qualitative rather than quantitative in nature. This type of variation refers to the constitution or nature of the individual, in other words, their overall health and wellbeing is manifested by differences between individuals of the same breed and between different breeds.

In regard to the character of flesh, some are hard, such as American Games and others soft, such as Plymouth Rocks.

In regards to health and constitutional vigor, birds of the same breed may differ in their power to withstand cold, or endure extreme heat. Also, individuals may differ as to their power to resist certain communicable diseases. The greatest service in the breeding of American Games is their close associated with form, function and beauty; this is all dependent on their level of constitution vigor.

Meristic variation: Meristics is a process which relates to the counting of quantitative features, or the progression of quantitative features occurring in sequence, and can be used to describe a particular species of bird, or used for differentiation of species and populations. Also it can be used to identify an unknown species.

For practical purposes a meristic (countable trait) represents alternations in the form or in the repetition of parts. It usually manifests itself by a departure from the normal systematic or specific plan of the birds. For example, the normal chicken has two legs; the addition of other legs would constitute a meristic variation in the type. Meristic variations are of little importance to most cockers and backyard breeders, as they usually appear as abnormalities, which have no value, so they are quickly culled. To the student of biology, however, meristic variations open up a vast field concerning the real nature of living matter. Practical uses of meristic variation for the cocker and backyard breeder may include the number of feathers in the wings and tail, and the number of spurs.

Functional variation: This relates to alteration in the normal activity of the various parts of the birds body, such as muscular activity and ability, and the like. It has to do, not with the form of the bird, but with their functions. The best examples of functional variation are the individual variations of a cocks pit performance, not to mention, the variation in prepotency and their power to fertilize a given number of eggs, and reproductive performance and ability of hens.

Functional activities are influenced, and variations are caused by many factors, among the more important of which are exercise, feed, improper environment, and care. All of these should be regulated by the careful cocker and backyard breeder, if his efforts in mating and breeding are to be followed by the fullest development and improvement.

THE ISOLATION OF GENES REDUCES THE "TOTAL POTENTIAL FOR VARIABILITY": This is an important concept to learn, for it will completely revolutionize the way you think about breeding and improving a strain. It will also make you rethink any ideas you may have about crossbreeding. This concept gives the practice of Selective Breeding a purpose.

Clearly, we recognize the fact that the random distribution of chromosomes and genes over the germ-cells, as a result of the reduction division, scatters genetic variability over the entire family of birds. While on the other hand, the isolation of genes of any kind reduces the "total potential for variability."

For example, if you were to buy a trio of American Games from a breeder, it is certain that this sample of the breeder's fowl would be less variable than his entire family of birds. It has occurred time and again that a breeder, who started with two or three birds, such as a breeding pair or trio, happened to find that the family of fowl he raised, from those few, was very excellent. If we were to import a new breed, and especially if we imported just a few good ones, our imported family of birds is certainly purer than it was in the country of its origin. In fact, the "potential for variability" of any species or breed must automatically reduce itself, unless the sample of germ-cells produced by the birds in one generation was entirely representative of what the preceding generation produced, and this is extremely unlikely. When the population of any plant or animal varies occasionally, the "total potential for variability" goes down. If we think of the way in which any breed or species continues from generation to generation, we shall see how the parents of the next generation are often a relatively small group.

It is for this reason we are able to create new breeds, varieties and strains. This also proves that if you can keep from adding or infusing new blood into your existing bloodlines, and you perform the practice of Selective Breeding by selecting superior individuals, while eliminating inferior ones, thru the practice of ruthless culling, uniformity is almost certainly assured.

VARIATION AND SELECTIVE BREEDING: Variation through selection is an effective tool for improving American Games. Although "variation" is responsible for producing the exceptional individual, "selection" is responsible for preserving it. Charles Darwin once said that there are two kinds of selection, one he calls "unconscious," the other "methodical."

In the case of "unconscious selection," this is the breeder, who, in the spirit of competition tries to outshine his opponent by breeding from his best birds. However, he does this without any attempt to establish a new breed or to preserve some new characteristic, or to improve an already established breed or variety.

On the other hand, methodical selection has to do with the evolution of the fowl. This is the fixing of new and desirable characteristics and the making of new breeds. The breeder who follows methodical selection is constantly on the lookout for new and valuable characteristics. He is not satisfied with following a standard of excellence. He sets up a new and higher standard. He believes in progress. He is looking for "sports" or "mutations" along certain lines and when they appear he makes them the basis of his breeding operations. The man who follows methodical selection would often achieve his highest purpose by breeding for characteristics of color or conformation of body.

Whether the improvement or evolution of the fowl is due more to one or the other method of selection, it would have been clearly impossible to evolve the fowl as we now have it, if, in the early centuries, an arbitrary standard had been set up, and all breeding made to follow along that line. For this reason methodical selection has probably done more for the improvement of American Games than unconscious selection. Even though unconscious selection has been at work longer than methodical selection, it is methodical selection that has improved them the most.

THE LAW OF MUTATION OR SPORT

Occasionally there may be individuals that show characteristics which differ quite noticeably from those possessed by their parents and distant ancestors. In short, they can appear radically different in conformation of body (type), color, or temperament from that of their own breed, variety or strain. These individuals or changes in genes are technically known as mutations or sports.

A mutation may be defined as a sudden variation, which is later passed on through inheritance, and that results from changes in a gene or genes. A Mutation occurs when a DNA gene is damaged or changed in such a way as to alter the genetic message carried by that gene. It could affect color of plumage or their conformation of body. Any trait or characteristic can be affected by change, and mutations are nothing more than a transformation of the norm.

HOW DIFFERENT BREEDS WITHIN A DOMESTIC SPECIES BECAME SEPARATED: Many people have some difficulty in understanding how the different breeds within a domestic species came to be separated. Some clarification of this point may be helpful

Since the domestication of the Wild Red Junglefowl of South East Asia, many mutations have occurred. These changes in the DNA have caused alterations in the phenotype, or appearance of the birds. Most mutations are recessive to the wild type. This means that a change in a single gene will not produce a visible effect until two birds are mated, both of which carry the same mutation. The effects of the mutation in homozygous form are then evident in a certain proportion of the progeny. If it is a simple mutation with full expression of the character, approximately one-quarter of the offspring of such a mating will show the new character resulting from the mutation. If the mutation be a dominant one with complete expression of its effects, the latter will be visible at once in the progeny of any bird carrying such a mutation.

One difference between a dominant and a recessive mutation is that the recessive will not manifest until two birds that carry it happen to mate, whereas the dominant mutation is recognizable in the next generation after its occurrence.

MUTATIONS ARE NOT THE RESULT OF SLOW CONTINUOUS SELECTION: Mutations are distinct from ordinary variations, and may be described as a sudden but accidental deviation from the normal type. It appears that mutations are unexpected and unanticipated new types, which do not come as the result of a process of slow continuous selection and fluctuation, or variation, and have no intermediate stage between the old type and the new. When it comes to mutations, there is a sudden change of form. It is impossible to predict their appearance and to the speediness with which they disappear. For some mutations, they are easy to perpetuate, while others, if inbred with the parents, they frequently cease to reproduce.

Although many new varieties of poultry have resulted from breeding mutations and sports, the better method for improving a family is the slow one of gradual selection, from time to time, of all variations which tend toward the ideal type. Whether or not mutations should be perpetuated will depend on the type of mutation.

THE ACQUISITION AND TRANSMISSION OF A MUTATION: A new character may appear unexpectedly in one generation and be transmitted through inheritance to succeeding generations. For instance, let's say you have a family of fowl, they are Black-Breasted Reds, for generation after generation they produced nothing but Black-Breasted Red offspring, but one day unexpectedly a white bird shows up. If you were to breed that white sport to another white bird, you would be able to create a new variety of the same strain. This is very easily done since sports breed very true.

Although mutations are rare, they are a permanent structural alteration in the DNA. In most cases, DNA changes either have no effect or cause harm; however, the good news is that occasionally a mutation can improve an organism's chance of surviving and passing the beneficial change on to its descendants. This is also true with sports. Like I mentioned earlier, sports usually breed very true, and therefore, if the sport happens to be of a desirable kind, and is what you're looking for, it may result in a much faster improvement than you could obtain by the more gradual process of selecting less obvious variations. A good example of this is the White Old English Games, which is said to have arisen or originated from white chicks produced from the breeding of Black-Breasted Reds.

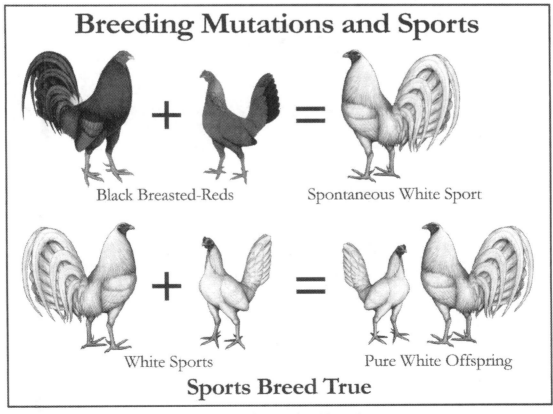

Breeding Mutations and Sports

Black Breasted-Reds

Spontaneous White Sport

White Sports

Pure White Offspring

Sports Breed True

Most sports and mutations breed very true.

Upon finding these individuals, breeders would mate these white sports until they came consistent, and eventually perfected them as a new variety of Old English Games.

The White American Games have many different breeds of gamefowl in their blood, but derived a majority of their blood from Old English Games. However, I'm sure there are some American Game Whites that have come about due to white sports arising from Black-Breasted Reds, and have contributed to the existence of the White American Game variety. In fact, I have received many phone calls from cockers who have experience this very thing, and I have always encouraged them to perpetuate it.

PUREBREDS AND THE EFFECTS OF MUTATIONS: It is true of purebred fowl, that once a very high quality is reached, good quality can be kept up without any real selection whatsoever, but only when the potential for variation in the strain is reduced to almost nothing. In most cases, we only need to stop introducing outside blood to keep the quality at the high level of purity that has been reached. Spontaneous mutations and natural changes of genotype would then be the only cause for the loss of quality, and mutation is definitely a rare phenomenon in strains which have been bred pure for a number of years. To guard against the results of mutation, any system in which one breeder continues the strain and keeps up a ridged selection practice, as well as inbreeding, will be ideal. There are many backyard breeders who now own very pure, very high-quality inbred strains of gamefowl. I suggest you search these breeders out when buying a strain.

THE LAW OF FORM AND FUNCTION

"It is therefore very desirable, before any man commences to breed, that he should make up his mind to the shape and qualities he wishes to obtain, and steadily pursue this object."

Charles Darwin

The most common expression of this phrase has always been that of "form versus function." However, when it comes to American Games, form must always follow function, without proper formation of the body they are nothing more than dysfunctional birds. To understand this we must look to its origins and the purpose for which they were bred.

With no designer, except that of the rough and tumble of evolution, the Wild Jungle Fowl of South East Asia would seem to have no purpose, other than serving as an evolutionary pathway for that of all the domestic fowl around the world. But that is not true for its closest domestic relative, the American Gamecock. In their case, it's the purpose of the bird which determines its design. Their form is largely determined by their overall function. Every part of the bird's body has a job, and every part equals the whole, which dictates its purpose.

FORM TO FUNCTION: This is an important concept to understand. The "Form" of the bird is best understood by standing back and looking at your bird from the side. Their profile is their form. A bird's form will determine how they use their body parts, such as their legs, wings and tail, not to mention the individual attributes of the head and neck. When assessing a bird's conformation of body, I like to view them by taking into consideration the phrase, "form-to-function." In other words, their conformation of body determines their functionality, and their functionality determines their overall form.

I want the body of my fowl to have the correct form, or structural appearance, so that the bird can perform the desired functions. To augment the function of the body, I then consider the birds form. I know this sounds a bit confusing, but just stay with me a moment. Over time, through Selective Breeding, I slowly change their form to draw out better functionality. By improving form, through changes of the bird's individual body parts, I thereby improve their body motions and actions, which improves their overall functionality. The result is a bird that is properly balanced.

The function of any bird is determined by his job or purpose. I shape the bird through the practice of Selective Breeding. When the bird is in the right form he will develop into a more efficient gamecock and he will function better in competition. However, when changing the birds form, I am very careful to stay in the boundaries of his desired conformation of body, so that no undesirable extremes in structure are introduced making them look odd or out of balance. Remember, they must always look, act and perform like an American Gamecock. If he lacks in any of these attributes he is incorrect for his breed. Like one of my mentors used to tell me, *"If he has the proper form and function he will be a picture in fluid motion."* I couldn't agree more.

"Differences apparently of very slight importance would certainly determine the survival of a form when forced to struggle for its own existence."
Charles Darwin

AMERICAN GAMES AND THEIR RELATIONSHIP TO OTHER BREEDS: Like every other breed, variety or strain, the American Game belongs to one of five major groups, each carrying with it a very special gene pool, one of form, function, and beauty. Combined, they determine their overall purpose. There is no doubt that their form indeed follows their function.

The five major groups I was just referring to include:
- The commercial egg breeds
- The commercial meat breeds
- General-purpose breeds
- Ornamental or exhibition breeds
- And of course, breeds bred for sport

As you can see, each of these groups have very little to do with the other. Their pathways from that of the Wild Jungle Fowl have traveled in very opposite directions. Along with a difference in their functions, they have very different forms as well. What they do have in common is they carry with them very special characteristics and traits that are important to their breed and variety, as well as their function and purposes.

FORM VERSUS FUNCTION: Although there are some breeds that emphasize form over function, or function over form, American Games cannot afford this luxury. For example: exhibition or show type strains tend to emphasize on traits that involve form, such as color, conformation of body, or special phenotypical characters and traits which are unique to the breed. While commercial poultry producers concentrate on hens which lay large number of eggs throughout the year, or meat producing strains, which produce enough meat to butcher and package in 5 to 6 weeks. In this case, the emphasis is on function rather than form.

However, when it comes to the general-purpose and gamefowl breeds, both "form" and "function" are combined. This is what makes these breeds so very special.

When you look at the form and function of American Games, and compare it to those of general-purpose breeds, such as, Plymouth Rocks, Rhode Island Reds, Wyandottes, and Orpingtons, which are the most popular, although there purpose does deviate, and in very opposite directions,

This is a comparison of the three most common production breeds (meat, general purpose and egg) with that of American Games. Here we can see how form and function helps to shape their purpose.

Comparing the most common types of poultry, we can see how function shapes purpose.

these breeders do share two very important characteristics:

- First, both try to maintain a low profile at all times; backyard breeders, because they practice the quiet production of home produced eggs and meat, and cockers, because the sport of cockfighting is illegal in most states.

    - Note: Both are high profile targets for organizations such as Animal Rights, which have a problem with anything that has to do with animal usage. Legal or illegal, they are against the butchering for meat just as much as they are of the sport of cockfighting. Their only purpose is to turn the general public against the raising of chickens in any way, shape, or form possible.

- Second, the backyard breeders and cockers share the task of maintaining important genetic pools that have the most amounts of maintainability and future potential. This is important, not only for American Games and General-Purpose breeds, but for the future of all chickens.

On the other hand, breeders of commercial poultry and exhibition breeds have bred for such an extreme in production and appearance that they may have done permanent damage to the maintainability of their genetic pools.

In a proper breeding program, the breeder selects traits that are important to the improvement of his fowl. While he emphasized these traits, he ignores the unimportant traits, and he culls the traits that are harmful or destructive to the improvement of his family. As certain traits are perpetuated and others are selectively bred out, it is the breeder's goal to eventually eliminate the undesirable traits, ones that are disadvantageous to his breeding program and create something that is very special. If achieved, his name will certainly live on.

Barred Plymouth Rocks.

To understand the degree of damage that can be caused by improper breeding practices let's look at six different characteristics American Games possess that commercial poultry and exhibitionist have deemed unimportant and disadvantageous to their fowl. Here are six characteristics that have been bred out of most commercial poultry and exhibition breeds:

Orpingtons.

1. <u>Constitutional Vigor and Fertility</u>: These are traits that represent not only a good resistance to disease and adaptability to their environment, but also the ability to reproduce strong, healthy offspring. The most vigorous and fertile among all chickens are, in fact, American

Wyandottes.

Rhode Island Reds.

Games. These are fowl which must be hardy to stand up under the rigors of derby's and shows, yet, surprisingly, constitutional vigor and fertility are too often not a breeding priority. While everyone agrees that good constitutional vigor and fertility are indeed important, these traits are not high on everyone's list when selecting broodfowl. Most American Games have inherited constitutional vigor and good fertility as a result of their durability and longevity. In a proper breeding program only the strongest individuals should live on to the second year. And only the best producers of high quality offspring should live on any further. It is the broodfowl with the best constitutional vigor and good fertility that should pass those traits onto their offspring. To maintain good constitutional vigor and fertility, it is important to maintain a sufficient population within the family that is used for breeding. To inbreed using only a small population of fowl, only to focus on one or two traits at a time, can lead to a loss of constitutional vigor and fertility.

2. Temperament: This is a trait that is of little priority to most breeders. In fact, they place the importance of other traits over that of temperament when selecting their broodfowl. As a result, their hens are prone to panic and are usually nothing more than nervous and flighty birds. Their cocks become aggressive towards people and are difficult to handle. American Games should be selected and bred for good temperament at all times. This will improve the breeders/cockers enjoyment, and guarantee the safety of his family, especially that of his children. While exhibiting American Games for shows, good temperament is essential, since birds that are composed show better than flighty or mean ones. Breeders of American Games should select broodfowl that are good-natured and gentle around people. Cocks that tend to attack people are referred to as manfighters.

3. Foraging ability: This is the ability to search for food. For American Games, foraging is an important function of exercise and nutrition. Foraging is also important as a means of reducing the cost of feed, which can be pretty high at times.

4. Broodiness: For American Games, the hen's purpose is to perpetuate her strain, and this is achieved by laying a clutch of eggs and hatching them. Her job also consists of caring for her chicks until they reach sufficient age to be weaned. One of the things that attracted me to American Games was the fascination of having hens that would hatch and care for their young.

5. <u>Conformation of body and size</u>: These are essential traits when it comes to American Games. Since breeders of commercial and ornamental/exhibition breeds tend to select against variation, little diversity in type exists within each strain. Developing a strain with good conformation of body involves inbreeding, line-breeding, and good selection, which if done improperly, may lead to loss of fertility, incorrect form and a loss of functionality. Size is also very important for American Games, for they must conform to the sometimes subjective standard of sizes and weights designated for this breed. Extremes in either direction, tend to destroy fertility, and in turn, their functionality. Among American Game strains, size is closely associated with agility and quickness, and 5 pounds is considered the ideal weight for this breed.

6. <u>Color of Plumage</u>: The greatest variety in feather color occurs among gamefowl breeds. In traditional gamefowl strains, plumage color retains its original survival purpose. Any color other than white offers camouflage for foragers and setters. Among cockers and gamefowl enthusiasts, plumage color also identifies established bloodlines and strains, which at one time were in Old English Game strains, but in reality have become different varieties of American Games.

> *"The English game-cock has not only been improved during many years by man's careful selection, but in addition, by a kind of Natural Selection, for the strongest, most active and courageous birds have stricken down their antagonists in the cockpit, generation after generation, and have subsequently served as the progenitors of their race."*
>
> *Charles Darwin*

<u>FORM, FUNCTION AND PURITY OF BLOOD - THE TOTAL PACKAGE IS WHAT COUNTS</u>: There may be differences in their feather coloring or even markings, which would make up separate varieties within its own breed. A good example of this would be that of the American Game - Black-Breasted Red, a breed of fowl with an extraordinary conformation of body, and is extremely athletic in nature. Nobody would deny that, but to compliment it's form as well as its function, he should have nice long wings that are carried low, amply covering the thighs; he should have a long sweeping full tail that's carried fairly upright; a flat, heart shaped back with the proper slope or angle; a short well curved beak that's hawk like; long strong neck; and legs of medium length with good angulations.

It's very important that you understand this in order to become proficient at breeding American Games, because breeding is more than just putting two birds together, it is knowing the outcome before those birds are put together. It takes a lot of thought and planning to produce a great family of gamefowl, especially ones that come from a consistent and uniform strain.

When breeding gamefowl for their fighting characteristics, most cockers breed and select gamefowl for their power, speed, cutting ability, brains, temperament and heart, in other words their "Gameness." These are all important things to consider that will better prepare the bird for the job at hand, but these same people seem to neglect the things that really complete the bird's total makeup, such as their conformation of body and color of plumage. It is the total package that counts.

THE LAW OF LIKE BEGETS LIKE

"If animals and plants had never been domesticated, and wild ones alone had been observed, we should probably never have heard the saying, that "like begets like." The proposition would have been as self-evident as that all the buds on the same tree are alike, though neither proposition is strictly true. For, as has often been remarked, probably no two individuals are identically the same."

Charles Darwin

This is a common phrase used by many breeders. It simply means that there is a strong similarity between the parents and their offspring, and in some cases, of that of their distant ancestors.

When creating a family, through the practice of Selective Breeding, don't be surprised when two fowls of the same breed or variety, which are from the same family of fowl, and have had no foreign blood introduced for a considerable amount of time, when mated, their offspring all, or nearly all, resemble the parents quite closely. In most cases, the likeness of the offspring to that of the parents is so strong that it is easy to see who their parents are among a large family of birds. If bred close enough, through the practice of Selective Breeding, they will begin to look like the others of the strain from which they originated. This is especially true when certain breed or variety characteristics are concerned, with respects to some of the individual peculiarities of one or both of the parents. Because of this, the offspring are likely to inherit, in some degree, the same attributes of the parents. This includes the conformation of body, color of plumage or plumage type, and other similar, but uniquely, distinctive characteristics and traits.

DOES LIKE ALWAYS BEGET LIKE? One of the greatest problems for the successful breeder of American Games is the inability to select broodcocks of the required type. This brings up a good question, does "like always beget like," as the old saying goes? In general, the logic behind this is true, but there are some that say that it is not always so. The fact that there is a difference of opinion; it has become a subject worthy of study.

There are many breeders who believe that there are limitations to this theory. That it is foolish to believe that it is an absolute. I can see where they are coming from. Let's take this apart and look at it with an open mind.

We often see children who resemble and act like one parent, let us say the father, while others resemble and act like the mother. And yet some children will be like neither of the parents, nor like any of their immediate family. I have experienced this first hand. I have three daughters, all three are distinctly different, not only in looks, but in their personalities too. My oldest daughter, Megan, looks and acts just like me. She takes after the Troiano side. My youngest daughter, Tawny, looks and acts just like my wife, Nancy. And my middle daughter, Sammy, looks and acts nothing like me or Nancy. But, they all three look very much alike, as sisters should. Breeders of dogs and horses, as well as cattle, and other types of livestock are fully aware of the variations in offspring in this respect, and it is probably because of their persistent quest for knowledge along these lines that they have made so much more progress in scientific breeding than the average backyard breeder.

Among those who have never given mating nothing more than a casual thought, and there are many out there that are like that, there is the belief that winning cocks are bound to produce chicks which will develop into winners. In their minds, to produce a winning strain all that is necessary is to test the progeny, and breed only from such cocks that have achieved a certain performance record. This is a step in the right direction, the idea is a splendid one, and makes for careful selection. But, unfortunately, it does not go far enough. In the first place, we cannot test the hens, which have the greatest influence on our stags. Moreover, pedigree, while useful and essential, is not alone a sufficient basis for the selection of that element, which is to dominate future generations, and probably the success or failure of the cocker or backyard breeder.

<u>THERE ARE SOME EXCEPTIONS TO THE RULE</u>: When it comes to American Games, we would like to believe that the hereditary transmission of physical characters and traits to their offspring are true and absolute. In most cases it is, if you understand the laws of inheritance, such as the function of chromosomes and genes, dominant and recessive characteristics, chromosome segregation, hybridization, sex-linked inheritance, sex-determination, and phenotype vs. genotype, the results are very predictable. But when you do not understand the laws of inheritance, it's like playing pool with your eyes closed and having your hands tied behind your back.

To illustrate this further, consider the man who purchases a strain from a master breeder of American Games, who truly has high quality fowl. He gets pure blood that is true to type and starts to carefully breed them. Fully expecting every chick to be like the parents in color, conformation of body, and size, as well as, functional qualities, it takes but one season to show him his error. In this case he simply lacks the knowledge of the family. He is not acquainted with their special individual characteristics, and knowing which broodcocks to breed with which broodhens and why. It takes a certain familiarity of the family and knowledge of the laws of inheritance to be as successful as the original breeder.

It is true that the longer you inbreed, line-breed and maintain a closed yard, the more uniform they will become and the more they will resemble their parents. Will they all have the same color, conformation of body and temperament? In a strain of fowl, which have been inbred true to color and type, will every chick come completely uniform? Certainly not! There will always be an exception from time to time. This is called variation. It doesn't matter what characteristic or trait you are attempting to perpetuate and propagate, an exception from time to time will occur. If it is station, and the tallest fowl are used as broodfowl, some short stationed fowl will appear from time to time. No matter how long may be the pedigree of the hen from the highest station of blood, there will be some exceptions in the offspring.

<u>WHICH PARENT HAS THE STRONGEST INFLUENCE</u>? It must be understood, however, that it is impossible to select parents that are identical in their characteristics, and as each parent has an influence upon their offspring, it can be easily understood why the offspring may not be identical with one or either of the parents. It must also be remembered that the grand-parents and great-

132

grandparents, as well as, their ancestors of long ago, all exert some influence which tends to bring about variation. However, this is nothing to be feared but only something to watch out for. If used the proper way, variation can be a very positive force, for variation is the main equation for the improvement of the strain.

THE INFLUENCE OF HEREDITY AND LIKENESS: A Shamo Gamefowl may be hatched from eggs of the same size as American Games. The chicks may be the same size when hatched, but from that time on the influence of heredity will be shown in the larger growth of the chick that has an ancestry showing large size. For instance, when a purebred American Game is mated to a purebred American Game it is almost a certainty that the offspring will be fowls of smaller size than the Shamo.

Here is another example: when the male offspring begins to crow, it does so because of this same law; its male ancestors for thousands of years have crowed. Sometimes the breeder, and often the nearby neighbor in the early hours of the morning would prefer that this law was more flexible and that it were possible to breed chickens without a crow, but the breeder knows by experience that there are certain characteristics that have become fixed and that if he attempted to change them he would get nothing for his effort.

So is egg-laying a fixed characteristic? It is a law of nature or heredity that the hen lays eggs. The practical breeder is guided by this law of "like begets like" first and foremost. But while the law of heredity is persistent and inflexible, while like begets like, there is the strange contradiction in

The Influence of Heredity

American Game   Shamo

Baby chicks may be the same size and shape when hatched, but from that time on the influence of heredity will be shown in their size and shape at maturity.

This is a comparison of American Games and Shamo's.

nature that no two individuals are alike. The male chickens all crow; they are alike in that respect, but there are differences in the crow which are easily discernible. So the females are alike in regard to laying eggs; they all lay eggs, but there are differences in the size and shape of the eggs and how often they lay them.

Once a particular characteristic is "fixed" within your strain, meaning most of the birds in the family, if not all, possess this characteristic, a high proportion of the offspring will also possess this desired characteristic. As a result, this characteristic will become the trademark of the strain. The repetition of noticeable characteristics is what has led to the principle of "Like begets like." As a family, they will start to look quite different from other unrelated fowl that are from the same breed and variety, and begin to take on a look of their own.

IS IT POSSIBLE TO PRODUCE "PERFECTION" IN A FAMILY OF FOWL? Unfortunately, undesirable characteristics are also inherited in exactly the same way, so that the mating together of birds with the same fault will perpetuate the undesirable. Within closed strains there will obviously be a greater degree of uniformity than that of unrelated fowl, so that the amount of "likeness" to related fowl is greater.

The skillful breeder should have a strain where all the "fixed" characteristics are desirable, and the variation occurring within the strain allows the future blending of all desirable qualities on to a single bird. In other words, it is ultimately possible to produce perfection, however, two birds, both of which possess the same desirable characteristic, may produce offspring of which a proportion does not possess the same characteristic. Why? The answer is simple. The undesired alternative to the desired characteristic has been "carried" undetected within the strain until two such carriers have been mated together.

One of the most common of such occurrences is the production of straight (*single*) combed offspring from pea-combed parents. This most often occurs on the mating of an offspring back to its parent, both of whom must be carriers to produce the undesired result. The utilization of such sports in future breeding plans is very risky in that even as the undesired alternative may disappear in the next generation one is increasing the likelihood of such sports in the future. In the sense that a strain can have carriers of a certain fault for many generations before such a fault appears, then if possible, all such sports should be eliminated as and when they occur.

THE LAW OF THROWBACKS
Reversion, atavism or simple degeneration?

"Domestic races have often been intentionally modified by one or two crosses, made with some allied race, and occasionally even by repeated crosses with very distinct races; but in almost all such cases, long-continued and careful selection has been absolutely necessary, owing to the excessive variability of the crossed offspring, due to the principle of reversion."

Charles Darwin

When the offspring of American Games resemble some remote, rather than immediate ancestor in a noticeable degree to that distant ancestor, we refer to it as a "Throwback." However, the correct terminology is "Reversion or Atavism." In other words, a throwback is a characteristic or trait that appears in the offspring that does not exist or appear in their parents or known ancestry, but in actuality, did exist in some of the ancestors many generations before. This is a common occurrence, and is generally well accepted and understood by the most experienced breeders. These are breeders that know the benefits of a throwback or reversion, as well as, the pitfalls.

Some look at throwbacks or reversions as a form of degeneration. In some cases, they are right. The appearance of offspring resembling remote ancestors has long been regarded by some cockers and breeders to indicate and imply a so-called impurity of breeding. In some cases this is true. However, there are times when a throwback is just what the breeder needs to improve his fowl. This is referred to as "The Advantages of Variation," which we will discuss shortly.

As a matter of fact, throwbacks and reversions have a simple Mendelian explanation. In the chapter "Color and Uniformity," which I wrote in my first book, it has been observed that when a white variety, such as the American or Old English Game White, is crossed with the American or Old English Game Black-Breasted Red, the F_1 birds are colored, and resemble that of the wild type, Gallus Bankiva. Instead of there being impurity in either the Whites or Black-Breasted Reds, to account for the results, it is pointed out that the Whites lack a gene for the production of color, which the Black-Breasted Reds provides, and the Black-Breasted Reds lack the gene for the production of white, which the Whites provide. In cases such as these, the term reversion would seem to have no standing in present-day discussions on inheritance. However, Whites do appear from time to time in an apparently dominant Red family.

Muffs   **Tassels**

Throwbacks can appear in many ways.

A good example of a more common throwback or reversion is the appearance of tassels or muffs on gamefowl that normally don't show this trait. This happens in spite of the fact that clean headed birds were used for many generations as breeders, and a tassel or muff still appeared. The appearance of these feathers undoubtedly is a throwback to birds that were heavily feathered on the head or under the beak, but used at some distant time in making the original breed.

Reversion is likely to appear in crossbred forms or infusions. The more recent the cross or infusion of such birds used in a breeding program, the more frequent and troublesome these throwbacks could be.

Such reversions are due to a recombination of certain genes. The most common are throwbacks to the grand-parents. However, there are times when the reversion can go back so far that the unexpected characteristic, which comes from some distant ancestor, is a complete and total surprise. This may have come from a bird so many generations back that the breeder has no knowledge that such characteristics ever existed. Hence, the result of this reappearance of such characteristic only leaves the breeder scratching his head in wonder. It is for this reason that heredity is not a matter, which involves only the individuals mated, it involves all the ancestors of the individuals as well! Each individual displays only a part of the characteristics he inherits. Therefore, he is capable of transmitting characteristics which he apparently does not possess.

To understand "Throwbacks" and "Reversions," study the effects of variation. It is the effects of variation which causes the "throwback" to appear. Variation is an important part of breeding. If the variant is a desirable characteristic, it behooves the breeder to take advantage of the characteristic. If the variant is undesirable, it would be unwise to use these individuals for breeding, particularly if the undesirable "throwback" is frequent in appearance. This undesirable characteristic would cause the family to degenerate.

Read the book: *"The Variation of Animals and Plants Under Domestication,"* By Charles Darwin. In Darwin's own experiments, crosses of various breeds of chickens occasionally produced fowls resembling Gallus Bankiva. He considered this a reversion to the ancestral type, the most prevalent of throwbacks of them all, the Wild Jungle Fowl.

A while back I received an email with a question concerning "Throwbacks and Gameness."

<u>Question from Christopher</u>: If at some point in breeding American Gamefowl we get the throwback qualities of the Wild Jungle Fowl, could it be one of the reasons why we get runners, even when we are assured of a long generation of gameness in the line (maybe in inbreeding also)? Jungle Fowl = non-game = runners?

<u>Answer from Kenny</u>: We see throwbacks coming from the Wild Jungle Fowl all the time. Some are quite subtle, while some are huge. As far as "gameness," this is something we have to cultivate and develop constantly. Wild Jungle Fowl (as a rule) are not game. However, even Jungle Fowl show variation within the species

Wild Junglefowl.

towards this trait. It was only by breeding birds (perhaps Jungle Fowl) that showed this trait to a high degree that we've been able to perpetuate the trait in the first place. This is why gamefowl need to be tested on a regular basis. Whether or not this trait came from Wild Jungle fowl, I'm not sure. But what I do know is this, start breeding to non-game birds and before you know it, nothing will be game! A good breeder knows you must always test your progeny to maintain and improve your fowl.

A COMMON MISPERCEPTION CONCERNING THROWBACKS: There is a belief out there that cocks or hens, which express unusual physical qualities (because of the inheritance of certain characteristics and genetic traits from distant relatives) make the best foundation fowl. The main reason throwbacks are a fairly common occurrence these days is due to the widespread practice of crossbreeding, and not from sound breeding fundamentals. Almost all American Games we have today were created by highly crossed flocks of fowl.

In a properly bred family of American Games, throwbacks only occur occasionally, and they don't perform any differently from their brothers. Yet, against my advice, a number of my customers insist on buying them for breeding, in the belief that all throwbacks carry valuable genes, which will make them exceptional foundation fowl. If only breeding were that simple!

Remember, variation makes selection possible and selection makes improvement possible! It's the variants that you choose that will determine your success.

THE LAW OF PROGRESSION AND REGRESSION
Is it the royal road to perfection?
Or the unfortunate pathway to mediocrity?

Progression and Regression, two laws of opposing forces, which are simple to appreciate but hard to understand, one advances the strain towards perfection while one moves the strain towards a path of mediocrity. Either way, it is all about selection.

PROGRESSION: This is a term which simply means that the quality of the offspring, or the production of an occasional individual, exceeds the average of the stock from which the parents were selected. They are usually outstanding in quality of appearance (form) or performance (function) or both (form and function) as compared to the family in general. It is only by continually selecting breeders of a type better than the average of the family that progress can be made.

Progression applies to the individual rather than to the accumulation or mass of the offspring. An illustration of this principle is as follows: A cock and hen of good quality are mated, and as the result, one of the offspring develops into a specimen that far surpasses not only the parents in every aspect but is beyond that which is even occasionally produced or found in the family. This individual is an example of progression.

REGRESSION: By Regression, what I really mean is an eventual movement towards mediocrity of the strain. In this case, regression is the opposite of progression. It is when the general tendency of the offspring of a particular mating, on the average, is lower than the norm for that family. They are actually worse than their parents. If the parents are highly selected individuals of form, function and beauty, as they should be, who are well above the average, and their offspring have regressed, they will be poorer in quality than that of the parents, and may even be lower than the average for that family.

Here is a proven Troiano Red cock, owned and bred by Kenny Troiano. A fine product of good selection from a solid and well maintained family of Gamefowl.

An example of this principle can be observed by the following contrasting matings. Let's say you have a cock and hen, which have good conformation of body and a good medium-high station of leg. In this case, they are very good representatives of the family. You mate them, and the majority of the offspring from this mating are very apt to be like the parents. Now, conversely, here is where this principle is in full evidence, when the parents are shorter in station than the average for the family, in which case a greater percentage of the offspring are apt to average shorter in station than the parents, and that of the family as a whole, that is regression.

Regression is ordinarily not limited to one or a few individuals but appears in the mass or greater percentage of the offspring.

In breeding American Games, the goal is to always select individuals for the broodpen that are well above the average. It is that tendency toward a lower average in the offspring, which should be of particular concern to the breeder. He must continuously fight this tendency of the offspring to regress toward the average, producing offspring that are nothing more than mediocre fowl. To conclude, the breeder must continually select broodfowl that are of the highest quality. The best method for progression and preventing regression is to always select offspring that are better than their parents. If the offspring are not better than the parents, you are going in the wrong direction. I would rather not breed that season if the offspring are not better than their parents.

ALWAYS SELECT WITH THE GREATEST CARE AND NEVER STOP SELECTING:
It is this law of "Progression and Regression," which makes it necessary for the breeder to continue to select, with the greatest of care, even after he has attained a high degree of excellence in his family of fowl. For the minute he stops thinking that he has reached his highest level of perfection in maintaining high quality American Games, he will soon find out that he has quickly lost ground.

When no selection of any kind is practiced, the tendency is to regress toward the average. Selection, therefore, is absolutely necessary to maintain a certain standard of excellence, even if no further progress is desired.

SELECTION IS THE KEY:
In order to achieve progress, it is necessary for the modern cocker to be able to identify superior broodcocks and broodhens, and to mate them in such a way that they will produce the largest possible number of progeny possessing the desirable characteristics. The ability to identify cocks and hens of superior breeding worth is the first requisite of a successful breeding program.

In many gamefowl farms throughout the country, far too many birds of inferior breeding worth are used each year because many cockers apparently have never adopted a logical basis on which to select their broodfowl. The results secured from many matings are largely matters of chance, because in too many cases, the matings are made by guesswork, due to an insecure amount of evidence upon which to base the intelligent selection of the proper kind of cocks and hens to mate together.

BREED TOWARDS PROGRESSION NOT REGRESSION AT ALL TIMES:
Remember - perfection is the goal, not mediocrity. Unless you are very selective in the type of fowl you are using for broodfowl, your offspring will only be mediocre. Unless you are willing to cull ruthlessly, and I mean all fowl that are less than perfect, your fowl will regress, maybe even to its original wild state. All living things, wild or domestic, will regress if left to breed freely and naturally. In fact, it is my belief that if all chickens were released and allowed to breed freely among themselves, they would revert directly to their origins. They would look identical to the Wild Junglefowl of South East Asia. Of course, climate and environment of that particular area would have some effect on the birds.

<u>SELECTIVE BREEDING IS THE ANSWER</u>: It is through "Selective Breeding" that we have so many different breeds, varieties and strains of chickens, not to mention, all the different types of animals that exist. And it is through Selective Breeding that we are able to keep them this way. Just look at all the breeds of dogs that exist today. I am sure they evolved from the wild state, such as the wolf, coyote, and fox. In the course of many years, through the practice of Selective Breeding, their structure and appearance has evolved into the kind of dog that the breeder desires. Well, the same thing has happened to the chicken, and especially that of American Games. They have been bred to suit a certain purpose.

Some chickens are bred to lay lots of eggs; some are bred for meat production; some for ornamental and exhibition reasons. Although American Games were originally bred for cockfighting, they have found another purpose in the modern world, which is that of the exhibitionist. They are the show bird of all show birds! I feel this is a good thing, for it will only help to improve the breed, as well as preserve its existence for future generations.

<u>PROGRESSION AND SINGLE-MATING</u>: When breeding chickens, single-mating is the only way to improve any family or strain. All "Yard-Breeding" amounts to is an indiscriminate, haphazard breeding practice. Without a systematic approach to breeding, and having a definite ideal to selecting broodfowl, all you are doing is breeding towards mediocrity.

Each and every mating must consist of the most perfect and outstanding individuals that you can find and they must be bred to specific individuals to achieve a specific purpose or result. It is the only way to move forward. I do not believe that you can mass produce toward perfection.

<u>BREEDING TOWARDS "PROGRESSION" AND NOT "REGRESSION"</u>: This is the key to improvement. To be successful in breeding high-quality American games, you must constantly select and breed toward improvement; otherwise you are just raising chickens. Why do you think some thoroughbred race horses are in such great demand for stud service? It's because they are the

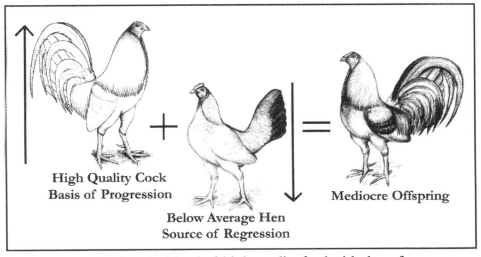

High Quality Cock
Basis of Progression

Below Average Hen
Source of Regression

Mediocre Offspring

When combining the blood of high-quality fowl with that of average or below average fowl, you will upgrade the average and downgrade the high-quality fowl.

finest individuals of their breed. They are the cream of the crop, the highest of quality, and they are superior to all they compete with. As a result, they are highly sought after to improve the breed. These are breeders who know the value of an outstanding individual, for they know that it is the superior specimens within the family that are able to best improve the breed. If these breeders did not do this, their horses would all regress back to mediocrity, and eventually they would revert to animals like those found in the wild.

THE DANGERS OF INTRODUCING OUTSIDE BLOOD: When you introduce one inferior individual into your breeding program, you have lost serious ground. As a result, you have moved toward mediocrity and away from perfection. You have regressed rather than progressed. Always make sure that the bird you infuse is much better than your own, in every way, or you will bring your fowl down to the level of whatever weakness that bird (which you are infusing) may have.

Here is a good example of what I was just talking about: - When you combine the blood of high-quality fowl with that of average or below average fowl, you will upgrade the average fowl a little bit, but you will also downgrade the high-quality fowl a lot. It's like water, eventually it will find its own level. You will never be able to pull the average, or below average fowl completely up to the level of the high-quality fowl, but you can pull the high-quality fowl down to the level of the average, or below average fowl. In this case, you are actually "breeding in reverse." You are tearing down what it has taken generations and generations of Selective Breeding to produce. You are breeding toward mediocrity.

Practice Selective Breeding and strict ruthless culling at all times. Do your part in preserving and advancing the breed by breeding toward more perfect American Games, do this through Progression and not Regression. Do not breed to mediocrity. Breed fowl that you can be proud of, and remember, Mother Nature loves mediocrity but breeders hate it!

THE LAW OF CORRELATION

"When parts stand in close relationship to each other, changes in the one are usually accompanied by modifications in the other, though not necessarily to the same degree."

Charles Darwin

There is no doubt that marvelous things can be done with chickens. Selective Breeding is a wonderful mechanism for creating and improving a strain, but there are factors which can seriously limit the breeder's efforts and effectiveness.

It is often said that - *"If we could just start with the individuals that we desire, being of the proper breed, variety and strain, and having the proper conformation of body, color, temperament, and ability, and have great prepotency, no matter the individuals they are mated with, within a few generations, it would be easy to fix or to eliminate any single characteristic or trait, and create the family or strain of our dreams."* But the reality is, no matter the quality of the individual or the individual that it is being bred to, when breeding to fix, maintain, or produce a particular type, it is necessary to consider many characteristics and traits at the same time. For instance, breeders of American Games are continually dealing with their family's constant and persistent tendency to go back to original type. They are bombarded with variations of characteristics, which strive to drive their families towards preceding ancestors at all times and in some cases right back to the Wild Junglefowl. At the same time, they are dealing with other factors, where some traits are directly affected by other traits. What we are talking about here is a factor known as "The Law of Correlation," or otherwise known as "The Correlation of Parts."

HOW IT WORKS: It is said that when a particular characteristic is closely linked or connected with another characteristic, there is a correlation between these characteristics. This occurs when selecting for a specific trait which has a tendency to generate changes in another trait. In other words, Correlation is the close association of certain characters with other characters. It is also the relationship which exists between the form and functions of various parts of the bird's body.

For instance, there is a close correlation between red earlobes and brown or tinted-shelled eggs, and white earlobes and white-shelled eggs, in that one of these characteristics is rarely found without the other.

CORRELATION OF CHARACTERISTICS: If each characteristic, in its various expressions, were absolutely independent of every other characteristic, the making and maintaining of new varieties within a breed would be a hopeless task. If there were no similarity from one variety to the next within a breed, how could they ever be standardized? Let me explain more fully.

The characteristics of an individual, being parts of another individual, are often unavoidably similar in certain forms, either throughout their total makeup or in closely related groups, or parts of the body. Without this fact the creation of new varieties, or even strains, within a breed would be impossible. Therefore, a correlation of characteristics is very important.

The welfare of the individual greatly depends on the adaptation of its parts to each other (its form), and to its conditions and mode of life (its function). Therefore, a family or strain is established, by being bred on a principle of selection of certain apparent correlations

Old English and Modern Game

A comparison of Old English Games (Carlisle type) with Modern Games.

of parts, which occur so regularly that, when considered only where they occur, they appear to indicate an essential unity, making the group of characters act as one. Thus, the body, legs neck, and head of a bird have, as a rule, a similarity of proportions.

Old English Game (Oxford type)

For example - a bird with a long body is likely to have a long neck, head, legs and wings. A bird with a short body tends to have short wings and a tail that is up, over the back. This is called "Squirrel Tailed." A bird with very short, strong bill and broad skull is likely to be short and heavily built throughout. To fully understand the impact of these correlations and their functions, just look at birds such as the Modern Old English Games, a bird bred exclusively for exhibition by breeders who did not understand the nature and makeup of the true Old English Games. Here we see an increased length in the neck and legs, which are quite out of proportion to the increased length of the body. As you can see, there is a natural, but general tendency to correlation in the structural character of bones and muscles.

CORRELATION BETWEEN CHICKENS AND AMERICAN GAMES: There is, without a doubt, a general correlation of characteristics between all poultry. However, American Games are very unique in all their characteristics and traits. They are very different from other fowl in their form and function. Just look at their conformation of body and color of plumage. No other domestic fowl has their stature or color, or their ability to defend their territory to the death. This is further evidence that Correlation does indeed exist, between all forms of animal life, and makes possible their systematic classification.

"Of all the laws governing variability, that of correlation is one of the most important."

Charles Darwin

CORRELATION AND SELECTION:
American Games are exceptional for studying features that are correlated, because they have many variable and easily defined parts. Some of the following are especially interesting correlatives.

The form and size of the individual is often proportional to the form and size of its parts. For example, a bird with a long neck is very apt to be "rangy" throughout. Long necks are closely associated with having a long body, long legs, long wings, and a snake like head. The reverse is also true, where a bird with a short, compact body and neck usually has short, stout legs, short wings, and a short, overly compact back, and their head is too short and compact as well.

Leghorns.

Correlation is a big issue when it comes to the breeding and selection of high-quality American Games, for there are many characteristics that usually go together. Therefore, the breeder must be very aware of these characteristics when selecting the ideal bird.

American Games.

EXAMPLE OF CORRELATION OF PARTS: Correlation can be very valuable when fixing things such as their conformation of body. On the other hand, it may prove troublesome. It is usually true that cocks, which are high stationed, are inclined to be too leggy and are also inclined to be flat or lacking in breast muscles. A high station bird and weak breast muscles are usually correlated, and it's extremely rare for individuals that are medium stationed to have weak breast muscles.

In breeds such as American Games, there is a definite relationship between the size and weight of the body and the development of wings. In the smaller but lighter strains, the results are great powers of flight, something that is lacking in the larger, heavier strains.

CORRELATION AND HEALTH: There is also a relationship between the color of the comb and wattles, and the health and vigor of the bird, the latter being associated with a bright red comb, and disease or lack of vigor with a dull color or lack of color.

THE LAW OF CONTAMINATION

"In improving a breed, if care be taken for a length of time to exclude all inferior individuals, the breed will obviously tend to become truer, as it will not have been crossed during many generations by an inferior animal."
Charles Darwin

THE IMPORTANCE OF THIS LAW - CONTAMINATION: The law of contamination has never been so widely considered, and its effects measured, as it is among breeders of gamefowl, particularly American Games. Reason being? Gameness! It is the one characteristic that can make or break an individual. Without gameness, Gamefowl would not fight; they would go at it for a short while but would soon quit and run. This is also the one characteristic that can be lost forever from one infusion with the wrong bird. Other traits can be affected from contamination besides gameness, but gameness is the most important characteristic to protect and preserve.

For the average poultry breeder, contamination is not that big a concern. They feel that since the chick does not develop to a substantial degree within the mother's body, and that a major part of the chick's development is done outside the hen (in the egg) that there is no such thing as a pure chicken. They also feel that it is impossible to pedigree chickens for this same reason. However, the preservation of gameness for over a thousand years has proven just the opposite. Cockers know just how easy it is to lose a trait such as gameness. With the slightest drop of the wrong blood (such as a Leghorn) in a family of American Games, and with no selection of any kind, especially through progeny testing and ruthless culling of the inferior progeny, gameness can be forever lost. All it takes is one time (contamination of the wrong bird) and gameness can vanish forever!

THE MISCONCEPTION OF CONTAMINATION: Many people believe that contamination is the breeding of a cock with a hen, where the cock has a lasting effect on that hen; as a result, any offspring produced as the result of such breeding, will bear a resemblance to the first or previous cock, even though she will be bred with different cocks later down the road. They also believe that once bred to a cock of another breed or variety she cannot be depended on to breed true ever again. This is not completely true. It is true that you should wait a while after the hen has been placed with a new cock before hatching her eggs. But usually, after a ten day period, her eggs should be okay for hatching. It is only in rare instances that eggs laid ten days after contamination, chicks hatched, will show in any way the influence of the foreign cock. There has never been a reported case of the influence of a cock of another breed persisting for months or years. So if you want to be really sure, it is best to wait 30 days.

THE TRUE MEANING OF CONTAMINATION: When we talk about "Contamination," what we are really talking about is the breeding, of let's say an American Game with that of a Leghorn. In this case, the influence of one breed would cause destructive results to the other.

As long as the hen and the cock were of the same breed and variety, except for color differences due to dominant and recessive traits and obvious defects, you would probably not notice a significant difference. But if the cock and hen were of a different breed or variety altogether, contamination would immediately have an important and a disastrous effect. For if there was such a contamination, as an American Game hen, for example, which had been bred to a Leghorn cock, her offspring would no longer have any value as breeders of American Games, even when mated to

American Game Hen and Leghorn Rooster

Contamination - When American Games are bred with Leghorns, the influence of one breed are sure to cause destructive results to the other.

other American Games, since they would show the influence of contamination due to that Leghorn cock. Needless to say, such an influence would have a measurable effect on the other.

CONTAMINATION AND THE AVERAGE BACKYARD BREEDER: The theory of contamination finds little substantiation or proof for the average poultry breeder, since they feel that there are no reliable or authentic records to support this idea. It is common practice for them to allow their hens to run with cocks of other breeds and varieties, rather than their own kind without the slightest effects of something bad showing up. However for the cocker, this would be a disaster, and should be avoided at all cost.

THE LAW OF ANCESTRAL INFLUENCES
The power of the parents and grand-parents over the offspring

There are breeders who believe that the parent of one sex has more influence on one particular trait or a combination of traits, while that of the other sex has an influence upon another trait or combination of traits, the most common of these traits being conformation of body and color of plumage. For American Games the most common of these traits include gameness and performance ability. Unfortunately, breeders are themselves divided as to which sex exerts a greater influence, and to what characteristics do they influence.

The fact is there is an equal inheritance from both sexes, and in all characteristics. The real exceptions include a few characteristics of various kinds, which are linked with sex in inheritance in such a way that there is no transmission from mother to daughters. These sex-linked characteristics are discussed later in this book.

Dominant and recessive characteristics can also seem to be influenced by one parent over the other, but in this case, it depends more on who is carrying the dominant characteristic and who is carrying the recessive characteristic and nothing more.

Exceptions may also occur from differences in the prepotency of individuals. It may happen in a particular mating that the cock is prepotent in one or two traits, such as conformation of body or gameness, or a combination of the two, while the hen is prepotent in color or ability performance or a combination of the two. But in another mating the situation may be totally reversed, or one parent may be prepotent in all respects. In short, there is no definite law connecting sex and prepotency.

THE INFLUENCE OF A PREVIOUS MATING: This is a term used to suggest that there may have been an influence from a previous mating on later offspring, which if true, would affect all succeeding matings as well. There are a number of breeders, who may, no doubt still be found, who firmly believe that if a hen has been bred by a mongrel or alien sire she is absolutely "spoiled" for the future "pure breeding" of her own kind. This approach has spurred an expression, which has become very popular among backyard breeders, which is the phrase - "The Power of a Previous Mating," also referred to as "Telegony." This attitude is quite widespread among all classes of breeders. The only problem is that there is no such thing as Telegony. The previous mating does not affect the succeeding mating in any way, so far as the cock is concerned. In the case of the hen, the influence of a previous mating will last for only a comparatively short period after the mating is broken up.

Once upon a time there was a poultry breeder who believed that if a Brown Leghorn rooster was mated with a White Leghorn hen, never again would the White Leghorn hen produce purebred White Leghorn chicks, even when mated to a White Leghorn rooster. The source of such a peculiar belief is probably due to the fact that in cases where a "foreign" rooster has mated with a hen, eggs have been saved for hatching prior to the time that all the spermatozoa of the "foreign" rooster had perished, even though the hen had later been mated with one of her own kind. As a result, there are many poultry farmers and cockers who firmly believe that if a purebred white cock is mated to a black hen, and then later mated to hens of his breed, that the black mating will have a lasting influence. There is no foundation for this kind of thinking.

This is the sort of attitude that prompts some breeders to put a hen with dunghill blood with a thoroughbred American Game cock, hoping to raise the "quality" in all her subsequent progeny. For one thing, it never seems to work out, and another thing, this is breeding in reverse. Or they will go the other way and dispose of the thoroughbred American Game hen that happen to be mated to a dunghill cock, hoping to eradicate the influence of the dunghill cock.

Some time ago, I was curious about this phenomenon. I was also curious about the apparent fluidity and unpredictability of the trait "gameness," which is so precious to our American Games. So I carefully carried out a systematic and methodical experiment to find out the truth. I bred a Rhode Island Red rooster to an American Game hen. I waited a month and I then bred the hen to another American Game cock, her own kind. I did not see an influence of the Rhode Island Red rooster in subsequent offspring, nor did I see an influence in the F_2 generation either. Such experiments failed to induce the phenomenon in question. There was no apparent influence of a previous sire of any kind. My conclusion? When a test such as this fails to produce the result in question, I will no longer believe it. I will look at it as nothing more than speculation and old wives tales.

Admittedly, however, breeders are perpetually meeting with strange experiences, which are perhaps at first sight hard to account for. In plain words, even the most remarkable cases of supposed telegony can doubtlessly be explained as due to reversion and variation. Reversion, or the reappearance of ancestral characters, is one of the most common occurrences experienced by breeders. But if breeders are not aware of the origin of their families or strains, the significance of the phenomenon is, of course, entirely lost upon them.

Again, variations of the most sudden and abrupt nature, better known as mutations, occur constantly. They also help to account for the phenomenon we've been dealing with, making it unnecessary to resort to the telegony doctrine.

As these subjects will be referred to at length in future chapters, we will dismiss them for now with the final remark that "telegony," fails to endure the searchlight of modern scientific investigation, and, like some other cherished beliefs of old-time breeders, proves itself to be built on foundations of sand.

THE LAW OF PREPOTENCY
The power to impress its characters or qualities upon its offspring

"Prepotency of transmission may be equal in the two sexes of the same species, but often runs more strongly in one sex. It plays an important part in determining the rate at which one race can be modified or wholly absorbed by repeated crosses with another."

Charles Darwin

This is a concept that can be hard to explain. Webster's dictionary describes it as: "Having exceptional power; authority or influence over another." Prepotency is a word used by breeders to describe the ability of an individual to impress its qualities and characteristics upon its offspring, and also, the ability of one parent's power over the other parent to pass on its characteristics onto the offspring. If used properly, the breeder, in time, can stamp or fix a certain character or several characters onto the family.

Therefore, it is easy to see why the matter of prepotency is of great importance and of utmost value to a breeder. It's the direct influence of prepotency that will improve his family or strain. Whether it's to improve form, function or beauty, or to improve its chances in competition in the pit, or in poultry exhibitions, prepotency is a valuable tool.

Here are some interesting points to consider:

- Not all broodfowl (cocks or hens) are capable, or have the power to transmit its own characteristics and traits.
- Parents vary greatly in their potency. In other words, either parent may be prepotent in transmitting to the progeny conformation of body, size, desirable color of plumage, or performance capabilities, etc.
- Full brothers or sisters sometimes vary considerably in their ability to transmit a certain characteristic to their offspring as well.
- Prepotency is not always measured by length of pedigree. Even though a cock or a hen has a fine pedigree, it is not a guarantee that the offspring will have the same characteristics as the parent, although the chances in such cases may be better due to purer bloodlines.
- Prepotency does not follow bloodlines. Although results are better when the individual is pure, from a well-established bloodline. When breeding a crossbred or mongrel to a purebred, it does not necessarily follow that the offspring will take after the purebred in all characteristics and traits.
- Prepotent breeders may transmit qualities and characteristics that may be either desirable or undesirable. In this case, although one parent is prepotent for some very good qualities, the other parent may be prepotent in its ability to impress certain undesirable characters, such as knock-knees, duck-toe, or wry-tail, etc.

- An individual may have all the attributes that a breeder could ever desire, with respect to certain characteristics, yet might not transmit these particular traits to its progeny because it lacks prepotency.
- Once a bird (either cock or hen) has proven its prepotency, it should be used as a breeder as much as possible.

An individual may be thought to be prepotent when it can transmit a certain character or set of characters to a considerable proportion to its offspring, but in a substantial and noticeable degree. However, this is also true when it can transmit a character or set of characters to one or a few offspring to a very high degree. For instance, let's take a Black-Breasted Red cock, such as a "Hatch," let's say he's outstanding in every way, but especially in type (which is another word for Conformation of Body). His excellence in type, if prepotent, could transmit this character to a high degree to his sons or daughters, which makes this cock very valuable for breeding.

Ordinarily, progress in breeding is slow, but by the introduction of a decidedly prepotent individual into a family or line, more may be accomplished in a single generation than in a long term of years preceding.

GETTING THE MOST FROM A PREPOTENT PARENT: As you can easily see, this quality of prepotency, when demonstrated in a desirable direction, is an extremely valuable one, and one of which the wise breeder takes full advantage.

Prepotency is increased in the individual and in the family with increased purity of blood; stronger constitutional vigor; and inbreeding. For instance, if the individual in consideration possess it, and has a particularly good combination of those desired traits or genes in concentration, he will then have the ability to transmit them in greater abundance to his offspring. This is more likely to occur when inbreeding and line-breeding is practiced, as in the breeding of pure families and strains, where there are fewer combinations of genes involved. I will discuss this system later.

Once a bird (either cock or hen) has proven its prepotency, it should be used as a breeder as much as possible.

When a single mating is found that consistently throws better than average offspring, that mating should be kept together for a number of generations without experimentation. This is important in order to save the progeny for future breeding, and in establishing new lines.

PREPOTENCY AND THE VALUE OF PROGENY TESTING: Although prepotency in individuals varies greatly, the only way the prepotency of an individual can be determined accurately is by observing its offspring. Prepotency is indicated both by the resemblance of the progeny to the parent and to one another.

In the case where egg production is desired, this will mean trap-nesting the daughters of a mating and pedigree-banding the sons. In the case where battlecocks are desired, it means testing the sons in the pit and evaluating their performance and pedigree-banding the daughters.

CERTAIN BREEDS ARE ESPECIALLY PREPOTENT: This is true with regard to some well-defined characteristics, such as conformation of body, color of plumage, temperament, as well as, brooding instincts. For example, American Games, when crossed with other breeds, such as Aseels, have been known to produce some of the finest battle-crosses. In most cases, American Games are able to transmit a good portion of their distinctive traits to a large percentage of the progeny.

PREPOTENCY AND AMERICAN GAMES: The gene is the unit of inheritance for all various characteristics. Therefore, there may be genes for high headedness and cutting ability. There may be genes for shuffling or for single-stroking, finishing a down cock, gameness, and genes for sulking or running as well. The genes are contributed equally from both cock and hen, but how they are eventually grouped together in the fertilized egg is a matter of chance. Although, when the more favorable genes exist in both parents, the chances are greater that the favorable genes will be those that will be in greater concentration in the offspring.

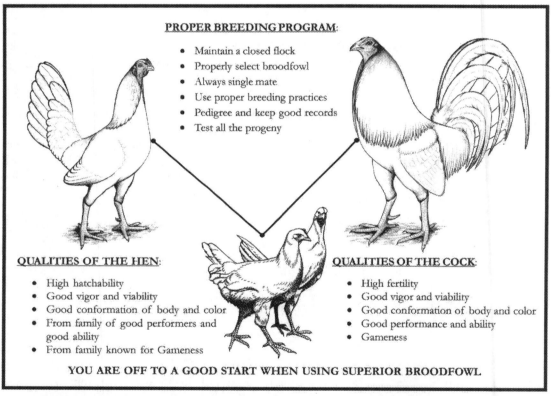

PROPER BREEDING PROGRAM:

- Maintain a closed flock
- Properly select broodfowl
- Always single mate
- Use proper breeding practices
- Pedigree and keep good records
- Test all the progeny

QUALITIES OF THE HEN:

- High hatchability
- Good vigor and viability
- Good conformation of body and color
- From family of good performers and good ability
- From family known for Gameness

QUALITIES OF THE COCK:

- High fertility
- Good vigor and viability
- Good conformation of body and color
- Good performance and ability
- Gameness

YOU ARE OFF TO A GOOD START WHEN USING SUPERIOR BROODFOWL

Breeding birds from a closed, carefully selected family will result in greater uniformity for those characters essential to a successful family.

THE PREPOTENCY OF THE COCK: There are many who believe it is the cock that is responsible for transmitting the most important characteristics and traits to his progeny, such as conformation of body, color of plumage, not to mention ability and gameness. The truth is, there are many contributing factors, which have a lot to do with Mendelian Genetics (most prominent are the dominant and recessive traits). However, if he can dominate certain important characteristics, is it not reasonable to assume that he may dominate all of them? Of course, we assume that to do so,

151

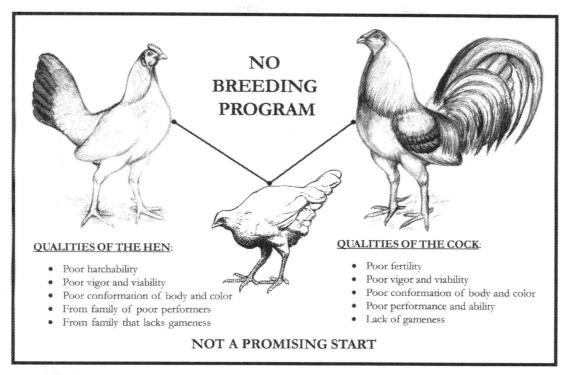

NO BREEDING PROGRAM

QUALITIES OF THE HEN:

- Poor hatchability
- Poor vigor and viability
- Poor conformation of body and color
- From family of poor performers
- From family that lacks gameness

QUALITIES OF THE COCK:

- Poor fertility
- Poor vigor and viability
- Poor conformation of body and color
- Poor performance and ability
- Lack of gameness

NOT A PROMISING START

The introduction of unknown broodfowl into a family, year after year, will not promote uniformity in the offspring.

his vitality and constitutional vigor are equally as strong as the hens, if not stronger. More than that, we assume that he possesses the faculty or capacity of transmitting his qualities.

THE PREPOTENCY OF THE HEN: If this is true of the cock, it is even more important in the hen. If one hen proves to be a producer of exceptional stags from the single matings of different cocks, she is considered a goldmine and more valuable than any cock no matter how spectacular his fighting abilities are. It is around such great individual hens that a successful strain must be built! The beginner must understand that the hen is the strain. Without the right hen, you have nothing!

This is also true for the average backyard breeder who is only interested in a steady production of eggs. In breeding for egg production, a hen must not only be a good layer herself, but must transmit the quality of good egg production to her sons, which in turn transmits that quality to his daughters, this is important for her to be considered a good breeder.

PREPOTENCY AND SELECTION: Ordinarily, progress in Selective Breeding and prepotency should not be confused. Progress through the practice of Selective Breeding, especially to a specific type, is slow, inch by inch, as it were. Let a prepotent individual appear, and its power be discovered, and in a single generation a breeder may make more progress through this one individual than he has made in all the years prior. Within another generation he may raise the average quality of his family to very near the average of the progeny of the prepotent individual. Within a few years the distribution of this family may have a noticeable effect and improvement in the specific breed and variety that it belongs to.

This is most noticeable in the early stages of the development of a family, when quality of characters is low or mediocre as measured by the approved standard, and individual differences are most noticeable.

Here is how it normally works. Let's say you are in the process of creating a family, but they have shown no unique or exceptional value or advancement for years. Then one breeding season it seems as if all the offspring from a particular individual are exceptional in every way. So you breed him exclusively, and cull everything else. To your surprise, they begin to improve, and improve significantly. Within a few more years you have created a family that you can be proud of. They are uniform and consistent in every way, and they have all the qualities and attributes that you've desired for so long. Wanting to know the opinion of your fellow cockers or poultrymen, you decide to attend a show, and to your amazement everyone is in admiration of your remarkable string of birds. Immediately your family is in great demand. Within a few years many breeders have made similar improvement due to infusions of your blood, or they have purchased some of your fowl direct. Before you know it your name is synonymous with greatness, and your fowl are in every backyard.

Although, progress by ordinary selection is always slow, hardly noticeable in the averages of consecutive generations, progress by the use of a prepotent individual is instantly noticeable and improvements are always significant.

THE LAW OF MOTHER NATURE
The effects of the environment on growth and development

"It is not the strongest of the species that survives, nor the most intelligent that survives. It is the one that is the most adaptable to change."
Charles Darwin

The environment can be your friend or it can be your enemy. It is your family's ability to adapt to its environment that is important. This brings up a good point; the conditions under which young gamefowl grows and live may affect their overall size and development, therefore, changing their conformation of body. The main question is, can it cause a modification in their genetic constitution. Charles Darwin once stated, *"Changes of any kind in the conditions of life, even extremely slight changes, often suffice to cause variability."* Does this mean that the environment has an effect on inheritance? We will discuss this subject and many others.

THE EFFECTS OF THE ENVIRONMENT: The environmental conditions, which most commonly affect American Games is the climate, which includes: weather, temperature, atmosphere, as well as the overall ambiance of the farm. It also includes the various practices of management, including: sanitation and overall health, housing and penning arrangements, feeding and watering, and care of the eggs prior to and during incubation, as well the care of the chicks during the growing and developing period.

Environmental conditions, particularly those of climate, may cause a modification of size or conformation, but only in preventing them from developing their inherited characteristics to the fullest extent. This does not interfere with their ability to transmit these characteristics to their offspring. These birds still have the ability to pass on these characteristics to their offspring no matter how they develop or mature.

Environment has the ability to modify a bird but not his gene pool. The only factors which can change the genetics of a family are random mutations, and the introduction of outside blood. However, an effort should be made in controlling or modifying the environment so that it will be more favorable for the full development of the desired characters, such as high quality offspring, which is inherited by the broodfowl.

"The possibility of selection coming into action rests on variability; and this is mainly caused by changes in the conditions of life."
Charles Darwin

BENEFITS OF A GOOD ENVIRONMENT: Through the years American Games have improved tremendously in their appearance, performance and in their overall disposition. The amount of variation traceable to heredity has been large enough to make selection highly effective. In fact, they went from being merely mediocre to something that is actually quite good.

Along with heredity, much has been learned about how to improve their characteristics and traits by simply providing a better environment.

These include the favorable effects of:

- Providing the best possible rations.
- Providing fresh water.
- Better constructed and reliable incubators and brooders.
- Free-ranging the young stags and pullets through the critical stages of their development, where they benefit from having access to fresh grass and bugs, and plenty of exercise.
- Providing teepees and barrels for cocks where they too can benefit from having access to fresh grass and bugs, and plenty of exercise.
- The availability of wormers and some medications.
- The construction of better broodpens, flypens, broody houses, which provide more comfortable quarters and protection from predators.

All of these are combined to increase the opportunities for improving overall quality and performance of our American Games through the influence of environment.

HOW THE ENVIRONMENT AFFECTS GENETIC INHERITANCE: Some say that the amount of individual variation traceable to environment increased so much that selection has approached the limit of its effectiveness. Also it is said that many of today's best bred birds and the amount of variation, that is directly traceable to heredity, is no more than twenty percent. I think this is hogwash and backward thinking. The environment plays an important role in the development of our fowl, but it does not take the place of good selection and genetic inheritance. Cockers and backyard breeders should always practice proper selection and concentrate on perpetuating desirable characteristics and traits. In conclusion, know that there is no such thing as a low degree of heritability, especially when it comes to the effects of the environment.

> *"Individuals, which are best fitted for the complex, and in the course of ages changing conditions to which they are exposed, generally survive and procreate their kind."*
>
> *Charles Darwin*

COMPARATIVE INFLUENCE OF ENVIRONMENT AND HEREDITY: The old question whether the influence of the environment is greater than that of heredity might well be asked with respect to body size. It is clear that the genetic potentialities for size are greatly limited in the newly hatched chick by the size of the egg from which that chick hatches. Other limitations may operate during the period of growth, but when the effects of these are not persistent or not too severe; the size attained at maturity is likely to be determined by heredity.

Chickens, which are retarded by hot weather, will usually recover by what is called "Compensatory Rapid Growth." They will eventually attain a size and weight normal for the strain. Similarly, if you were to put chicks on diets containing different levels of protein, their growth during the period of most rapid development, usually from hatching to 10 weeks of age, is usually directly proportional to the amount of protein they received. Lowering the protein content will slow down the rate of growth. Here is the interesting part, they will grow slowly in their earlier stages, but at 29 weeks of age, they usually make up the deficiency before they reach maturity.

IMPORTANCE OF THE ENVIRONMENT: Due to the fact that there are some inherited characteristics in the fowl that can be modified by the environment, it is essential to test the individuals of your family so that the differences caused by variations, induced by the environment, cannot affect the more important inherited characteristics that we desire to keep. This is called the "Progeny Test."

Clearly, the environment should be as uniform as possible for all birds. It is easier to give all birds the same feed, to house them in the same type of pens, and to do all the other obvious things around the farm the same. You want birds that can adapt to the environment at hand rather than for you to try and adjust to their idiosyncrasies and eccentricities.

In addition to such complications, there are others that may be entirely unsuspected. As for the expected differences, it is not so easy to keep the late-hatched chicks from getting coccidia, to which their early-hatched sibs are better able to develop resistance. In this case it would seem probable that the early-hatched chicks had escaped some influences that caused higher mortality in their later hatched sibs. There are some differences where you will have to adjust your methods.

One important environmental influence that must always be considered is the length of day or the amount of available light, especially during the breeding season. Broodfowl require fourteen hours of daylight for proper reproduction to occur (production of sperm and eggs). There are ways, natural and artificial, that you can do to make this happen.

THE ENVIRONMENT AND THE DEVELOPMENT OF THE CHICK: From the time the egg is laid it is susceptible to external conditions, such as temperature, moisture, and physical changes. These factors can be directly influenced or regulated by man. If the embryo is to develop normally and regularly during the incubation period, and the chick be successfully hatched, these external factors of temperature, moisture, and purity of air, as well as certain physical changes, must all be regulated.

The external conditions, such as shelter and feed, which exist immediately after hatching, influence to a great extent the characteristics of the progeny at maturity, and they affect indirectly the future breeding possibilities of the individual.

COMFORT IS THE ROAD TO PROPER DEVELOPMENT: All the problems of environment can be solved, by planning everything with the question of - are the birds comfortable? I can assure you, if they are not comfortable, their growth and development will not be up to acceptable standards.

Cleanliness and sanitary surroundings for the chicks are essential, as they tend to minimize the danger of communicable diseases and create an atmosphere of contentment.

Maintenance of favorable environment is very important during the brooding and rearing period, for a low brooder temperature will chill the young and cause crowding, which will result in weakly undeveloped chicks, if not, in their immediate death.

Later, during the growing period and when on the range, they need a large area of shade and an abundance of nourishment, including green feed. This is important if the ancestral blood elements, which they have inherited from their parents are to be given an opportunity for full development.

<u>NUTRITION IS AN ELEMENT OF THEIR ENVIRONMENT</u>: Another important factor in the environment of the chick, and later, the young stags and pullets, is the supply of feed, which must be sufficient in its amounts, wholesome, and as natural as possible, and of the right degree of concentration.

I have experienced instances in which the ration was not properly balanced, and when the birds reached maturity, during their first breeding season, they were so weak that the vitality of their offspring was not all that vigorous, many died or were underdeveloped later down the road.

Birds which are kept by man in a state of domestication are dependent upon him for food and shelter, which largely make up their environment, so a careful and proper regulation of this is essential if the inherited qualities are to be given opportunity for their highest development.

Well I hope this has given you a little more insight of the laws of breeding. There is a lot to consider when creating or maintaining a strain, and these laws will aid you in creating the best fowl possible, now and in the future.

SEEKING PERFECTION
It's good to have a healthy concern for the selection of your fowl

"Whether it is for pit or exhibition purposes, every cocker and breeder should try to increase both the reproductive and standard characteristics of his fowl each and every year, then and only then will good specimens become more and more numerous."

By Kenny Troiano

The originators of many of the most popular varieties of American Games, and indeed those who have produced outstanding strains, were known to combine intense observation with an inbuilt belief that all traits were inherited unless proven otherwise. Although they didn't know how genetics worked, they were very aware that many of their mistakes were caused by "factors" inherent in their strains. They certainly were not students of poultry genetics, and even if they were, they most likely would not have benefited from the knowledge that was available in their day. They bred their fowl with the understanding that each bird, fixed within it, already has the established genes required for both improvement and degeneration alike, and that it is the accumulation of minor genes (or modifiers) that matters most. For most of these breeders, all a study of genetics would have taught them was what they already knew – and that was, all things are inherited until proven otherwise. This knowledge led to a healthy concern in the selection of their broodfowl, a practice which all great breeders use to this day.

Today we have a better understanding of how genetics works. We are quick to share general knowledge on the subject, in sometimes interested but often in heated discussions. The observational powers of the successful breeders are therefore quite highly developed, and extend to other aspects of breeding not immediately obvious. For instance, many breeders have only a limited budget available, for the simple reason that they are self-financing. Many also wish to exhibit or pit their best fowl at peak fitness, usually for a particular event. Consequently they have to time their development to perfection so that their fowl are just right when it counts the most.

When it is all said and done, it is the enthusiastic and successful breeders that are willing to learn the practical rules of their trade, while the apathetic ones are left scratching their heads in wonder and utter failure. No longer can we ignore the powers of selection and the influence that modern genetics have on the success and failure of our breeding programs.

*Note: While much of the subject matter in this chapter is applicable to all species of poultry, because of space limitations, discussion and examples will be confined to the American Games.

KNOWING A GOOD BIRD WHEN YOU SEE ONE: The most important ability possessed by successful breeders is the ability to "see" the quality of the bird of which they are looking.

Recognizing attributes that are beneficial, while discriminating against the poor ones, is the difference between success and failure. But having this ability depends on the individual breeder. It is achieved by acquiring the proper knowledge and being committed to the purpose at hand. This can come from reading and studying books, having good mentors, and from personal experience, such as taking advantage of your successes, when they come, while learning and benefiting from your mistakes.

<u>Preference also plays a part in having this ability</u>: Everyone has in their mind what the ideal bird should look, act and perform like. If you were to ask ten people what their ideal bird was, you would most likely get ten different answers. It is important to understand what your ultimate aim is. Do you want to create your own strain of fowl, or do you want to improve an existing breed?

All breeders aspire to produce attractive birds, but what is the proper definition of an "attractive" bird? Once again, this all depends on the individual breeder. As they say, "One Man's Junk is another man's Treasure," or better yet, "Beauty is in the Eyes of the Beholder."

Here is a proven Troiano Red cock, owned and bred by Kenny Troiano. A fine product of good selection from a solid and well maintained family of Gamefowl.

In creating a strain you must have the ability to breed and develop fowl for very specific qualities of form, function and beauty.

If your aim is to improve an existing breed, and you accept the interpretation of the "Standard of Perfection" as your ultimate guide, it will give you the picture of the ideal bird that is required for showing. However, be aware that these standards are so brief and to the point in their descriptions that they do not permit a sufficiently detailed explanation of "all" the attributes of a true champion. Some of it is left to your imagination and your knowledge of genetic inheritance.

<u>They must be balanced</u>: The American Gamecock is the Olympian athlete of its species, a gladiator of sort. Therefore, all the parts of his body must be put together and arranged in such a way that it comprises a well-organized, efficient and proficient killing machine. Every characteristic, trait and attribute has a specific function and purpose. As a result, the underlying

A cock that is extremely out of balance.

essential quality of a top-class gamefowl is balance. Without balance no bird can be really attractive and competent for which it was bred. Without balance it cannot help but appear and act awkward or clumsy in some way. The further out of balance the bird, the more awkward looking it appears. For this reason, it is essential to assess your fowl while on the ground, as well as, in the hand. You must understand and appreciate that no matter the bird, they are either balanced or they are not. There is no grey area when it comes to the form and function of a bird.

<u>Improving balance in a family</u>: In order to breed birds that are well balanced, the breeder must select broodfowl that are well balanced. However, what if the breeder has no choice but to breed to something that is somewhat imbalanced? In this case, the breeder must have the ability to assess the reason for the imbalance. In most cases, the reason is quite simple, it stems from defects of the skeletal system. Parts of the skeleton may be the wrong shape or size, or are in improper angles. Although the answer may be obvious, where everyone has difficulties is deciding how or where it is incorrect. This is not as easy to ascertain as you might think.

The most important single reason for imbalance is:

- Incorrect positioning of the shoulders, causing undesirable alteration in the carriage of the wing, which then alters the relative distribution of weight.

- To be balanced, the length of shank and thigh is another very important feature. The shank should be slightly shorter than the thigh. It is rare that the length of thigh over exceeds that of the shank to the point that it causes an imbalance. The imbalance is almost always the other way around. Elongated shanks lead to stiltiness, because the fowl pivots about its hock when walking, with the result that a stiffness develops to counterbalance the incorrect distribution of weight over the feet. Elongated shanks also lead to cocks that are less powerful and less accurate in battle.

Imbalances are mainly the result of faults observed in the extremities of the bird, such as the length of their wings and legs, and the size of their tails, which may simply be out of position, or the result of imbalances in the shape of their backs, positioning of their legs and shoulders. However it is possible for a bird to be faultless in all these areas and still be completely out of balance. The lengthening or shortening of any and every bone alters the weight distribution and stance, therefore the balance. Consequently, it is not surprising that we frequently hear people saying, about winning birds, that they are "Conformationally Sound." By this they simply meant that all parts of the bird are in proper proportion to each other.

PERFECT FEATHERS MUST GROW FROM PERFECT BODIES: One of my mentors used to always tell me that *"Perfect feathers must grow from a perfect body. If you neglect the body, or the selection for the perfect body, they, the family, will eventually lack the proper feathers as well."* And usually that was the case. I also noticed that good plumage can never make up for a faulty conformation of body. If the conformation or carriage is wrong, it won't matter what color they are or how good a plumage they may have, it is still wrong. They simply do not look right.

For perfection to be achieved, they must be perfect in every way, from their conformation of body to the condition of their plumage. Once again it's all about balance. Nevertheless, balance in conformation of body cannot be achieved until they are in good feather too. Therefore, when it comes to American Games, the feather plumage is very important. For instance, when we look at the feathers of an American Gamecock we can plainly see that it is his body armor, his protective shielding from other cocks that happen to threaten his territory. For the American Gamehen, feathers are her natural camouflaging for hiding from predators and for protecting her chicks. For both, the American Gamecock and hen, feathers are their protection from the elements of Mother Nature, such as, the heat of the day and the cold of the night. Feathers are their natural rain coat during rainy weather. And let's not forget maybe the most important asset, feathers are their natural means for expressing dominance, used especially for sexual selection. Survival of the fittest is a real factor in the life and daily existence of American Games, and their plumage plays a major part of that survival.

Note: sexual selection can account for many traits. However, most of them are sexually dimorphic, such as comb size, body size, feather shape and feather color, which is usually completely different from the hens. For instance, look at the Black-Breasted Reds. The cocks are black-breasted and red, while the hens are partridge colored. In the wild, it was the hen who determined the color of the cock.

Uniformity of color is also essential: We just talked a bit about the importance of a good plumage, but to complete the picture, it is important to also focus on the proper color, which is needed in the feather. Uniformity of color and markings is essential if an impression of quality is to be created in a family.

For perfection to be achieved, broodfowl must be perfect in every way. Therefore, balance is important.

When we are dealing with breeds or a particular stain, which are very uniform, any obvious variations will destroy the overall effect. For uniformity to occur in any family or strain it is essential that the variations within the birds of the family are properly selected for, or properly culled. The development of a family, which has been properly selected, due to favorable variations can have far-reaching benefits for the future of any family.

*Special note: No matter what their type, condition or color of plumage, all attributes must be right for their breed and variety.

INTERPRETATION OF THE STANDARDS: The problem most beginners face is that almost all breed standards that are available are, at best, incomplete in regards to their description of feather. The color pattern is well documented but the quality and quantity of plumage is not described very well. Some actually give the breeder the impression that the authors of these standards have avoided the issue altogether.

The feathering must compliment the body in forming the shape of the bird and the desired outline. Unfortunately some breeders tend to compensate for a body with a narrow back or a thinly or flat sided breast, instead of having the necessary heart shaped back and round football shaped body, by perpetuating broodfowl that are excessively abundant in plumage, so much so that the overall balance of the bird is ultimately incorrect. This approach is doomed to failure because the increase in mass, due to the accumulation of excessive feather, also adds mass in unwanted areas, knocking the balance of the bird completely out of whack.

The precise feather shape, which the breeder seeks to attain, will depend on the type of markings which the chosen bird ought to possess.

THE MIXTURE OF BIRDS IS SOMETIMES NECESSARY: Most master breeders know that in order to breed a bird of true quality it is sometimes necessary to form a mixture of birds. This is the crossing of fowl which are superior in many respects; it is also the crossing of fowl in the expectation that they will balance each other in many ways.

The finding of the correct combination is the true secret of breeding, but the search for such a blend is not very easy. The right bird can do wonders for a family while the wrong bird can absolutely destroy a family. However a vision of the desired end product, with a good knowledge of the faults in the existing stock, coupled with the ability to predict the possible outcome of matings, and incorporating disease resistance so that the offspring may attain their full potential, is a sound basis with which to start.

Having a determination to succeed, and by persisting with the best broodfowl available and hatching plenty of youngsters so to have plenty to select from, will steadily bring the goal closer to fruition.

PROPENSITY OF BREEDING

Knowing the breeding tendencies of your fowl will help in eliminating the little imperfections when they arise

Different strains of the same breed and variety may, and usually do, have different breeding tendencies. These tendencies are nothing more than little variations, which arise from time to time, within a close bred family. Some are dominant while others are recessive. Some are good while others are bad. Just what these tendencies are can be determined only by you, the breeder, and by having an intimate relationship and knowledge of the fowl in question. This means that you must closely study the results of every breeding on your yard. You must also work with the same family of fowl for a long period of time. Such knowledge is essential for success, and the breeder, who fails to study his fowl to this extent, with a definiteness of purpose, will not attain the highest level of success.

LEARNING THE BREEDING TENDENCIES: Probably the most difficult problem in connection with improvement by breeding lies in learning the breeding tendencies of the individuals within the family. We may have a good looking hen, but she may not produce good looking offspring. Or we may have a high quality cock that is proven in every way, but his sons may not show any evidence of their father's traits. While there is a tendency for like to produce like, as the old rule of breeding goes, there are enough exceptions to the rule to completely upset the results of any breeding, especially in the improvement of a family. This is accomplished only by knowing the breeding tendencies of each individual bird on your farm. The question to ask yourself when putting together your broodpens, is, *"Is this bird, which I plan to use for breeding, beneficial or unbeneficial to my breeding program?" "Will this bird help or hurt the family?"* When breeding American Games, it is important to always move forward, never backwards. In other words, ask yourself, *"Are this year's offspring better or worse than their parents?"* This is important. The offspring should always be better than their parents, every year, even if it's just a little better. If the offspring are not better, don't breed them!

The benefits of knowing the breeding tendencies of your fowl: This enables you, the breeder, to count upon those tendencies which are "strong" in the right direction, and at the same time allows you to take special care in guarding against unwanted tendencies. This is very important, especially when putting together your broodpens. Having the knowledge of the breeding tendencies that are possible in your family will often have an important bearing on the selection of individual birds that are to be used in mating, and makes the selection of the individuals as breeders much less of a matter of guesswork.

For example, let's say you have a family of Black-Breasted Red - American Games that have been known to produce individuals showing wry-tails from time to time, it would be highly undesirable and unwise to use a bird from yours or another's yard that is showing this defect, even if they possess certain other qualifications of an outstanding character. The idea is to perpetuate the desirable traits while eliminating the undesirable ones, and you cannot do this if you are breeding birds that show this trait. If they show it, they carry it! If they carry it, then they can pass it onto their offspring! There are no "if's, and's, or but's" about it!

Success requires a keen observation and careful attention to all details: Then there is the problem of determining the result of a particular union of a cock and hen. The cock, for instance, may be a good overall specimen and a good breeder for the particular characteristic and trait desired, but the hen to which he is mated may nullify, by cancelling-out or reversing, all his good points. In this case, the breeder has achieved nothing. As you can see, breeding fowl properly requires keen observation and careful attention to all the little details in order to get a good understanding of your fowls breeding tendencies.

Anticipating and correcting bad trends: To be successful, the breeder must be quick to see any bad trends that may creep its way into his family of fowl, and he must take decisive steps in his breeding program to correct them. The quicker he notices these tendencies and anticipates their eventual arrival the easier it will be to eradicating them. If you fail to recognize the dangers, of undesirable characteristics and traits, until they show strongly in your fowl, you will have a hard time eradicating them. This again emphasizes the necessity for the breeder to continuously study his family of fowl in the minutest of manners. He must, in effect, be thinking and planning well ahead

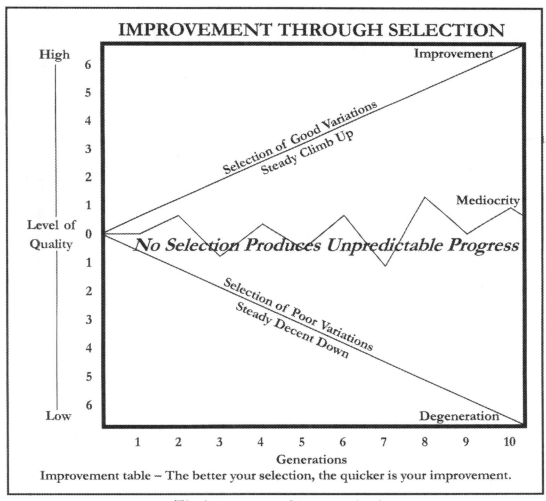

The importance of proper selection.

before putting together his broodfowl and broodpens. I like to plan five years in advance. I do adjust these plans as time goes on, but it gives me a solid foundation which to build on, and a direction and goal to work towards.

<u>What to lookout for</u>: These tendencies could be anything from their ability and style to their level of gameness in competition, or even their conformation of body, or color and condition of their plumage. For example, a breeder of Black-Breasted Red Games, such as a "Hatch" family, may notice a troublesome tendency toward white in the wings and tail creeping into his family of fowl. Or let's say they are starting to show a tendency towards duck-toe, or wry-tail. They never showed this before, but suddenly it has become a problem. He must then immediately become more rigid in his selection against these tendencies in those areas, and use no birds showing these tendencies, if it can possibly be avoided. In any case, it would be wise for the breeder to take precautions by culling the questionable birds and make special mating of birds that are strong in desired areas, so that he will have a number of young stags and pullets available to him, especially strong in this particular area, from which he can select breeders to use in future matings and stop this troublesome tendency.

<u>In Summary</u>: Remember that "Breeding Tendencies," of any kind, are simply variations of characteristics and traits carried within the family gene pool that are either dominant or recessive. This is important, for the reason that these tendencies are what make selection possible. Indeed, if it wasn't for selection we would not be able to improve the characteristics and traits of our fowl.

Also, it can be put down, as a general rule, that the greater the number of ancestors exhibiting the breeding traits that you desire, which occur successively, uninterrupted in the pedigree of any breeding specimen, the more likely that specimen is to transmit the beneficial traits to its offspring. In other words, the longer you perpetuate the trait, by breeding individuals carrying that trait, for many generations, the more prominent that trait will become, in the family and in the individuals of that family. Eventually the trait will become a dominant trait.

Whatever you do, don't get discouraged, even an experienced breeder, who purchases the best fowl obtainable, may still be unable to keep the quality of the fowl up to that attained by its former owner, at least for some years. This is due to the fact that he is unfamiliar with the family's breeding tendencies, and must breed that family of fowl for several years before learning just what the real breeding tendencies actually are and what to do about it.

PUTTING AN END
TO IMPERFECTIONS
The importance of eliminating defects
and disqualifications, large or small

"Indomitable patience, the finest powers of discrimination, and sound judgment must be exercised during many years. A clearly predetermined object must be kept steadily in view. Few men are endowed with all these qualities, especially with that of discriminating very slight differences; judgment can be acquired only by long experience; but if any of these qualities be wanting, the labour of a life may be thrown away."

Charles Darwin

As long as the maintenance of breed and variety standards are considered important for the best interests of all American Games, and the Gamefowl industry as a whole; and as long as purebred fowl are in popular demand, it will be necessary to maintain a working standard. Cockers and backyard breeders, therefore, must always be on the alert in guarding against undesirable characteristics from becoming established in their families and strains. These undesirable characteristics that are sometimes found in purebred birds are called either "defects" or "disqualifications." It is important to understand the difference between the two, and to learn what they are and what to do about them. Later in this book I will give you a complete list of all the defects and disqualifications, as well as their definitions.

Here is a list of subjects that we will cover in this chapter:
- The Importance of Eliminating Defects and Disqualifications, Large and Small.
- Recognizing Common Defects and Disqualifications.
- The Regressive Nature of Little Flaws and Imperfections.
- Common Defects and Disqualifications and Their Genetic Influences.
- The Most Common of these Defects and Disqualifications.
- The Most Uncommon of these Defects and Disqualifications.
- Variations and Abnormalities Which Affect Their Plumage.
- The Elimination of Undesirable Traits.

WHAT ARE DEFECTS AND DISQUALIFICATIONS: First of all, before we go any further, what is the definition of a defect? It is the lack of something necessary for completeness. It is also an imperfection or fault. For American Gamefowl, a defect is any characteristic that makes a bird less than perfect. Although some are environmental, nearly all defects are inherited.

What is the definition of a disqualification? It is a term applied to a deformity or a fault, sufficiently, or serious enough to exclude a fowl from an award, or for consideration as a breeder. Like a defect, disqualifications are usually inherited, but can also be caused by the effects of the environment it lives in.

What constitutes this level of perfection? Well, it is a combination of the "Standard of Perfection," which is established by the agreement of a committee, and by you, the breeder. In comes down to, what characteristic and traits do you want to perpetuate and which ones do you want to eliminate?

"When man attempts to make a breed with some serious defect in structure, or in the mutual relation of the several parts, he will partly or completely fail, or encounter much difficulty; he is in fact resisted by a form of Natural Selection."

Charles Darwin

A PERFECT SPECIMEN EXCEPT FOR ONE SMALL, ALMOST UNNOTICEABLE DEFECT: In judging American Games, my experience has shown me that not only are no two birds alike, but also that, all birds carry a defect of some kind. It can be in one or more parts of the body. Therefore, you just have to locate them and determine their importance. For instance, some defects are obvious while others are discreet. Some defects are minor while others are more serious. A bird may be desirable in every respect, except that it has a crooked back; or has a duck-toe; or there may be feather-like growths or stubs on the shanks, or bits of down may appear between the toes; or the tails of some birds may depart so much from the normal shape that they are either wry-tailed or squirrel-tailed. Furthermore, it could be some other deformity altogether that you would not notice if you did not get them in the hand to inspect them, such as a poorly indented breastbone. A cock may seem to be almost a perfect specimen except for one small, almost unnoticeable defect. It is up to you to locate the defect and determine whether it is serious or minor.

Some of the defects mentioned above are transmitted and all of them, as well as others described in the Standard of Perfection, are regarded as serious departures from the ideal shape and color standards desired for American Games. As a result, these defects are called "disqualifications." A bird possessing any one of them should be barred from winning a prize in the showroom and should not be used in the breeding pen. Some birds may have certain shape and color defects, which do not constitute disqualifications but should still be excluded from the breeding program.

Here is a good example of a cock with white streamers in the tail feathers.

SOME DEFECTS ARE OF MINOR IMPORTANCE, SOME ARE NOT: For American Games, there are many defects which should be guarded against and eliminated from the breeding program as soon as they are identified. However, there are some defects which, should not be ignored, but are of relatively minor importance compared to other more serious defects. These include such things as scaly legs; an abnormal number of points on a straight (*single*) comb; and in some cases, the color of their plumage. For instance, in some birds, such as Black-Breasted Light-Reds, white plumage in the tail can be considered a defect. Some judges would disqualify this bird, while others would just knock off a few points. And then there are those, judges, which like white streamers in the tail.

Another example would be that of the American Game Dom, similar to the Barred Plymouth Rocks, solid black feathers in the body plumage could constitute a defect, although some judges will overlook it.

One more example would be that of "shafting" in the feathers. When it comes to American Games, the hens are notorious for this trait. In most breeds this would be a disqualification, but for American Games they all pretty much have it. Try finding a Black-Breasted Red – partridge hen that doesn't have it. As a judge, about all I can do is make sure I give high marks for hens that don't show shafting or show it the least.

Here is an example of an American Game Black-Breasted Light-Red cock with white streamers in the tail feathers. For some judges this can be a defect.

TOO MUCH ATTENTION ON "USELESS FORM" AND TOO LITTLE ON "PURPOSE AND FUNCTIONALITY": American Games must excel, not so much in production, unless we are talking about the production of broodfowl, battlefowl or hatching eggs, but in the proper conformation of body, color of plumage, temperament, and performance qualities. To accomplish this they must be standard-bred. What does this mean? Well, your family and strain must be selected and bred with a very specific criterion of characteristics and traits, and all defects and disqualifications must be eliminated as soon as they are detected. At the same time, if they are, for instance, a Black-Breasted Red they must look like a Black-Breasted Red as described in the standard.

These days this is very rare, for there is too much attention placed on characteristics of minor importance, such as, on the pattern of the scales on the legs; an extremely high station of leg; and the number of feathers a cock has in his tail, just to mention a few. There is too much attention on "useless form" and too little on "purpose and functionality." This type of breeding has resulted, in the past, in several different varieties of gamefowl, which eventually lost their place in popularity. I think fowl, known as "Sweaters" are heading in that direction as well.

Barred Plymouth Rock and American Game Dom

A Barred Plymouth Rock and an American Game Dom, both have the cuckoo feathering.

WHICH DEFECTS ARE "MAJOR" AND WHICH ARE "MINOR"? When dealing with defects and disqualifications, it is necessary to recognize which are "major" faults and which are "minor." Unfortunately, in some cases, the issue is not always as straight forward as we would like. For example, a very short tail on an American Gamecock is a major defect, but to be fair, allowance would have to be made for the time of year. If a cock is just through the molt he may not have grown his tail to the full length and, therefore, should not be disqualified as a broodcock. On the other hand, a few missing feathers from the tail and wings would be of a minor concern, but would be classified somewhat differently if many of the wing feathers were broken as well. This may indicate a plumage that is brittle or fragile, which usually results from a hereditary defect or from feeding too many carbohydrates in the yard feed, such as corn. It is important to understand that some defects are conditions which may be caused by an unbalanced diet or their environment, but can be genetic as well.

From these observations it should be apparent that the degree or extent of the fault may have an important bearing on whether they should be used for the broodpen or culled. However, the very presence of certain defects, which I will list shortly, should exclude a bird from being used as breeders.

THE PRINCIPAL IDEA IS TO PRODUCE STOCK OF HIGH QUALITY: In addition to the foregoing paragraphs, the ultimate purpose of breeding should be always kept in mind when selecting breeders for the broodpen. In other words, know beforehand what it is you intend to accomplish, and select broodfowl accordingly. If the principal idea is to produce stock of exhibition quality, select broodfowl nearest to the standard in conformation of body (known as type) and color markings, or a combination of these qualities so as to produce birds that will most nearly approach the ideal standard. In addition to these standard requirements, if the purpose of mating is to produce battlefowl, birds that possess all the attributes necessary for good performance in the pit, such as good conformation of body, temperament, ability, and gameness, birds that have all the necessary attributes should be selected as broodfowl. In the selection of breeders for the reproduction of future stock, breeders should be chosen that are all-round good fowl, or are the sons or daughters of all-round good fowl.

Standard-bred fowl should always be single mated. That is, both cocks and hens are secured which conform to the standard requirements of the breed and variety from one mating. While the production of both cocks and hens of standard quality is possible as the result of single mating, many master breeders have departed from this plan and have resorted to one mating to secure exhibition cocks and another mating for exhibition hens. This system is known as double-mating, and is becoming more and more accepted every day.

RECOGNIZING COMMON DEFECTS
And Disqualifications

*"It is one of the most essential requisites that appertains to the welfare
of producing an unexceptionable breed of cocks, to detect with anxious
attention even the slightest traits of change in the constitution."*

W. Sketchley

Undoubtedly, you know what a "chicken" looks like. But how closely and carefully have you really looked at them? Have you observed the details of the head, face and beak? Have you ever noticed the scales on the legs? Do you know where a bird's knee is or its ankle or hock joint? What about its prop-toe? Do you know the particulars of the wing, such as the primary and secondary wing feathers, the primary and secondary coverts, wing bow, wing bar, and axial feather? What about the tail? Are you familiar with the main tail feathers, sickles, lesser sickles, and side hangers? Not to mention, the shape and structure of the body and carriage. Every bird has a distinctive body shape and you, the breeder, should know what that is.

According to the American Standard of Perfection, a disqualification and defect is a fault sufficiently serious to eliminate the bird from competition or the breeding program. Disqualifications and defects are faults that should be taken into consideration at all times, but especially when selecting fowl for the broodpen. To qualify as high quality broodfowl, the birds must be completely free (not reasonably free, but completely free) from all disqualifications and defects. Any birds in question should be eliminated from the breeding program and culled.

The principal goal of this chapter is to help you understand the basic form of an American Game, and the defects and disqualifications to guard against. This knowledge provides a framework within which you will be able to identify, describe, compare, and eventually classify the different parts of the bird. Also, you will be able to identify and eliminate the various defects that can and do exist.

For all intents and purposes, the bird's body is arbitrarily divided into ten major regions; each of these, and their major parts, are considered in turn. When examining your bird, first note the shape of the body; how it slopes and how everything tapers nicely to the tail. Observe its athletic posture and stance.

**Here is a good example of a proper
American Game.**

Then identify and observe the details of the ten main parts of the bird, such as: - eyes, head, beak, comb, neck, body, wings, tail, legs and feet. Once you have completed your observation of the ten major parts, observe the bird's plumage, size and weight, behaviors, health, and general condition. These observations will help you to better understand the reasons why American Games are structured as so.

American Games are both pit and show birds, therefore, their function should complement their form and vice versa. Although this may be something that is overlooked in other fowl, such as commercial or ornamental breeds, when it comes to American Games, the breeder should always aim at producing fowl that have all the finer points and requirements of both. Therefore, a strict watch should be carried out to identify any deviation from the norm.

THE SERIOUSNESS OF DEFECTS: Different varieties of gamefowl have their own peculiar defects. These defects are serious handicaps to the specimen's worth, and are of even greater detriment if allowed to appear in the broodpens. Many cockers and backyard breeders are unaware of the seriousness of breeding from defective birds, and do not realize how their fowl will regress from a higher quality if defects are not culled from the breeding program. Show birds, pit birds, or even broodfowl, if they have a defect, they should be culled and culled ruthlessly. While, there may be some instances for retaining birds having these defects, for whatever reason you may find important, they should never be allowed in the broodpen.

Once you have decided to purchase broodfowl, it's a good idea to look them over really good. Look for essential points other than the obvious ones, such as, their conformation of body and temperament. Look for breed defects that you would not want to perpetuate.

Every cocker and backyard breeder should try to increase both the reproductive and standard characteristics of his fowl each year, then and only then will good specimens become more numerous and more prevalent in the future. Whether it be for exhibition, pit, or breeding purposes, eliminating defective birds is a must.

BECOME FAMILIAR WITH DEFECTS AND DISQUALIFICATIONS: It is important to understand that if defects occur in a family or strain, it is "Selective Breeding" that is necessary to eliminate them. To aid in the selection of high quality fowl, on the following pages is a list of the more common defects that are known to exist in today's gamefowl strains, especially in American and Old English Gamefowl. Cockers can do much to improve the quality of their gamefowl by becoming familiar with these defects and disqualifications, and eliminating as many as possible from their broodpens, and only entering those individuals in poultry shows and the pit that are free from such defects. By being persistent you will eventually eradicate these defects from your family or strain.

WHICH ARE SERIOUS AND WHICH ARE NOT: The question I get most often about defects and disqualifications is – *"which defects are serious and which are not?"* My usual answer is this - *"Any imperfection or fault that departs from the standard or overall health of the bird is a serious defect."* Another answer I will give is this – *"if the characteristic or trait, which is in question, is not an attribute that you want to perpetuate, it is a fault, a defect."*

Every part of the bird's body must complement the other. In other words, their form must compliment their function. If we were to look at commercial egg layers, it is easy to understand why they must have a body that compliments the ability to produce a lot of eggs. If we were to look at the commercial meat chicken, we would quickly understand why they must have the ability to gain weight in a short amount of time. If we were to look at general-purpose breeds, there is no question that they must have the ability to produce a fair amount of eggs, but also have a body that can produce enough meat to satisfy the average family. And if we were to look at the American Games, we can plainly see why they must have the body of an avian athlete, the mind of a gladiator, and the actions of a skilled magician. If they were to lack any one of these attributes, they would be eliminated fairly quickly. Out of all the fowl in the world, it is the American Games that are affected most by what we call "survival of the fittest." It is for this reason that they must be as perfect as possible. A so-called "little imperfection" could mean certain death to an American Gamecock in the pit.

When it comes to form and function of the bird, defects and disqualifications only hinder the bird's ability to perform properly. This could include such things as being out of condition; having the wrong shape; or having features which are quite alien to American Games. For example, an excessively feathered bird, known as a feather duster; a bird with a small tail; or a bird with a large head; or an absence of the proper carriage, such as a properly sloping back. It could be a health issue, such as a lack of constitutional vigor or exhibiting signs of disease or a physical disability.

SOME DEFECTS REQUIRE A SUBJECTIVE JUDGMENT: Although, these all constitute major faults, there are other faults which may call for culling but often require subjective judgment in deciding whether the defect is bad enough to warrant the maximum penalty. For instance, what constitutes a red eye? The true red eye is fiery and clearly quite red, but there are shades which are so near that most judges would not penalize an excellent bird because the eye is slightly pale. Defects of the comb as well as white earlobes are in this category. Is it a defect when the comb will be eventually dubbed anyways? When it comes to white earlobes, most breeders just trim the white parts off. The best thing to do is to use your own best judgment. Ask yourself, is this a trait that you "do" or "do not" want to perpetuate?

Here is a list of some of the more serious defects and disqualifications of American Games. The following defects must be guarded against when examining or selecting fowls for the breeding pen. Birds having the following defects should not be included in a "choice" breeding pen. If upon examination, the following defects are found, throw the bird out:

DEFECTS OF THE EYE: One means by which a bird can react to the environment is through the use of its special senses. The eyes of the bird are the most important of all these senses. The eyes of birds are located on the sides of the head. This lateral placement, plus the great mobility of the head, gives birds an extremely wide field of sight.

The particularly important role vision plays in the life of birds is reflected in every facet of the eye's anatomy and physiology. For instance, the eyes of birds make up a larger proportion of the head than those of mammals. Relative to their body size birds have enormous eyes.

Although the avian eye is quite similar to the eyes of mammals, the eyeballs of birds are flatter than the commonly spherical eyeballs of mammals. Even though birds have by far the keenest vision of all vertebrates, their visual acuity is not much greater than that of humans. Birds have the ability

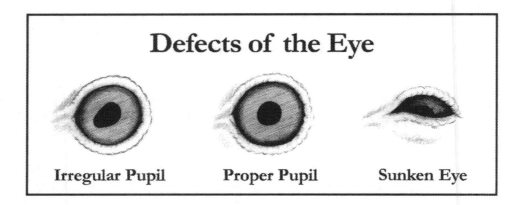

Defects of the Eye

Irregular Pupil **Proper Pupil** **Sunken Eye**

to process visual cues much faster than humans, but they do not see images much clearer than humans, they can only see the images more rapidly.

<u>Interesting note</u>: All birds possess color (chromatic) vision.

The eye demonstrates, very well, the bird's functionality, overall health and vitality. During an examination, this is the part of the bird that I will look at first. If there happens to be a defect of the eye, there is no reason to look any farther. I will cull the bird at that time. The most usual of these faults are as follows:

- **Odd Eye**: Where the two eyes are not alike, such as in the color of the eye and the size of the eye. They should be identical.
- **Irregular Eye or Pupil**: An eye that is malformed in any way (See illustration).
- **Sunken Eyes**: When the eyes are sunken into the eye socket, making the eye look hollow and depressed, or otherwise dull looking (See illustration).
- **Daw or Pearl Eyed**: This is a bird that has a very light-colored eye. In other words, a creamy white or very pale bluish gray colored eye. Dawed colored eyes are common in Oriental breeds such as Aseels, but are serious defects in American Games. Although it can be genetic, it can also be signs of a liver disease known as Lymphoid Leukosis.
- **Color Discrepancies**: This is any color other than the natural one for the breed, according to breed standards. Some judges may regard wrong eye color as a serious defect, while others just want to see that the eyes are identical.

DEFECTS OF THE HEAD: The standard descriptions of the head include – the skull, face, beak, comb and wattles (it also includes the eyes; however, we discussed this in the section prior to this one).

In spite of the remarkable consistency of chicken anatomy, from one class to another, each breed of chicken has evolved unique physical characteristics and traits (known as form) to compliment its purpose (otherwise known as its function). Although American Games have a very distinctive head shape, their comb type determines the size. Since the head is the most individualistic and the most characteristic region of a chicken's body, it is in its finer points of shape, size, as well as minuteness of details, such as eye color, comb type, face color, shape of beak that are often the best indicators of their genetic makeup, which determines, in a large part, their main purpose and function, as well as their general health and well being.

Most defects, which affect the head also affect their vision, and how well they are able to defend themselves against predators and in defending their territory against rivals. Most are defects that Mother Nature would eliminate naturally in the wild. The most usual of these faults are as follows:

Here is a good example of Crow or Snake Head.

- **Beetle Browed**: Where the eyebrow hangs heavily over the bird's eye, destroying the bird's peripheral vision. This is caused by a prominence or projection of the skull. This is best seen in breeds such as Malays. (See illustration).
- **Thick Headed:** Otherwise known as a "Beefy Head." This is a defect that is usually seen in fowl that have straight combs.
- **Crow or Snake Headed**: This is a head and beak that is narrow and shallow, like a crow. This is a serious defect.
- **Defects of the face:** Such as a foreign face color. A considerable white in the earlobe of American, English or Asiatic breeds and varieties of Gamefowl, or a considerable red in the earlobes of Mediterranean breeds and variety, is not desired. This is not so much a defect but a disqualification.

DEFECTS OF THE BEAK: Perhaps no other structure in the vertebrate world has been as variously adapted and modified as the avian beak. Chickens depend on their beaks, not only to obtain food, but also to preen their feathers, build their nests, perform courtship, and defend themselves from predators or rivals. Aside from feathers, the beak is surely the most quintessentially birdlike feature of the avian body.

Consisting of an upper and lower mandible, the beak is composed of a bony framework that is covered by a tough jacket of keratin that forms the visible shape of the beak. This light but effective horny covering of the jaws compensates for the loss of teeth. In proper form, the upper beak slightly overlaps the lower beak when the beak is closed. Birds have the ability to tear, rip, and crush food in their beaks, but the difficult work of chewing is performed by the gizzard in the stomach. Birds have thus moved much of the heavy business of chewing food

Defects of the Beak and Head

Beetle Browed
(Boney mass over the eye)

Twisted, Crooked or Crossed Beak

Sparrows Beak
(Long, narrow beak)

Gapped or Open Beak

toward their center of gravity, where the weight of the gizzard is less important to balance and maneuverability.

Most defects which affect the beak also affect the way they eat and drink, and how well they will be able to defend themselves against predators and in defending their territory against rivals, or in battle. These are defects that Mother Nature would eliminate naturally in the wild, and in short order too. The most usual of these faults are as follows:

- **Beak Deformities**: Such as broken; twisted; crooked or crossed beaks, where one mandible crosses over the other and do not meet squarely. These are defects that can interfere with the birds eating, thereby making it hard for the bird to eat enough food. It can also hinder his performance in the pit. This is not so much a defect but a disqualification (See illustration).
- **Sparrows Beak**: The shape of the beak should be crooked or hawk-like, pointed and strong at the base. American Games must have a good strong beak. If the beak is too long and not very wide, there's no strength. This is what is called Sparrows Beak (See illustration).
- **Gaped Beak**: Otherwise known as "Open Beak," this is where the upper and lower portions of the beak do not meet. In other words, there is a decided gap or space between the upper and lower mandibles, thereby making it hard for the bird to eat, drink, or get the proper bill hold in times of need, such as, when exhausted and fatigued in the pit (See illustration).

Double Pointed Comb.

DEFECTS OF THE COMB: The comb is the fleshy protuberance on top of the head of the fowl. Larger in the cocks than the hens, they come in various forms for different breeds and varieties of fowl; usually red in color they can also come gypsy or purplish-red. There are many varieties of combs, such as pea, straight (also known as single), rose, buttercup, cushion, strawberry, V-shaped, and walnut. However, the most common for American Games is pea and straight (*single*) combs.

Thumb Marked Comb.

For American Games, the condition of the comb is of very little concern. Normally the comb is eventually dubbed or trimmed by the time they are one year of age. However, you may still want to eliminate defects that affect the comb. The most usual of these faults are as follows:

- **Side-Sprig**: Side-sprig or otherwise known as "sprigs" is a well-defined pointed or projection, a fleshy material or growth, that is coming out of the side of a straight (*single*) comb, rather than the top of the comb. This is a fault in all straight (*single*) combed varieties. This is not so much a defect but a disqualification (See illustration).

Split-Comb.

A cock with a Side-Sprigged comb. Can you see how one little defect changes the look of an otherwise good bird?

A cock with a Lopped-Comb. Again, can you see how one little defect changes the look of an otherwise good bird?

- **Lopped-Comb:** This occurs when the comb of a straight (*single*) combed cock falls over to one side, far enough to obstruct his vision (See illustration).

- **Thumb-Marked Comb:** A disfiguring depression or indentations in the blade, which sometimes appears in the sides of a straight (*single*) comb. This is a defect (See illustration).

- **Split-Comb:** This is a defect where there is a definite division or split in the rear part of the blade of a straight (*single*) comb, or a divided comb that falls over on both sides. In some cases, the two parts overlap (See illustration).

- **Twisted Comb:** In this case, the front or rear of the comb is abnormally twisted, taking away from its normal shape and form. This is a defect that should be culled.

- **Other Miscellaneous Comb Defects:** A pronounced fold; a double pointed or a high blade on a straight (*single*) comb; absence of the spike or a telescope spike on rose-comb breeds and varieties, also a lopped rose-comb. A telescope spike is one that appears to be pushed back into the comb. These are all defects that should be culled.

- **Comb Foreign to the Breed:** Each breed must have the type of comb that is standard for that breed. Any comb foreign to the breed or variety should be rejected.

- **Poorly Dubbed Individuals:** In many cases, an unimpressive appearance is the result of a poorly dubbed bird. This is not so much a fault but of poor presentation, and affects the reputation of the breeder more than anything else. It shows everyone, who sees it, the level of your skills. Indication of poor dubbing is where the comb is trimmed either too high or is trimmed to close to the head. Another indication of poor dubbing is a head that looks course or has ragged edges where the wattles and earlobes were located, rather than a smooth, refined look. Although these examples indicate poor dubbing techniques, this is not so much a defect but a disqualification.

DEFECTS OF THE NECK: Birds have such large eyes in proportion to their skulls that they have largely lost the ability to move the eyeball within the eye socket of the skull. To restore their ability to see the world around them, and to compensate for the loss of the pectoral limbs for grooming feathers, which require constant maintenance, and other daily functions, birds have evolved long, strong, flexible necks, with complex muscular systems surrounding the cervical vertebrae. This allows the head and eyes to be moved very rapidly and effectively.

The muscles that surround the cervical spine are numerous. Adapted both to support the cervical vertebrae and to provide precise control over movement, they are important for the birds overall survival, in defending itself from predators and during battle with other cocks for territory. Defects of the neck affect the bird's strength, endurance and coordination. The most usual of these faults are as follows:

A cock with a Twisted-Comb. Can you see how one little defect changes the look of an otherwise good bird?

- **Thin or Poorly Developed Neck**: A thin neck indicates a weak neck.
- **Wry or Twisted-Neck**: Normally this is a neurological disorder, but can be genetic as well. Either way, it should be culled.

DEFECTS OF THE BODY: When discussing the body, we are talking about the portion which contains the trunk, the part exclusive of the head, neck, wings, tail, thighs, shanks and toes. The trunk of birds is rather compact and is divided into the back, rump, breast, belly, sides, and flanks. Often the sides and flanks are partly concealed by the wings and visible only when the bird is flapping his wings.

The most common fault is a back that is not broad at the shoulders, compact and flat. They are usually too long, narrow, and rounded, or they are simply too short. Another common fault is that of the incorrect angle of the body. This is due to the fact that the bird's skeletal system lacks the proper bone structure, and prevents him from standing properly, which knocks everything else out of balance. When showing American Games for exhibition, especially birds that are well formed and of good conformation, it is essential for them to be "pen trained." This will ensure that their posture (the bird's body and tail) is at the correct angle while being examined.

The breastbone is another common fault to be watchful of. They tend to be pointed and excessively deep or crooked, all faults that should be culled.

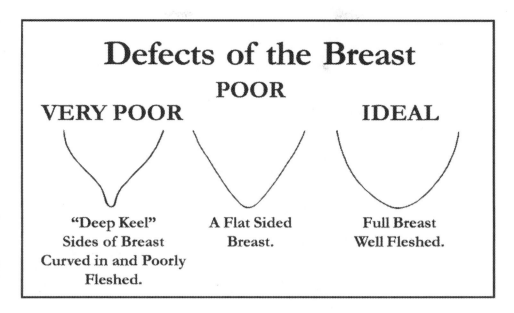

The most usual of these faults (defects of the body) are as follows:

- **Flat-Sided Breast:** This is a defect where the body lacks the normal curvature of the sides, which usually indicates a narrowness of the body. The bird's breast is long, deep and pointed, and the sides of the breast are flat. The proper breast enables the bird to have the correct formation of body. But in this case, the breast is irregular (See illustration).

- **Pointed Breastbone:** Also known as a Deep-Keel, this is where the keel bone extends well beyond the muscles of the breast (See illustration).

- **Crooked Keel or Indented Breastbone:** Usually caused by roosting too early, this is a condition that may or may not be inherited. Either way, it is a defect that is extremely undesirable in either sex. Look for a breast bone that is soft and flexible, and not crooked.

- **Shallow or Narrow Breasted:** Also known as "Weak-Chested. This is a breast that is neither prominent nor muscular, and is flat. The muscles of the thorax support the rib cage, power respiration, and fix the pectoral girdle to the body. In birds, the relation of the pectoral girdle to the chest wall musculature is crucial, for the "massive muscles of the breast" power both the down stroke and the upstroke of flight. For those of you that admire high breaking cocks, this is essential. Therefore, cocks that have a flat chest also have weak pectoral muscles. This is a serious fault.

- **Crooked or deformed Back:** Also known as a Raised Back, Wry-Back or Roached-Back, this is a defect where the back is crooked or arched near the hip joints, just before the tail, making them look humped back. This also creates a tail that has an incorrect angle. To inspect for this defect, simply run the palm of your hand over the birds back and observe whether the back is crooked or humped. In most cases, if you stand back and look at the bird, you will see a distinct "hump" on the back. Although this is not so much a defect but a disqualification, this is a serious fault.

Differences of Body Structure

These birds have:

- Bad carriages and are poorly balanced
- Cobby structures
- Long backs
- Wings that are high up the body (Known as Angel-Wings)
- Short station of legs
- Weak tails

These birds have:

- Proper carriages
- Properly balanced
- Proper backs
- Proper wings
- Proper station of legs
- Proper angle of tail

These birds have:

- Bad carriages and are poorly balanced
- Long, lengthy structures
- Short backs
- High station of legs
- In most cases, squirreled tailed too

Differences of Body Structure between members of the same family. This is especially the case with hybrid-crosses.

- **Round Back**: This is a back that is rounded instead of flat. American Games should have a nice flat back that is shaped like a heart.
- **Long Back**: This is a long, slim back that makes the overall body measurements look "out of balance." Overly long wings usually accompany this defect.
- **Cobby**: This is a body that is too short, round or compact in build. Birds such as this tend to be squirrel tailed as well.

Poor Carriage.

- **Rumplessness**: Basically, this is a bird that is without a tail. The rump is the part which carries and supports the tail feathers. Rumples birds have no tail, or a tail that is devoid of a full set of feathers.
- **A Proper Tail in Relation to the Body**: This is a defect where there is an absence of an abrupt break between back and tail. This is sometimes referred to as "Down Tail."
- **Poor Carriage**: This is a trait which is shown by their "out of balance" appearance. Fowl that have a bad carriage also have poor action and activity.
- **Poorly Developed Abdomen**: This is an abdomen that is large or one that is overly shallow, or one that is sagging and flabby. There is a term used to describe the proper abdomen that is called – "*to be Tucked-Up or Well-Tucked*," which simply means that the abdomen makes a straight upward turn from the end of the keel to the pubic bones, and is firm.
- **Other Defects of the Body**: Wrong shaped body, which includes a body that is lacking the proper cone shape. In other words, a body or back that does not taper properly from shoulders to stern; one that is too long or too short; a bird that looks dumpy and lacks good conformation and balance.

DEFECTS OF THE TAIL: The tail of an American Game is an integral part of the composition of the bird, and may make or spoil a particular specimen. When we think of birds we naturally focus on the wings, but the tail also plays an important role. Although a good tail is a must for balance, the tails main function seems to be to act as a rudder to help the bird steer properly when in flight or when breaking into the air. Long tails help birds maneuver as they fly, whereas short tails have a reduced ability to steer.

The tail of a bird is technically a small bony and fleshy structure marking the end of the vertebral column, but most people, including ornithologists, use the term "tail" to mean the feathers arising from the "official tail." The

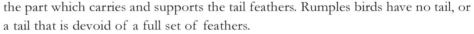

The Proper Tail of an American Game Cock and Hen

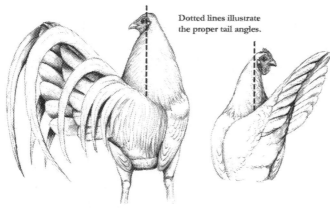

Dotted lines illustrate the proper tail angles.

Wry Tailed Cock and Hen

A cock with a Squirrel-Tail. Can you see how a defect such as this changes the overall look of a bird?

Split Tail.

feathers of the tail consists of good strong mains or primaries for support, good sickles, with good lesser sickles and side-hangers to protect the primaries.

Being that the tail is a complexity of form, function and beauty, it is therefore essential to understand the standard relating to the proper structure of the tail and its proper angle, as well as the correct color. The most usual of these faults are as follows:

• <u>**Wry-Tail**</u>: Simply put, wry-tail is where the main tail feathers are turned or carried permanently to one side of the body. In a much broader sense, it is a tail that is asymmetrical or lopsided, carried well out of kilter to the right or to the left side of the continuation of the backbone or vertical, instead of being straight behind the head, in line with the body. This is a serious defect (See illustration).

• <u>**Squirrel-Tail**</u>: Simply put, squirrel tail is a defect in which the main tail feathers are carried at an angle of more than 90 degrees. In a much broader sense, it is a tail that projects forward, well over the cocks back, past the 90 degree angle, toward the head, and extends beyond that of a perpendicular line. This is a line that is drawn through the base of the tail and is perpendicular with the ground. There are some cases of squirrel-tail where the tail bends sharply over the back, so much so, that it touches, or almost touches the head, like that of a squirrel. To allow for any inconsistencies, the tail must be carried at an angle of 75° degrees not exceeding 90° degrees. Therefore, a tail that is carried over 90° degrees is to be disqualified and culled (See illustration).

• <u>**Split-Tail**</u>: Also known as a divided tail, this is a defect in which there is a distinct and decided gap between the main tail feathers. This gap usually extends all the way down to the base of the tail. This results from the permanent absence of a feather or feathers, or from the improper placement of main tail feathers resulting in disarrangement. This is a serious defect in young birds and a disqualification in both adult cocks and hens (See illustration).

- **Gamy Tail**: This is a tightly folded, slim, tapering, whip like tail. This is a defect in American Games.
- **Faulty Tail Feathers**: This is a fault where the tail is not fully developed or grossly underdeveloped. For example, in cocks, where the sickle feathers of the tail lack the proper curvature; or the sickle feathers are carried at an incorrect angle; or is a tail that is loose, that is, one not closely and tightly folded. Another example would be the absence of sickle feathers.
- **Dropped Tail**: Also known as a

A cock with a Dropped-Tail. Again, can you see how a defect such as this changes the overall look of a bird?

Droopy Tail. This is a fault in American Games, but is the standard for such breeds as Malays, Aseels and other Asian Games (See illustration).

DEFECTS OF THE WINGS: Like the tail, the wings are an integral part of the composition of the bird, and may make or spoil a particular specimen. For American Games, it is the source of his power and propulsion while flying and maneuvering in the air, as well as in battle. It can be said that *"the bird with the best wings always wins."* It is therefore essential to understand the standard relating to the proper form and function of the wings.

As in most anatomic structures, the surface of the wing is determined largely by the supporting structures of the skeleton. The skeletal structure of the wing also provides the basic definitions of the two major flight feather groups of the wing, the primary feathers that are attached to the bones of the metacarpus, and the secondary feathers that are attached to the trailing edge of the ulna.

The feathers of the wing consist of the primary and secondary flights, the primary and secondary coverts, the wing bow, wing bar, shoulder butt and axial feather. The most usual of these faults are as follows:

- **Short-Wings**: This is a defect where the wings are so short they are carried above the tail. Also known as "angel's wings," this is a trait more common in hens than in cocks.
- **Long Wings**: This is a wing that is too long. It doesn't happen very often, but a wing that is too long is more of a hindrance than it is beneficial. The wings should meet easily in the rear area just below the tail, any more than that is an impediment and a defect.
- **Split-Wing**: One in which the feathers of the wing are so irregularly developed that a gap (or distinct separation) shows between the primaries and secondaries of the wing feathers. This abnormal division between primary and secondary feathers results from the permanent absence of the "Axial Feather." This is a disqualification. <u>Note</u>: Permanent absence of the axial feather is determined by the absence of the

feather follicle itself. Some say that split-wing is simply a slipped-wing that is carried to the extreme. This would be true if the axial feather was intact and undamaged. This is not so much a defect but a disqualification (See illustration).

- **Slipped-Wing**: This is a wing that does not fold closely nor held firmly in its proper position. There are a few ways to identify this problem. For instance, the individual feathers may overlap in a reverse order, such as over instead of under each other from outer to inner; or there may be a permanent tendency for the entire section of the wing (mainly the primaries) to be held outside or below the secondaries, instead of under and well tucked up. In other words, the primaries will simply sag (carried in a drooping position) when the wing is folded. Either way, both are serious defects. This condition is often associated with split-wing, in which primaries and secondaries show a very distinct segregation. This is not so much a defect but a disqualification (See illustration).

- **Goose-Wings**: This is a defect where the butts of the wings appear above the back, similar to that of a goose.

- **Angel-Wings**: This is a defect where the wings are carried up on the birds back. This is normally caused by wings that are too short. The wings of American Games should be carried low, enough to cover the thighs, as if they were protecting the thighs like a gladiators shield.

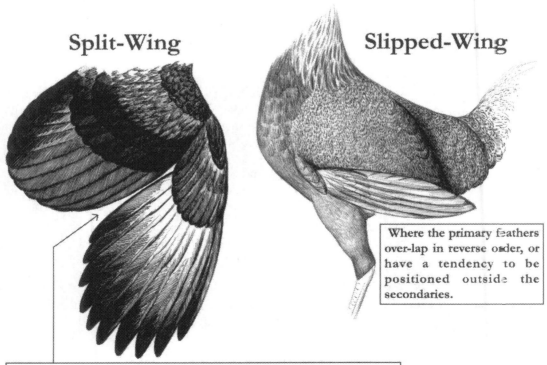

Split-Wing

Slipped-Wing

Where the primary feathers over-lap in reverse order, or have a tendency to be positioned outside the secondaries.

Where there is a distinct separation between the primary and secondary feathers, resulting from the permanent absence of the axial feather.

DEFECTS OF THE LEGS: Most breeders of American Games think that the legs consist of only two parts, the thighs and the shanks. But what they don't realize is that the thigh is divided into two parts, and has two functional sections.

Like most birds, the structure of the American Games hind limbs has four divisions: the upper thigh leg (femur), which is rather short and often hidden by body feathers; the lower thigh leg (tibia), which is elongated; the shaft (metatarsus); and the foot.

Note: if you were to look at a skeletal picture of a bird, you would notice that birds knees bend in the same direction that yours do, but the actual location of the knee can be confusing. Just as the actual length of the neck is hidden by their posture and feathers, so, too, is the thigh hidden from sight, making the ankle appear to be the knee.

The legs are an important asset to American Games. They are used for walking, running, scratching, propelling into the air, and for shuffling or fighting. It is the legs that put the action in the athlete, and the weapon in the warrior. The legs must be powerful and precise in every move they make. Without good legs the bird is completely useless. When it comes to the legs anything less than perfect is a fault. The most usual of these faults are as follows:

- **Cow Hocks or Weak Knees**: These are knees that are weak. They tend to slip out when the bird is in motion or is standing still. (Also known as slipped-hock or slipped-tendon).

- **Bow-Legged**: A deformity in which the legs are farther apart, or bowed, at the hocks than at the feet and knee-joints. A disqualification if a noticeable angle is evident at the hock when viewed from the front or back. This is a serious defect (See illustration).

- **Knock-Knees**: (Also known as "Knocked-Kneed" or ""In-Kneed"): A deformity in which the legs are closer together at the hocks than at the feet. A disqualification when a noticeable angle is evident at the hock. This is a serious defect (See illustration).

- **Straddle Legged**: Also called "Splayed Legs." This is a defect where the legs are slightly spread out at both sides as they stand or walk. Sometimes confused with knock-knees, except the hocks are farther apart. This can certainly be genetic, but can also be caused environmentally. Usually caused in the incubator or brooder by having a floor that is too slippery of a surface while the chicks are still young. Newly-hatched chick's legs slip and spread out and have difficulty standing. Unfortunately, this carries onto maturity. To reduce the environmental ricks of this infliction, use paper or coarse-woven cloth in hatch trays, and plenty of litter, such as wood shavings, in the brooders. This preventing the chick from slipping and helps them to stand upright.

- **Stork Legged**: This is a defect where the legs are straight, lacking the natural bend. In this case, they resemble that of a stork than an American Game. There should be a proper angle to the legs and thighs. One of my mentors, Tony Saville, likes to call it "Angulation." This is a serious fault, which is more common with birds that are high stationed (See illustration).

Proper Leg Angulation (front view)

Knock-Kneed

Proper Leg Angulation (side view)

Bow Legged

Stork or Straight Legged

Defects of the legs.

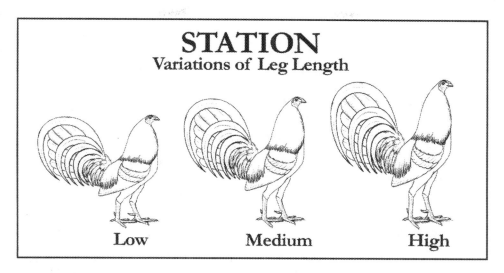

STATION
Variations of Leg Length

Low   Medium   High

- **Thin or Poorly Developed Thighs**: Underdeveloped thighs are a fault that affects the bird's strength, coordination, and accuracy when in battle, and encumbers the bird ability to evading predators as well. This is normally caused by the "Selective Breeding" of birds that are too high in station. When you elongate the leg, you elongate the muscles in the thighs, which in turn cause the muscles in the thighs to become thin. When the muscles in the legs become thin you weaken them.

- **Too Long Legged**: These are legs which are "overly long and slim," known as "Stilty." Some call this a bird having "High Station." Normally, they are weak and do not have the correct bend, one that follows the line of the body (See illustration).

- **Too Short Legged**: This is a lack of station. A serious fault with American Games (See illustration).

- **Stilt-Legged**: This is a defect where the bird walks stiff legged or with a gated step. By not moving their joints properly they lack agility and grace of movement.

- **Flat Shanks:** A term usually applied to a shank that is decidedly lacking in roundness of bone.

- **Scaly-Leg**: A faulty condition of the shanks and toes of a fowl caused by a small burrowing mite, and results in an encrustation or deposit upon and beneath the scales. This is not so much a defect but a disqualification (See illustration).

- **Rough, Uneven Scales**: This is a good indication of either old age or a bird that is raised under unfavorable conditions. To make sure you aren't getting an old, worn-out broodcock or hen, look for legs that are smooth and clean. This is not so much a defect but a disqualification.

- **Faulty Leg Color**: Color in the shanks is dependent on the breed, and may be white, yellow, olive, black, slate, carp, willow or some other specified shade. This may be varied by things such as feeding, conditions of their environment, the age of the bird and, whether a hen is in the lay. A laying hen will tend to lose pigment during the laying season. The type of land on which the birds are kept also affects the color, as does the natural food available. Running on grass tends to keep legs very clean and bright, but can be spoiled with mud and other unfavorable conditions.

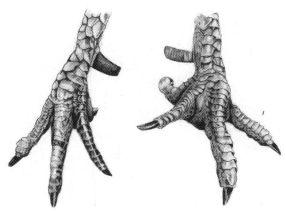

Legs affected by scaly-leg mites.

However, there are times when the foreign color is caused by hereditary influence. In this case, the shank, foot, or toe is of foreign color to the breed. A good example of this would be an olive leg with one yellow toe. This is not so much a defect but a disqualification. Another example would be that of dark spots on the shanks or toes of white or yellow-shanked varieties. This fault is in fact, a defect.

• **Feathered Shanks:** Another fault, although uncommon, is feathered shanks. These are featherlike growths on the shanks, feet, or toes of breeds required to have unfeathered shanks. This is normally seen in breeds such as Cochins. However, American and Old English Gamefowl have been known to produce offspring with feathers in the shanks and feet from time to time. These feathers are so small and are hard to see. Often they appear as small stubs or quills one--sixteenth to one-eighth of an inch long. This is a serious fault for all breeds and varieties that are known to be cleaned legged, especially American and Old English Gamefowl, and should be discouraged at all times. Keeping such birds out of the broodpen will eventually insure a family or strain that is practically free from this fault. This is not so much a defect but a disqualification (See illustration).

• **Other defects of the legs:** These are birds that are stiff legged or lacking agility; or birds that have thick, clumsy Legs; or birds that do not stand square on their legs; or have weak or buckled hock joints. These are all serious defects.

DEFECTS OF THE SPURS: Just as important as the legs they are attached onto; spurs have evolved into lethal armaments, and are used for both offence and defense. Although they are essential to the American Gamecock, this is one part of the bird that can be easily overlooked, as they are normally trimmed. There are some details of the spur, however, that should not be ignored. The most usual of these faults are as follows:

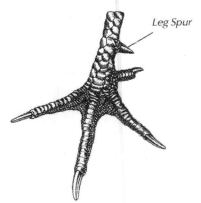

Leg Spur

The leg spurs of fowl: males, and sometimes females, develop bony outgrowths of the lower tarsometatarsus known as leg spurs, which are used as weapons during aggressive interactions with rival males.

• **Soft Spurs:** This is when the sockets of the spurs are soft and can be easily moved about by the fingers of the handler. This applies to cocks, not stags.

• **Missing Spurs:** Also known as a "slip-legged" bird, this is a cock that has had one or both spurs broken off even with the shank. Normally seen in hens, but sometimes occurs with cocks, missing spurs are also a heritable disorder.

- **Double Spurs**: This is a common trait for breeds such as Sumatra's, but for American and Old English Games is a serious fault.
- **Faulty Spurs**: Spurs can come in many sizes and shapes; they can also develop and point in many different directions. What you are looking for is that classic spur, one that is not too small or not to large in diameter. Look for spurs that point in the proper direction and have a slight curvature to them. Don't go by the length or condition of the spurs. Spurs can be easily twisted and slipped off, leaving a brand new one in its place. This is an old peddler's trick.
- **Position of the Spur on the Leg:** Also, look for spurs that are low on the leg. The lower the better.

DEFECTS OF THE FEET AND TOES: The feet and toes are constructed in such a way to give the bird proper support and balance. The foot and toes consist of the primary toe, the middle toe, the third toe, and the prop toe.

The feet are the bird's most immediate physical contact with their environment. For American Games, the feet are used for walking, running, scratching for food, and roosting. In the wild, they can fly, but only for a short distance, they spend most of their lives on the ground and in trees. The most usual of these faults are as follows:

- **Duck-Toe or Duck-Footed**: This is a weakness of the rear toe, known as the prop-toe. Duck-toe is a defect that disables the bird from propelling himself upward and forward into the air properly. Evidence of duck-toe, where the prop-toe, instead of laying spread out and flat on the ground, and positioned directly behind the foot, and straight back as it should, it lays close to the foot and points forward, thus resembling the foot of a duck. It is not really a disease in itself, but in American Games it is a serious defect. It is not wise to breed from birds exhibiting the condition. Some breeds are more prone to the trouble than others (See illustration).
- **Crooked Toes**: The toes are not straight, and are twisted or curled abnormally to one side or the other. Usually they are pointed inward when the bird is standing or in motion. Other times, the toes on the ends are pointed slightly outward. A bird with crooked toes is likely to be handicapped while scratching and foraging for food, as well as during mating (See illustration).
- **Web-Foot**: A condition in fowl, other than waterfowl, known as webbing of the toes. This occurs when the web unites the toes for a greater part of their length. This is not so much a defect but a disqualification (See illustration).
- **Splayed Toes**: These are toes that are overly spread and too wide apart (See illustration).
- **Long Slim Toes**: Toes that are overly long can be weak. It is true, the longer the better, as long as they are strong.
- **Down or Stubs between the Toes**: No feathers, whether they have quills (and are called stubs) or have no quills (down) are allowable between the toes of any bird in the gamefowl class.

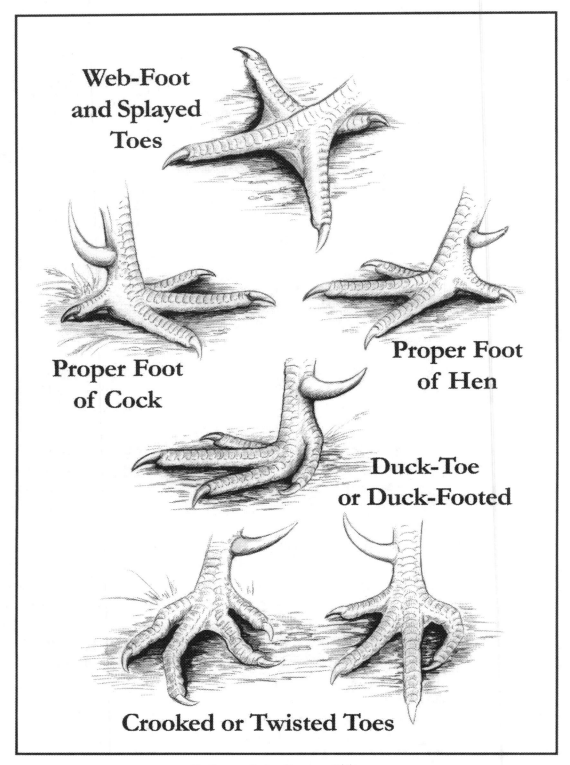

Web-Foot and Splayed Toes

Proper Foot of Cock

Proper Foot of Hen

Duck-Toe or Duck-Footed

Crooked or Twisted Toes

Defects of the Feet and Toes.

- **<u>Open Scaling On Shanks At The Approach Of The Toes</u>**: Indicating coarse and heavy insteps of the feet and toes, which is not conducive to good activity. This is not so much a defect but a disqualification.

- **<u>Long Nails</u>**: Long nails on a bird are an indication of inactivity and, if on free range or in a run, it is certain that the bird in question is a loafer and should be culled. If kept in an inside training pen for too long the nails will grow because the bird cannot forage, and therefore, when judging it becomes difficult to know whether to penalize. However, it is a duty for the breeder to ensure that nails are kept short so they should be penalized. This is not so much a defect but a disqualification.

Bumble Foot.

- **<u>Bumble Foot</u>**: A symptom of bumble foot is where the ball of the foot and area around the toes will be swollen and full of pus. It will cause birds to be lame. This is a condition to the feet, which is caused by birds dropping to the hard ground from the roost, without using their wings. It starts out as a bruise and swells. It eventually opens and becomes a sore and gets infected. This is caused by a bacteria know as staphylococcus.

- **<u>Other Examples Are</u>**:
  - Color of Legs and toes that is foreign to their breed, variety, or strain.
  - Thick insteps on the feet and toes.

<u>DEFECTS OF THE PLUMAGE</u>: The term plumage is the collective feather covering of the entire body of a fowl, including the head, neck, wings, and tail, and anywhere specified for breed requirements. Although very colorful, the plumage of fowl is used for protection from the elements and for camouflage. Plumage is a good indication of health and vitality, as well as heritable traits. The most usual of these faults are as follows:

- **<u>Poor Neck Hackles</u>**: These are cocks with hackle feathers that are sparse, inadequate for the breed or variety, or excessively short. Sometimes the hackle feathers are twisted.

- **<u>Poor Sickles</u>**: Poorly developed sickle and lesser sickles in the cock.

- **<u>Twisted Feather or Feathers in Wings or Tail</u>**: This is a defect where the shaft and web of the feather are twisted out of shape. This is a serious problem if found in the wing primaries or secondaries; the main tail or sickle feathers. The term "Twisted Flights" is a fault or imperfection of the main wing feathers. This is not so much a defect but a disqualification.

- **<u>Short Tail Coverts</u>**: This is a defect seen in the hen.

- **<u>Broken, Soft or Rotten Plumage</u>**: This, I'm sure does not need a whole lot of explanation. However, this condition can be caused environmentally but certainly has a genetic basis as well. This is not so much a defect but a disqualification.

- **Missing Tail Feathers**: This is a defect where the sickle feathers or main tail feathers are permanently missing or broken.
- **Loose Feathering**: In American Games feathers, especially that of the body must be hard, short, and rather tight.
- **Feathering Not Tight**: This is especially true in the breast area.
- **Curved Sickles on a Hencock-Type Bird**: (Also Known as a Henny) In this case, all feathers (color and shape) should resemble that of a hen. Henny's should be devoid of all sickles, lesser sickles, and side hangers.
- **Shafting**: Also known as a bird that is shafty. This is a color characteristic in which the shaft of a feather is either lighter or darker on the stem than the color of the web. A standard requirement in some breeds; a defect in others. <u>Note</u>: The shaft is the stem or base of the feather, and the extension of the quill, which runs the entire length of a feather to which the barbs are attached.

An example of shafting. This is a defect that occurs in Stippled varieties.

PLUMAGE COLOR: For the selective breeder, there are great opportunities in the matter of plumage color. All he must do is decide what color he wants to carry on. Yet he must remember that each breed has a preferred color and he should strive to reach that perfection. Each breeder should decide for himself the exact shade which he wants his birds to have, and select constantly for that shade. Only by constant selection for this ideal will he be able to eliminate color variations in his family or strain. With that said, there are matters of plumage color that are important to consider.

- **Foreign Color**: This is a matter of the wrong color or a partial wrong coloring. In other words, it is a color, in any part of a fowl, which differs greatly from the color prescribed by the standard. Such as a bird with a black tail showing white marks. This may be acceptable if there is a strong element of white in the bird. For example, a Black-Breasted Red American Game with white legs and is Pile bred. This can be a disqualification in some cases and a defect in others. Either way, the standard must be the final word. Other examples include:
  - **Black Quills in White Varieties** – This is a fault where black appears in the quills of the primaries or secondaries of white varieties. This is not so much a defect but a disqualification.
  - **Foreign Color In Any Part Of The Plumage** – A good example of this would be that of foreign color appearing anywhere in the plumage of white varieties except slight gray ticking. This is not so much a defect but a disqualification.
  - **Brassiness** - A term descriptive of a light yellowish metallic cast, commonly found in the plumage of white and partially-white varieties, usually on the back and wings.

- o **Foxiness** – A term used to describe a shade of rusty or excessive redness, on the wing-bay of partridge hens. This is a trait that is undesirable, and should be accepted as a defect. May be hereditary or environmental, such as affected by exposure to sun or affected by certain substances in the diets (such as too much corn).
- o **Mossy** - Confused or indistinct marking, smudging, or peppering. A defect in most breeds.
- o **Sootiness or Smoky Undercolor** - This is a defective grey or smokiness creeping in where it is not wanted, usually in the undercolor of a bird.
- o **Creaminess** - A fault normally seen in white birds.
- o **Smut** - This is a defect where there is a Dark or smutty color in an undesirable place, such as the breast or in the undercolor of the bird. For example, there may be black feathers, which are uncharacteristic for the breed (Such as Yellow Birchens, Gingers, Blues, Whites, and Piles), showing up in the breast. Although, most American Games are Black-Breasted, any color foreign to the breed is a fault.

DEFECTS OF WEIGHT AND SIZE CHARACTERISTICS: Normal weights for an American Gamecock are 4 lbs 12 oz to 5 lbs 8 oz. Cocks that run much bigger than the norm for the strain are usually loose feathered, clumsy fowl. Hens normally weight 4 lbs to 4 lbs 14 oz. The most usual of these faults are as follows:

- • **Weight Loss of American Games:** Cocks that fall more than 1½ lbs. below their standard weight; and hens that fall more than 1 lb. below their standard weight. This is not so much a defect but a disqualification.
- • **Weight Loss Of General-Purpose Breeds**: Roosters and hens, such as Plymouth Rocks, Rhode Island Reds, New Hampshire's, and Wyandotte's that fall more than 2 lbs. below their standard weight.
- • **Extremes in Size**: These are birds that are noticeably too small (stunted) or birds that are extremely large, also known as "Shakes or Shakebags," Fowl that are stunted cannot attain full size, and usually lack strength, vigor and good health. Larger cocks cannot be matched in Derby's or Mains because of their large size. Usually over 6 pounds. If Shake cocks are matched, it is done without any regard to differences in weight.

DEFECTS OF DISPOSITION AND BEHAVIORAL CHARACTERISTICS: Darwinian Theory provides a powerful approach to studying the evolution of all living things. The theory suggests that the attributes of species, including their behaviors, have evolved through reproductive competition, and therefore should help individuals reproduce successfully. This behavioral trait, such as fighting for territory, helps an individual to leave as many surviving descendants as possible.

Consider the fact that birds are often aggressive toward other members of their species, especially during the breeding season, as they stake out breeding territories. Some territories are small, some are large. For American Games, it is wherever they are standing at the time. If two contestants for a territory come in contact with one other, an all-out fight will ensue. For most chickens, physical aggression is resolved without serious injury between the opponents. Even when a bird, who has no territory, invades another's territory, the intruder typically flees at once when challenged by the occupant of that territory. However, due to the fact that American Games territory is so large, and its boundaries change constantly, fighting usually results in death.

For American Games, this is a trait that has been perpetuated for more than 2,000 years. This dominance of territory, which we call gameness, is something they must have in order to be true American Games. Whether you are a cocker or a gamefowl enthusiast, they must maintain the characteristic of gameness. I believe if they lose their desire to defend their territory (also known as function and purpose), conformation of body (also known as form) will disappear as well. Before you know it, not only will they act like the average barnyard chicken, they will look like one too.

Although they must be game, they must also have good temperament, this is important in both the cock and the hen. They should have a good disposition around people at all times. The most usual of these faults are as follows:

- **Lack of Gameness**: Any Signs that would indicate a lack of gameness, such as hacking, sulking, running, or a total lack of interest in other cocks. For American Games, this is a serious fault. Cocks such as this are also called dunghills. The name derives from that of "manure piles" on oldtime farms.

    o **A Sulker:** is a cock that, after fighting for a time, stops, and does not fight, even though he is able to continue.
    o **Hacking or Under-Hack:** this is a cock that will not show or fight. He will not put up his hackle feathers. Sometimes this is due to being fought at an early age, they are simply too young. This also occurs when there is dunghill blood in the family.

- **Manfighting**: The best time to identify this fault is when they are young stags and pullets. Look for young birds that are highly strung, to the point that they are "crazy" acting whenever you come near their pens. When you pick them up they have a wide-eyed look of fear, and they never settle down. What you will find is, as they mature, the hens will continue to be highly strung and crazy acting, but the cocks will turn that fear into aggression, and become manfighters. They will attack you at every opportunity. Birds with bad temperament of any kind can be caused by genetic or environmental influences. Any birds which have a tendency to be aggressive or have aggressive behaviors towards their handlers should be culled. Birds such as these are dangerous and problematic at best. Furthermore, if not eliminated from the breeding program the behavior will be reproduced in their offspring.

- **Nervous or Skittish Behavior:** Birds that are high-strung and easily excitable are a burden and nothing but trouble. Hens with these problems tend to produce pullets and hens that are just like them, and produce stags and cocks that are usually manfighters.

- **Poor Mannered Cocks**: The cock must be courteous and considerate with the hens and chicks at all time. Cocks that compete for food, bully the hen, or harm the chicks, are cocks which should be culled.

DEFECTS OF HEALTH AND ENVIRONMENTAL CHARACTERISTICS: These are disqualification which can be eliminated by providing proper care. If you get a chance to visit the breeder in person, stop to listen for any coughing or sneezing throughout the yard. When a chicken catches a cold, chances are good the whole yard will come down with it. I knew an old cocker who would whistle whenever he walked through his yard. This would cause the birds to pause in their tracks, allowing coughs and sneezes to be heard more easily. The most usual of these faults are as follows:

> • **Any Sign of Disease or Sickness**: Broodfowl must be constitutionally sound at all times. Any indication of weakness in health, such as stamina, lack of activity and alertness, or lack of constitution and vigor must be culled.

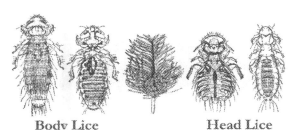

Body Lice   Head Lice

Lice Eggs (Nits)
on Base of Feathers

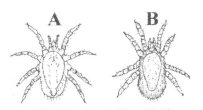

(A) Northern Fowl Mite
(B) Common Red Poultry Mite

The most common external parasites.

> • **External and Internal Parasites**: A well-kept bird of any age is always parasite-free, which you can check by looking under the wings and around the vent. External parasites such as lice and mites, as well as feather mites (evidence by damaged web of feathers), and fleas, or any other pest that might be on the bird can be easily seen. An infestation of internal parasites, such as, worms often causes diarrhea that will stick to their vent feathers; the bird will also display loss of weight and a pale face. This is not a defect but is a disqualification at the shows.

> • **Missing or Malformed Appendages**: This includes toes, spurs or eyes, or in the case of a slipped beak, where the upper mandible has been lost and never heals hard again. This is not so much a defect but a disqualification.

GENERAL CONDITION OF THE BIRD: It is not the purpose here to discuss selection in general. However, when selecting future broodfowl, remember, the only bird worth keeping is the one that meets practical requirements, such as standard breed characteristics and traits that are beneficial to the owner. The general condition of the bird determines their overall value. Look for these signs:

> • **Out Of Condition**: This is a bird that lacks balance, fitness, or alertness. For example, a bird that looks mopey or mellow eyed, or has a listless poise, or a dull looking comb, or a bad carriage or action. Any bird that is lacking in fire and spirit indicates a weakness of constitution and should be culled. This also includes birds that have too coarse of bone, are soft fleshed, or are not well muscled.

Other Defects And Disqualifications: The most usual of these faults are as follows:

- **Fowls That Are Deformed In Any Manner**: Any other evident sign of weakness or deformity or defect, which is in opposition to the Standard of Perfection. Such as, wrong conformation of body, also known as "type." Wrong color of plumage, one specified by its breed and variety. Evidence of crossing with another breed (such as an American Games with that of an Aseel).

- **Color Abnormalities**: Also known as "Sota" (Pronounced So-tah), a term used to describe a bird that has different colored toes, legs, or eyes. For instance, a bird might have a yellow leg and a green leg; or green legs with yellow toes; or different colored eyes. This is a defect.

- **Any Evidence of Physical Weakness**: For example: injury; sores; or sickness. This is not so much a defect but a disqualification.

Here are defects that should be taken into consideration when selecting and judging fowl, but understand that the following defects are not serious enough to eliminate the bird from your breeding program.

- Eye injured or destroyed.
- Eye color that is required to be red, but is lighter shaded to orange.
- Broken or missing feathers.
- Broken or slipped beak, normally caused by fighting through the wire.
- Broken or missing toes, normally caused by fighting through the wire.
- Broken or missing spurs, but only if caused by the environment, not genetic.
- White streamers in the tails of Black-Breasted Reds and Light-Red varieties.
- Poor barring or black feathers in American Game Doms.
- Hens with green colored legs that come from a yellow legged strain, but only if this color is sexed linked.
- Foreign color legs in a Spangled bird.
- Comb with too many or too few points.
- Loosely fitting earlobes.

These are very common defects seen in many of our American Gamefowl families. Birds possessing these undesirable characteristics either inherit them or have been grown under unfavorable conditions.

Everyone who breeds chickens and gamefowl should examine their birds carefully for defects and disqualifications. As a good friend of mine once told me - *"The overall*

When selecting future broodfowl, the only bird worth keeping is the one that meets standard breed requirements. Then and only then, can such characteristics and traits be beneficial to the owner. Remember, the general condition of the bird determines their overall value.

assessment of a bird should be that of a "downgrading or reduction," with the result that he is placed below birds, which do not have decided defects or disqualifications, or have features which are exaggerated, but present a combination of superior characteristics and traits of the appropriate quality and excellence." Whatever you do, do not use birds for breeding that have any of these faults. You will only perpetuate the fault. Also, only enter fowl for competition in poultry shows, or the pit, that are free of these faults. They should be the exemplar of form, function and beauty, and a good representative of American Games.

*Note of interest: Although there are numerous defects that occur in different varieties and strains of American Games, which are given in this chapter, another place to find information on defects and disqualifications is the Standard of Perfection. When birds are judged at exhibitions, the "cut" or amount deducted from 100% (the perfect score) is indicated in the Standard.

THE REGRESSIVE NATURE
OF LITTLE FLAWS AND IMPERFECTIONS

Different breeds and varieties have their own peculiar defects, and American Games are no different. These defects are serious handicaps to the specimen's worth, not only as broodfowl but for exhibition and pitting purposes as well.

Many cockers and backyard breeders are unaware of the seriousness of breeding from defective broodfowl. They often fail to realize how their family lines will regress from the high standard we all look for and count on to something very mutant and malformed. If allowed to appear in the broodpens, defects can become a great detriment to your breeding program, even if done just once. If defects are not culled from the broodpen, you will transform them from the true American Game to just a mere chicken, and in a relatively short amount of time.

I have a lot of cockers and backyard breeders telling me – "*how hard it is to cull something that looks so good, except for that one little defect.*" I know the feeling, believe me! As a young man, I remember having a stag that was perfect in every way, let me tell you something, he was beautiful! The only problem was, he had a defect, called duck-toe. So I decided to use the "Blanket Theory," by breeding the stag to a hen that I knew was free of duck-toe. The result was interesting. Half the offspring had the duck-toe the other half did not. So I decided to cull the ones showing the defect and keep the others. The following season I took the best of the best from the offspring I produced and I bred

the best stag to a hen of a different family and a pullet to a cock of a different family, and what did I get? All the offspring came out duck-toed. I was forced to cull the whole lot of birds. Could you imagine what would have happened if I would have breed them haphazardly into my family of fowl? The whole family would have been ruined.

Years later, I got another stag that was beautiful in every way but he had the duck-toe defect. Having a hard time culling him, I held onto him for three years trying to make up my mind what to do. Finally, after some recollection of what had happened years before, I decided to cull him, and let me tell you something, I am glad I did! You must understand that if you do not cull that individual from the breeding program, you are only perpetuating the defect. Before you know it, your whole yard will be filled with birds that carry that defect.

There are times when breeding to recessive characters is a good way to go. For instance, birds that are red, green legged, and straight combed are ones that will breed true for those characteristics, every time.

MOST DEFECTS AND DISQUALIFICATIONS ARE RECESSIVE IN NATURE: which means, once in your yard they are very hard to eliminate. That is why it is best to cull them as soon as they are identified. Breeding to a defective bird will certainly perpetuate the fault, and, as I said earlier, if you are not careful, your entire flock will express the fault, forever!

Remember, breed a dominant trait to a dominant trait and you will get a dominant trait. As long as they are homozygous (same) for that trait, it will be expressed as a dominant trait every time. Breed a dominant to a recessive, such as a defect, and the dominant trait will be expressed, but it will now carry the recessive trait (or defect) as well. They are now heterozygous (different) for those traits. The recessive trait (or defect) will remain hidden, but only until it is bred to another who carries the same recessive trait (or defect). Once that happens, both the dominant and recessive traits are expressed, which means half the offspring will look fine but half will express the defect. If you should breed two individuals that express the same recessive trait (or defect) the dominant trait will be eliminated forever! It would no longer exist in that family, and the recessive trait (or defect) will be expressed by your entire flock as a homozygous (same) trait forever. That is what happens when you decided to breed fowl that carry defective traits. Most defects tend to be recessive, which means they are easy to introduce into the family, but very hard to eliminate.

Do not get caught in the trap, thinking that – *"Gee, the bird is so perfect in every way except for the "small" defect. I will just breed him this one time and no harm will be done."* Think again!

HOW DO DEFECTS REACT TO SELECTION WHEN TRYING TO ELIMINATE THEM? Defects which persist in a family or strain, in spite of constant selection against them, are usually recessive. Recessive traits can be troublesome simply because they are capable of staying hidden, until they are mated with another bird that carries the same recessive trait. Dominant traits are much easier to eliminate. Any dominant defect can be eliminated, at once, merely by excluding it from the broodpen. Since any birds carrying a dominant trait must show the trait, by eliminating the trait from the broodpen, it prevents its being transmitted to future offspring. This is not true of recessive traits, since they may be transmitted by birds not showing the trait at all.

The recessive nature of the More Common Traits: As far as dominant and recessive traits are concerned, it is good to know that straight (*single*) combs are recessive in a pea-comb variety, and pea-combs are recessive in a rose-comb variety. Also, Red plumage is recessive to Grey plumage, and green leg is recessive to yellow leg, and yellow leg is recessive to white leg. We will talk more about this later in the book as well.

WHEN YOU HAVE NO CHOICE BUT TO BREED BIRDS WITH KNOWN DEFECTS: I advise anyone who discovers a defect or disqualifications of any kind to cull them, and I mean cull ruthlessly. In general, it is unwise to breed birds showing defects or disqualifications. In the first place, a disqualification, if reproduced, causes the birds to be unfit either for exhibition or for the pit; in the second place, disqualifications are likely to be defects which are more or less common and troublesome to the breed or variety, and therefore, quite likely to be reproduced later down the road. With that said, I will continue…

There are times when it is impossible to cull that bird. Mostly, for reasons such as (except for the defect or disqualification) the bird is extraordinary and shows excellence in many ways, more than the other birds in the family. Or, more importantly, you lack the number of specimens to select from, and you would rather breed the defective bird rather than bring in outside blood. In either case, the bird is obtained for breeding, and although the consequences are many, here are your choices of action.

The judgment goes to the individuality of the breeder himself. He is the deciding factor. He must determine whether this is wise or not. The advisability of breeding birds with defects really depends largely upon the frequency of the occurrence (which is the tendency toward producing the same defect or disqualification), and the seriousness of that particular defect or disqualification of the family as a whole. If the bird, which possesses the defect or disqualification, is an outstanding individual in all other respects, and there are no other birds that can take his place, it is often advisable to breed it. But there are times when it is better to discard than to use it, especially if the family shows a tendency toward this defect or disqualification. In any case, when such a bird is used, the opposite sex of the mating should be selected with special care to offset the defect or disqualification.

Many defects and disqualifications are due to accident or certain forms of deformity. For instance, a crooked breastbone, which is usually due to too early roosting, or the "occasional" crooked or roach-back that is thrown by normal individuals shouldn't cause the breeder too much concern.

However, defects, such as duck-toes, wry or squirrel-tail or even split-wings are defects that should always be culled. Always! These are common and are inheritable in some breeds of gamefowl, while in others it is very rare and less inheritable. In any case, only a superior of excellence of a disqualified individual justifies its use as broodfowl.

COMMON DEFECTS AND DISQUALIFICATIONS
AND THEIR GENETIC INFLUENCES
The hereditable qualities of faulty and defective characters and traits

Here in this part of the chapter, some of the more important defects and disqualifications are discussed and briefly considered. Here we will be able to better determine whether they are genetic or environmental. And if they are genetic, we will learn their genetic nature and whether they are dominant or recessive. This is important to know when breeding and perpetuating a strain or special line of fowl. The idea is to perpetuate the desired traits and eliminate the undesirable traits, the defects and disqualifications, which are certainly detrimental to the family. However, some defects are harder to eliminate than others.

The knowledge you will gain in this part of the chapter will aid you in the selection and breeding of your fowl. Remember this phrase – *"Selective Breeding Is the Only Cure."* As one of my mentors once told me, *"It is through Selective Breeding that you have all the power!"*

THE BENEFIT OF EXHIBITING YOUR FOWL, AND WHY THE JUDGE IS YOUR BEST FRIEND: At exhibitions, birds which possess defects and disqualifications are prohibited from winning a prize, and for good reason too. The reason for this? When you win a prize, what the judge is telling you, is that your bird is a good representative of its breed, that your bird is excellent in every way, and is a good specimen for perpetuating his blood. He is also telling you that all his attributes are worth repeating, generation after generation.

Birds that are disqualified should never be used in the breeding pen. They are not specimens that you want to perpetuate. By following the advice of the judge, he can save you years of trial and error, and certainly some hardship. So praise the judge that has the guts to disqualify your bird, don't criticize him. He is on your side more than you will ever know.

MANY DEFECTS AND DISQUALIFICATIONS ARE INHERITED: In addition to the more common defects and disqualifications already mentioned in this chapter, there are a number of defects which are heritable, which should be eliminated from all breeding improvement programs. These are very common to all fowl, especially in American and Old English Games, but should be culled as soon as they are identified.

Some of the more common of hereditary defects and disqualifications are caused by recessive genes, meaning they show up only when two birds are mated that carry the same gene. However, there are some that are dominant, which is good news. This means that they are easier to eliminate.

THE MOST COMMON OF THESE DEFECTS AND DISQUALIFICATIONS

Here are some of the most common undesirable traits that are influenced by hereditary factors, which can be perpetuated or eliminated by Selective Breeding of dominant and recessive traits, these include:

THE INHERITANCE OF - "LACK OF PIGMENT IN RED-EYED BREEDS": This is rather common, but is an inherited weakness. Brown or dark eye color is dominant to red, especially in crosses between American Game Black-Breasted Reds and other varieties of American Games, such as Blacks, Black-Breasted Black-Reds and Brown-Reds. It is also controlled by a sex-linked gene.

Pearl or Daw eyed birds inherited this trait from Oriental fowl, such as Aseels. However, a more alarming factor is that it can also be caused by disease as well, such as Liver Leukosis complex.

THE INHERITANCE OF – "CROW-HEAD": Otherwise known as sparrows head. However, don't confuse this with sparrow's beak, they are a little different. This is a defect which is caused by a delayed lethal condition, which has an effect on the skeletal development of the bird.

Birds with this condition are normal at hatching time but develop abnormally from eight weeks of age to maturity. There is a progressive shortening of the head bones and beak during development, thus leading to the "crow-head" appearance. Inheritance is believed to be recessive. Studies have discovered, from mating broodfowl, where both showed the trait, that 20 percent of the offspring were crow headed.

A Crow-Headed bird.

THE INHERITANCE OF – "BEAK ABNORMALITIES": There are several types of defective beaks that are known to be inherited in chickens and gamefowl. The most common are expressed in chick embryos, but the majority of these are never seen because they die during the later stages of incubation, although, a few do hatch. Many of these, such as the absence of the upper portion of the beak; the shortened upper beak; and the defective lower beak, are largely lethal to the developing embryo. They simply cannot pip their way out on the shell at full term. Most of the time these defects are not detected unless unhatched eggs are broken and the embryos are examined.

This abnormality is usually caused by a lethal gene, but also results, as do other conditions, from an accident in development, sometimes induced by an unfavorable environment. As you can see, such factors can be contributory to poor hatchability and tend to complicate any analysis of the inheritance of hatchability.

THE INHERITANCE OF – "CROSSED-BEAKS": Also known as "crooked-beak," it's a more common type of beak deformity, and is found in many breeds of chickens and gamefowl. This type of beak abnormality is greatly influenced by incubation conditions but is inherited as well.

A Crossed-Beak bird.

This defect usually does not develop until the chick is one or two months of age, with maximum expression developed by the time they are three or four months of age. These are chicks that were normal at hatching time and developed the abnormality later.

There are various types of expression of this condition, some of which are slight, and others which are rather extreme. The abnormality may affect either the upper or lower beak, but the upper beak is more often the affected part. It will develop a lateral bend more often to the right, which may vary from only the tip being affected to the whole upper beak being affected.

Like I mentioned earlier, the lower beak is usually unaffected, except that, since it is not used for pecking, the end is not worn down as much as in normal fowls and one side is worn more than the other. At maturity the tip of the upper beak tends to curl downward.

In some birds, where the upper beak is normal, but the lower one is twisted, there is very little known of this condition or its causes. However, birds with the upper beak straight or normal, but much shorter are sometimes found in families showing crooked or crossed-beaks, and the two forms are probably genetically identical.

This makes it necessary to examine every breeder carefully in families where the deformity is troublesome. In the most extreme expression, the upper beak crosses the lower one so much that the bird has difficulty eating. In extreme crossing the lower beak becomes elongated, thus aggravating the problem of eating.

The genetic factor: Crooked or crossed-beak is inherited, but they are not sure of its exact mode of inheritance. A condition described as "twisted-beak" was found by Mr. Hutt, in 1932. He suggested, based on his own data, that it was probably inherited as a simple autosomal recessive. Since then, further studies, which were very extensive, showed that this type of crooked or crossed-beak is indeed hereditary and recessive, but is of a somewhat complicated inheritance. Apparently only a small proportion of the birds homozygous for crooked or crossed-beak are visibly affected.

Another type of crooked or crossed-beak was studied, in which chicks exhibited the defect at hatching. They found this congenital type only in White Leghorns and crossbred birds of Leghorn ancestry. It differed from other types only in that some chicks with crooked or crossed-beak became normal as they advanced in age. Crosses between this congenital type of crooked or crossed-beak and the late onset type produced only normal birds. When birds with congenital crooked or crossed-beak were mated, they produced a higher proportion of affected offspring than did the late onset type.

Conclusion: Birds with crooked or crossed-beaks can survive, especially if the beaks are trimmed. The variation in which the upper beak is straight but shortened is more likely to be fatal before maturity, because of the difficulty in feeding.

Ordinarily, if all birds showing even the slightest indication of the deformed beak are eliminated from the broodpens, this defect can be controlled to the point that it will not cause any great trouble.

THE INHERITANCE OF – "A SHORT LOWER BEAK": Also known as a "short mandible," this is a condition in which the lower mandible is shortened to about half the length of the upper beak. In some cases the ramus of the mandible, or rami, located in the mid-region of the skull, will buckle up or down, and when bowed up will result in a right-angle bending of the shortened mandible (right angles to the normal plane). This situation will cause the mouth to be permanently propped open.

About 50 percent of affected embryos will hatch, but few of the chicks will survive, normally due to the inability to eat or drink. Those that do survive, once they reach 5 or 6 months of age, will have a lower mandible that is slightly shorter in length than their sibs. However, due to a persistent downward curving of the upper beak, they will have to be trimmed frequently.

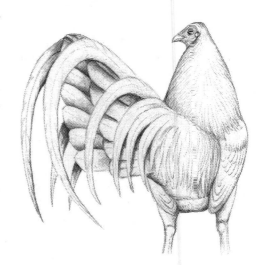

The genetic factor: In studies, where a series of matings were carried out using birds that were (1) carriers of the trait but did not show the trait; (2) birds that were normal; (3) and birds that were affected, all showed that the trait was inherited as a single autosomal recessive character. Other studies, where the mating consisted of birds that both were affected (short lower x short lower), out of a hundred eggs that were incubated, only 42 hatched. Out of the ones that hatched 3 chicks were normal and 39 chicks were affected with the defect. What does this tell us? It indicates that the trait is variable in its expressivity. The 3 exceptions suggest that some birds may not show the character though they are homozygous for it. Short mandible must be classified as a semi-lethal mutation.

A cock with wry-tail.

THE INHERITANCE OF – "A SHORT UPPER BEAK": This mutation affects the upper beak as well as the long bones of the appendages, such as the wings and legs. However, the wing bones are less affected than the leg bones. Although the shortening of the leg bones is the most common characteristic of this trait, it is most apparent in the tarsometatarsus.

Although the upper beak can be shortened by amounts varying from one-sixteenth of an inch to half its total length, there seems to be no correlation between degree of beak shortening and degree of limb shortening.

Studies showed that out of a hundred eggs incubated, only 14 of them hatched. Out of the ones that hatched very few survived. Early mortality was high due to eating difficulties. Of those surviving to maturity, the beak remained short in some, while it developed to a normal length in others. Some developed a crossed beak with the upper beak curvature being more frequently to the right.

The genetic factor: Genetic analysis of this condition shows that it results from the action of a single autosomal recessive gene. By selecting against the lethal action of this gene, in five or six years, you may be able to increase their hatchability to 75 percent. However, the best remedy is to cull in favor of normal beaks.

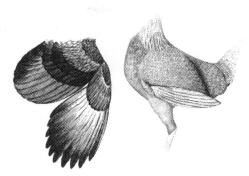

Defects of the wing.

THE INHERITANCE OF – "WING DEFECTS":
These include defects, such as split-wing and slipped-wing. The genetic factor concerning these traits is really quite simple. They appear to behave as recessive traits. Which means, if you breed two individuals that carry the trait but don't show it, they will produce 50 percent of the offspring that have the defect and 50 percent that don't. If you should decide to breed individuals that happen to show the trait, you will perpetuate the trait in such a way that it would be almost impossible to eliminate down the road. So always, select and cull in favor of proper wings.

Split Tail Squirrel Tail

THE INHERITANCE OF – "TAIL DEFECTS":
These include defects, such as wry-tail, squirrel-tail, and split-tail. This is a condition in which the main tail feathers lean or twist to one side, or where the main tail feathers are carried at an angle of more than 90 degrees, or where there is a distinct and decided gap between the main tail feathers. These are defects which are due to a fault in the vertebrae that holds the tail. These are recessive traits that usually show up as the tail feathers grow and develop. The same rule applies to tail defects as do wing defects, as mentioned above, select and cull in favor of proper tails.

THE INHERITANCE OF – "CROOKED-TOES" AND "DUCK-FEET":
This condition is where its toes are curled inward, underneath the foot, causing difficulty in walking. This is usually caused by close, careless inbreeding, or by careless turning of the eggs in an incubator. However, it can be caused by a genetic influence of the mother and father.

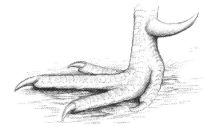

An example of duck-foot.

Duck-foot is another defect of the toes and feet that must carefully be watch for. In fact, it affects the rear prop-toe. These are autosomal recessive traits, so always select and cull in favor of proper toes.

THE INHERITANCE OF – "CROOKED BREASTBONES":
Also known as "Crooked Keels," this is a defect which is found in varying degrees and in many families of American and Old English Games.

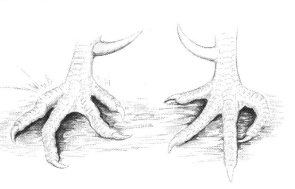

An example of crooked-toes.

For a long time I have heard fellow cockers argue about the causes of crooked breastbones. Some say it is caused by the environment in which the bird is raised, such as improper roosting conditions and climatic circumstances. Some say it is caused by heredity factors. And then there are those that think it is cause by improper diet or poor nutrition. I am here to inform you that all of these conditions and factors are more or less responsible. To what degree, we will soon learn.

Simple anatomy: Birds are characterized by the presence of a lower sternum, a projecting blade, which is attached to muscles operating the wings. This part of the sternum, known as the "keel," is normally straight, but in American and Old English Gamefowl, as well as, chickens of the ornamental and commercial varieties, are often found to be crooked. The abnormality is a serious fault to cockers and backyard breeders, and can be the source of loss for commercial meat industry.

Skeleton of a Cock
Showing the Location of the Sternum.

Birds are characterized by the presence of a lower sternum, a projecting blade that is attached to muscles operating the wings. Also known as the "keel," it is normally straight but is often found to be crooked. The abnormality is a serious fault to all gamefowl and chickens.

Causes of the abnormality: It is now clear that the abnormality results from hereditary susceptibility to faulty ossification in the sternum, but that environmental and nutritional influence are very important in determining the extent to which the hereditary weakness is expressed.

Note: Ossification is a medical term that is synonymous with bone tissue formation.

Another contributor to this problem is the rate of calcification of the bone. Research shows that, and I have noticed this from observations of my fowl throughout the years, that the rate of bone calcification is slower in stags, making them more subject to breast defects than are pullets.

*Note of interest: Calcification is a medical term that is often confused with ossification. However, Calcification is the process in which the mineral calcium builds up in soft tissue, causing it to harden. The consequences of Calcifications may be determined by whether or not there is a good mineral balance. Calcification is synonymous with the formation of calcium-based salts and crystals within cells and tissue. Calcification is a process that occurs during ossification, but not vice versa.

Usual age of abnormality: Crookedness of the breastbone ordinarily does not develop until after the chick is about 6 weeks of age. However, a large percentage of the crooked breasts can be detected as early as 3 months of age and more so after the age of 4 months. There are a small number of individuals that will develop the deformity well later in life. You must examine your fowl on a regular basis. I normally check the breastbone every time I pick up a bird, it's the first thing I do. These days it's automatic, I do it without thinking.

Form and structure of the defect: The keel may be bent to the right or left; may show various degrees of concavity; or may be both concave and bent. These different forms and the different degrees of abnormality all result from the same underlying condition, hereditary susceptibility to faulty ossification in the sternum, brought on by poor nutrition or unsatisfactory environment.

*Note of interest: Bending to the right side is more common than bending to the left.

The genetic factor: This character is so variable in its expression, and so subject to environmental modification that in some matings no hereditary susceptibility may be apparent. Thus when normal cocks are mated with hens having keels that are (1) noticeably crooked, (2) slightly curved, or (3) completely straight, the proportion of crooked breasts among the offspring is not usually significantly different within the three groups. However, when breeders from a close family are selected on the basis of whether they have, or don't have, crooked keels, the influence of heredity is immediately apparent in the first generation.

A proper breast-bone is the foundation for a good conformation.

The results will look something like this:
- Crooked-keeled parents from families with many affected birds will produce offspring of which 80 percent will most likely develop the defect.
- Straight-keeled parents from families with few crooked keels will produced, at the same time, progeny of which only 4 percent will have crooked keels.
- With Selective Breeding for straight-keels, in a closed flock family, you will notice that after approximately six generations, you will observe a slight decrease in the incidence of crooked keels, to which approximately 2 or 3 percent (3 out of 100) of the cocks will show the defect, even under roosting conditions conducive to maximum development of crooked keels.

The tendency to develop crooked breasts seems to behave as a recessive trait. Therefore, elimination of crooked breastbones will be easier in some strains than in others.

Reduction of the frequency of this defect is most likely to be accomplished, as with other multiple-factor conditions, by Selective Breeding and a consistent use of the progeny test. However, try to select breeders on the basis of the family record rather than on their appearance or performance of the individual. Mass selection is important, that is, the elimination of all birds with crooked breasts from the breeding pen; but in some cases it is not enough. It is quite possible that the exceptional straight-keeled bird from a family in which the majority has crooked breasts may transmit more genetic susceptibility to the defect than the occasional bird with a crooked keel from a family in which all the rest are normal.

Factors affecting expression of crooked keel: It has been shown that under identical rearing conditions, strains will differ radically with respect to the tendency toward crooked breastbones. However, sex seems to be a deciding factor. In most cases, more cocks are affected than hens. The difference is probably due to the fact that the rapid growth of chicks slows down sooner in pullets than in stags and ossification is completed earlier for the pullets than the stags. Since most of the crooked keels appear after that age, it is natural that more cocks and stags should be affected than hens and pullets.

Roosts: It is well known that the expression of this condition is dependent upon proper management. Expression of an inherent susceptibility to crooked keel is noticeably enhanced in chickens that have sharp roosts and are allowed to roost too early, which tends to aggravate this condition. Obviously, wide perches are desirable, but my observation has shown that the incidence of the defect is more likely to be lessened by Selective Breeding than by modifications of the roosting conditions.

It is evident from this that improvement of the genetic constitution of the bird provides a means of eliminating crooked keels that is much more effective than any attempt to control the problem by removing the roosts.

Best age for roosting. In the case where the cocker or backyard breeder is raising chicks that he purchased from a hatchery or from another breeder, he is unable to control the breeding except by exercising care in the choice of his stock and giving preference to breeders who are doing the right kind of breeding. In such an enterprise, the owner of the growing birds must use every means at his disposal to reduce the incidence of crooked keels. One of these is the provision of wide perches. Another is the withholding of roosts till a comparatively late age.

Interesting facts concerning crooked keel:
1. There is a tendency for the earlier hatched birds (November to January) to be affected more than chicks that are hatched in the spring (March to May).
2. A nutritional deficiency, especially that of vitamin D, will also cause crooked breastbones, but this sort of defect bears no relationship to the inherited type. Therefore, in most cases you will not prevent crooked keel by changing the amount of calcium, phosphorus, vitamin D, or protein in the diet.
3. Most birds that develop crooked keels later in life are usually heavier at 8 weeks than those which did not. This suggests that birds growing very rapidly are most subject to the deformity.
4. Since crooked keels may be considered as indicating softer bone and faulty ossification, a similarity to rickets may be evident. But the truth is crooked keel is not the same as rickets. The abnormality results from a specific weakness in the sternum. Birds with crooked keel are no more susceptible to rickets than those with normal keel.
5. Birds with crooked keels on normal diets have abnormal ossification in the sternum. Crooked keel results from a specific weakness in the sternum, not from faulty metabolism of calcium or from generally defective ossification throughout the body.
6. Birds of the crooked keel strain are more susceptible to abnormal ossification of the sternum than those of the other strain.

*Note of interest: Whatever you do, don't get this confused with a condition known as breast blisters. The so-called blisters on the breast of growing chickens may be very large, though not entirely, controlled by roosting conditions.

<u>Conclusion</u>: Although crooked breastbones seem not to handicap most birds in growth or performance, it is well to select against the deformity. If the roosting conditions are normal and the vitamin D in the diet is adequate then birds possessing crooked breastbones should be avoided as breeders.

Through the years I have noticed that American Games have shown that, through Selective Breeding, strains that show a low incidence of crooked breastbones can be developed.

If eliminating crooked breasts from among the breeders does not adequately reduce the deformity in the family, it may be necessary to resort to family selection for solving the problem (I will talk more about this later in the book).

Side-Sprig.

THE INHERITANCE OF – "COMB DEFECTS": Comb defects are rather numerous. Although they are not a concern for most breeders of American Games, due to the fact that the cocks are dubbed, they should be culled and selected in favor of breeders that have proper combs. Even though the cocks are dubbed, the hens are not. Defects of the comb include (especially in the straight (*single*) combed varieties) – side-sprigs, split-comb, twisted-comb, lopped-comb, thumb-marks and others. Then you have the telescoping-comb.

<u>Side-Sprigs</u>: A side-sprig, which is a well-defined, pointed growth on the side of a straight (*single*) comb, is regarded as a disqualification, and as a result, selection should be made against this variation rather than toward its preservation. These lateral projections near the posterior end of straight (*single*) combs vary from small tubercles to an almost complete splitting of the blade.

Lopped-Comb.

<u>The genetic factor</u>: Side-sprigs appear to be a dominant defect. In fact, the inheritance of side-sprigs are due to the interaction of two dominant autosomal genes, which are complementary in their action, so that when both are present either in the heterozygous or homozygous condition, side-sprigs are produced.

A study conducted by Mr. Asmundson, in 1926, eliminated any possibility that side-sprigs might be caused by a single gene, either dominant or recessive, and indicated strongly that side-sprigs resulted only when two complementary dominant genes are present. This would explain why many offspring with side-sprigs may be produced by parents that don't show it or are absent of the defect altogether.

Twisted-Comb.

Further studies conducted on the effects of side-sprigs, where the results were secured from reciprocal matings, indicated an absence of sex-linkage.

Other comb defects include:
- <u>Split-comb and Telescoped-comb</u>: which are most likely caused by a recessive character.
- <u>Lopped-comb</u>: which appears to depend upon the presence of two dominant complementary genes.

Split-Comb.

THE MOST UNCOMMON OF THESE DEFECTS AND DISQUALIFICATIONS

THE INHERITANCE OF – "TWISTED NECK": Also known as "Crooked-Neck," it results from the curvature of the spine or "scoliosis," and occurs as the bird grows.

Crooked-neck develops when the chick is a few weeks of age. The bird is so badly handicapped that it usually dies early, but if not, it should not be included in the breeding pen. It usually happens to a group of related birds, and is particularly common among American Games.

The genetic factor: Some indication that the crooked neck might be inherited as was found among the progeny of carrier parents. In 1926 a study was performed on the inheritance of hen-feathering in Brown Leghorns (hennies) at the U.S. Animal Husbandry Experiment Farm, Beltsville, Maryland. An inadvertent discovery developed. Seven birds appeared to have crooked necks. The simultaneous appearance of seven such abnormal birds led to an analysis of the results, and it was found by Mr. Morley Jull that these abnormal birds were produced by one rooster and three different hens in a total population of 39. It became apparent at once that not only was the crooked-neck condition inherited but also that it was probably inherited on a monohybrid basis.

Note: When a cross is made between one pair of contrasting characters, such as black and white, the cross is called a monohybrid cross.

The conclusion: Crooked-neck is inherited as an autosomal recessive character.

THE INHERITANCE OF – "WEBBED-TOES": Another defect, although uncommon, found in gamefowl and chickens is the webbing of the toes, sometimes referred to as "syndactylism." The webbing is usually between the two outside toes and may be enough to interfere with walking. Like many other defects, this trait is inherited as a recessive trait. The degree of webbing may vary. In family's and strains where this defect is found all breeders should be examined critically for any indication of the webbing, and if all defective individuals are eliminated, the incidence of the webbing condition can be reduced to where it will cause no great trouble.

An example of webbed-toes.

THE INHERITANCE OF – "STUBS ON THE SHANKS OR TOES": Stubs are short partly grown feathers on the shanks and feet that appear in breeds that are normally clean-legged. It is a difficult trait to study since down on the leg at hatch may or may not lead to stubs in adulthood. Likewise, clean-legged chicks may develop stubs at a later age.

Although, not a common occurrence in breeds such as American and Old English Games, they have been known to appear from time to time, and is regarded as a disqualification when it is present in breeds having nonfeathered shanks.

Stubs are usually found either on the sides of the toes or on the web of skin between the toes, usually between the middle toe and the outer one, and may sometimes be found on the outer sides of the shanks. Sometimes only a single tuft of down is present, but it is not unusual to have the whole web covered. Frequently, instead of the quill portion of a feather, down may be present, the amount varying from almost complete absence as observed by the naked eye to a complete covering of the web between the outer toes.

Recognition of this trait can sometimes be difficult and subject to some error because some of the tufts are extremely tiny, and as every breeder of feather-footed fowl knows, the down is so easily removed that even an encrust of sticking mud might pull it out.

The interesting fact is that, while chicks with down nearly always had down at maturity, many of those without down at hatching would later show it as adults. My advice to breeders of clean legged fowl, especial that of gamefowl breeds, is to always inspect your fowl for down or stubs, no matter their age.

The genetic factor: In American and Old English Games, it is concluded that the presence of down or stubs on the toes and shanks behaves as recessive to normal. However, the method of inheritance is rather complex. They are produced by two independent autosomal recessive genes, with homozygosity at either locus, which causes the production of stubs.

In a study done on this trait, it was reported that there was a deficiency of females showing the stubs, which leads to the suggestion that the trait may be partially sex-limited.

I read another study done by a gentleman named Mr. Warren, in 1930, where he developed, by selection, a strain of White Leghorns in which a high proportion of the progeny had down on the legs and toes, and another strain of White Leghorns in which none of the progeny had down. These two strains were crossed and the results showed that the presence of down is more or less recessive in its behavior, and that more than one autosomal gene is involved.

What's the simple explanation? Stubs are caused by a recessive gene, whereas clean shanks and toes are caused by a dominant gene.

Heel-Tuft - type of feathering: A trait that is similar to stubs is known as "heel-tuft feathering." Today it is referred to by most poultry enthusiast as "stubs on hocks." This trait is expressed as small stubs, or as tiny feathers appearing in the region just below the tibiotarsal joint, on the inner surface of the shank.

Feathered shanks are common in such fowl as Langshans, Brahmas and Cochins.

Although the "heel-tuft" type of feathering can be attributed to a single autosomal dominant gene, it is very difficult to analyze by its phenotype. While it may show in some chicks at hatching, other fowls may have clean hocks for 2 years but still develop stubs after that age.

THE INHERITANCE OF – "FEATHERS ON THE FEET":

This is a trait similar to stubs, but in this case instead of stubs, fully developed feathers are formed. Feathers on the shanks or feet are an important characteristic for some breeds, such as Cochins, Brahmas, Langshans, and Silkies. This is called "feathered shanks" or "feathered feet." Since the feathers are on the toes and the metatarsal region, the term "feathered feet" seems more appropriate than the commonly used "feathered shanks."

The extent and degree of the feathering vary greatly from breed to breed, and in some cases, bird to bird, within the same breed. In general, the majority of the feathers are down the outer side of the tarsometatarsus and on the outer toe. In feather-footed breeds there is a certain proportion of uniformity of feathering on all the toes and feathers on the inside of the tarsometatarsus.

As we talked about earlier, some birds have only a few tiny feathers between the toes or on the "hocks" called "stubs," and, according to the "Standards of Perfection" which is produced and governed by the American Poultry Association, they constitute a disqualification from the show ring in breeds not supposed to have feathered feet. So, for breeds which are clean legged, make sure to cull in favor of clean legs.

Langshan
(Feathered Legged)

Leghorn
(Clean Legged)

The breeding of feather legged fowl with clean legged fowl.

The genetic factor: From a number of genetic studies of feathered feet, there was no understanding of the trait, which satisfactorily explained all the different types and degrees of the condition. In crosses between "feathered feet" and "clean-footed" fowls, the F_1 generation was usually feather-footed.

In 1918, Punnett and Bailey crossed a Leghorn with a Langshan and the results were interesting. They found a complete dominance in the F_1 generation; a 3 to 1 ratio in the F_2 generation, and a 1 to 1 ratio in the backcross to clean-footed fowls. Their conclusion of the study was that a single dominant gene was responsible, and that variability in the F_1 generation and backcross was caused by modifying genes. They also showed that some of the results in earlier investigations with Brahmas and Cochins, which have more feathers on the feet than Langshans, could be accounted for by duplicate genes, with the dominant allele of either pair causing feathered feet.

THE INHERITANCE OF – "SURPLUS OF PRIMARY FLIGHT FEATHERS": Normally there are ten primary flight feathers on each wing. Some breeds and strains are known to have more than ten. This condition was fairly common in breeds, such as, Rhode Island Reds and Barred Plymouth Rocks. However, American and Old English Games are rarely affected. In studies of the inheritance of surplus primaries, they concluded from crosses using birds that are known to have a surplus of primaries and White Leghorns that it was due to the complementary action of two completely dominant autosomal genes.

THE INHERITANCE OF – "SURPLUS OF MAIN TAIL FEATHERS": A normal tail has only six main tail feathers on each side, plus the main sickles, lesser sickles, side hangers, and tail coverts. I have seen some fowl, in which the birds had seven main tail feathers on each side of the tail, plus the main sickle feathers and some extra lesser sickle feathers. Sometimes they would have an eighth tail feather, but only on one side. This trait is caused by a single autosomal recessive gene with incomplete dispersion. In a family that carries the gene, the rate at which it is distributed and expressed varies.

THE INHERITANCE OF – "VARIATIONS IN THE SPUR": It is safe to say that the "Metatarsal Spur," also known simply as the "Spur," has evolved by Natural Selection as a useful weapon of offence and defense. However, since the domestication of the chicken, and the wide-ranging significance of cockfighting, which is practiced in all parts of the world, the metatarsal spur we see today is a product, more or less, of the effects of Artificial Selection.

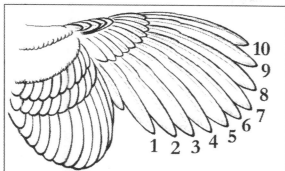

Normally there are ten primary flight feathers on each wing. Some breeds are known to have more than ten.

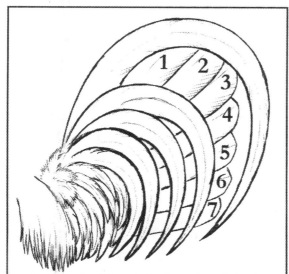

A normal tail has only six main tail feathers on each side, plus the main sickles, lesser sickles, side hangers, and tail coverts. Some fowl have seven main tail feathers on each side of the tail, plus the main sickle feathers and some extra lesser sickle feathers. Sometimes they would have an eighth tail feather, but only on one side. This trait is caused by a single autosomal recessive gene with incomplete dispersion.

The form, function and development of the spur: The structure of the metatarsal spur of an adult bird is elongated, tapered, and pointed at the end. The spur consists of a bony core surrounded by softer spongy tissue and covered on the outside by a cornified layer. Like a human finger nail, the length of the spur increases with age in both cocks and hens. Eventually the outer layer either wears off or comes loose and falls off, and is replaced from below by a new spur. However, if the spur should be broken off at the base, it will not grow back.

The formation of the spur can be detected as early as the tenth day of incubation. The position of the spur is indicated by a small papilla, which is confined to the epidermal layer of the leg. At one day of age, spur caps composed of hard keratin are present in both sexes. As they grow older, spurs begin to develop out of the spur caps.

At about six months of age, a growth of bone inward from the epidermis meets a bony outgrowth from the shank, and the two fuse with the tarsometatarus to form the spur and becomes permanently attached to the skeleton. Spurs continue to grow throughout the bird's life.

Metatarsal spurs in hens: Spurred hens are found more frequently in American and Old English Games, Leghorns, and other Mediterranean breeds. Heaver breeds such as Rhode Island Reds, Plymouth Rocks, and other general-purpose breeds very seldom produce hens that are spurred. For American Games, spurs are most common in older birds but may develop in the first year.

The fact that selection of the metatarsal spur is normally confined, almost entirely, to cocks may account for the fact that in present-day chickens, spurs develop in all normal cocks, but not usually in hens. However, spurs do develop in some hens. This suggests that a lack of selection for spurs in that sex, together with a few thousand years of Natural and Artificial Selection for good spurs in cocks may be responsible for the sexual dimorphism that we see in our fowl today.

Are spurred hens masculine? It is commonly believed that spur-bearing hens are somewhat masculine and that they do not lay as well as normal hens. This idea is quite erroneous. Studies, which were conducted on the inheritance of the metatarsal spur in hens, have shown that there are no abnormalities of the ovary or of other endocrine glands in hens that are spurred, and that spurred hens reproduced and grew as well as did the non-spurred hens. Histological examination of the ovaries of such birds revealed no testicular tissue and only normal structure.

The genetic factor: Although there was no real difference between the two types, it was concluded that spur development in hens had a genetic basis. In other words, this trait is indeed inherited, and by selection, the development of a strain in which most of the hens will develop spurs is certainly achievable. It was suggested that inheritance of the metatarsal spur in hens was recessive.

The study I read also talked about an experiment they made by breeding an American Pit Game broodcock, whose hens are spurred, with hens from light breeds, such as Leghorn, who were spurred. The cross produced offspring that were mostly spurred.

My own experience: Through the years, in an attempt to increase the expressiveness of hens with well formed and properly developed metatarsal spurs, I have proven that with the use and practice of Selective Breeding, this is indeed possible. Through selection, I have increased the percentage of spurred hens in my own fowl and in a comparatively short time too. The proportion of hens with metatarsal spurs has been increased to about seventy percent from the thirty percent expressed when I first acquired them. It is my goal to create a strain where all hens will be spurred.

Metatarsal Spur

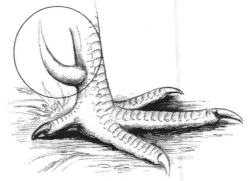

The structure of the metatarsal spur of an adult bird is elongated, tapered, and pointed at the end. The spur consists of a bony core surrounded by softer spongy tissue and covered on the outside by a cornified layer.

Hens Metatarsal Spurs

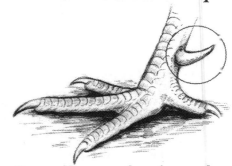

Spurred hens are found more frequently in American and Old English Games, Leghorns, and other Mediterranean breeds.

Spurlessness: This condition prevents the development of a spur on one leg. Although, it can occur with cocks from time to time, this is a condition most common with hens, where they will have one good spur on one leg and be spurless on the other leg.

In this condition, you will notice that the epidermal spur papillae are absent in day-old chicks, or represented only by an enlarged scale. In other words, the enlarged scale takes the place of a spur. In some cases, spurlessness is often accompanied by the absence of scales along the inner surface of the shank.

At sexual maturity, pullets may develop slight protuberances at the spur sites. At first they may appear to be normal spurs. Some of these may break through as the birds get older, however, they usually developed into bony outgrowths from the shank and resembled short deformed spurs, but the epidermal portion of the spurs is always and totally lacking. These are frequently outgrowths from the tarsometatarsus and lack that portion of the spur which normally develops from the epidermis. It was thought by some that sexual dimorphism might be a factor at maturity.

The genetic factor: Spurlessness is inherited as a single recessive gene. It is autosomal, but since its effects are more evident in pullets and hens rather than stags and cocks, it seems to be partially sex-limited.

Double Spur: Occasionally a bird is found with a double spur on one leg or on both. The dichotomy usually involved both legs, but sometimes only one is affected. One of these spurs is directly below the other, and both point in the same direction. The upper spur is usually longer, but sometimes both are of the same length, and in some cases the lower may be the longer. Each spur has its own bony core and attachment to the rather large bony outgrowth of the tarsometatarsus, from which both arise.

Some breeds have hens that are spurred and some don't. American Game hens are known to have both.

The genetic factor: Inheritance of this trait is influenced by unknown factors, which indicates that this condition might just be a mutation. However, it generally behaves as an autosomal recessive.

Multiple Spurs: The Sumatra breed is unique in having multiple spurs. Mature cocks usually have three spurs on each shank, consisting usually of a large central spur with a smaller one immediately above it and another below. While a triple spur is usual, in some birds there are as many as five, three of which are below the longest spur.

All spurs point in one direction, and each spur has its own bony core, but only the longest ones are directly attached to the tarsometatarsus. The smaller, lower ones terminate in a bony projection running downward from the normal site of attachment of the spur.

In newly hatched chicks, as well as in adult females, the normal single spur papilla is replaced by 3 to 5 enlarged and flattened scales. For this reason, it is possible to identify this condition with great accuracy at hatching.

The genetic factor: Multiple spurs is inherited as a single autosomal dominant mutation, with heterozygotes usually having two spurs and homozygotes having three to five.

The proper care and management of long spurs: Long spurs are undesirable on broodcocks because they may injure the backs of the hens during mating. They may also cause damage among aggressive, quarrelsome cocks if they are accidently thrown together or if one should get loose and they fight between the wire. Not to mention, the damage and injury they often inflict on their handlers. Such spurs may and should be sawn off.

Beware however, that some studies have shown that if the spurs are sawed off to early in their development that the development of the spurs may be prevented with devastating results. I don't usually use cocks as breeders until they are 18 to 24 months of age. So I will trim their spurs for the first time at that age.

THE INHERITANCE OF – "RUMPLESSNESS": One of the most unique structural variations existing among domestic fowls is the condition known as rumplessness, in which the birds have no tails. This defect is the result of the absence of some of the tail bones. In fact it is an apparent lack of all, or part of the tail feathers. Although this is a characteristic trait for breeds such as Araucanas, it is a serious fault for American and Old English Games.

Although not very common, I have seen this from time to time in American and Old English Games. Needless to say, it left the breeders profoundly and utterly confused as to what actually happened. The defect can occur sporadically in many strains of chickens, and sometimes appears not to be inherited.

The normal chicken: To understand the significance of the rumples bird, we must first compare it with that of the normal one. In the normal chicken there are sixteen synsacral vertebrae, which are fused with the pelvis, five free caudal vertebrae, and six vertebrae, which are fused to form the pygostyle. The normal chicken also has twelve main tail feathers, along with two sickle feathers, a series of lesser sickle feathers and side hangers, as well as tail coverts. They also have an uropygial oil gland.

Three types of rumplessness: There are three types of rumplessness – hereditary recessive, hereditary dominant and nonhereditary accidental.

Specimens of all three types resemble each other more or less, but differences among them are manifest from their breeding results, owing to the fact that in one type the trait is not inherited, whereas in the other two types, in which it is inherited there are differences in their structure. The principal difference between a normal bird and a rumpless one is a deficiency in parts of the skeleton of the tail.

On a rumples bird, a few tail feathers may or may not be present, and the backbones range from being almost normal to an almost completely rumpless condition. The difference between the accidental and hereditary rumpless types being the presence or absence of certain vertebrae's in the tail.

Accidental Type: The accidental type of rumplessness is somewhat different from the hereditary type, in that it is completely rumpless. In this type, the pygostyle is lacking except for the last two vertebrae, and one or two vertebrae are missing from the center of the synsacrocaudal vertebrae. In this type, rudimentary oil glands appear in only twenty-five percent of the offspring.

*Note of interest: The accidental type is not genetic. Rumpless birds that sporadically appear in various flocks are usually of the non-hereditary type, that is, when mated to normal birds they produce nothing but normal offspring.

Hereditary Types: The recessive and dominant forms appeared outwardly to be the same, the posterior of their bodies are round, and they both lack an oil gland and tail feathers. Examination of the vertebrae, however, shows that they are indeed different. The dominant rumplessness condition is characterized by a lack of all but the last two pygostyle vertebrae; they lack all the free caudal vertebrae, and one or two vertebrae from the center of the five synsacrocaudaul vertebrae. The recessive rumplessness differed from both of the others in that all the free caudal vertebrae are present although they are fused together irregularly.

The genetics factor: The recessive gene of rumplessness is not regularly expressed, and, although the dominant gene is involved, especially when it comes to breeds known for rumplessness, it's probably not the one commonly causing all the troubles. Normally, rumplessness, in a family of fowl not normally known for rumplessness, is caused by the accidental type.

Here is the genetic foundation for most hereditary types. Mating of rumpless cocks to rumpless hens will produce F_2 progeny in the proportion of three rumpless to one normal bird. These results indicate the dominance of rumplessness on a monohybrid basis. Furthermore, when this same type of rumpless bird was mated to normal birds, rumpless and normal progeny were produced in approximately equal proportions. These results indicate that the hereditary type of rumplessness usually encountered, is in a heterozygous condition.

It is wise, therefore, to avoid as breeders, birds showing rumplessness since certain types are inherited. Merely the elimination of defective birds from among the breeders will probably be adequate.

Rumlessness and its influence on fertility: Fertility problems resulted from purely mechanical reasons. The lack of tails, which act as balancers in the act of copulation, resulted in incomplete copulations.

THE INHERITANCE OF – "DWARFISM": There are two types of dwarfism, although both are recessive, one is sex-linked and the other is characterized as the lethal type.

Dwarfism - sex-linked type: I have read a number of studies concerning a main type of dwarfism, one that is caused by a single sex-linked recessive gene. Females with this gene tend to weigh about thirty percent less at maturity than their normal sisters.

Although this mutation is still being studied, some facts concerning it are already evident. For instance:
- There is no sign of dwarfing when the chicks are hatched.
- Some of them are recognizable as dwarfs at eight to ten weeks of age, but classification is most accurate when the birds are five months of age or more.
- Apparently it is completely recessive.

Contrary to the type of dwarfism of the lethal type, which we will discuss next, these dwarfs mature sexually, and both sexes reproduce normally.

Dwarfism – lethal type: Research has shown that out of a hundred eggs incubated only seventy-five percent hatched. Out of the ones that hatched, half died before reaching four weeks of age, and the remainder died between four and twenty weeks of age. The condition can therefore be considered as an obligate lethal character, with delayed lethal action, or perhaps as a semi-lethal one.

Here is a description of the typical characteristics of this type of dwarfism

- These dwarfs show a general retardation of growth, which is recognizable at 2 to 4 weeks of age.
- The outer toe is usually curled backward, and this is sometimes evident at hatching.
- The skull is broad and high in relation to its length.
- The upper beak is bent downward.
- The tissues around the eyes appear swollen.
- The tongue is shortened and swollen.
- The legs are shortened, more so in the tarsometatarsus than in the femur and tibiotarsus.
- The sacrum is disproportionately small and high, so that the tail seems abnormally high on the body.
- There is almost no endochondral bone in the shaft of the long bones.
- None of the dwarfs became sexually mature, therefore they cannot reproduce.

The genetic factor: Dwarfs of this type are evidently homozygous for a recessive autosomal gene.

THE INHERITANCE OF – "WHITE EARLOBES": The color of the earlobe, in the case of many breeds, is a breed characteristic, which means that all birds belonging to a certain breed must have the same color of earlobe. It is normal for earlobes to be white in breeds of the Mediterranean classification, especially in breeds such as Leghorns, Minorcas, Anconas, and Blue Andalusians. In fact, all Leghorns, regardless of variety, have white earlobes. However, white earlobes in American and Old English Games are a serious fault that should be culled for and eliminated from the breed at every opportunity. These breeds must have red earlobes in order to meet proper standard requirements.

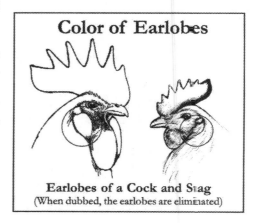

Color of Earlobes

Earlobes of a Cock and Stag
(When dubbed, the earlobes are eliminated)

It has been the thought of many cockers that white earlobes in an American Game demonstrates a Mediterranean influence, which at one time, Leghorns may have been infused to strengthen color. I can't say for sure whether this is true or false, but there seems to be a genetic connection.

White in the earlobes, known as "enamel," tends to appear in red earlobe birds from time to time. Cockers and backyard breeders should consider this a serious disqualification to the breed, and make special efforts to exclude birds with this defect from their breeding pens. On the other hand, poultrymen breeding other varieties should be equally alert in excluding from their show stock and breeding pens birds with any red in the earlobes that should be all white to conform to breed standards.

The genetic factor: Since white earlobes constitute a breed characteristic for some and a fault in others, the condition is unquestionably hereditary. An analysis I read concerning white earlobes showed that the genetic basis or inheritance of earlobe color is very complex, and that multiple factors are responsible. The results indicated that earlobe color is dependent upon the action of several genes, neither white nor red being dominant. The F_1 generation from crosses of "white earlobes" x "red earlobes" were mostly intermediate, but in seven of the ten F_1 populations there were birds with white earlobes and others with red ones, in addition to those with a mixture of both colors. *An interesting note: Breeds with white earlobes usually lay white-shelled eggs.

VARIATIONS AND ABNORMALITIES
Which Affect Their Plumage

FLIGHTLESS: There is a mutation in the plumage which causes the shafts of the remiges and rectrices to break off. As a result, the birds become incapable of flight and cannot even fly up to their roosts at night. Some of the larger feathers of the body are also broken. After a molt, the new feathers break off as soon as they become dry. This condition is referred to as "flightless." The condition is identifiable in young chickens as early as six weeks of age, by which time some of the wing feathers are broken and others are of uneven length.

The genetic factor: Research has shown that all fowls, which expressed the trait, were heterozygous for a dominant gene.

RAGGED-WING: This abnormality, to some extent resembles the flightless mutation, and is not as uncommon as you would think.

Form and function of the trait: In its most extreme form, the mutation eliminates all the remiges from the adult plumage. In its most simplest of expression, all the feathers are present but extremely shortened. Between the two extremes are the more common types, where some of the flight feathers are present, while others are missing. In regards to the two wings, they are often uneven.

Ragged-wing birds are not recognizable until the adult remiges begin to grow in at eight to twelve weeks of age. Those showing abnormal wing feathers are abnormal at maturity.

The genetics factor: This abnormality is an autosomal recessive mutation.

How ragged-wing differs from flightless: I mentioned earlier that they resemble one another. The difference in the two is that the remiges of the ragged-wing bird are not broken off but are either absent or shortened. The rectrices of ragged-wing birds are not affected, whereas in flightless ones both tail and wing feathers are broken.

FRAYING OF THE FEATHERS: This is an abnormality of the plumage, which is usually confined to the large feathers of the wing and tail. In extreme cases, other feathers may lack smoothness and show a "ropy" appearance. Chicks normally show no signs of the defect at hatching, and very little in the first set of chick feathers. However, the mutation is quite evident in the second set of juvenile feathers and in those of adults.

The genetic factor: The frayed appearance of the feathers results from defects in the barbules, particularly in the distal ones and their hooklets. As a result, there is an imperfect interlocking of anterior and posterior barbules, and the barbs are not held together as it is in normal feathers. This is considered to be a simple recessive character.

THE INHERITANCE OF OTHER DEFECTS: There are many other deformities which are inherited and may be troublesome in certain families and strains, which include irregular eye or pupil, sunken eyes, beetle browed, crooked or deformed back, knock-knees, and short legs. These also include traits, such as twisted feathers in wings or tail and shafting. We talked more about these defects earlier in the book. However, what I can tell you about the genetic factor concerning these traits is they are really quite simple. They appear to behave as autosomal recessive traits. Which means the defect can be expressed in both the cocks and hens. Not only that, if you breed two individuals that carry the trait but don't show it, they will produce fifty percent of the offspring that express the defect, and fifty percent that don't, but are carriers. If you should decide to breed individuals that happen to show the trait you will perpetuate in a way in which it would be almost impossible to eliminate it down the road. So always, select and cull in favor of proper attributes and characteristics.

EVERYTHING COUNTS: Many cockers and backyard breeders believe these types of traits are of so little importance that they give it no consideration in their breeding programs. This is a mistake! If there is one thing I have learned, it is that EVERYTHING COUNTS!

It is essential that you do not use birds with any of these defects as breeders. Your breeding program depends on you, the breeder, to cull any and all breeders that you can identify as being unattractive or carry any undesirable recessive genes that can have a negative effect on the outcome of the family or strain. Most of these defects can be somewhat controlled simply by rigid elimination of defective birds from the broodpen. Selection against such traits in the broodpen will help to reduce the frequency with which the defects appear in the family or strain, however, be aware that such breeding methods will seldom eliminate the trouble entirely.

THE ELIMINATION
OF UNDESIRABLE TRAITS

This is accomplished by a systematic testing to detect birds which carry but do not show the trait. If the undesired trait is known to be a recessive trait, it is usually more practical to eliminate the problem by getting rid of the birds that show the defect, as well as those that carry it. Although the necessary procedure may seem impractical at the time, it eliminates completely the problem of being overwhelmed with a certain percentage of surplus bird's that may be nothing more than carriers of the defect. As long as the impure or defective family is maintained, you must keep the potential for variation small, which means only keep the birds that are free of the defect and are valuable to your breeding program.

YOUR REPUTATION AS A BREEDER IS ON THE LINE: It is important to deal with the defects as they arise. The persistence of certain defects, though they might be of a minor nature, may reflect unfavorably on the reputation of your family or strain, and on you, the breeder. Your reputation as a breeder is your number one job. Protect it! It is important that your clientele can trust you. Sometimes this means the elimination of the whole family and starting new with another. But only use this as a last resort. You may end up with a family that has more problems than your original family.

TESTING BROODCOCKS FOR UNDESIRABLE RECESSIVE TRAITS: First of all, you must pen all broodcocks individually. Although this is normally the case for American Games, putting together individual sire pens for all broodcocks is essential in order to perform this test properly. If you do not know who the parents of each chick is on your farm, in this case the broodcock, you cannot eliminate undesirable traits.

Secondly, enough cocks will need to be tested to obtain a sufficient number of non-carriers in order to head the family the next breeding season. To determine how many cocks must be tested, it can be estimated that the percentage of carriers in the flock will be greater than the percentage of those showing the recessive defect. If the incidence of the defect is low, as is usually true, then the number of carriers will be considerably larger than the number showing the defect.

For example, if only one percent of the birds in a pea-combed flock have straight (*single*) combs, then only about twelve percent of the pea-combed birds will be carriers of the straight (*single*) comb tendency, or in other words, approximately eighty-eight percent of the pea-combed birds will be true-breeding [non-carriers of straight (*single*) comb] for pea-comb. If a pea-combed family shows sixteen percent straight (*single*) combs, then only forty-three percent of the pea-combed birds will be true breeding for pea-comb. Thus, in this family it can be expected that more than half of the birds tested will be discarded because they are carriers of straight (*single*) comb. If you have decided that you will need fifteen broodcocks, then about forty cocks will need to be tested for you to be assured of having enough sires that will breed true for pea-comb. I am only using pea-combs as an example; this can be used for any trait.

TESTING BROODHENS FOR UNDESIRABLE RECESSIVE TRAITS: The same rule will hold for testing the broodhens, but in this case they can be carried in a large family mated to several straight (*single*) comb broodcocks and the chicks individually pedigreed by dams only. In the case of straight (*single*) combs, the defect can be identified in the day-old chick and requires no further checking. If the trait is not expressed until later in life, then wing banding of the chicks will be necessary.

FOR TESTING BOTH: In order to demonstrate that a prospective breeder (either broodcock or broodhen) is free of a recessive defect, or in other words, is a non-carrier, it is required to have at least ten offspring, all of which fail to show the defect. This figure is based on the assumption that the trait is expressed in both sexes. Thus, when testing a pea-combed bird for purity by using a straight (*single*) combed mate, it must produce ten chicks, all of which have pea-combs, to demonstrate that the bird will not transmit straight (*single*) combs. One chick with a straight (*single*) comb condemns the pea-comb parent as a carrier regardless of how many pea-comb offspring it may have. On average, half of the offspring will show straight (*single*) combs and half pea-combs if the bird is a carrier of straight (*single*) comb. Therefore, the

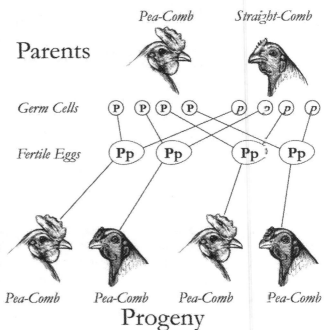

This illustration shows what happens when you breed a pure pea-comb bird with a straight (single) comb bird. The results are revealed in the offspring, all of which show the pea-comb trait.

proposed total of ten chicks should be sufficient to avoid the chance of failure to identify a carrier. It is exactly the same odds as pitching pennies, since they should fall heads up half the time and tails up half the time. It is possible even by chance to have runs of heads or tails only, but it is highly unlikely to get either heads or tails ten times in succession.

THE ELIMINATION OF RECESSIVE TRAITS - IT'S ESSENTIAL TO KEEP INDIVIDUALS THAT CARRY THE DEFECT: In order to perform the proper test of identifying possible carriers of a particular recessive defect, it is necessary to retain some individuals which carry the recessive trait. If this trait should happen to be a straight (*single*) comb appearing in a pea-comb variety, then you should have some straight (*single*) combed birds. They may be individuals that appear, from time to time, in the family that you are attempting to purify, which is the better way to perform this test, or they may come from infusions or importations from some other straight (*single*) comb breed or variety, which I would only use as a last resort.

Either way you decide to go, remember that these individuals, which are carriers of recessives or defective traits are only used for the test, not to permanently infuse into your family. All offspring produced by the test should be culled, discarded, or given away as non-pure or potentially blemished fowl. And not sold as broodfowl.

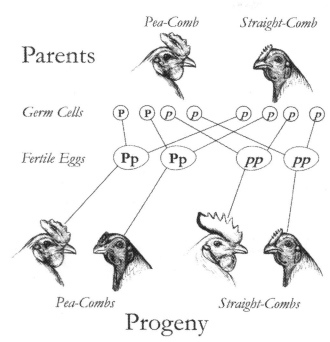

Parents

Pea-Comb   *Straight-Comb*

Germ Cells

Fertile Eggs

Pea-Combs   *Straight-Combs*

Progeny

This illustration shows what happens when you breed a non-pure pea-comb bird with a straight (single) comb bird. The results are revealed in the offspring. Fifty percent of the offspring show the pea-comb trait and fifty percent of the offspring show the straight (single) comb trait.

Inheritance creates a problem of elimination: The procedure necessary for creating a family that is free of an undesired recessive trait does require considerable effort, and if done in the regular breeding season will involve considerable loss of time. It can be worked into the regular breeding program but is slow and difficult to obtain complete elimination by this method.

The progeny test method will locate carriers of the defect, but if this method is followed, it should be emphasized that the production of a single offspring with the defect lays blame on both parents as carriers. An example illustrating this case is one where several broodhens are mated with a single broodcock, and only one hen produces offspring showing the recessive defect. This means that both the cock and the one hen are carriers and should be discarded. It is probable that the rest of the cock's mates are true breeding for the absence of the defect.

THE ELIMINATION OF UNDESIRED DOMINANT TRAITS: As you can plainly see, it is understandably difficult to eliminate undesired recessive traits and easy to eliminate dominant traits. In a family of fowl that is throwing both pea and straight (*single*) combs, you must go through the somewhat involved program described above to get rid of the straight (*single*) combs. If you choose to get rid of the pea-combs, to establish a true breeding straight (*single*) comb family, it is merely a matter of eliminating the pea-comb individuals from the broodpens for only one year. For the same reason, it is easy to fix a desired recessive trait. In this case, it is a matter of mating only individuals showing the recessive trait.

MAKE THEM PURE, KEEP THEM PURE: When you have found a sufficient number of breeders, which are proved to be non-carriers of straight (*single*) comb, or whatever recessive trait or defect you desire to eliminate and use them only to reproduce your entire family, you will no longer be troubled with your pea-comb variety throwing any more straight (*single*) combs. If the conversion cannot be made in a single year, then make up one or two broodpens of proven individuals, which you can, in another year, obtain enough broodfowl.

There is only one problem connected with this breeding program of elimination, and that is you, the breeder, are significantly limiting your bloodlines and you must be certain that you are not intensifying some other undesired trait. This problem may be handled by restricting the testing to birds relatively free of other defects.

222

Once a family is freed of an undesired recessive trait, care must be exercised when bringing in new breeding stock to make sure that such individuals do not carry the undesired recessive. Such individuals should be tested as described above before using them in the broodpen.

The method outlined above for eliminating straight (*single*) comb may be used for eliminating any recessive trait, but it should be kept in mind that one must build up, or obtain elsewhere, at least a small family of birds showing the defect, which you will use as testers for proving the non-carriers.

WHEN TO CARRY OUT THE TESTING PROGRAM: Probably the most effective and practical, and maybe even economical method of elimination is to carry out the testing in the late fall and early winter by mating the birds in question to recessive testers. Like I mentioned earlier, the stock produced in the test should be culled, discarded, or given away as non-pure or potentially blemished fowl. Most importantly, they should not be sold as broodfowl. Since all of the birds produced in the test have one parent showing the defect, they are of no value as future broodfowl.

If the test is started early enough, it may be completed without interfering with the regular breeding program (usually in late winter or early spring) and utilize the broodpen facilities at a season when they are not otherwise needed. Actually, individual broodpens will be needed for testing cocks only, since the hens to be tested can be carried in a larger broodpen and group-mated or stud-mated to a group of cocks showing the recessive, which are individually tethered on string-walks. These hens must be trapnested and the chicks produced identified with their dam.

THE IMPORTANCE OF SELECTING BROODFOWL THAT IS FREE OF DEFECTS: When it comes to the breeding of American Games, most breeders will spend a good portion of their time on the selection of the broodcock. They will put very little thought in the right broodhen. This just may be the biggest mistake they will ever make. If anything, it is wise to select the hen just as carefully as you would the cock. Whatever you do, never neglect to select the proper hen.

I understand where most breeders are coming from; the cock is indeed the show piece. It is because of his attributes that we are attracted to the sport, so it stands to reason that it is the cock that we would want to clone the most. However, there is a statement that has often been made that says: "*although the cock is half of the flock, the hen is so much more.*" Therefore, great care should be exercised in selecting both the cock and hen for breeding purposes.

There is one thing to keep in mind, and that is, it is the hen that will have the greatest influence on her offspring, especially the stags. She will determine more than ever the quality of her entire family, for she is the strain. Therefore, more defects and faults can be improved on, or eliminated, by selecting the proper hen.

Although the hen has the most influence, the cock should be as free from all breed defects and disqualifications as well. In a well-bred strain of birds, one poor broodcock may do as much as twenty times the damage as one broodhen in a single season by the introduction of some undesirable characteristic or trait. Fortunately, Mother Nature has a tendency to provide a large number of cocks to select from. In fact, the normal ratio of cocks to hens is close to one to one. Therefore, there are usually many more cocks, which are produced than will ever be used as breeders. With so many cocks to choose from, and through the process of elimination, we should have no trouble selecting the right broodcock for the job.

Every cocker and backyard breeder should know the standard defects and disqualifications of his particular breed, variety and strain, and should always use cocks and hens that are as free from these defects as possible. Time and care spent in the selection of broodfowl that are free from defects is a sound investment.

WHEN SELECTING BIRDS FOR BREEDING: Once you have gone through your fowl, eliminating any and all defective birds, and have selected all perspective breeders, you will find it helpful to put all the potential broodfowl in one place or area so you can easily and carefully compare them. If they can be brought together you can better judge them. If a few drop-pens are available, a comparison can be easily made. Just line the pens up, place the birds in these drop-pens and start comparing them with other birds of the same sex, as well as, birds of the opposite sex. Then, begin to match them up.

The hens and cocks can then be brought side by side, studied and handled, and a more intelligent selection can be made than if the birds are separated in different pens and you try to rely on your memory as to what they look like. Close comparison is best for this purpose of selection.

BREEDING FUNDAMENTALS
The Breeding of American Games
Modern Techniques for the Modern Cocker

"So then if you are desirous to breed a cock of the Game, whose delicacy of shape and excellency of heels, whose admirable hardness and most exquisite deportment in all respects may not only prove pleasing but also profitable to you, imprint these subsequent lines on your memory, that when you come to breed a bird of this sort you may not be wanting or unacquainted in those mysteries practised by the ablest masters in the world at this day in the noble art of cocking."

Harrison Weir

INTRODUCTION

"Breeding American Game is an inexact science. We never really know just how good the offspring will turn out when we plan the mating each spring. This makes breeding American Games an exciting and interesting phase of our hobby."

Kenny Troiano

As you well know, the aim of practically every cocker and backyard breeder is to create the best family or strain. We are all trying to make the breeding of American Games as successful as possible. Why else would we do it? What's interesting about this is that we all have different ideas of how to accomplish this. Some rely on "old wives tales" that were passed down from generation to generation; some play the "let's see what happens game." Then there are those who trust in the principles developed through scientific theory to guide their practice. Is one better than the other? All I can say is that the answer is somewhat subjective in nature, in other words, it depends on who you are talking to.

What I can tell you is this, the collective achievements of breeders all over the world, in originating, developing, and conserving specific breeds, varieties and strains, not mention, highly specialized lines, did not happen by accident or by random luck. They occurred as a result of the basic interest and determination to succeed, which all achievers must have. What secures this success? What do these breeders all share in common? Well, for the modern cocker, it's really very simple. It occurred because breeders had the ability to accurately assess the true breeding potential of their fowl, and to relate their observations of form, function and beauty into the creation of a bird (American Games), which has been developed through Selective Breeding for a specific purpose. Today it is the preservation and perpetuation of the breed. More importantly, it is the safeguarding and maintenance of their unique form and function.

We must never forget the purpose for which they exist and were originally bred for. Their purpose dictates their form, which in turn allows them to function properly. In short, "they must look, act and perform as a gamecock should." A lack in any one of these three criteria's spells disaster. They must also show the pride, honor and courage for which they are known to possess and are so famous for. We call this Gameness!

The breeding of American Gamefowl is very important, and may be carried on with any of the following objectives in mind:

- For the production of standard-bred, high quality American Gamefowl, primarily to preserve their true form, (which is very well illustrated in the American Gamefowl Standard of Perfection), and to secure its rightful place at the shows and in history as the king of all fowl.

- For the production of hatching eggs, and that of healthy, viable baby chicks. To secure the American Gamefowl for future generations.

- And that of the production of hybrid crosses (known as battlefowl), to secure their true function for which they were originally bred by our forefathers, for the purpose of competition and for survival of the fittest.

Whatever may be the objective, the incentive is always the same, to produce offspring that are better than their parents, year after year, generation after generation, and it is the fundamental principles of breeding that will determine your results.

It is my hope that the following information will be valuable and useful in all your endeavors to create, improve and preserve your fowl for future generations. And that you will take what I have taught you and pass it on to others, hopefully improved and enhanced for even better success, for I believe, as the old saying goes, a true Master is not the one with the most students, but one who creates the most Masters; a true leader is not the one with the most followers, but one who creates the most leaders; and a true teacher is not the one with the most knowledge, but one who enables others to become more knowledgeable.

Here is a list of subjects that we will discuss:
- A Brief History on the Breeding of Chickens
- Definition of Breeding
- The Practice of Selective Breeding
- The Importance of Variation
- The Importance of Selection
- The Practice of Inbreeding
- The Practice of Line-Breeding
- The Practice of Crossbreeding
- The Practice of Infusion - The Introduction of New Blood
- The Practice of Outcrossing
- The Practice of Grading-Up
- The Practice of Breeding By Means of Compensation

A BRIEF HISTORY ON THE BREEDING OF CHICKENS

"The several kinds of dogs are almost certainly descended from more than one species, and so it is with some other domesticated animals. Hence the crossing of aboriginally distinct species probably came into play at an early period in the formation of our present races."

Charles Darwin

The breeding of chickens probably began about 6000 B.C., when man first domesticated the Wild Junglefowl. These birds originated in South East Asia. However, it has been said that fowl were first bred and raised for cockfighting about 4500 years ago. Cockfighting, which is known as the first spectator sport, was popular throughout Asia, Africa and throughout Europe. At that time, practically no attention was given to the development of chickens for meat and egg production. I'm sure fowl were used for their culinary value, but in minute quantities and in remote areas.

In 1849 cockfighting was outlawed in England, not for reasons of morality but for political reasons. The royals were worried that cockers were plotting against them at the pits. Soon cockfighting was outlawed in many other countries as well. Here in America, although cockfighting laws were passed from state to state, there were four states that lasted until the late twentieth century.

Until the late eighteen hundreds, most poultrymen, especially cockers, were not interested in raising chickens for meat or egg production. They emphasized color and pattern of feathers, comb type, size and shape of body, and general attractiveness. Cockers would take this a step further and emphasize on traits such as ability, style and gameness. Many of the breeds in existence today were developed by the backyard breeder.

Once man learned the value of the chicken, they began to breed the chicken for a specific form and function, first for cockfighting and later for commercial reasons. Soon exotic breeds would be developed as well. In this short amount of time many new breeds were created, for a multitude of outcomes. It was for this reason that poultry shows became popular and numerous. Chickens went from being bred for sport to being bred for production; they were no longer bred just for hobby. Before you knew it, the demand for birds increased with the number of breeders. It wasn't long after, that chicken production became a profitable enterprise.

During the period from about 1890 to 1920, chicken raisers began to stress meat and egg production qualities in selecting their breeding stock. Chicken breeders relied largely upon the breeds that backyard breeders had developed. Improvement in egg and meat production was neither rapid nor great. Some breeders selected birds for egg production. Some were primarily concerned with meat qualities. Others tried to develop a general-purpose chicken for both meat and egg production. Eventually they were successful, and the chicken industry has never been the same.

The commercial hatchery business came into existence around 1920. Hatcheries at first relied upon backyard breeders to supply them with eggs. Later, many hatcheries took over the management of breeding flocks in addition to hatching eggs. Today hatcheries, in the effort to save on expenses, are looking again to the backyard breeder for their eggs.

It was also at this time the Old English Game, which was popular at the time, began to change as well. Soon other breeds of gamefowl would be introduced, such as Irish Games, Aseels and Spanish Games; this would set the way for the development of American Games.

Whether for sport, ornamental, or for commercial reasons, poultry breeding today is big business. The cocker and backyard breeder is likened to the modern-day scientist, who uses proven principles and practice, but is breaking new ground as well. Modern technology has developed breeders that are scientifically trained. New strains are developed all the time. Strains of existing breeds are maintained. Crosses of strains and breeds are being made. In fact, crossbred and hybrid chicks have become an important commodity for all areas of poultry breeding and raising.

The cocker and backyard breeder of today, whether sportsmen or farmers, who specialize in a particular breed or variety, must understand the principles and practice of breeding in order to be successful. This chapter is designed to help you in accomplishing just that.

DEFINITION OF BREEDING

The breeding of American Games is both a science and an art. It is a vocation or an avocation open to more people who are interested in developing their own strain than is true of any other breed of poultry. I would speculate to say that more than eighty-five percent of all backyard breeders in the United States keep gamefowl of some kind, and a majority of them raise American Games. Some are interested in the birds because of the eggs and meat that they produce, and others breed and raise American Games purely as a hobby (sport and exhibition).

There are certain characters possessed by American Games, which make small-scale, as well as large-scale operations, possible and interesting:
- First, the individual bird is small and a great deal of variation exists. Six to a dozen birds take up only a little space.
- Second, the time of reproduction is short and many progeny can be obtained from a single mating in any one year.
- Third, the life span is relatively short, compared to other animals.
- Fourth, progress comes easily.

For these reasons, a great many people, old and young, derive much pleasure from the breeding of American Games.

The breeding of American Games may be defined as the reproduction and inherent improvement of domestic birds. Reproduction is primarily concerned with the replacement of older individuals with individuals that are younger. Many cockers and backyard breeders are in the business of multiplying stock with little or no emphasis on improvement. Others, by the use of various breeding techniques, are making an effort to replace their birds with stock that is inherently better.

Actually, only a limited number of cockers and backyard breeders are in position and have the qualifications necessary to carry on a breeding program, which will result in noticeable hereditary improvement. Through the reading and studying of the contents of this book, you can be one of them.

THE PRACTICE OF SELECTIVE BREEDING
"Artificial Selection or Domestic Evolution"
Which method of breeding are you practicing?

"When practicing the art of Selective Breeding, you should breed in such a way that natural and Artificial Selection works hand in hand. This, I believe, is the foundation for success."

Kenny Troiano

Domestically bred animals are known as breeds. Within each breed we have varieties, and within each variety we have strains, and within each strain there are a series of lines, all, which are selectively bred for a particular form and function. This is a process that is normally done by a professional breeder for improving a family under domestication. He knows that if he is successful, his fowl will make a significant impact on the breed as a whole. And it will rise his reputation to great heights.

Many of us cockers can remember a time when there was a breed or variety that was better than the rest. I have often thought to myself, "How did they get them so good?" I have also noticed that there are breeders who are making an effort at improving or bringing back a particular breed or variety. Many of them will cross to something completely different in an effort to achieve their goals. This is not always a good idea. I do realize, of course, that crosses were a necessary evil used to make a certain breed or variety, but it is hard to determine the exact cross that was originally used in the creation of that breed. In this case, all we can hope for, when trying to reproduce it, is to come close. As you can see, knowledge of a breed is very important.

My principles for Selective Breeding is simple - breed and raise many offspring, cull ruthlessly, and select individuals that have variations which are desirable or advantageous, introducing new blood only when absolutely necessary. If we can follow these guidelines, we can usually improve the quality of what we have. That was the way it was done in the past, and the reason why many of us can remember birds of superior quality to this day.

We must also acknowledge that progress can be slow. In fact, many breeders spent a lifetime working to improve or create a new breed or variety. My advice would be to set a goal, create a plan to achieve that goal,

Potential for Variation

Defects   Diversity

Disease   Poor Ancestry

SELECTIVE BREEDING IMPROVES

- Health and Vigor
- Resistance to Disease
- Livability
- Longevity
- Fertility
- Hatchability

- Uniformity
- Purity of Blood
- Conformation of Body
- Plumage
- Disposition
- Performance

The importance of selective breeding.

and learn to recognize improvements, even though they may be very small. Most importantly, never give up, for the satisfaction of improving or creating a breed or variety can be beyond measure.

As many of you know, I breed American Games and Homing Pigeons; both are a great resource for learning how Selective Breeding operates. I have bred birds for over thirty-five years and have learned a lot about the process. I've learned how to create new variants and how to maintain ones already created.

It is my intention, with the information in this chapter, to help you in maintaining or creating fowl that you can be proud of. More importantly, fowl that will last well into the future. I hope you have much success in all your breeding endeavors.

WHAT IS SELECTIVE BREEDING? The term Selective Breeding is synonymous with Artificial Selection. For thousands of years, new breeds and varieties of domestic chickens have resulted from Selective Breeding for particular traits, or combination of traits. Some Selective Breeding techniques include Artificial Selection, where individuals with desirable traits are mated to produce offspring with those traits. A variation of this process traditionally used is inbreeding, where the offspring produced by Artificial Selection are mated with one another to reinforce those desirable traits.

Charles Darwin, the author of "Origins of Species."

In fact, Selective Breeding was used by Charles Darwin as a springboard to introduce the theory of Natural Selection, in which the differential reproduction of organisms with certain traits is attributed to improved survival or reproductive ability. This is known as "Darwinian Fitness." Selective Breeding was used by Darwin and other breeders to help support his theories. In his book, *"Origin of Species,"* Charles Darwin discussed how Selective Breeding had been successful in producing change over time. As opposed to Natural Selection, where the environment acts as a filter through which only certain variations can pass, in Artificial Selection, humans favor specific traits that they believe are beneficial or advantageous.

The first chapter of the book discusses Selective Breeding and domestication of such animals as pigeons and dogs. He even references chickens and their direct relationship to the Wild Junglefowl.

How does "Selective Breeding" support Darwin's hypothesis? Selective Breeding supports Darwin's theory because organisms adapt to their environments, and whoever is compatible with the environment for which they live will pass on their traits, even if that means outside their own species.

Although Natural Selection is guided by different influences other than that of Artificial Selection, they operate in similar manners. We, as breeders of American Gamefowl, may not breed outside the known species, but we do breed outside the known breed in creating new and more improved breeds. In fact, American Games have many breeds within their blood, such as, the Wild Junglefowl, Phoenician Games, Greek Games, Roman Games, Old English Games, Irish Games, Spanish Games, and Aseels, which carry in their bloodline breeds such as, Sumatra and Malay Games. However, as Darwin put it: *"As each breed is slowly improved, the inferior varieties are first neglected and finally lost."* When it was all said and done, we were left with the fowl we have today, the American Gamecock.

230

"If several varieties are grown together, and is indiscriminately selected,
it is clear that the hardier and more productive kinds will, by a sort of
Natural Selection, gradually prevail over the others."

Charles Darwin

NATURAL SELECTION VERSUS ARTIFICIAL SELECTION: To understand Artificial Selection, we must first understand Natural Selection. It should be emphasized however, that there is no real difference in the genetic processes that are fundamental to both Artificial and Natural Selection, and that the concept of Artificial Selection was used by Charles Darwin as an illustration of the wider process of Natural Selection.

The selection process is termed "artificial" when human preferences or influences have a significant effect on the evolution of a particular population or species. However, when it comes to Natural Selection, it's quite a different story, for there is a war of nature, where individuals are in a struggle for existence. The strong survive and reproduce, while the weak die and go extinct. Given enough variation, this selective pressure is enough to bring about slow incremental evolutionary change, a process mirrored perfectly in the breeding of chickens.

Although species or populations evolve, Natural Selection does not act directly on them as a whole. Natural Selection acts only on individuals. Each individual lives or dies accordingly, but it results in the evolution of species. Furthermore, Natural Selection acts on the whole individual. Because each individual is the sum of many different genetic traits, the relative advantage of each trait depends on its genetic context. For example, a trait increasing the growth rate of a tree's trunk and branches is useless, possibly even detrimental, unless accompanied by a trait to increase the growth of the roots.

Likewise with chickens, a trait that increases the length of the wings would be useless, possibly detrimental, unless accompanied by a trait that would lengthen the neck, body and legs, and increase the size of the tail. A bird such as this would be imbalanced.

Although, Natural Selection occurs due to predation and environmental influences, which often acts on minute differences between individuals producing slight changes from one generation to the next, Artificial Selection is the process of "selection through variation." This requires controlled mating for the production of specific traits that the breeder desires to perpetuate. In other words, it requires genetic variation on which to act. Sometimes it's through culling the undesirable traits that produces the biggest change, and in some cases it's much faster too.

<u>Note of interest</u>: If the variation in a trait is strictly environmentally induced, then the selected variants will not be inherited by the next generation.

Here is a proven Troiano Spangled-Red cock, owned and bred by Kenny Troiano. A fine product of good selection from a solid and well maintained family of Gamefowl.

Animals that are easily manipulated, such as Wild Junglefowl, were easy targets for Artificial Selection and domestication. The fact that it only takes a short time between generations facilitates the process of Artificial Selection, by speeding up the response to selection.

Is the nature of Artificial Selection irreversible? Artificial Selection differs fundamentally from Natural Selection in that it favors alleles (forms of a gene) that do not contribute favorably to survival in the wild. Such alleles are usually recessive; otherwise they would not persist in wild populations. Artificial Selection is essentially a process of increasing the frequency of rare, recessive alleles to the point where they usually appear in homozygous form. Once the wild-type alleles are eliminated from the population, the process of domestication has become irreversible and the domestic species has become dependent on humans for its survival.

Then again, if you were to take all the fowl that have been directly created from the Wild Junglefowl, it is the American Games that still, to this day, retain many of their natural instincts of their wild ancestors. You could put these fowl in the wild, on their own, with no assistance from humans of any kind, and they will survive and flourish. They will endure the elements of their environment. I would suspect that they would evolve as well. To what? Who knows? Maybe even revert back to their wild ancestors and retain the exact type and color of the Wild Junglefowl. Interesting thought.

"Facts in sufficient number have now been given showing that Natural Selection often checks, but occasionally favours, man's power of selection. These facts teach us, in addition, a valuable lesson, namely, that we ought to be extremely cautious in judging what characters are of importance in a state of nature to animals and plants, which have to struggle for existence from the hour of their birth to that of their death,—their existence depending on conditions, about which we are profoundly ignorant."

Charles Darwin

"From the occasional appearance of abnormal characters, though at first only slight in degree; from the effects of the use and the disuse of parts; possibly from the direct effects of changed climate and food; from correlation of growth; from occasional reversions to old and long-lost characters; from the crossing of breeds, when more than one had been formed; but, above all, from unconscious selection carried on during many generations, there is no insuperable difficulty, to the best of my judgment, in believing that all the breeds have descended from some one parent-source. Can any single species be named from which we may reasonably suppose that all are descended? The Gallus Bankiva apparently fulfills every requirement."

Charles Darwin

HOW SELECTIVE BREEDING FUNCTIONS: Today we live in a world of exquisite diversity, with more breeds and varieties of chickens than we can possible count. Why so many? Why so different? The answer is through the process of Selective Breeding.

Approximately 6000 B.C. in the countries of India and South East Asia, Gallus Bankiva, otherwise known as the Wild Junglefowl, were first known to be domesticated. As we well know, Wild Junglefowl eventually gave rise to gamefowl. As new breeds of gamefowl arose, they gave rise to other breeds, and as they did so, they changed. The change was so minute and subtle, but given enough time the results were spectacular. Today, we have more breeds of fowl than we can observe or even appreciate.

Many have mentioned, in wonder, the magnificence of the domestic chicken, but none have been more magnificent than that of the Games. Gamefowl are the exemplar of honor and courage, and they are the reason for the diverse assortment of fowl throughout the world. I wouldn't be surprised if gamefowl were someday called upon to save the domestic chicken from the devastating effects of genetic erosion. The heroes of the day will be those cockers who practice Selective Breeding.

Selective Breeding, also known as Domestic Evolution, is the process of inbreeding, line-breeding and outcrossing. It is the selection and breeding of animals for particular genetic traits. That is the obvious explanation, but what are the mechanics of the process?

- All chickens at birth are split up from each other according to the characteristics and traits for which they express.
- Breeders select birds which carry traits that are highly desirable, and they cull the rest.
- The birds selected for their special features will survive and reproduce
- The desirable features accumulate from generation to generation and eventually become exaggerated.
- Eventually they will evolve and become a new breed, or variety within the breed.

In short, Selective Breeding is the remarkable process of a breeder developing a superior breed over time, and selecting qualities within individuals of the breed that will be best to pass on to the next generation. Furthermore, it is the intentional breeding of birds with desirable traits in an attempt to produce offspring with similar desirable characteristics or with improved traits.

"Domestication, even when long continued, occasionally causes but a small amount of variability. The slight differences, however, which characterise each individual would in most, probably in all, cases suffice for the production of distinct races through careful and prolonged selection."

Charles Darwin

WHAT IS THE PROCESS OF SELECTIVE BREEDING? Today, nearly all breeding of domestic animals is "selective" as opposed to "random." Years ago, before the era of scientific genetics, breeding was done more by phenotype than by pedigree. Race horses tended to be bred by the stopwatch. Gamefowl tended to be bred by their performance in the pit, and why not? That was where the money was! Later, it was recognized that breeding together closely related animals tended to speed up the process of "fixing" the desired traits within a few generations.

Today, Selective Breeding has become a scientific practice, one that is a three method process, which includes: Isolation, Selection, and proper Breeding Techniques, such as inbreeding, line-breeding, and outcrossing. Let's discuss them now.

Isolation - There must be a period in which the members of the group are isolated before they can be relatively fixed. Without genetic isolation, the differentiation that creates a new breed cannot take place. Charles Darwin puts it like this: *"The prevention of free crossing, and the intentional matching of individual animals, are the corner-stones of the breeder's art. No man in his senses would expect to improve or modify a breed in any particular manner, or keep an old breed true and distinct, unless he separated his animals."* He goes on to say that: *"The killing of inferior animals in each generation comes to the same thing as their separation."*

Artificial Selection - Breeders must prevent random mating from coming about, and limit mating to those individuals who exhibit desirable characteristics. One logical consequence of this isolation is the next characteristic, "inbreeding, line-breeding, and out-crossing."

Inbreeding, line-breeding and out-crossing - Ordinarily, those who are controlling the breeding through Artificial Selection will find it necessary at some stage to utilize a certain degree of inbreeding or line-breeding, to facilitate the weeding out of undesired characteristics and the fixation of desirable traits. Inbreeding and line-breeding are controversial aspects of Artificial Selection, but have been practiced for centuries. Although there comes a time when the introduction of genetic material is necessary, outcrossing is always a better alternative to crossbreeding. Here is a better explanation of these methods of breeding:

- Inbreeding (mating closely related individuals) - Inbreeding is breeding between relatives, which results in a homozygous population. Breeders often practice inbreeding to "fix" desirable characteristics within a population.

- Line-breeding (mating within one bloodline or strain) – This is a form of inbreeding. It is used by breeders to "fix" certain desirable traits, while leaving out the undesirable traits that happen in inbreeding.

- Outcrossing (infusion of distantly related individuals) – This is the process of introducing genetic material from distant relations into a breeding line. This creates a certain amount of genetic diversity, which greatly reduces the probability of gaining a genetic disorder. It is used in line-breeding to restore size and fertility to a breeding line. Gregor Mendel used outcrossing in his experiments with flowers in his breeding stock.

Benefits and concerns:
- Benefits – The benefits of Selective Breeding is that breeders get to choose which birds fit their criteria, so more of the right kind of birds can be produced.

- Concerns – The overuse of Selective Breeding can result in genetic disorders, such as inbreeding depression, which occurs when an inbred individual shows lower health and fitness levels.

> *"As conspicuous deviations of structure occur rarely, the improvement of each breed is generally the result of the selection of slight individual differences. Hence the closest attention, the sharpest powers of observation, and indomitable perseverance, are indispensable."*
>
> *Charles Darwin*

SELECTIVE BREEDING IN ACTION: Breeding high quality American Games begins with superior broodfowl, used for the purpose of planned breeding.

When individuals are looking to breed high quality American Games, they must look for certain valuable traits in order to attain a certain purpose, preferably in purebred fowl. Some will use crossbreeding to produce a new strain, with different and presumably superior abilities in a given area.

234

Here is a proven Troiano Red cock, owned and bred by Kenny Troiano, a fine product of selective breeding.

To breed American Games, a typical breeder will start by buying a brood trio, or young juvenile birds. He may even purchase baby chicks or hatching eggs. It is for this reason that it benefits the breeder to study different breeds, varieties and strains of gamefowl, and analyze what can be expected from a certain set of characteristics before he or she starts breeding them. When purchasing initial broodfowl, the breeder should look for a group of birds that will most closely fit the purpose for which he intends to breed and raise them.

Purebred breeding aims to establish and maintain stable traits that the fowl will pass to the next generation. By breeding the "best to the best," utilizing a certain degree of inbreeding, considerable culling, and selection for "superior" qualities, one could develop a bloodline superior in certain respects to the original bloodline. Such birds should be pedigreed with some sort of record keeping.

However, single-trait breeding, which is the breeding of only one trait over all others, can be problematic at best. For instance, when cocks are bred for high station of leg - speed, power and accuracy is sacrificed. Their thinly developed, weak muscled legs can't perform properly, so they are quickly killed. This is known as the "law of correlation." This happens when a particular characteristic is closely linked or connected with another characteristic. When selecting for a specific trait, you must be careful that it does not have a tendency to generate changes in another trait.

"We see what selection, though acting on mere individual differences, can effect when families of the same race, have been separately bred during a number of years by different men without any wish on their part to modify the breed."

Charles Darwin

<u>SOME IMPORTANT PRINCIPLES OF SELECTIVE BREEDING</u>: The following are a few fundamental factors to consider in selecting high quality breeders of American Games:

1. Breed only from purebred birds of a well-established breed. By following this procedure a breeder gets uniformity of progeny.

2. Breed only from hens that lay eggs of the proper size, shape, and strength, and lays consistently from day to day throughout the breeding season, or until they go broody. Also, breed only from cocks that are virile and fertile. If culling has been accurately and persistently carried out, the remaining birds will usually be very good reproductively, and safe to use in the broodpens.

3. Breed only from mature birds, both cocks and hens. Mature birds produce offspring of better vigor and vitality.

4. Practice line-breeding wherever possible. This means breeding within closely related bloodlines. This practice combines and intensifies the good qualities of any strain. Wherever it is necessary to introduce new bloodlines, great care should be used to see that the birds, through which they are introduced, carry all the desired attributes of the original bloodline in a very definite degree.

5. The breeding from hens, which as pullets, were excellent layers and carry all the attributes mentioned earlier, such as proper size, shape, and strength of eggs, and they laid consistently from day to day throughout the breeding season, or until they became broody, is a good practice.

6. Breed from hens that molt late and finish early. Hens which molt early and take a long time to change their plumage are generally poor producers of eggs during the breeding season, and should never be used in the broodpens. Late molters are quick molters and almost universally great producers of high quality eggs during the breeding season.

7. Breed from birds, cocks and hens that are active and have good appetites, and have well-formed, athletic looking bodies, capable of digesting and transforming large quantities of feed in a short period of time.

8. Breed from birds which are early risers and are the last ones on the perches at night. Such habits indicate a healthy bird, for that bird is busy searching and scratching for feed.

SELECTIVE BREEDING AND HYBRIDIZATION: Although crossbreeds are a mix of two purebreds, hybridization is a process of Selective Breeding that is much more involved. This involves crossing two individuals with different desirable traits to produce offspring with a combination of both desirable traits. An example of this is the crossing of two gamefowl strains in the production of battle-crosses. They share many common traits, such as gameness and performance ability, but it also produces offspring that are bigger, better, faster, stronger and smarter than either of their parents, or the original blood from which they came.

Another example would be that of the Cornish-Cross chickens, which were developed by breeding White Cornish fowl with that of the White Plymouth Rocks, which provide good meat in a relatively short period of time (normally five or six weeks). Today the Cornish-Cross chicken is the mainstream of the commercial meat industry.

WHAT ARE THE SIMILARITIES BETWEEN SELECTIVE BREEDING AND GENETIC ENGINEERING? Many ask me, is Selective Breeding similar to genetic engineering? My answer is no, not at all. Genetic engineering is the combining of DNA from different species, and can only be done in the laboratory. Selective Breeding uses natural biological means to alter genetics. An example of this is using a bird from one strain to fertilize another strain and so "cross" the gene pools. Genetic engineering artificially goes into the chromosomes to edit them, this is an unnatural process.

There are some similarities, however. For instance, both genetic engineering and Selective Breeding result in modification of an organism's genotype. In other words, the organism's genes are changed in some way. If one or more genes from another species are introduced, the resulting genome consists of recombinant DNA.

In both processes, humans are in control, rather than Natural Selection. So humans decide which individual animals to retain in each generation. And in both processes, the purpose is to make the birds better from a human point of view.

WHAT SELECTIVE BREEDING HAS ACHIEVED: Unbelievable though, as it may seem, these gorgeous but inbred aristocrats of the avian world, the American and Old English Games, which include muffs, beards, and topknots, are all descendants of the Wild Junglefowl of Southeast Asia. In time, they have developed into a wide assortment of breeds and varieties of all colors and types, and the best part is, we are not even through, for evolution has no end. Just look at all the different breeds of chickens throughout the world. The possibilities are enormous.

I'm sure there are some who enjoy the activity of developing a new breed or variety, which is fine. However, my interests and desire for others is to take existing breeds and make them better. If you have one of those rare breeds, rather than being the last one to have them, why not spread them around. Encourage other breeders to do the same. It would be great to see some of these rare varieties of American Games make a comeback.

THE IMPORTANCE OF VARIATION
For it is the mechanism of all improvement

"Good gamefowl are multidimensional. When the attributes of appearance, temperament, and performance, harmonize to form one cohesive unit, it's as if it was created by the hand of God!"

Kenny Troiano

If you have followed my writings throughout the years, you know that I cover this one quite a bit, for I feel that variation is of extreme importance to the breeder of American Games. In fact, I consider variation a law; the ultimate law of breeding, for it is the basis of all improvement. Charles Darwin considered variation to be the mechanism of evolution; well it is also the mechanism for which Selective Breeding operates. Without variation, progress in breeding would be impossible. Without variation, the selection of superior individuals would be impossible. Without selection, improvement is impossible. In other words, variation makes selection possible and selection makes improvement possible. Charles Darwin put it like this: *"This want of uniformity in the parts which at the time are undergoing selection chiefly depends, to a certain extent on the continued variability of the parts which have recently varied. That the same parts do continue varying in the same manner we must admit, for if it were not so, there could be no improvement beyond an early standard of excellence, and we know that such improvement is not only possible, but is of general occurrence."* He goes on to say: *"As a consequence of continued variability, all highly improved races, if neglected or not subjected to incessant selection, soon degenerate."* In other words, selection should be continuously practiced by the breeder or his fowl will suffer degeneration.

Note: I quote Darwin quite a bit it this book, especially in the next two sections. I feel his work on "The Variation of Animal and Plants under Domestication" sums up, very well, what I believe about Selective Breeding. It is my hope that his insight in this area will help you is breeding better fowl.

Variations are often due to distribution of traits among the offspring according to a definite method of inheritance. While the offspring of any single mating may be uniform and resemble the parents quite closely, they are almost never exactly alike. A group of offspring from the same parents will differ among themselves, and some, or all of them, may differ from their parents. When I have fellow cocker visit my farm, they are always amazed on how uniform and alike my fowl actually are. They can't tell them apart, but I can. Although I do believe my fowl are extremely uniform and consistent, in all their attributes, every bird has their own special features and personalities. Although minute, I see the variations throughout my yard. I know they are extremely uniform and consistent, but there are differences from one bird to the next.

"Variation has been led along certain beneficial lines, "like a stream" along definite and useful lines of irrigation."

Charles Darwin

LAW OF VARIATION: As I mentioned earlier, I do believe this to be a law. This law may be defined as the tendency of individuals to produce progeny, which differ in type from either parent. Whatever the cause of variation, the fact that there is great difference among fowls is of particular significance in inheritance, for it is constantly working in opposition to the law of heredity, and might be expressed as the law that "like does not produce like."

If all the individuals in a family of birds were exactly alike, with reference to their reproductive cells, further selection would be useless, as no improvement could be expected. Thank God that is not the case, for I am always looking for ways to improve my fowl, and I look to variations in order to do this.

In the light of modern knowledge, the causes of variations can be difficult to understand. It will be noted, however, that in many cases, the progeny are not like the parents. In some instances, the differences may be slight and exhibited only in one or two characters, while in others, the variations may be very noticeable and cover a great variety of characteristics and traits, not to mention forms and functions. The fact that individuals do vary makes improvement possible through selection and breeding, which would otherwise be impossible. Indeed, without this factor there would be no chance for either improvement or deterioration. The type would be fixed in all its characteristics.

THE SOURCE OF GENETIC VARIATION: The variability between individuals of the same close family ultimately arises from mutations, actual changes in the basic structure of DNA. Mutations can arise spontaneously, but also are induced by radiation and certain chemicals. Although mutations can occur in any cell in the body, only those in the cells that produce sperm and eggs can be passed on to an individual's offspring.

If you were to study the Wild Junglefowl of South East Asia, in which all chickens originated, including American Games, in the last thousand or so generations, I would bet many mutations have risen. Neutral and advantageous ones may persist, while disadvantageous ones may die out. Over time, a great deal of variability may be produced in a population. Evidence of this is seen in the fact we have so many different breeds and varieties of chickens presently in the world.

A key point that is misunderstood by many is that mutations are random. They arise by chance, not for a purpose. For instance, the variation in the flight speed of Homing Pigeons (if you have pigeons, as I do, you know exactly what I'm talking about) did not develop because a need for faster birds arose, but because either:

1. By chance, a range of flight speeds existed in the population before predation by Cooper's Hawks became a survival factor.
2. Or a mutation increasing flight speed arose randomly in a Homing Pigeon, allowing it to more readily escape hawk predation.

Let's say you and a friend are walking in the woods. All of a sudden a bear shows up. Both of you begin to run. To survive, you do not need to be faster than the bear; you just need to be faster than the other guy. In time your descendants will become faster and faster and they will be the sole survivors. The rest of the population will be eaten and go extinct. This is a crude example, but it shows how variation works for Natural Selection, and artificial selection works in a very similar way, only man decides which birds will continue to breed and procreate and which ones will be culled. Once the variability exists, Natural Selection proceeds in a very nonrandom fashion, but the type of variability that arises in the first place is random.

The random nature of mutations explains why evolution is often so slow. Nearly all mutations are detrimental. As I was once told, *"Think of any living thing as a finely tuned watch. What is the chance that dropping your watch will improve its function?"* Natural Selection proceeds slowly because it has no predetermined purpose, it is not goal oriented. Natural Selection works on the random efforts of a "blind watchmaker."

Although mutations are random, "Artificial Selection," or as I like to call it, "Selective Breeding" is anything but random or slow. Within a short time, it can produce a masterpiece of characteristics and traits, from colorful, elaborate feathers to the amazing performance qualities and gameness that we see in our American Games. And it's through variations that randomly appear within the family that this is possible.

"On the whole we may conclude that whatever part or character is most valued, that character will almost invariably be found to present the greatest amount of difference both in kind and degree. And this result may be safely attributed to man having preserved during a long course of generations the variations which were useful to him, and neglected the others."

Charles Darwin

<u>VARIATION - THE MECHANISM FOR IMPROVEMENT</u>: The object of every serious breeder is to establish not only a good strain but one better than any thus far produced. Breeders select desirable features to survive and reproduce, and cull the rest! The desirable features accumulate from generation to generation and become exaggerated. Whether he is breeding for form or for purely functional qualities, his actions are concentrated in an attempt to exaggerate some already exaggerated characters or "points," which he believes will add to the beauty or the performance of the strain. Although the breeder is fully aware that some features help the bird while others hinder it, it is through the remarkable process of "Selective Breeding by means of Artificial Selection" that birds are quickly modified and transformed into an astonishment of form, function and beauty. This can be achieved through the selection of any trait, whether on purpose or by chance. For instance, if a breeder of American Games, without any thought of making a new breed, simply admired, for example, short-beaked birds more than long-beaked birds, he would, while reducing the number of fowl, generally cull the long-beaked birds. As a result he would, in the course of time, modify his strain. Thanks to this process, it is now possible for the breeder to accomplish his aim in a limited period of time, whereas in earlier times it would have taken a lifetime in the creation of a strain.

There are three chief ways in which new varieties of American Games can be formed, which we will discuss at this time.

<u>The first sort of variation</u>: In the first case, a sudden variation or sport (now better known as mutations or discontinuous variations) appears in the breed, such as the appearance of a crest or feathers on the head, the appearance of feathers or fluff under the beak, as in muffs, as well as many other cases.

As breeders are very quick to make a secret of a unexpected but valuable new variation, treating it as though they have, by some miracle, created a new breed or variety, it is sometimes difficult to trace the exact origin of any really original variation. It seems to be fairly certain, however, that the same sport is at times frequently repeated in a breed or variety, proving that, although from an unknown cause, is a common occurrence.

A close study of American Games has also impressed me on the idea that variations, when they come, are very quick to take the form of a character normal to some of the wild species, such as the

Wild Junglefowl of South East Asia, or species of the same family. Also, the larger the family, the greater the variation among the members of the family. Many American Games have their counterpart in different strains all over the world. The breed is so large, therefore, variations in American Games is extensive.

There are two kinds of variability - "The changes of characters that are highly exaggerated, which consist of the acquisition of new genes, or the loss of already existing ones." The cause of variation, if not its nature, remains a great mystery. But all agree that it is due to the omission or introduction of a genetic factor. I heard it put once that - *"How the pack is shuffled and dealt we can only observe; but what are the cards?"* Wild and mysterious the question may sound; genetic research may answer it yet.

All scientists, whatever their background, have always agreed that mutations are hereditary. Therefore, where is the proof that varieties, which are called "sports" are not fixed. On the contrary, they are often transmitted to successive generations with curious persistence.

The length of time a character has been in existence in a breed gives us no clue as to its hereditary behavior under given conditions. It was once thought that the genetically older character was the dominant or prepotent one. New technology, however, has revealed that this is not true, though it seems to be pretty well accepted that when the new variety is recessive, it is clear that the variety occurs in consequence of the error of a genetic factor.

The point of practical importance to breeders is the fact that we get a key to the methods, it is necessary to adapt in order to establish a breed from a "sport" basis. When such birds are mated with the only available type, the wild one, the progeny almost invariably come of the wild coloration. As an element (pigmental) is missing in these sports, we now know that they may be expected to be recessive; and we also know that the possibility is that if we mate together their wild colored progeny, a proportion of "sports" will return among the offspring, which, when mated together or with the original sport, will breed true to the new type.

The second sort of variation: This is brought about by the slow process of the selection of extremes or fluctuations. This is a class of variation which closely affects the modern cocker and backyard breeder, and is best described as "Fluctuations," which are limited to increase and decrease of what is already available.

The third sort of variation: As we shall return to a consideration of fluctuating variability further in the book, we may pass on to the third and last, but by no means least, important way in which varieties may be formed. This is by the recombination of already existing material.

> *"It has been boldly maintained by some authors that the amount of variation to which our domestic productions are liable is strictly limited; but this is an assertion resting on little evidence. Whether or not the amount of change in any particular direction is limited, the tendency to general variability is, as far as we can judge, unlimited."*
>
> *Charles Darwin*

Variations are limited by the processes of selection: Although there seems to be almost no limit to the possible number of variations, they are, as everyone knows, strictly limited by processes of Natural and Artificial Selection. Man allows greater license than Nature in the genetic materials that he controls. But even he cannot tolerate the monstrous or the absolutely useless. Hence, the limit is set to the degree of variation that he permits. In creatures like American Games, in which almost every possible variation seems to be already in existence, these days the only originality is those produced by a reshuffling of the cards. In other words, a recombination of the gene pools. The result is apparent in the numberless breeds differing from one another, only in one or two characters, and in their degree of purity.

It is possible, as we have already seen, to graft a new character on in two or three generations, such as a different comb or a different feather. The "purity" of the result depends mainly upon the breeder's knowledge of the laws of heredity, and the modesty of his ambitions. Obviously the greater the number of points the breeds crossed differs in, the longer will be the time taken to reestablish the uniformity and constancy of the genes of the new combination.

Discovering which class of variation the breed originated: In establishing a strain, the first points of importance are to discover from which class of variation the breed originated, and its degree of uniformity. If the breed originated from a recessive sport, we have already seen the steps that are necessary to take in order to perpetuate it. If the breed is of crossbred origin, then it will be necessary to determine the exact statistical relationship of every "point" or character. A variety formed from two breeds, which differ in a great number of characters may be exceedingly difficult to make "pure" or uniform. This can only be reached by analyzing each character separately on the Mendelian system. It is presumably possible in a cross between diverse breeds to get all the phenomena (dominance, blended inheritance, reappearance of ancestral form, etc.) exhibited in the various characters of the crossbred, as it is also possible to get entire dominance of one form over the other, in which case, the recessives would be as pure as their original grandparent.

"Breeding Out" a wrong quality in a variety: Cockers and backyard breeders are often puzzled at the difficulty which may sometimes be experienced in "breeding out" a wrong quality in a variety. When pea-combed varieties of gamefowl became the fashion, sometime in the middle of the twentieth-century, the earliest and best strains were still of the Old English Games that were imported from England, the country of their origin. The only problem was that they always threw straight (*single*) combed offspring. Birds with these so-called faults, but good in other respects, were sometimes used in the broodpen, and the straight (*single*) comb was seldom inherited.

We now know that straight (*single*) comb is recessive to pea-comb. Therefore, no bird with straight (*single*) comb should ever be permitted in the broodpen, if it was desired to eliminate this trait altogether.

That these qualities were in existence in the American Games at all, at the period of which we speak, is testimony to the want of proper selection, in the earliest days of the establishment of the breed, for the characters under consideration were no doubt first derived from an Aseel cross made to secure the pea-comb trait, and might have been eliminated by careful selection on a sufficiently extensive scale.

The possibility of eliminating an undesirable character: What breeders of many years ago failed to realize was that it was possible to entirely eliminate an undesirable character. It was taken for granted that features would keep cropping up, as we know indeed will, if genes representing them still exist in an active state in the germ cells; and we of the present day are the richer for the knowledge that definite characters can be totally suppressed by eliminating from the broodpen all individuals which possess them or carry them in their germ cells.

242

<u>VARIATION PROVIDES GREAT OPPORTUNITY FOR THE BREEDER</u>: Some fowls of the same breed or ancestry vary in their features; it may be in the finer points of conformation of body, size and weight of the body, or station (length of leg). It may be in the color of their eyes, or the color of their plumage, etc. Although this is the very essence of variation, there is good news. Variation provides a great opportunity for the breeder. The problem that confronts him at the outset is first to recognize the limitations due to heredity, and, second, to discover wherein certain points or characteristics may be improved by taking advantage of variation.

Variations are of two kinds, those which increase the usefulness of the individual and those which are undesirable, or create an inferior condition. It is the responsibility and purpose of the breeder to select and intensify desirable variations whenever possible, while eliminating the undesirable.

The questions I get most are - "*How may desirable variations can be fixed?*" "*Is it an evolutionary process?*" In other words, "*is it a process of breeding that requires years to accomplish, or will it happen all at once?*" When it comes to American Games, three general principles should be considered:

- All traits and characters vary to a considerable extent in inheritance.
- Variation, as a phenomenon of inheritance, is probably not (although it could be) caused by the sudden cropping out of a distinctly new and different character.
- Variation is the result of changes taking place in existing characters, due to the changing relation between characters.

<u>Interesting as they may be, these three principles tend to raise the following questions</u>:
- Will the immediate parent transmit his or her qualities to the offspring, or will the influence of all the ancestors be apparent?
- Is it a variation that is called continuous, because it has been gradually evolved, step by step, or is it discontinuous, appearing suddenly, having none of the characteristics of its immediate ancestors?

The old theory of breeding was that "all variation was continuous," or, if a sport or mutation did appear, it would suddenly disappear. In other words, all improvement was the result of selection, selecting the best, generation after generation, until finally the desired type or characteristics became firmly fixed. This was the theory of Charles Darwin, but it has been shown that all improvement is not a slow evolutionary process, that it's not all a matter of selection, but that a new type may suddenly appear and start a new breed or a new variety.

The vast majority of "sports" or mutants may not breed true. They may disappear as suddenly as they appeared, but the breeder with a good knowledge of the breeding tendencies of his family or strain will carefully test any variations that point to higher excellence.

There are many breeds of fowls that owe its existence to the appearance of a mutation or mutant bird. American Games that are white are nothing more than a "sport" that came from a Black-Breasted Red breed and resulted in one of our popular breeds. The occasional mutant may humiliate the breeder who is breeding for uniformity, but the breeder who wishes to perpetuate new and desirable characteristics, or establish a new breed must be on the lookout for and carefully preserve such characteristics when they appear.

A white individual from a red family may or may not breed true. Some of them may and some may not, but the progressive breeder will take his chances. So far as it is now known, it is a chance, and the sure way to determine whether they will breed true is to test them in the broodpen.

"It is, also, highly important that many individuals of the breed which is to be improved should be raised; for thus there will be a better chance of the appearance of variations in the right direction, and individuals varying in an unfavourable manner may be freely rejected or destroyed. But that a large number of individuals should be raised, it is necessary that the conditions of life should favour the propagation of the species."

Charles Darwin

THE LOSS OF VARIATION AND THE BEGINNINGS OF A GENETIC BOTTLENECK:
Many know that I promote the creation and breeding of pure families and strains. However, there are some dangers to this practice that you should be aware of. Although uniformity is the name of the game, some variation is actually a good thing. You do not want to eliminate all variation. Remember, variation makes selection possible, and selection makes improvement possible. It's all about eliminating the bad variations while taking advantage of the good.

When creating or maintaining a family, you want to make sure to have a good number of birds to work with. In some cases, the larger the population the better.

When a population becomes very small, three things begin to happen that will cause a loss of genetic variation:

1. Merely accidental, some alleles, beginning with the rarest ones, disappear altogether.
2. The rate, at which new alleles crop up, in the population as a whole, declines, because there are fewer individuals in which new mutations can occur.
3. Opportunities to pair with genetically dissimilar individuals become reduced, so that close inbreeding begins to occur more frequently.

The resulting loss of genetic variation, in the family as a whole, then leads to both a decrease in hatchability and an increase in mortality, due to birds that have a poor resistance to disease. Therefore, extremely small populations are subject to an ever-worsening spiral - as each succeeding generation fails to replace itself fully, more alleles (forms of a gene) are lost and the population becomes even more inbred, or genetically homogeneous. Families such as these are said to have experienced a genetic bottleneck.

"Unfavourable conditions of life overrule the power of selection."

Charles Darwin

EFFECTS OF THE ENVIRONMENT:
The breeder must always keep in mind that, variations are of many kinds and are due to many causes. Except for most of the color characteristics and certainly of the morphological characteristics, the actual differences between two individuals are caused partly by environmental influences as well as by heredity. In fact, many variations are due to environmental influences, such as differences in heat, light, moisture, and food, as well as many other factors.

Environmental influences exercise their effects on such characteristics as the size and weight of the bird, reproductive qualities, such as good egg production of the hen and good fertility of the cock, not to mention proper egg size and shape. It also influences the rate of hatchability and viability in the chicks, as well as proper growth rate and overall development of young stags and pullets. Therefore, an individual in its definitive form is the result of both hereditary and environmental influences. This creates a big problem when it comes to selecting broodfowl. It makes it more difficult because the modern cocker may mistake the effects of the environment for the effects of the genes, and as a result, save some birds that will prove to be poor breeders.

THE IMPORTANCE OF SELECTION

"The importance of the great principle of Selection mainly lies in this power of selecting scarcely appreciable differences, which nevertheless are found to be transmissible, and which can be accumulated until the result is made manifest to the eyes of every beholder."

Charles Darwin

"Know that the cock which you intend to breed from must be a bird well descended, rightly shaped; he must also be most healthful, fresh, and full of feather"

Harrison Weir

We have just discussed the importance of variation, now we will discuss its relationship to selection. For, variation is highly effective through selection. However, it would be wise to remember that although variation is responsible for creating the exceptional individual, it is selection that is responsible for preserving it.

Selection, or the practice of picking superior birds for breeding, is the most fascinating process in all breeding endeavors. By selection, what I am talking about is the process of choosing the fowl (both cock and hen) that will eventually be used in the broodpen, the idea being to select those individuals with desirable qualities, which are prepotent with regard to these qualities.

Consistent selection year after year, with a clear idea of purpose in mind, will bring about a continual improvement or trend toward a common goal or objective. For most cockers, the ultimate aim in breeding and selecting American Games is to improve the bird's competitive advantage, and in turn, their winning percentage. Since pit performance is the fundamental purpose for which most American Game breeding is directed, the average cocker and backyard breeder's principle concern is in breeding for traits to improve that function.

Although traits concerning performance must be emphasized, let's not forget about conformation of body. Conformation is the part of the bird which allows him to carry out the function for which he was bred, and to achieve true superiority as a gamecock.

"A species may be highly variable, but distinct races will not be formed, if from any cause selection be not applied."

Charles Darwin

<u>Using selection to change the probabilities in your favor</u>: Not even the best breeders in the world can say they have produced a family of gamefowl that are successful 100% of the time. But if a breeder can change the probabilities in his favor through proper selection and superior breeding techniques, as well as non-genetic factors, like good management and proper nutrition, he will be in a much better position than his opponent. Suffice it to say that a well-bred, well-put together cock is more likely to win if pitted against one that is not as well put together as it is.

If your interest is to improve conformation of body, then you must select broodfowl that possess characteristics or traits that will improve conformation of body, and use a breeding system that will allow them to perpetuate these traits.

Now that we have a basic foundation, let's talk about the many facets of the selection process.

> *"Unless some degree of selection be exercised, the free commingling of the individuals of the same variety soon obliterates the slight differences which arise, and gives uniformity of character to the whole body of individuals."*
>
> *Charles Darwin*

<u>SELECTION AND THE PURPOSE OF THE BREEDER</u>: Regardless of the extent or the method of breeding, the modern cocker and backyard breeder always has, at his command, the power of selection. This is the real source of improvement. Nevertheless, it is only made possible by variation, and is responsible for many of the most well-known developments in poultry breeding.

By selection, what we are really talking about is the ability to choose broodfowl for propagating purposes, which possess desirable qualities, and which are prepotent with regard to these characteristics, so that, with proper care, the resulting progeny will be of a high standard of excellence, which can be maintained for generations. To select consistently and bring about definite improvement, a breeder must have a clear idea of his purpose, and work continuously toward it. He must know the breed with which he is working, as well as its ancestry. He must understand the principles that are fundamental to the selection process, and use judgment in departing from certain well-defined lines.

As far as the various physiological characteristics are concerned, it is safe to say that any two birds will be genetically dissimilar to a greater or lesser degree. The problem for the modern cocker or backyard breeder is to be able to identify which of the two is superior in its ability to transmit the desirable genes to their offspring. It should be kept in mind however, that selection can do nothing toward creating new genes. Nevertheless, the selection of the best individuals for future breeding purposes makes possible the separation of desirable genes from each of the parents, and the recombination of these desirable genes in the progeny.

In selection, there is an important but fundamental advantage, which results in absolute improvement of quality. Selection accomplishes two well-defined results:

1. It increases the quality of individuals, thereby making it possible to secure superior families.

2. It stimulates the average performance by raising the average of the mass, by eliminating the poor specimens, and by substituting superior specimens in their place.

It is important to understand that, although, selection is an effective method for elevating a family to a higher standard, it is not achieved through the elimination of the lower or average members.

> *"An animal of little value and bred by poor people, there has been no selection, and distinct races have not been formed... But when selection is brought to bear, all is changed."*
>
> *Charles Darwin*

246

THE ABILITY TO IDENTIFY GREAT INDIVIDUALS IS THE FIRST REQUISITE OF A SUCCESSFUL BREEDING PROGRAM: In order to achieve progress, it is necessary for the modern cocker to be able to identify superior broodcocks and broodhens, and to mate them in such a way that they will produce the largest possible number of progeny possessing the desirable characters for which the family is being bred. The ability to identify cocks and hens of superior breeding worth is the first requisite of a successful breeding program. This is just as true in breeding for perfection in standard-bred excellence as in breeding for excellence in pit performance.

In many gamefowl farms throughout the country, far too many birds of inferior breeding worth are used each year because many cockers apparently have never adopted a logical basis on which to select their broodfowl. The results secured from many matings are largely matters of chance. In too many cases, the matings are made by guesswork due to an insecure amount of evidence upon which to base the intelligent selection of the proper broodcocks and broodhens.

How to eliminate some of the guesswork in selecting broodfowl and how to mate cocks and hens of superior breeding worth for the development of superior strains is discussed in the following pages. I am confident that if you follow these techniques, you will be successful in your breeding endeavors.

"Whenever and wherever selection is not practised, distinct races are not formed..."

Charles Darwin

SELECTION IN BREEDING: When breeding American Games, future progress depends largely upon the breeder's ability to control heredity, and heredity can be controlled and directed best only when the knowledge of the breeder develops sufficiently to enable him to select broodfowl that will transmit their most desirable qualities to their offspring. It was once said to me that - "*Selection is the keynote in the program of future development.*" Therefore, refinement in the "Methods of Selection" is a very important quandary, which confronts all breeders of American Games.

History dictates that the breeding of American Games rest at the very foundation for which they were originally bred, which is for the purpose of cockfighting. Every facet of selection is used towards that end, whether in practice (the pit) or as an illustration as in poultry exhibitions. The many diversified varieties and strains of American Games that are in existence today, which have been produced from a very small number of originally ancestral forms, is striking evidence of the degree to which man has developed and extended his control over the natural processes of reproduction.

When you look at the modern domestic chicken, and its great diversification, you can plainly see that man's interest has led to the production of many of the standard breeds and varieties known to us today. The satisfaction of having developed something new has become the best incentive in man's efforts to understand the laws of inheritance.

In a practical world, however, which we find ours to be, there has been a growing demand for high quality gamefowl, fowl that meets our needs as well as our interests. The production of high quality American Games becomes more important as the number of cockers increases. Therefore, the modern cocker and backyard breeder is ever more confronted with the question: "*How can I best select and breed my fowl to produce offspring possessing the most desirable qualities?"* The answer to this question is obvious, in, that the rather haphazard and experiential methods of procedure in breeding American Games must be superseded by a thorough and systematic study of the inheritance of factors associated with form, function and beauty, and the selection thereof.

"A fancier who wished to decrease the size of his bantams would never think of starving them, but would select the smallest individuals which spontaneously appeared."
Charles Darwin

Selection by appearance: The system of breeding for the development of a high quality strain involves the fundamental principles of inheritance. Yet, the practice of many breeders is that they base their breeding solely on the selection of the best looking cocks to mate to the best looking hens, on the theory that "like tends to beget like." The only problem with this practice is that the degree of success or progress achieved under this system of breeding is usually very slow.

In the case of performance ability in fowls, experience has shown that the selection of broodfowl based on their appearance only proved to be an exceedingly unreliable guide to their real breeding worth. Conformation of body and color is only one part of the equation. There are many more parts to consider.

Select for standard-bred quality: In the breeding of American Games, reasonable care must be taken to maintain standard-bred qualities, particularly breed type (conformation of body) and plumage coloration, as well as, freedom from defects and disqualifications, such as, duck-toes, stubs on the shanks, squirrel tails and wry tails, just to name a few.

Many cockers ask me what are the possibilities of breeding a number of different birds of various strains, and combining characteristics of type, ability, and style? Such is a possibility, although evidence has shown that the greater the number of desirable characters being bred for, the more complex becomes the breeding program. As in the breeding of other types of livestock, proper consideration must be given to breed standards, as many factors as possible should be taken into consideration when selecting both the broodcocks and the broodhens, for proper selection is the keynote to further progress.

Select good body type: The proper size and shape of the head, a solid beak, and a pair of prominently developed bright eyes are characteristics of good vigor. Good football type body that is corky to the feel, with a back that is flat and wide at the shoulders and tapers nicely at the tail is desirable too. The keel should be of good length to give proper support to the abdominal muscles, but not be deep or pointed. The legs should be placed well apart, knock-knees being particularly objectionable since they are an indication of constitutional weakness. While ruggedness is desirable in both the broodcock and broodhen, extremely coarse looking birds should not be selected as broodfowl. Broodfowl should possess "quality," using that term in a very general sense to indicate refinement in their body characteristics and applied particularly to smooth scales on the shanks.

Select for Hatchability and Livability: The selection of broodfowl based on the progeny test should also take into consideration the results obtained in respect to hatchability of the eggs and the livability of the chicks. A cock might be selected as a broodcock because he was out of a multiple winning cock or may be a multiple winner himself, or out of a hen that came from a multiple winning line, but he might prove to be a poor breeder because he carried genes for low hatchability.

Select broodfowl for constitutional vigor: Every breeder appreciates the importance of selecting broodfowl which possess an abundance of constitutional vigor, but do they actually select in favor of it? The vigor of the family must be kept up. If this is not done, bad results will be obtained in fertility, hatchability and the rearing of the young offspring. Success, whether in the pit or in exhibition, or the combination of the two, depends upon these factors:

- The ability to keep the family healthy.
- The ability of the birds to breed.
- The ability of the eggs to hatch.
- The chick's ability to grow and develop properly.

Selection for vigor is, therefore, most important. In fact, it is fundamental. The basis of selection often differs among breeders because there is little definite information regarding exactly what constitutes vigor. If you asked ten breeders what they think, you would probably get ten different answers. The breeder must not be blinded by excellence of color to the necessity of vigor, strength and constitution. The breeder must always be aware of fowl that look weak and listless and fails to develop properly. It is not always possible to select the most vigorous birds, but the appearance of the fowl and their actions are a pretty reliable indicator to their health, vigor and overall condition.

A good indication of health and vigor are fowl that have bright colored eyes; well proportioned head parts; glossy, clean plumage; good conformation of body; always active, energetic, and alert to their surroundings; and have made good, continuous growth. Fowl such as this are usually strong, vigorous individuals. A well-proportioned bird is much more desirable than a long-legged, knock-kneed specimen, or one that is obviously weak.

Avoid fowls which show:
- Sunken eyes.
- Long, narrow, snaky heads.
- Toes, which are long for the breed.
- Listlessness and are inactive.
- Whose growth has been slow, uneven or unbalanced.

Cocks, especially those over one year old, sometimes become weak in their hock joints. They show this by standing unsteadily on their legs and raise their feet unusually high in stepping. Cocks which are too long in the leg (high stationed), in a family that is not known for this trait, seem to be more susceptible to this condition. Such birds should not be used as breeders.

Although there is relatively little definite information regarding the extent to which various characters are associated with performance and ability, the breeder of American Games can at least eliminate the fowl that are obviously unfit.

Select broodfowl on the basis of ancestry: A bird's ancestry gives considerable information of value regarding the relative worth of the bird as a prospective breeder. Of two good birds that have won the same number of competitions of approximately the same conformation of body and color, the bird with a good ancestry is to be preferred to the bird with a poor ancestry. The chances that the bird of good ancestry will produce progeny possessing the desirable characteristics being bred for are greater than those of the bird with poor ancestry. Although the chances are greater, there is no guarantee that a good bird of good ancestry will always produce good progeny.

Good ancestry is an important factor in increasing the chances that the selected bird will give better results in breeding. But in order that the breeder may make the best selection of his broodfowl, he needs to consider more than the characters, which the bird itself possesses and its ancestry; he should also consider the kind of brothers and sisters the bird has.

Select on the basis of the birds siblings: The selection of a bird as a prospective breeder on the basis of the kind of brothers and sisters it has is the next progressive step in the selection of broodfowl. Of two good birds that resemble each other closely, the one belonging to a good family is likely to give better results as a breeder than the one belonging to a poor family. Of two good cocks each with a good ancestry, the one with six good brothers should be a better breeder than the other one with six poor brothers.

Other things being equal, a hen that produces good eggs of size, shape and strength, healthy vigorous chicks, and offspring that are exceptional in conformation and color, not to mention exceptional in competition, and had six sisters all of which are very similar, each should be a better breeder than a hen that is even better in all areas, but had six sisters none of which were worth a damn.

One of the most effective steps that a breeder can take when breeding for excellence in performance and ability is to select broodhens according to the performance of their full-brothers. The kind of brothers and sisters a bird has is often of greater value than its ancestry in determining a bird's worth as a prospective breeder, particularly if the reproductive performance and kind of progeny produced by any of the bird's brothers and sisters that were used as breeders are taken into consideration.

Select on the basis of reproductive performance: In the selection of broodfowl, some consideration should be given to the reproductive performance of the ancestry as well as of the bird itself, if it has been used as a breeder. The reproductive performance of a bird, when bred, provides a good indication to the relative number of fertile eggs produced, the relative number of fertile eggs that hatched, and the relative number of chicks that lived and grew well. If they prove to be good in all these areas, keep breeding them, if not, cull them!

Fertility is not inherited, but high fertility in the eggs produced by a given mating is desirable in order that as many progeny as possible may be obtained. On the other hand, hatchability is inherited, and in selecting birds for the broodpen the hatchability of the ancestors of each bird should be taken into consideration. If the bird itself was used as a breeder then the results in hatchability obtained from the mating, in which the bird was used, should be carefully considered before deciding to use the bird a second time. If one hen among twelve mated to a cock gave poor hatchability, as compared with good hatchability of the other eleven, there is no good reason for using the hen showing poor hatchability a second time, regardless of how good she may be otherwise. A hatchability of seventy-five percent of the fertile eggs produced is a good minimum to use as the basis of selecting broodfowl.

Selection on the basis of viability and growth: The viability and growth of chicks produced by a bird's ancestors are other factors that should be taken into consideration in the selection of broodfowl. A bird representing a family of chicks, most of which died or grew very poorly, should never be used as a breeder, regardless of how good it may be in other respects. So, if the bird itself upon being bred the first time produces a family of chicks, most of which die or grow poorly, it would be a bad idea to use the bird again as a breeder.

"I do not feel myself liable to contradiction when I assert that nothing is more common than to breed from a cock, after having fought not only one battle, but several; the more battles he has been engaged in, the greater recommendation to make use of him as a brood cock."

W. Sketchley

Select on the basis of the progeny: The supreme test of the worth of a bird as a breeder is the kind of progeny it produces. When a bird is selected as a breeder for the first time, the progeny test cannot be applied, because no progeny has been produced. However, what should be done then is to consider the kind of progeny produced by the bird's ancestors. To some extent this is the same thing as considering the kind of brothers and sisters the bird has, but the kind of progeny produced by the bird's grandparents should also be considered. A bird whose parents and grandparents produced a relatively high proportion of good progeny is much more likely to produce good progeny than a bird whose parents and grandparents produced only a relatively few outstanding individuals.

The progeny test should be applied to the bird itself, providing it meets the requirements concerning the standard breed characteristics, performance quality, constitutional vigor, good ancestry, and has a high proportion of brothers and sisters that possess the desirable qualities being bred for. These various requirements should be met in order to insure that the bird to be tested is a superior individual, for it is only a waste of time to apply the progeny test to a mediocre specimen.

To apply the progeny test to a bird, use it as a breeder one year and keep careful records regarding the kind of progeny produced. Focus on the standpoint of the performance quality of the sons. From the daughters, evaluate the size, shape and strength of eggs, to include, conformation of body and color of plumage within both (son and daughters). The kind of progeny produced the first year is the only way of determining a bird's real worth as a breeder, and those that produce superior progeny should be used as long as they live.

> *"During the formation or improvement of a breed, its members will always be found to vary much in those characters to which especial attention is directed, and of which each slight improvement is eagerly sought and selected. So it is in every case; and the large price paid for first-rate animals proves the difficulty of breeding them up to the highest standard of excellence."*
> *Charles Darwin*

BREEDING BY SELECTION: In order to create and maintain a strain one point must be carefully considered. This point is, "special matings for special breeding purposes." These are best made right before the breeding season, usually in January or February, by selecting the finest hens and mating them with choice cocks, both of known pedigree and within the same family, preferably multiple winners and sisters of multiple winners. Such matings should be made early enough to allow at least four weeks to elapse before the eggs are saved for hatching, so that the effects of previous matings are gone, and a higher degree of fertility will be assured.

To secure the best results, broodfowl should be single mated. Whenever single mating is practiced, more care and attention can be given to individual breeders. Such matings are advisable for many reasons, the following being the more important:

1. By breeding from the best progeny, in accordance with the laws of heredity, it will not only resemble the parent in many respects, but will be of higher type than if the entire family had been used for breeding.

2. Group or mass breeding does not assure superiority; in other words, when eggs are selected, year after year, from those of the entire family, all that can be expected is to maintain, in a succeeding generation, the same degree of perfection which was attained by the parent. In breeding for performance and ability, Natural Selection is of no value. In fact, experience seems to show that it tends to cause retrogression.

When breeding from the mass, many fowls will fall below the standard in type (conformation of body) and performance ability.

3. It is impossible to study individuality when large families are used for breeding. The possibility of future improvement lies in a study of the individual and efforts to raise the average in form, function and beauty. This can best be done by single mating for breeding purposes. Such matings should be based not only upon external characteristics, but upon performance and ability as well. When you are working with a smaller number of birds, it requires very little amount of labor and expense.

4. In matings of this kind, a high percentage of fertility will be realized, from the fact that greater care can be exercised in picking both the broodhens and the broodcocks. It is also much easier to keep track of the condition of the breeders and to eliminate anything which might tend towards infertility.

5. The handling and selection of eggs from pens of this type will be more careful. The percentage of eggs hatched and the resulting progeny depend to a great extent upon the care and handling of the eggs after they are laid. Where a cocker and backyard breeder has a small number of eggs of high value, as is the case with these single matings, he will naturally give them closer attention than where he has to handle an enormous quantity, due to group matings.

Cockers and backyard breeders, when breeding their prospective broodfowl, should seriously consider the advisability of making special broodpens. By so doing the breeder is making it possible to gradually improve the quality of his birds with little effort and expense. He can also eliminate the very poor individuals from the family. It is by discarding such birds and breeding from the best that superiority is ultimately brought about.

> *"Should the owner observe any slight variation in one of his birds, and wish to obtain a breed thus characterised, he would succeed in a surprisingly short time by careful selection. As any part which has once varied generally goes on varying in the same direction, it is easy, by continually preserving the most strongly marked individuals, to increase the amount of difference up to a high, predetermined standard of excellence."*
>
> *Charles Darwin*

POINTS TO CONSIDER IN THE SELECTION OF BROODFOWL: In the selection of desirable birds, both cock and hen, for the broodpen, the first consideration should be whether the resulting progeny is to be purebreds, crossbreds, or both. No matter which way you choose to go, only the most ideal birds in these respects should be chosen. You must first decide upon the ideal birds that will best fit your needs and desires and keep this clearly and plainly in your mind, well before you set up your broodpens. You should base your selection not only upon temperament and performance abilities, but upon external appearance, such as conformation of body and color of plumage, and any attributes which you consider desirable. Since uniformity in this respect is important, make sure to select offspring that carry the same desirable traits as their parents.

Purchasing broodfowl (foundation stock): The ancestry or pedigree of the birds is important and should be considered, however, this can be difficult when you are purchasing broodfowl, especially from an unknown breeder. At the beginning, due to lack of records, it will be impossible to know the exact ancestry of your new broodfowl, in this case external appearances must count for a great deal. But, when possible, the best plan is to purchase broodfowl from a reliable breeder who is known to carry the best birds for which you desire. Even if they cost a considerable sum of money, good broodfowl are worth their weight in gold, and can mean a great deal to the future of the family. Take your time and find the right fowl for you, and make sure that you have made a worthwhile investment.

> *"In the choice of your hens let them be rightly plumed to your cock: nor let your choice fall upon those that are large but rather suffer the cock to make up deficiency in the hens being small: their shape should be similar to the cock-lofty necks-short and close feathered. A true blood hen is seldom or never gummy in the bone of her leg, but clean, sinewy, and, in length, proportionate to the rest of the body, with a well-set thigh, long, clean, and taper toes, so that they may, as far as is practicable, be as near in every respect to your original brood, as the nature of breeding will admit of."*
>
> W. Sketchley

<u>Selection of the broodhen</u>: It is often said that a good broodhen is worth half the flock, but if you ask me, she is worth a lot more than that, for I believe she is the strain. It is my experience that more can be accomplished by line-breeding to the hen than to the cock.

On paper, she may equal fifty percent of the blood of the progeny in the first generation, and if she is prepotent as to her characteristics, and is bred to her sons, she then represents three-fourths of the blood of the progeny in the second generation, and seven-eighths of the blood in the progeny in the third generation, and fifteen-sixteenths of the blood of the progeny in the fourth generation, and thirty-thirty-seconds of the blood of the progeny in the fifth generation. This is what you would see on paper when line-breeding, but there is much more to this practice than you might think.

When line-breeding the hen to her descendants (sons, grandsons and great-grandsons, etc.), and with the practice of proper selection and ruthless culling, progress is certain. If you are careful to select for uniformity, her attributes are quickly replicated. If this method is followed continuously, it is possible to raise fowl that will inherit almost entirely the attributes of that hen. It is at this point that purity of blood is achieved. This happens much faster when line-breeding to the hen than when line-breeding to the cock.

> *"In order to enable you to judge of the constitution of the brood-cock you mean to select, he should have every apparent feature of health: such as a ruddy complexion-his feathers close and short-not cold or dry-flesh firm and compact-full breasted, yet taper and thin behind-full in the girth-well coupled-lofty and spiring -a good thigh-the beam of his leg very strong-a quick large eye-strong beak, crooked and big at setting on-not more than two years old, put to early pullets, or a blooming stag with two-year-old hens-and when a cock, with pullets of his own getting. "*
>
> W. Sketchley

<u>Selection of the broodcock</u>: Although it is my opinion that the hen is the most essential part of the equation, never neglect to select the right broodcock. He should be as perfect as possible. It is important to choose cocks for the broodpen, not only for their excellence in conformation of body and fine plumage color, but for their high excellence in performance and ability, which greatly represents the functional worth of the family. They should have won a number of competitions and a good proportion of them impressively. The cock should be descended from excellent performers and have a good ancestry. In this way, high performance will be inherited from both parents. If the ancestry is good, then you stand a good chance that the individual cocks will be good too.

<u>Prepotency of the pair is also of prime importance</u>: They should not only possess the desired characteristics, but the power of transmitting them to their progeny. This trait can be studied for a number of generations by means of pedigree records, and is shown by the resemblance of offspring to their parents. If a bird capable of excellence in performance is not prepotent, and there are many that are like this, they are of little value in the broodpen.

<u>Selection for good form</u>: External characteristics should be considered, yet not be given greater weight than that of their functional qualities. For instance, birds should not be introduced into the broodpen only for their external qualities, nor should a bird be discarded from the broodpen because their color markings are not of the best. But as much as is possible, you should select birds which conform to the standard of the breed, such as conformation of body, color of plumage, temperament, and performance ability.

> *"If hens and cocks have not completed this renovation, and fully arrived to their health and bloom, both the one and the other are unfit for the purposes of breeding."*
>
> *W. Sketchley*

<u>The health of broodfowl is important</u>. No bird should be put in the broodpen that has shown signs of disease. I make it a rule to cull all sick birds. If this seems a bit extreme, you may want to mark, with color bands, any birds in the family that have ever been afflicted with disease so that you will not forget that this bird has been sick and to remember not to use it as a breeder. For birds such as these, even after they recover, do not make good breeders. In the case of certain hereditary diseases, there is always the danger of transmitting them to the progeny. Hence, the health of both cock and hen in the past, as well as the present should be noted. Only birds of good constitution and vitality, and free from contamination of disease should be used.

WHEN TO START THE SELECTION PROCESS: Selection is a continuous process, starting with the baby chicks at hatching time and continues during the lifetime of the bird. As long as they live and make up a big part of the family, they should be examined for proper functionality and productiveness.

In reality, the selection and culling of fowl should begin with the shape, size, and condition of the egg before incubation, and when the chicks are first taken from the incubator. Baby chicks showing any abnormality or deformity should be eliminated as soon as they are noticed. It's a good idea to pay special attention to their growth and development throughout the brooding period. The next systematic selection may come during the penning of the young stags and pullets, usually around five months old.

> *"Successful competitors breed largely, and keep the best. I breed many, and hang many. As they belong to poor people, and are mostly in small lots, they never can be improved."*
>
> *Charles Darwin*

THE RELATION OF SELECTION AND CULLING: Although frequently used as synonyms, the terms "selection" and "culling" are strictly opposite in their suggestion. The foundation of breeding is accomplished through selection and culling. A family of fowl, if consistently culled and inferior birds are eliminated will contain only those which are the superior individuals. It is from these superior individuals that the breeders are to be chosen.

254

Listed below are the differences between selection and culling:

- Selection aims at progress. It is positive and constructive in nature. It deals with the very cream of the crop. In most case, it includes the top ten or fifteen percent of the offspring.
- Culling, on the other hand, is negative in nature, and has no necessary relation to breeding. It deals with the least desirable part of the family, and is aimed at the prevention of retrogression rather than at progress.

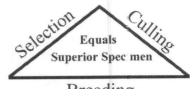

Breeding
The three most important functions required to produce superior quality offspring.

Selection and culling should be continuously practiced and carried out simultaneously to achieve the same goal, not only in the broodpen but in the elimination of weak or sick birds throughout the entire brooding and growing period. Birds which show, at any time, a lack of constitutional vigor will never be beneficial to the future of the family.

> *"The conditions favourable to selection by man are,—the closest attention to every character,—long-continued perseverance,—facility in matching or separating animals,—and especially a large number being kept, so that the inferior individuals may be freely rejected or destroyed, and the better ones preserved."*
>
> *Charles Darwin*

> *"Length of time is all-important; for as each character, in order to become strongly pronounced, has to be augmented by the selection of successive variations of the same kind, this can be effected only during a long series of generations. Length of time will, also, allow any new feature to become fixed by the continued rejection of those individuals which revert or vary, and by the preservation of those which still inherit the new character."*
>
> *Charles Darwin*

NO TIME TO BE WRONG IN THE SELECTION OF BROODFOWL: As compared with the larger classes of livestock, American Games are relatively short-lived creatures. The modern cocker and backyard breeder do not have the time to waste, especially while trying to figure out their breeding programs. They have to make progress and they have to make it right now. When they find an outstanding individual their natural tendency is to clone him or her. They want more just like them. This is understandable to say the least. However, the only problem they face is that they don't have the time to be wrong in their selection of broodfowl.

The fact is, when it comes to the productive lifespan of the cock and hens, it is very short-lived. The hen's ability to produce eggs declines steadily each year with advancing age, and fertility steadily declines each year with the advancing age of the cock. Before they realize it, the window of opportunity is closed. The average age of productiveness is about five years. The cock may last longer, but the hen is only good for four or five years. For more information on this subject, go to "Best Age for Broodfowl."

> *"Fanciers, whilst admitting and even overrating the effects of crossing the various breeds, do not sufficiently regard the probability of the occasional birth, during the course of centuries, of birds with abnormal and hereditary peculiarities; they overlook the effects of correlation of growth—of the*

long-continued use and disuse of parts, and of some direct result from changed food and climate, though on this latter head I have found no sufficient evidence; and lastly, they all, as far as I know, entirely overlook the all-important subject of unconscious or unmethodical selection, though they are well aware that their birds differ individually and that by selecting the best birds for a few generations they can improve their stocks."

Charles Darwin

UNCONSCIOUS AND METHODICAL SELECTION: Charles Darwin once said that there are two kinds of selection, one he calls "unconscious," the other "methodical." To the "unconscious" he acknowledges, in large part, the evolution of the fowl. In this case the breeder, who in spirit of rivalry tries to surpass his competitors by breeding from his best bird, without any attempt to establish a new breed or improve an established breed. Nor is there any attempt to preserve some new characteristic. Here is how Darwin puts it, *"This unconscious kind of selection will more especially come into action with animals which are highly serviceable to man; for everyone tries to get the best dogs, horses, cows, or sheep, without thinking about their future progeny, yet these animals would transmit more or less surely their good qualities to their offspring. Nor is any one so careless as to breed from his worst animals. Even savages, when compelled from extreme want to kill some of their animals, would destroy the worst and preserve the best."* He goes on to say that, *"During this process the best or most valued individuals are not separated and prevented from crossing with others of the same breed, but are simply preferred and preserved; yet this inevitably leads to their gradual modification and improvement; so that finally they prevail, to the exclusion of the old parent-form."*

"Methodical" selection, however, has to do with the making of new breeds and varieties, and the fixing of new and desirable characteristics. This assumes the breeder knows what he is doing, and that he has a good knowledge concerning the principles of breeding, and what it takes to properly breed American Games.

Charles Darwin put it like this, *"We know well that of late years methodical selection has greatly improved and fixed many characters…"* The breeder who follows methodical selection is constantly on the lookout for new and valuable characteristics. He is not satisfied with following a standard of excellence. He follows the beat of his own drum and creates a new and higher standard. In other words, he believes in progress.

While the man who is satisfied to beat his competitor in the show room or the pit, by discarding everything in his broodpen that does not conform to the standard setup by others, the man who follows methodical selection often achieve his highest purpose by breeding for characteristics or type that would be culled by others. This is a breeder who is looking for "sports" or "mutants" along certain lines, and when they appear, he makes them the basis of his breeding program.

Some would say that when it comes to American Games, there has always been a standard of excellence, written or unwritten, and we cockers have been unconsciously following it throughout the centuries. However, according to Darwin, unconscious selection has done more for the improvement of fowls because it has been at work longer than methodical selection. *He also said, "We have every reason to believe that unconscious selection, carried on for many generations, will have steadily augmented each new peculiarity, and thus have given rise to new breeds."*

Whether the improvement or evolution of the American Gamefowl is due more to one or the other method of selection, it would have been impossible to evolve the fowl as we now have it, if in the early centuries, an arbitrary standard had been set up and all breeding was made to follow along that line.

"Selection, whether methodical or unconscious, always tending towards an extreme point of all useful and pleasing qualities... Together with the neglect and slow extinction of the intermediate and less-valued forms, is the key which unlocks the mystery of how man has produced such wonderful results."

Charles Darwin

SELECT THE MOST IMPORTANT CHARACTERISTICS FIRST: One of the inherent difficulties involved in the breeding practice of American Games, is that the modern cocker usually considers several different characteristics simultaneously when he is making his selections. What he should keep in mind is that the larger the number of characteristics on which selection is based, the lower the intensity of selection for each of the characteristics that he is trying to improve by selection. In other words, the more attention paid to unimportant characteristics, the less valuable is the selection for the more important characteristics.

Since the average cocker and backyard breeder is eager in maintaining excellence with respect to each of several characteristics, such as conformation of body, color of plumage, station of leg, temperament, ability, style, and gameness, it is obvious that a very large number of genes is involved. Although, there are probably a large number of genes responsible for the development of each of these characteristics, rarely does any individual bird excel in all or even most of these characteristics. In fact, most birds excel in but a few characteristics. It follows, therefore, that the genes that determine these characteristics are in varying degrees of heterozygosity (meaning different in their genotype and phenotype) in practically all birds. The object of the modern cocker and backyard breeder is to produce birds each having as many as possible of the desirable genes. In other words, the desired goal of every modern cocker and backyard breeder should be to achieve homozygosity (meaning same in their genotype and phenotype) in their family of fowl, which is the uniformity of desirable genes in each and every bird.

There are several obstacles, however, that prevent the average modern cocker and backyard breeder from being able to select from among all the birds he has available to him, those which when used as broodfowl would produce the kind of progeny that possess to a high degree the various characteristics and traits, and qualities that the breeder most desires.

The difficulty of deciding upon how much importance should be attached to minor points of breed and variety characteristics, such as the color of leg; comb type, whether they are pea comb or straight comb, or whether or not they have the proper number of serrations on the comb, in the case of straight *(single)* comb birds; as well as other characteristics and traits that ultimately mean nothing, such as the number of feathers in the tail or the formation of the scales on the leg. Characteristics and traits such as these often lead to the sacrifice of birds of real value from the standpoint of transmitting qualities of importance.

Selecting birds on the basis of their relative perfection in breed and variety characteristics is commendable enough in itself, but the object lesson for the modern cocker and backyard breeder is that the more attention given to these matters, the less progress can be expected in breeding for more important qualities, such as conformation of body, color of plumage, station of leg, temperament, ability, style, and gameness.

Selection is key.

"Selection, guided by utility for a single purpose, has led to convergence of character. Continued divergence of character depends on, and is indeed a clear proof of the same parts continuing to vary in the same direction."

Charles Darwin

STARTING WITH GOOD BROODFOWL: Most cockers would experience better results from their fowl if they started with fowl that were better bred. Also, less culling would be necessary.

Does culling produce the best breeders? By properly culling you are enabling the family to strive and flourish. However, the greater the amount of culling that is necessary for a family to maintain excellence in performance abilities; the less valuable may be the remainder of the family for the purpose of breeding. Let me explain this further.

In the case of American Games, after the culling process is completed, only the best performers are left in the family. If they are used for breeding purposes, you may find that they vary a great deal in their ability to transmit, to their progeny, the desirable characteristics they themselves possess. The important point to keep in mind is that judging fowl for their performance ability alone is somewhat different from selecting the best breeders. If fact, the results of their progeny are quite different.

THE IMPORTANCE OF PROGENY TESTING: Another obstacle in selecting the best broodfowl is that their individual performance record can often serve as a very poor measurement of their breeding worth. When performance is the only measure of a birds worth, the pedigree of that individual can often give a false sense of security. There is no guarantee that just because they are good performers they will be good breeders, and will pass those desirable traits to their offspring. This makes performance a poor measurement of a birds breeding worth, especially when it is their only means of evaluation.

Usually the pedigree contains information of, not only the qualities and breeding worth of the individual's immediate relatives, but the qualities and breeding worth of the entire ancestral line.

The most reliable measurement in evaluating the breeding worth of the cocks and hens that are used as broodfowl is the "Progeny Test." Progeny testing can be used for morphological characteristics, which are the form and structure of any of its parts, as well as for various physiological characteristics, which is the normal functioning of those parts.

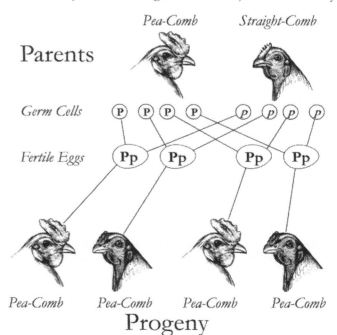

This illustration shows what happens when you breed a pure pea-comb bird with a straight (single) comb bird. The results are revealed in the offspring, all of which show the pea-comb trait.

In other words, it can be used to select for the performance and ability of the bird as much as its appearance.

There is nothing mysterious about progeny testing for the selection of future broodfowl. This principle can be illustrated by reference to practical experience, mine. I had a family of Lacy Roundheads that were pea-combed, but when bred to some straight (*single*) combed birds that I had at the time, occasionally birds with straight (*single*) combs would appear amongst the progeny. Since pea-comb is dominant to straight (*single*) comb, there being but a single gene difference, it was obvious that the broodfowl I received were heterozygous (impure) for pea-comb. They each had a gene for pea-comb and for straight (*single*) comb, but had pea-combs because the gene for pea-comb is dominant to the gene for straight (*single*) comb.

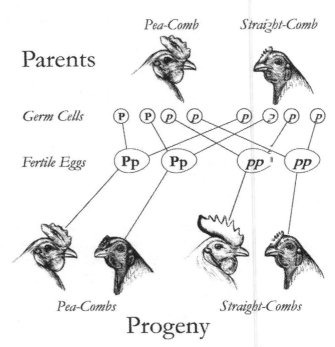

This illustration shows what happens when you breed a non-pure pea-comb bird with a straight (single) comb bird. The results are revealed in the offspring. Fifty percent of the offspring show the pea-comb trait and fifty percent of the offspring show the straight (single) comb trait.

It is most important to bear in mind the fact that these Lacy Roundheads, heterozygous (impure) for pea-comb, could not be distinguished in appearance from Lacy Roundheads that were homozygous (pure) for pea-comb. The only way they could be distinguished is by a breeding test, by breeding a pea-combed bird with that of a straight (*single*) combed bird. Birds homozygous for pea-comb when mated to other birds homozygous for pea-comb would produce 100% pea-combs. The birds heterozygous for pea-comb, when mated together, would produce progeny in the proportion of three with pea-combs to one with straight (*single*) comb. Birds homozygous for pea-comb when mated to straight (*single*) comb birds would produce only pea-comb progeny, but birds heterozygous for pea-comb, when mated to straight (*single*) comb birds, would produce approximately equal numbers of pea-comb and straight (*single*) comb birds.

The progeny test will always show the breeder the genetic constitution of the parental stock. In my case, the progeny test showed me the genetic constitution as far as comb type was concerned, but it can be used for just about any characteristics or trait that the breeder is interested in perpetuating.

So it is with respect to practically all other characteristics, which the breeder desires to develop in a strain. Neither the performance record nor the pedigree serves as a reliable evaluation of the breeding worth of an individual, although both provide useful information when considered in relation to the results obtained from progeny testing.

Pedigrees are necessary if the modern cocker and backyard breeder wishes to practice inbreeding or line-breeding in the establishment of a pure family or strain.

CONCLUSION: The foregoing discussion naturally leads to the question, what is the limit to the possible amount of variation, and, is there any limit to what selection can effect? I say, although there seems to be no limit to the amount of variation that can occur in our fowl, gamefowl can only get so tall (station of leg) or fly so high (breaking ability) before they become totally useless.

"If an architect were to rear a noble and commodious edifice, without the use of cut stone, by selecting from the fragments at the base of a precipice wedge-formed stones for his arches, elongated stones for his lintels, and flat stones for his roof, we should admire his skill and regard him as the paramount power. Now, the fragments of stone, though indispensable to the architect, bear to the edifice built by him the same relation which the fluctuating variations of organic beings bear to the varied and admirable structures ultimately acquired by their modified descendants."

Charles Darwin

THE PRACTICE OF INBREEDING

WHAT IS INBREEDING? Simply put, inbreeding is the mating of individuals that are closely related. It is a practice commonly used by breeders for the purpose of concentrating the blood of an individual or family, which shows the desired characteristics and traits, or qualities of form and function. Inbreeding has a definite influence on the composition of future generations, mainly due to its nature of isolation. Whether inbreeding works towards the betterment of the family or not, is for the individual breeder to determine. Depending on who you talk to, inbreeding can be a great tool or a recipe for disaster. In the following paragraphs, I will give you my view of its function and use.

Inbreeding is a long-term breeding strategy, which is sometimes used for several successive generations. It is most useful as a way to strengthen and preserve valuable genetic information in a bloodline. Practically every successful family of fowl has been made with a considerable amount of inbreeding. Commercial flocks have been improved, and have made great strides through the practice of inbreeding. As a matter of fact, inbreeding has been practiced to some extent in nearly all commercial flocks where high egg-production has been developed and maintained. Inbreeding was practiced rather extensively in the development of some of the more outstanding strains of horses, cattle, sheep, and swine as well.

This big move towards improvement of poultry began sometime in the 1940s. In fact, advancements, such as these, have made substantial improvements in all breeds of chickens, including American Games. Inbreeding of American Gamefowl has made possible in creating better varieties and strains, some which bare the names of their creators, for example Mr. Harold Brown, Mr. Colonel Givens, Johnny Jumper, and probably the most famous cocker, Lord Derby of England. This is due to the intensification or purification of the blood of outstanding or especially valuable individuals or families, and these breeders knew the value of inbreeding.

Such an intensification of the blood targets at and results in the blending of characteristics, improving the quality of the individuals and their families. This causes them to breed more true, and if done properly, will develop a line of fowl, which when crossed will give the progeny the highest level of ability and performance capabilities.

WHAT IS THE PURPOSE OF INBREEDING: Many breeders believe wholeheartedly in the practice of inbreeding, while others are opposed to it without understanding its real purpose. Charles Darwin once stated that *"close interbreeding, if not carried to an injurious extreme, far from causing variability, tends to fix the character of each breed."* Today, the purpose of inbreeding is to accomplish the same objective, to intensify and fix desirable qualities. To express the same idea in another way, the real purpose of inbreeding is to develop birds whose genes are in a homozygous condition for as many desirable characters as possible.

In the development of a strain, it is required to have broodfowl, where all of them are in possession of the desirable genes. Does each bird need to possess all of the desired qualities? Not necessarily. One bird may possess the genes in a heterozygous condition for two of the characters, and another bird may possess the genes also in a heterozygous condition for two of the other characters. By mating the progeny of the two birds and then practicing inbreeding, it should be possible to develop birds possessing the genes in a homozygous condition for all four characters.

If a superior cock or hen is found, one that possesses in a high degree certain points of value to the breeder, it is advantageous for him to breed that cock or hen to their offspring (sons or daughters), where their characteristics will be more quickly fixed in the offspring than would be the case by any other system of breeding. The points of superiority may be purely on form, such as, conformation of body, color of plumage, shape or type of comb, station of leg, and shape of body. Or it might be for functional reasons, such as ability and performance qualities. Or it could be for matters which only concern the hen, such as the shape and size of her eggs. Not to mention, various other points that the breeder wishes to fix in his strain.

If the cock has proved to be an excellent performer, the theory of inbreeding is that by breeding him to his daughters, and later to his granddaughters and great-granddaughters, there will be more probability of getting greater performing stags and cocks than if he is mated to a hen of no relation.

If you are breeding for better color or conformation of body, it is more likely that inbreeding or line-breeding will give a larger proportion of offspring strong in those areas than would crossbreeding or outcrossing, even though the hens in either case are equally good in those areas.

HOW CLOSE IS TOO CLOSE: Inasmuch as inbreeding is the mating together of related individuals, it is obvious that the closer the degree of inbreeding, the greater the number of genes in a homozygous condition you will see in the progeny, for the simple reason that the more closely related the parents are, the greater is the number of similar genes that are brought together in the mating.

The most common practices of inbreeding consist of mother to son, father to daughter, grandmother to grandson, grandfather to granddaughter, great-grandfather to great-granddaughter, great-grandmother to great-grandson, aunt to nephew, and uncle to niece, as well as cousin to cousin. However, the closest form of inbreeding is the mating of full-brother to full-sister, and is sometimes called in-and-in breeding.

Although there may be fewer different ancestors, and in most cases, no common ancestors, in the pedigree of a bird whose parents are unrelated, this is not always a good thing, especially when breeding chickens and gamefowl for uniformity of a strain. The pedigree of a bird, obtained from any of the closely inbred matings listed above, shows the same ancestor appearing in the pedigree more than once. The importance of this fact is that, not only do the individuals of the family or strain, which have been inbred, have a common ancestor; they tend to produce offspring that have more genes in a homozygous condition than individuals that do not have common ancestors. It is for this reason, and only this reason, that they are uniform and consistent in all their characteristics and traits.

The question is, how close is too close? To give you an example of what can be done while inbreeding, and without any harm or damage to your fowl whatsoever, a friend of mine who is a fine breeder, started out with a trio of birds, and has bred those fowl for over twenty years, and has done so without the introduction of new blood, not even a drop. During this time he has improved their conformation of body, station, ability and performance, temperament, and color, and has not seen nor developed any weaknesses, which can be attributed to inbreeding.

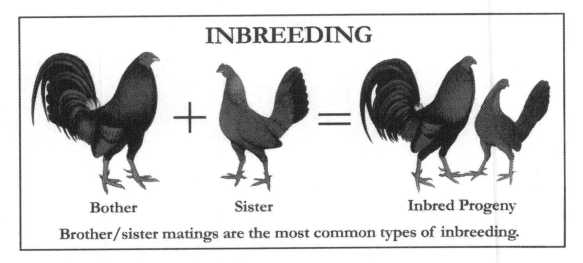

INBREEDING

Bother + Sister = Inbred Progeny

Brother/sister matings are the most common types of inbreeding.

THE UNCERTAINTIES OF INBREEDING: Inbreeding American and Old English Gamefowl is of great interest to the modern cocker and backyard breeder, but has become something that he fears rather than embraces. A matter of fact, he frequently finds himself in a dilemma as to whether he should use broodfowl within his own family or strain, or purchase broodfowl from an outside source. He also finds himself in a dilemma as to whether or not he should mate cocks and hens that are related. If this is what he desires to do, to achieve certain results or for a particular purpose, there is still the question as to how closely related the cocks and hens may be in order to obtain the most acceptable results. Should a father be mated to his daughters, mother to son, brother to sister, cousin to cousin, nephew to aunt, or niece to uncle, in an effort to improve conformation of body, color of plumage, station of leg, temperament, ability, style, or even gameness in a flock of birds? These are some of the questions in the minds of most modern cockers and backyard breeders with the approach of every breeding season.

THE EFFECTS OF INBREEDING: Inbreeding, if practiced properly, is not necessarily harmful, and in fact is often very advantageous. Great caution must be exercised, however, in the selection of broodfowl; otherwise very harmful results will follow.

It must be realized, for instance, that the results of inbreeding are to intensify the good qualities of an individual it also results in the intensification of all the characteristics and traits which that individual carries with him. It is here where the danger of inbreeding lies, for if there happens to be, as there usually are, bad characteristics or traits, or even weaknesses in an individual, it will be intensified as well, and may be transmitted from generation to generation.

Inbreeding increases the number of homozygous genes, therefore, it is important for the modern cocker and backyard breeder to understand that inbreeding does bring together desirable, as well as, undesirable genes, equally. Since many recessive genes have less desirable effects than dominant genes, inbreeding has the effect of unmasking the presence of these undesirable recessive genes, whose effects were masked by the presence of desirable dominant genes. It is when these undesirable recessive genes occur in a homozygous condition that they are able to produce undesirable characteristics, especially with such characteristics as hatchability of eggs and viability of chicks, as well as poor conformation of body and carriage, shorter station of leg, bad temperament, and lack of the most important trait every gamecock should have, which is unquestionable and absolute gameness. Not to mention many other characteristics and traits that may be desirable or undesirable.

Since inbreeding intensifies undesirable characters as well as desirable ones, it is even more reason to take great care during the selection process. While selecting individuals to be used for inbreeding make sure they are vigorous and have a strong constitution and have no bad traits. Rigid selection must be in use to prevent degeneration. Without special care of these individuals, this system of breeding is sure to fail.

What the great majority of cockers and backyard breeders do not realize about inbreeding is different results are to be expected when different kinds of stock are used, especially in the beginning.

Special note of interest: If inbred fowl are mated, and the progeny display undesirable traits, both parents and offspring should be removed from the breeding program, because the parents are both carriers for the recessive, undesirable gene that is expressed in the offspring.

INBREEDING AND THE POTENTIAL FOR VARIATION: When a population of fowl is variable in its genetic makeup, it has the potential for unpredictability. This creates a high certainty of variation in the characteristics and traits of the offspring. This means, in respect to many genes, some will be homozygous and others will be heterozygous.

Since chromosomes and genes are constantly being shuffled and recombined in every generation, the smaller an isolated group of birds is, the smaller its potential for variability there will be. This is especially true when we are mating small groups of closely related individuals. Birds that are closely related have more chance to be alike in regard to any gene than birds that are not closely related, or are from a larger group of fowl.

The purification, which goes on in a population of birds, which is constantly being renewed from only a few closely bred birds goes on slowly but surely. It is when new blood is constantly infused that the potential for variability is high and uniformity is never reached. For example: ordinarily, a cocker will practice a certain amount of inbreeding or line-breeding, and without realizing it he will reduce the amount of variability in his family. This will continue for a few years until some neighbor swaps a bird or a setting of eggs. It is at that moment that he is starting over. The potential for variation just went through the roof, so to speak.

Keep it simple by breeding only one family: If we look at the effect of inbreeding, we must realize that it is almost impossible to keep track of what happens during several generations, especially in a large population of birds. It is simplest to follow the fortunes of just one inbred family. Keep a few selected lines, but lines that belong to the same inbred family. Breed to the offspring (their direct descendants) of a few selected birds, and so on, but disregard the rest of the group. In other words, keep it simple and keep it small at all times, and the potential for variability will be small too.

In chickens, the smallest group is one pair. Let's take a look at what would happen if we started from one pair of birds. If we were to take just one cock and one hen from among their offspring (brother and sister) to continue the line, this would be inbreeding. There are many backyard breeders that are breeding in this way, substituting a pair or a small group of chicks for their parents every season. There is an unknown quantity of genes in respect to which the two original birds were both pure and identical. It is probable that (with the exception of the genes on the sex chromosome in respect to which no hen can ever be homozygous) an overwhelming majority of genes are the same in both.

Next there may be some genes which only one of the two possesses, while the other lacks them. This difference may be of different kinds; to put it in formula, one may be AA, the other aa. Or one Aa, and the other aa. And there are certain to be several genes in respect to which both are heterozygous, Aa, Bb, Cc, Dd, Ee, Ff, and so on. As we will see, the result of continuing such an inbreeding program, in succession, must therefore be a program of purification, and we can follow this best by looking at just one single gene, gene B. Here are the possibilities: BB x Bb, BB x bb, Bb x Bb, and Bb x bb.

What kind of chicks can we expect from each possible sort of mating?
- BB x Bb will give equal chances of BB and Bb offspring.
- BB x bb will give only Bb.
- Bb x Bb gives a 25 percent chance BB, 50 percent chance Bb, and 25 percent chance bb.
- Bb x bb will give equal chances of Bb and bb offspring.

If we are simply continuing from one pair of birds in every following generation, and calculate the chance for variation in respect to "B" to persist, we realize that in this loss of potential for variability, we are dealing with a "ratchet" mechanism, a tightening of potentially inheritable traits. Every time we happen to mate two BB birds together, or two bb birds, the strain we are creating becomes more pure, homozygous, in respect to gene B. This will happen at least once in eight times, one chance in sixteen that both will be BB, and one in sixteen that they will both be bb. This means that if we start from material that is variable in respect to a large number of genes, inbreeding (brother to sister matings) will reduce the potential for variability.

In larger groups of birds this "automatic reduction" of the potential for variability (number of genes for which every member is not alike and pure) will be smaller due to the large number of individuals. This means that on a farm that has ten breeding pens only twenty percent of the potential for variability would disappear per generation, if no selection were practiced. Selection according to individual quality of the cocks and hens (trap-nest selection) might help a little, but even if this were fifty percent effective, which it certainly is not, progress towards purer fowl and a better expectation of good quality chicks will still be extremely slow. Even this very slow purification would only be expected provided the breeder stopped importing and infusing new blood, and just rotated the cocks, the sons of one pen heading pens of hens from another group.

If, however, this breeder, that has ten broodpens, should start to keep ten parallel lines and stopped crossing his birds, filling house number three with a young brood pair derived from old pen number three, and so all along the line, the picture would change entirely. For now in each line a succession of just one male per generation would be kept, and a good proportion of the remaining variability will get worked away per generation. Those ten lines will then become more and more pure, and will certainly become different.

If we just blindly bred ten separate lines, those lines would all become pure slowly for different sets of genes. There are many who say they are breeding pure lines but are practicing this method of breeding. This is called "Maze-Breeding." Their method is to produce a multitude of pure families first, without bothering about their quality, in order to try, usually through good fortune, to later find strains which, when crossed, will give them good battle-crosses. The quality of such (blindly) inbred lines is generally low. If we inbreed without selection, starting from the usual extremely variable fowl that are available, there is a good chance that valuable genes, in respect to which the original material was impure, will get lost.

It is quite possible to take advantage of the purifying influence of inbreeding, while we guarantee ourselves against the loss of valuable genes, by directing our attention to homozygosity in the cocks (in hens this is practically impossible).

THE PREREQUISITES OF INBREEDING: It should also be understood that, although, most results are obtained from inbreeding experiments done on commercial fowl, using the closest forms of inbreeding, the modern cocker and backyard breeder who has a relatively large number of broodfowl to use each year could safely practice inbreeding with practically no inverse results, but only if he practices strict selection and ruthless culling of any fowl considered for future breeding purposes, whether they are young or old.

Whenever you are inbreeding, a lot of attention should be given in order to discover the first signs of weakness, not so much an individual weakness, but a family weakness. This is one where the weakness is perpetual throughout the family. If a weakness such as this should appear, it is at this time you should abandon such a close inbreeding and attempt to introduce new blood, or better yet, outcross to another line of the same family or strain.

Special note of interest: If undesirable characteristics appear in inbred birds, it is because undesirable genes existed in the original broodstock. In other words, both parents carry the same undesirable characteristic.

Inbreeding Chart

HOW TO INBREED: American Gamefowl, the really pure forms, are very rare and often very expensive, and with the shipping crisis as it stands today, makes it even more difficult for some to obtain these very special bloodlines. For those who have them and wish to preserve what they already have, they may find it better to inbreed their families or strains and establish a number of lines to maintain their purity of blood.

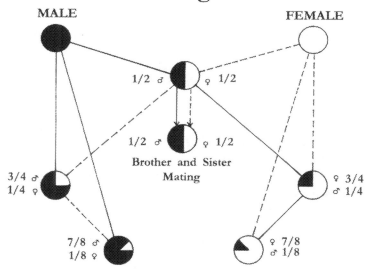

Inbreeding chart showing the distribution of inherited characters. The black represents the bloodlines of the cock, and the white represents the bloodlines of the hen. The solid black lines represent that a male has been chosen from the group from which they start and the dotted lines that a female has been chosen. Inbreeding is traced through four generations and the results are shown at the bottom of the chart.

Inbreeding is the mating of brother to sister; Mother to son or Father to daughter; grandparent to grandchild; great-grandparent to great-grandchild, it is the breeding of Aunt to nephew or Uncle to niece, or cousin to cousin. These all constitute inbreeding to some extent. Yet, breeding brother to sister is the most extreme form of inbreeding. Some breeders have been known to inbreed using brother to sister for six to seven consecutive generations in order to fix a new strain.

The advantages of inbreeding:

- Inbreeding, if accompanied by intelligent selection, makes rapid improvement possible because superior families can be readily separated from inferior families.
- The appearance of undesirable characteristics in inbred strains makes it possible for the modern cocker and backyard breeder to eliminate, rather quickly, numerous undesirable characteristics from his family of fowl.
- It allows for the fixing of characters and traits within a family, making them more uniform and more predictable.
- Individuals produced from these inbred bloodlines are valuable for producing hybrid battlecrosses.

The disadvantages of inbreeding: Some of the common evidences of too close breeding with a particular family are:

- Inbreeding depression
- Degeneration
- And reduced egg production
- Reduced hatchability
- Slower growth
- Increased weakness in constitutional vigor
- Increased mortality rate
- Increased age at sexual maturity

When the flock is large, the appearance of some of the above undesirable characters is more likely to be due to inadequate rations, poor management, disease, or neglect of properly selected broodfowl. With small flocks, however, the appearance of some of these undesirable characters may be due to inbreeding. Since there is extremely limited opportunity for selection in small flocks of 50 to 100 birds or even up to 500 birds, undesirable characters may build up.

INBREEDING DEPRESSION OR SIMPLE DEGENERATION: Continuous, close inbreeding can cause phenomenon's known as "Inbreeding Depression" and "Inbreeding Degeneration." In general, this is caused by the exposure of harmful recessive genes through matings between close relatives. Here we will discuss the effects of these phenomenon's, and how to prevent it and maybe use it to our benefit.

Most breeders of American Games are very much afraid of inbreeding, because they fear inbreeding as a cause of Inbreeding Depression or Degeneration. Are their fears justified? Maybe, maybe not! In most domestic animals, the system of perpetual crossbreeding, buying and using "new blood", is both the remedy against the dangers of inbreeding and the cause of those same dangers. In birds, however, it can be a bit more complex.

Some families are so pure that they are completely "inbreeding resistant." Inbreeding will not change or harm them. Then again, there are some families that when Inbred can cause the family to be genetically inferior or mediocre. In this case, when some birds are put through an inbreeding program differentiation usually sets in. This causes a segregation of the characters. In other words, there is a considerable amount of genetic variability of the individuals within the family, and the family as a whole. After several generations, the offspring will contain a heterogeneous mixture of lines. There will be a few good ones, but most lines will be of little value and many will be highly substandard.

For some families, the only thing which makes pure lines "inbreeding resistant" is their purity. Through Selective Breeding, selecting the good traits while eliminating the bad, in time, causes the family to be stronger genetically. The result is a family that does not carry hidden impurities. Therefore purity and the resistance to inbreeding degeneration is the result of inbreeding! Here we have a paradox, which always tends to confuse breeders who are not familiar with genetics. Inbreeding is frequently the cause of the production of inferior individuals and strains, and yet the only way to avoid all this trouble is by inbreeding!

Inbreeding, the mating of closely related birds, may be the cause of the production of unwanted recessives, not because those birds were closely related, but because they both were heterozygous for the same important hereditary factor. And when such heterozygotes are relatively rare, the chance that full brother and sister or first cousins whose common ancestor carried the impurity will have such recessives in their offspring is also heightened.

Now, there is one very significant fact in regard to inbreeding degeneration, and that is that we never get into trouble by inbreeding in regard to the qualities we desire and deem important for which we select our birds. It is quite common to find that in some highly valued and very successful strain of American Games, the egg production is very poor. Poor layers of exceptional conformation of body have obviously been chosen by the breeders in preference to others that were less "typey" but laid more eggs!

On the other hand, breeders of American Games often disapprove of the fact that in our most successful strains, the conformation of body or color of plumage has deteriorated. Again, the explanation is the same, the breeders, when having the choice between beauty and excellent performing individuals in their selections have given preference to excellent performance, disregarding conformation of body and color of plumage entirely.

It is certainly true that all sorts of faults of appearance, temperament, and performance qualities in American Games, as well as other breeds and strains, are recessive (due to the absence of important genes), and that for this reason, such faults tend to be found when we start inbreeding. Inbreeding too close is a sure way to increase your family's hereditary weaknesses, which include reduced hatchability, which is usually the first sign of inbreeding depression, later signs are fewer and fewer eggs laid, and cause of death of embryos, or chicks lacking in "constitutional vigor," meaning they're droopy and unthrifty, and may or may not die soon after hatching.

For some families, the obvious remedy against all such troubles is adding "new blood" and the reason for why this is helpful is fully explained in the chapter of crossbreeding. The "hybrid vigor" so obtained may be very interesting, and is of small wonder, in the light of this that "inbreeding" has a very bad reputation. Then again, it must be emphasized that the only way to avoid inbreeding trouble is by inbreeding, combined with a very efficient selection process and ruthless culling.

Inbreeding troubles will almost always appear where inbreeding is carried out. Wherever we carry out an inbreeding program, however, we see that such troubles, when we understand their nature, can easily be bypassed, and in practice, where we have to carry out an inbreeding purification program, such troubles become less and less serious.

The idea that inbreeding should always bring along lack of vigor and lack of fertility is probably simply due to faulty observation and to unwarranted generalization. In the first inbred generations from highly variable crossbred stock a high proportion of weaklings, badly viable embryos and sterile individuals may be expected, but you will see that if we breed enough and discard the bad lines, this trouble will soon pass. On the other hand, close inbreeding should always be avoided when it is suspected the breed is unpredictable, as most breeders must avoid the production of a deformed, sterile or otherwise valueless young chick. In fact, the only reason for taking inbreeding risks must be an attempt to "fix" the quality of really first-class breeding stock.

For American Games, there are two reasons for inbreeding. In the first place, to obtain high quality and to produce strains of great purity, high hatchability and free from the necessity of culling; and in the second place to retain this purity and high quality, once we have obtained it.

In the matter of fertility and hatchability we meet with the usual paradox when inbreeding. When a strain is highly unpredictable, inbreeding may cause the beginning of many embryos of poor constitution, and resulting in low hatchability. For example, a high percentage of chicks will be dead in the shell. But, on the other hand, it is very interesting that families that are inbred for a large number of generations are noted for the surprisingly high hatchability of their eggs. Through the breeding of my fowl, I have practiced inbreeding and line-breeding for more than two decades, and I have obtained a 100 percent hatch rate in my family of Troiano Reds. This is really what we should expect if the viable embryos are genetically superior. In a strain where the potential for variability has been bred out, if one embryo hatches, they should all hatch.

As you have probably noticed from the information in this chapter, I do not deny the danger of inbreeding, especially in ordinary crossbred stock. But at the same time, I insist that inbreeding, when carefully worked in combination with selection and progeny testing, in respect to purity, will be essential to produce the kind of stock in which "Inbreeding Degeneration" will cease to occur.

EVIDENCE OF TOO CLOSE INBREEDING: As previously mentioned, in all families and strains there are many undesirable characters. Many of these are recessive in inheritance and their effects are largely covered up by dominant characters and by controlled outcrossing. Under a system of inbreeding, a larger proportion of the birds become homozygous for these hidden weaknesses, which then change and take over their appearance.

Test by outcrossing: The practical test to determine whether inbreeding is producing undesirable effects within the family or strain is to outcross. Care should be taken in selecting fowl for the outcross, and it should be done in a limited way. If a noticeable improvement in fertility, hatchability, chick viability and adult viability result from outcrossing, there is very good evidence that the family may be too closely inbred.

After the progeny from the outcross test has proven themselves to be superior to the original broodfowl, more extensive outcrossing may be undertaken. From the genetic standpoint, it would be safer also to restrict the outcross to but one strain as long as that strain proves acceptable.

THE PRACTICE OF LINE-BREEDING

Among the various ways in which "Inbreeding" can be carried out, is by the use of a breeding technique known as "Line-breeding." This is the practice of breeding that produces birds from a single line of descent from a common ancestor, one that is closely related. To be more specific, it is used in the breeding plan by breeding one individual repeatedly to his or her descendants for many generations.

Just like "Inbreeding," this is a process whereby relatives are bred to one another, each having a lineage limited to some closely related lines of origination, but for a specific purpose and for a specific result.

Line-breeding is a long range plan that a breeder is required to have, using an ideal individual, which is firmly fixed in its characteristics and traits. It is a systematic method of cloning, which enables the breeder to replicate, or "set," the special characteristics and traits of one particular bird into the progeny.

Although line-breeding, in all reality, is simply a special method of inbreeding, it is one of the best ways of creating and maintaining a family or strain that is uniform and consistent in every way. For line-breeding to be successful, the breeder must be willing to pursue that ideal regardless of any breeding fads that might dictate otherwise.

Cattle breeders have been known to use a certain bull for several generations, and horse breeders have, at times, done the same thing with an outstanding stallion.

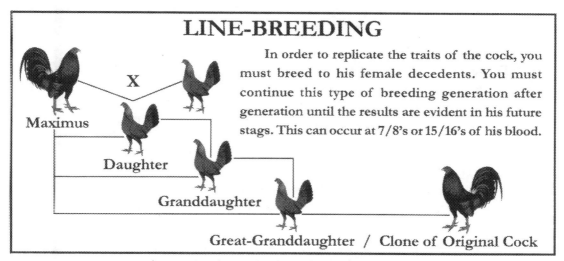

LINE-BREEDING

In order to replicate the traits of the cock, you must breed to his female decedents. You must continue this type of breeding generation after generation until the results are evident in his future stags. This can occur at 7/8's or 15/16's of his blood.

Maximus   X

Daughter

Granddaughter

Great-Granddaughter / Clone of Original Cock

A systematic method used for line-breeding.

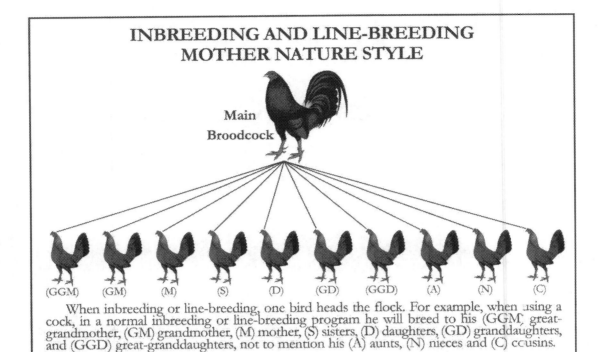

INBREEDING AND LINE-BREEDING MOTHER NATURE STYLE

Main Broodcock

(GGM) (GM) (M) (S) (D) (GD) (GGD) (A) (N) (C)

When inbreeding or line-breeding, one bird heads the flock. For example, when using a cock, in a normal inbreeding or line-breeding program he will breed to his (GGM) great-grandmother, (GM) grandmother, (M) mother, (S) sisters, (D) daughters, (GD) granddaughters, and (GGD) great-granddaughters, not to mention his (A) aunts, (N) nieces and (C) cousins.

MANY SPECIES INBREED AND LINE-BREED NATURALLY: Although many species inbreed and line-breed naturally, as part of their survival, many don't due to the sheer number of available mates. Junglefowl, which American Games originated from, are among these that do. In a normal flock of wild Junglefowl, one cock heads the flock. Although there are young stags among the flock, he is the King of his harem. In that harem, he will breed to his great-grandmother, grandmother, mother, sisters, daughters, granddaughters, and great-granddaughters, not to mention his aunts, nieces and cousins. Once he gets too old, however, or is killed by a predator, or challenged and beaten by a competing cock, usually a younger and stronger one, he will be replaced, whereby the new cock will breed to hens of the same relationship as the other cock. This is inbreeding and line-breeding Mother Nature style.

SHOULD I LINE-BREED? Any decision to create and breed a family should occur after a lot of thought and research. It should not be something that is undertaken lightly.

These are the sorts of questions you need to consider:

- Are the birds I want to line-breed of good quality? (This quality should be proven in the broodpen, show pen, and the pit).
- Do I have photos of the birds that go back several generations? (This will help you see the characteristics that they carry, and which characteristics are worth perpetuating).
- What will I do if the breeding is a disaster and none of the progeny has the characteristics I am looking for?
- Am I breeding to the most suitable birds for my lines?

What are the advantages of line-breeding?

- When line-breeding, you know what you are getting (most of the time).
- Line-breeding gives the breeder more control over what traits they want to perpetuate and carry on and pass along.
- It gives you the opportunity to "set" desired characteristics in your lines, which you hope will be easier to replicate in future generations.
- If the birds have good ancestors there should not be a lot of unexpected results.
- Cautious and careful line-breeding improves the lines, gives cause to breed more lines, and insures the future of the entire family or strain.
- If you have birds with no genetic defects to start out with, the chance of perpetuating future defects into the family is nil, unless you add some new blood from a defective family.
- Line-breeding does not add to the lines, but integrates the best characteristics of the lines being bred.

What are the disadvantages of line-breeding?

- Sometimes the breeding does not go as planned, and the characteristics you wanted the progeny to inherit do not come through.
- Sometimes it doesn't work, and none of the progeny are worth carrying on with. In such case, it is best to cull the progeny.
- Sometimes it does "set" some characteristics in your lines that you don't want. These then are usually very hard to lose.
- Some previously recessive (or hidden) characteristics can come out unexpectedly.

LINE-BREEDING AND SELECTION: When line-breeding American Games, the breeder must use selection as a rigid tool in the process. Unless this is adhered to, the breeder will never attain his goal, and the program will be doomed to failure. From what I have seen, there are very few productive line-breeding programs being practiced, and very few bloodlines that can be successfully line-bred. In most cases, breeders are trying to line-breed fowl that do not have the proper foundation. These are fowl that are the production of a cross. In other words, their characteristics are neither fixed nor set. Broodfowl must have characteristics and traits that are homozygous, in other words, uniform and consistent.

The general definition of a breed, which can also be used to describe a strain, is "a group of birds or animals that have certain inherited characteristics that they pass on generation after generation." The basis or bottom line in a group of bird's ability to pass these traits on is the genetic state known as homozygosity. We inbreed to set the desired characteristics by increasing homozygosity, which allows breeds to pass their traits on to generation after generation.

The characteristics and traits that must be selected for and maintained at all times are good health and wellbeing of the flock, refinement in their conformation of body and color of plumage, fertility, good disposition, and good performance qualities.

The most significant part of the selection process begins with the foundation broodfowl. Many breeders of success believe that the hens are the strongest part of the line-breeding program, and that the cocks are merely providers of genes of a secondary nature. They are indeed important, but inconsequential when compared to that of the hen. I tend to agree with this way of thinking. I

BALANCE and STABILITY

A well balanced bird is what you want. A problem with one side of the triangle can cause the whole thing to fall apart.

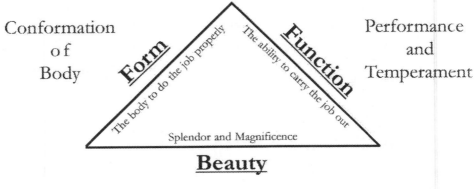

Conformation of Body

Performance and Temperament

Form — The body to do the job properly

Function — The ability to carry the job out

Splendor and Magnificence

Beauty

Appearance

**They must have the complete package to be successful.
(Form, Function and Beauty)
Which means they must look, act and perform well.**

believe the hen is the strain, that most, if not all line-breeding programs should be lead by the hen and not the cock.

Whether you decide to use the broodcock or the broodhen as the foundation of the line, they must be of a common ancestry with that of the fowl that you plan to line-breed them with. This will make the journey towards the ideal offspring much shorter. Otherwise the breeder will experience the need for additional generations of breeding if the ancestry is not common among the foundation broodcock and broodhens.

EXAMPLE OF LINE-BREEDING: Line-breeding is used to create or maintain a strain. Once the breeder has the individuals that he wishes to work with, he will begin to form his family or strain. He will, at this point, develop what's called "Family Lines." These lines are each separate elements of the same family. Each will be selected for specific characteristics and traits. Most breeders like to maintain a minimum of four lines, but it is best to keep as many as you can manage successfully. So let's say you have established your four lines, for reasons of simplicity let's call these lines – "Line A," "Line B," "Line C," and "Line D." Mine are called the "Maximus Line," the "Tecumseh Line," the "Proximo Line," the "Cochise Line," and the "Black Pearl Line." You can call them whatever you like.

From this point, there are many ways of practicing line-breeding. One is to simply breed a very special cock or hen to their sons or daughters, then the following year to their grandsons and granddaughters, and the following year after that to their great-grandsons and great-granddaughters. You will do this until the special attributes of the original bird are recognized.

Another example of line-breeding would be to breed "aunt to nephew" or "uncle to niece."

LINE-BREEDING

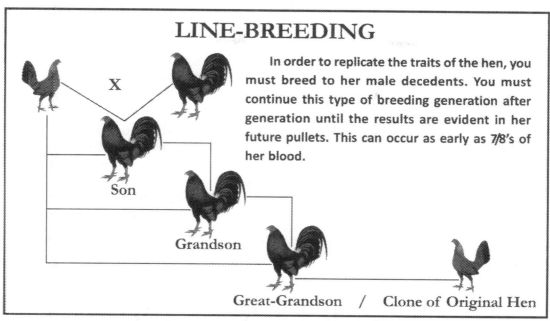

In order to replicate the traits of the hen, you must breed to her male decedents. You must continue this type of breeding generation after generation until the results are evident in her future pullets. This can occur as early as 7/8's of her blood.

X

Son

Grandson

Great-Grandson / Clone of Original Hen

A systematic method used for line-breeding.

Family Lines
Example - The Troiano Reds

These lines are unique, but each is a separate element of the same family.
Each will be selected for specific characteristics and traits.

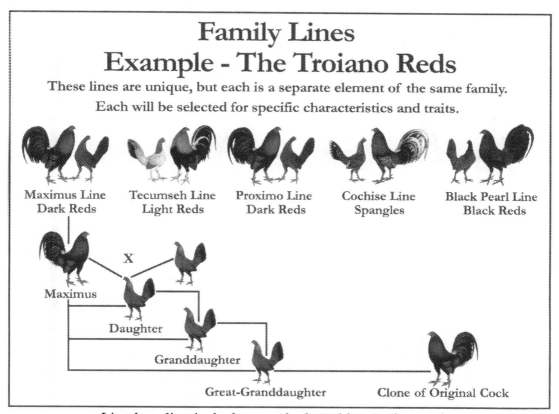

Maximus Line
Dark Reds

Tecumseh Line
Light Reds

Proximo Line
Dark Reds

Cochise Line
Spangles

Black Pearl Line
Black Reds

Maximus

X

Daughter

Granddaughter

Great-Granddaughter   Clone of Original Cock

Line-breeding is the best method used in creating strains.

The first step in line-breeding: As I mentioned earlier, you must start with broodfowl that have a good foundation. For instance:

- They must come from a good bloodline.
- They must have characteristics and traits that are uniform and consistent.
- They're genes must be fixed or homozygous, and not from the production of a cross.

The first step in most line-breeding programs is the mating of full brother to his full sister. This has been known to be repeated, by the best of breeders, up to six consecutive generations. I recommend that you only do it for three though. The result of the first brother/sister mating will be the second generation, resulting in sons and daughters. The next generation resulting in offspring being sons/grandsons and daughters/granddaughters.

Some like to start by breeding half-brothers and half-sisters. However, I would rather start with brother to sister. The results are much faster. Either way, if the foundation hens are of common ancestry with that of the foundation cocks, uniformity will be apparent in the offspring.

Line-Breeding Chart

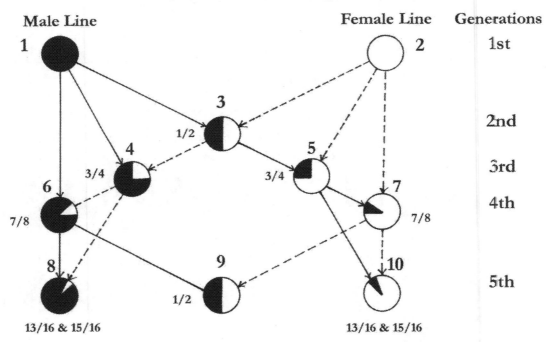

Line-Breeding Chart: The circles represent individuals or groups of individuals used in the breeding or resulting from the matings made. Black represents the cock's line and white represents the hen's line. The relative amount of black and white in a circle as well as the fractional figures at the side indicating the relative amount of each blood carried. The large number at the top of each circle is given to make the discussion of the matings in the article easy to follow. A solid black line connecting one circle with an-other indicates that a cock from the first group was used in the breeding to produce the second group, while a dotted line indicates that a hen was used.

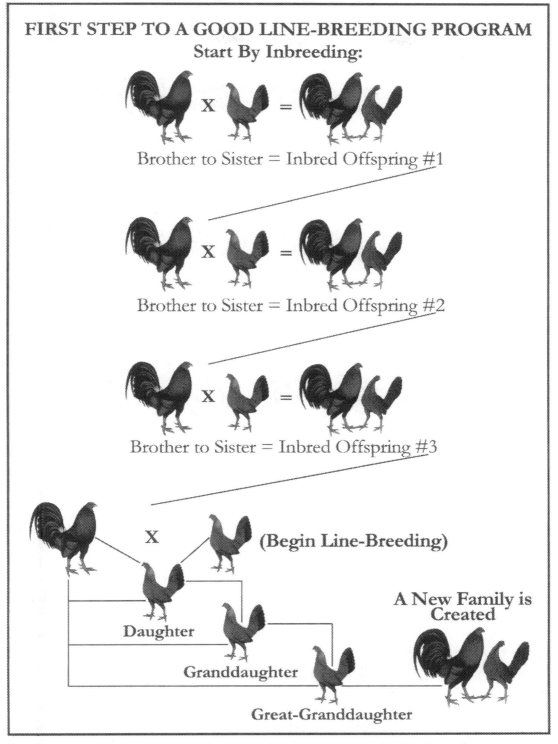

FIRST STEP TO A GOOD LINE-BREEDING PROGRAM
Start By Inbreeding:

Brother to Sister = Inbred Offspring #1

Brother to Sister = Inbred Offspring #2

Brother to Sister = Inbred Offspring #3

X (Begin Line-Breeding)

A New Family is Created

Daughter

Granddaughter

Great-Granddaughter

A systematic method used prior to the implementation of a line-breeding program.

One must not try to line-breed to more than one common ancestor. The sons/grandsons and daughters/granddaughters will be genetic sons and daughters of the foundation broodfowl (broodcock or broodhen). If each parent gave the next generation 50% of their genes, the sons/grandsons and daughters/granddaughters would carry 50% of the genes of the foundation broodfowl. But because of the random division of genes in the parents, the influence of the four grandparents may not be transmitted in equal portions. The offspring may bear a relationship to any one of the grandparents greater or less than the normal 25% relationship.

Another example of attempting to maintain the same relationship as the sons/grandson or daughters/granddaughter is mating a son/grandson and daughter/granddaughter. The result would have the same great-grandfather with four different great-grandmothers and the relationship would still possibly be a genetic son or daughter of the great-grandfather.

I was once told by a good friend of mine, a master breeder in his own right, *"The more superior a breeder's family or strain is to the average merit of its breed, the more reason he has to practice line-breeding to his very best birds or to the very best of the recent ancestors."*

The tool "selection" requires the breeder to eliminate many of the offspring developed in a line-breeding program. As you practice line-breeding it will be found that some broodfowl produce better daughters and others better sons. This makes selection even more important when determining the broodfowl. It will be also found that only a few of the lines from the foundation broodfowl will survive the process of selection over a long period of time.

In most cases, a breeder should not allow more than 87.5% of the genes of the foundation broodcock or hen to appear in any individual of the family, as this will avoid incestuous relationships, or worst yet, inbreeding depression. Other mating patterns can be the method of maintaining 37.5% of the genes from the foundation ancestor. An example of this is easiest explained as an aunt-nephew or uncle-niece mating. There are many methods that may be used to accomplish these results, but one must stay close to the foundation at all times.

It has been said that *"Line-breeding is similar to weaving a prize rug, and only a master breeder will survive the process. It will be found that after a lifetime of line-breeding only the surface will be scratched."*

WHAT CHARACTERISTICS AND TRAITS SHOULD I BREED FOR WHEN LINE-BREEDING?

When line-breeding, you want to breed for conformation of body (known as type) and color of plumage. This also includes the condition of the plumage as well. You must also consider the temperament, the health, the overall look, and the performance qualities of every bird you breed. If you want a specific conformation of body or color of plumage, then you must choose from quality birds that are known to produce those attributes. If you end up with something from breeding that does not fit or measure up to your standard, you should not breed that bird or pair again.

HOW CLOSE SHOULD I LINE-BREED?

Inbreeding is when you breed very, very closely, such as brother-sister. The fundamental question you need to ask yourself before every breeding is - why am I doing this, and what do I hope to achieve?

I would like very much to be able to give you a definitive answer to this question, but really, the answer will come to you after considerable thought and research. Breeding is not an easy undertaking, and it comes with considerable responsibilities. I think long and hard before I make such decisions.

Line-breeding involves broodfowl that have a wide range of attributes, all which complement each other, and all which are necessary for producing successful offspring.

DOES LINE-BREEDING INITIATE DEGENERACY? As we have mentioned earlier in this part of the chapter, families of fowl that are line-bred are usually started by mating the best cock to the best hens, and continuing the second generation by mating the original cock to his daughters, or the original hen to her son. Proceeding in a similar manner for the third generation, the original cock is mated to grand-daughters and the original hen to her grandson, which practically eliminates from each line its original respective sire or dam. It is difficult to explain this system of line-breeding in writing, but if you will make a chart of it and get down to actual figures, you will soon see that it is very simple.

Even with a system of breeding such as this there is no evidence to prove that line-breeding initiate's degeneracy, providing reasonable care is exercised each year in selecting only the best and most vigorous breeders, and there are a large number of fowls from which to choose. The danger becomes even more remote if two lines of the same blood are maintained year after year. This consists of keeping two distinct lines of the same strain, on the same farm, both of which have a common ancestry, but which grow farther apart every year.

WHEN IS IT TIME TO OUTCROSS? First of all, let's discuss what outcrossing means: For American Games, outcrossing is the breeding of different lines of the same family, for instance, every five years or so the cocks of one line are mated to the hens of the other line, and vice versa. For most other breeds of chicken, such as Plymouth Rocks, outcrossing is the breeding of other Plymouth Rocks outside the established family or strain, but of the same breed. I will discuss this in greater detail later in the book. I just wanted you to have a basic understanding before going any farther.

If you are an experienced breeder, eventually you may want to add an outcross to your lines. Once you have outcrossed new blood into the lines, you will take the result of the outcrossing and line-breed them back into your lines to maintain what you accomplished by the outcrossing in the first place. This would be called "backcrossing."

Different breeders have different opinions about line-breeding and outcrossing. Some feel by carefully adding new blood by crossbreeding, and breeding it into their lines they can get the same results as one could by outcrossing. Like I mentioned earlier, I would think long and hard before you make such decisions. For example, if you were to purchase a breeding pair or trio from a breeder, who has spent twenty years or more line-breeding his family to perfection, and you were to add some unknown non-verifiable bird, or a bird with any genetic defects in its background, you have pretty much turned what the original breeder had done into a total crap shoot. Why would you want to do something like that? I wouldn't. Before I were to make such a decision to infuse outside blood of any kind and add it to these lines, I would have to use a bird of superior blood with no defects or bad traits whatsoever in its background. But even so, this would not be an outcross, but rather a cross, which I will discuss later a well.

If you are new to breeding, or not as experienced as the breeders who have created your new family, have the common sense to get advice from those breeders. These breeders will teach you how to use quality birds with superior backgrounds for your breeding program.

Right now, I am undertaking a strategic move where I'm going to do an outcross with a bird from my "Maximus Line" with that of my "Tecumseh Line," and then I will breed the offspring from that mating back along my original lines. This is a decision based on the fact that I have a small gene pool, and my lines are getting very tight, but I do not want to infuse outside blood from other breeders, which in most cases are completely unsuitable for my needs.

If I were going to breed my "Maximus Line" to the "Tecumseh Line," and it's been at least ten generations since my last infusion, they most likely will have very little in common. This is called an "outcross." To breed a bird from the "Maximus Line" with a bird from the "Tecumseh Line," it is likely that the progeny out of such a breeding would

Every family requires an outcross from time to time.

be something great. However, if the progeny was put back to either the "Maximus Line" or "Tecumseh Line," the progeny from that mating would in all likelihood become even better than they were before. The idea is to infuse one line into the other, while maintaining the constitution of the entire family.

AN ALTERNATE METHOD FOR LINE-BREEDING: Here is a practical method of line-breeding, one that has been introduced to me that works on a much grander scale, and all it requires in the beginning is the acquisition of one great broodcock and a small group of well selected hens, and it works great! This system of mating is a five phase method that works best by using a large colony type broodpen.

- Phase one: Instead of following the usual method of mating, that of mating a number of cocks or stags of average quality to your entire flock of hens, one male, called the foundation broodcock, of outstanding quality, is purchased from a reliable breeder and is mated to twelve of your best hens.

- Phase two: The stags obtained from this mating are selected carefully and are saved for future matings with a select group of hens. The pullets obtained from this mating are put into the large broodpen with the hens selected from the previous year. During the second year of the line-breeding project, the foundation broodcock is again mated to the best hens kept over from the previous year. These may include a few two-year-old hens from the original matings and that of the best yearling hens, which are his daughters.

- Phase three: During the third year, the same methods are followed, and, since the mating consists mostly of the very best hens selected from the large flock, some of these hens should be not only daughters but grand-daughters of the foundation broodcock, provided, of course, that he actually proved to be a good breeder. These daughters and grand-daughters would have been produced in the first and second years of the line-breeding program.

- Phase four: During the fourth year, the foundation broodcock would in all probability be mated to a number of his daughters, grand-daughters, as well as his great-grand-daughters, hens produced by the mating of the foundation broodcock to selected hens in the first, second and third year of breeding.

- Phase five: If the foundation broodcock was used in the fifth and later years, he would in all probability be mated to related descendants only, unless a few four or five-year-old hens from the original flock were still on hand. As a result, some of the heritable characters of the foundation broodcock become intensified in the progeny of the whole flock.

This line-breeding program has the advantage of requiring the breeder to buy only one good broodcock for which he should be willing to pay a good price, instead of purchasing several medium-priced cocks and stags of mediocre quality. The program also has the distinct advantage of helping the breeder to select his best hens for the purpose of mating them to the foundation broodcock.

Another advantage is that the best hens of the entire flock are bred back to the foundation broodcock, making it possible in distributing the desirable heritable characteristics possessed by the foundation broodcock to every member of the flock.

A line-breeding project such as this can be carried on as long as the foundation broodcock lives and is able to produce a high proportion of fertile eggs, provided, of course, that he proves to be a valuable breeder as determined by the quality of his offspring. Should the foundation broodcock prove to be a poor breeder, another one should be obtained for the next breeding season. Never breed to a bird unless he or she has proven their worth.

THE PRACTICE OF CROSSBREEDING
Is crossbreeding the foundation for hybridization?
Or a source of variability?

"I have seen many of the best and most valued of the old strains lost entirely by falling into the hands of unskillful breeders, or those who have the inveterate propensity for constantly crossing with fresh blood, or a desire for something new, and striving after perfection, which was more certainly obtained by judicious mating and breeding a known breed in its purity with right selection, than by introducing fresh blood, however good, with its attendent uncertainties, and the certainty of throwbacks to faults and weakness long since bred out in both strains appearing in the fresh cross."

Herbert Atkinson

It is very remarkable that practically all our well-known breeds of commercial and ornamental chickens, even the very best ones, originated from gamefowl breeds. And if we trace back the history of those commercial and ornamental chickens, we find that the great majority of them were originally "just chickens" that somebody liked the looks of and imported, such as Leghorns and Rhode Island Reds, or the result of more or less haphazard backyard breeding "to see what would happen," such as Modern Old English Games, or deliberately bred in different colors for the shows. Even some of our best gamefowl, the Gingers, was just a breeder's sideline, selected entirely for color.

The real purpose of crossbreeding, especially for the modern cocker and backyard breeder, is to provide for the combination of desirable qualities from two distinct lines of blood. As a result of crossing different breeds, and selecting traits that were highly desirable it was possible to create new breeds, varieties and strains.

In this chapter, we will discuss the pros and cons of crossbreeding. That way you can decide for yourself if this is the best method for you.

WHAT IS CROSSBREEDING? Crossbreeding may be defined as the mating of birds that belong to different breeds, varieties, or strains. In simpler terms, crossbreeding is the mating of purebred cocks of one breed with purebred hens of another.

Although the natural tendency for most new breeders is to combine many different breeds from a wide range of sources, the best results of crossbreeding come from the breeding of two distinct and closely inbred lines that are unrelated, but share many common traits; this is where "Hybrid Vigor" comes from. I will explain this later in the chapter. A good example of this would be to breed a Hatch with that of a Sweater. This is crossbreeding one family or strain with another. Another example would be to crossbreed an American Game with that of Oriental fowl, such as an Aseel. This is crossbreeding one breed to another.

These days it is common practice to cross fowl when it is desired to secure a new combination of characteristics in the development or establishment of new breeds or varieties. Crossbreeding is also used with the hope of securing progeny that exhibit the desirable characteristics of both parents in one individual. Crossbreeding also produces offspring that are better than either of the two original broodfowl.

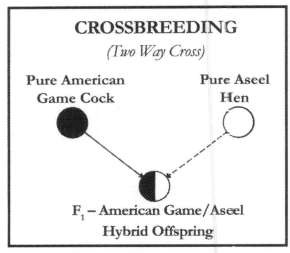

Here is an example of a two way cross.

This method has been popular in livestock breeding for hundreds of years. If truth be told, many of the American Gamefowl breeds and varieties that we have today originated as the result of crossbreeding. Although crossbreeding has contributed greatly to the existence of American Games, we must remember that it is just a tool. This is a tool that is riddled with benefits and dangers.

As Charles Darwin once said - "*The effects of too close interbreeding on animals, judging from plants, would be deterioration in general vigor, including fertility, with no necessary loss of excellence of form.*" That is, there will be a loss in vigor, but this may not be evident in the form or appearance of the fowl. He also says - "*The evidence convinces me, that it is a great law of nature that all organic beings profit from an occasional cross with individuals not closely related to them in blood.*" Again, "*The crossing of varieties adds to the size, vigor, and fertility of the offspring.*"

Mr. Edward Brown says: "*Recrossing very largely remedies deterioration, for it is found that first crosses between suitable breeds give us hardier and more useful birds than were either of the parents.*"

Mr. William Tegetmeier says - "*It is a generally received opinion that crossbred chickens are the hardiest and most easily reared.*"

THE FUNCTION OF CROSSBREEDING: The objective of crossbreeding is usually, in the effort of the breeder, to secure a new combination or blending of characters and traits of two original breeds, both in a pure state, in the development or establishment of new breeds, varieties or strains. The only other time this form of breeding is appropriate, other than in the formation of new breeds, varieties, or strains, is in the creation of fowl that can outperform or exceed their parents in overall functionality. It could be in utility, such as being able to lay more eggs per year, or to produce meat fowl that can gain enough weight for the purpose of human consumption in just six to eight weeks. Or it could be to improve overall performance abilities, such as the production of battlefowl used for sport purposes.

Crossbreeding is sometimes resorted to by breeders for the purpose of strengthening or improving characteristics of color or conformation of body (known as type). An example of this is the use of Black-Breasted Red Games on Silver-Duckwing Games to create the Golden Duckwing color, or breeding the Black-Breasted Red Games on Golden-Duckwing Games to strengthen the Golden Duckwing color.

Another example of this is to improve the birds overall build and level of ability. To produce a bird that is bigger, better, faster, stronger and smarter than either of his parents. These hybrid crosses are known in the cockfighting community as battlefowl.

There is a belief that the mating of fowls of different breeds or varieties, and consequently those which are absolutely unrelated, tends to produce offspring which are unusually strong and vigorous, in fact, more so than when crossing does not occur. There seems to be considerable foundation for such a belief. Therefore, crossing is sometimes resorted to for the purpose of increasing vigor or vitality. However, very little is to be gained by crossing fowl that have not been carefully selected.

THE EFFECTS OF CROSSBREEDING: The effect of its use is to "mix bloodlines and pedigrees" and to increase or improve form and function. However, when it comes to records of ancestry, all records, whether it be for performance or utility are lost or of no future value. For this reason, it is best that most breeders should not consider the crossing of their fowl to other breeds, varieties, or strains. This is not considered good practice, except where the resulting offspring are used for a specific function or purpose, and not used for future breeding purposes.

The effects of dominant and recessive genes when crossing: American Games, like other fowl, carry both dominant and recessive characteristics and traits. Which are dominant and which are recessive depends on the bird that they are mated to and the characteristics and traits that they carry. The real question is, are they homozygous or heterozygous? Since the characteristics of purebred parents are of the homozygous nature, they tend to be dominant as well. While crosses are due, for the most part, to the effects of dominant genes, it is obvious that the progeny of a crossbred mating contains many dominant genes, but in a heterozygous condition, some of the dominant genes having been received from one purebred parent and some from the other.

How do dominant and recessive traits come into play when crossbreeding? When dealing with traits that are dominant or recessive, as you attempt to add one trait you may also be inadvertently eliminating others. Controlling which traits are inherited or lost is tough enough, but when crossing two very different breeds or strains it becomes a great deal harder, maybe even impossible. For example: let's say one parent has a pea comb (dominant) and green legs (recessive), and the other has a straight comb (recessive) and is white legged (dominant). As a result, the offspring from this mating will show the combined dominant characteristics of both their parents, so therefore, they will be pea combed and have white legs.

Many dominant genes produce more favorable effects than do recessive genes, so that progeny produced by crossbreeding is usually superior in many characteristics over either of the parental breeds crossed. This superiority is said to be due to "Heterosis," or otherwise known as "Hybrid Vigor" (The term "hybrid" desig-nates the progeny of a crossbred mating).

"A cross becomes absolutely necessary; and such a one as may not only contribute to that end, but also be similar in feather, constitution, colour of the legs and beak, as your own; and by such a choice you bid fair to have them regular. The procuring a hen or cock every way calculated to meet your wishes, may be attended with some difficulty, but they are to be met with either by interest or money."

W. Sketchley

"There can be no doubt that crossing, with the aid of rigorous selection during several generations, has been a potent means in modifying old races, and in forming new ones."

Charles Darwin

Advantages of crossing:

(1) The crossing of two distinct breeds usually results in greater vigor. This is more apparent where purebreds have suffered from close breeding or inbreeding. Many commercial breeds of poultry have been destroyed from too close breeding. Once prominent, they are now practically extinct as a result of too much inbreeding.

This does not mean that close breeding is necessarily fatal. It's very possible, in the hands of expert breeders, to intensify special points of interest, or any other points, by long-continued inbreeding without destroying the breed. For some, inbreeding means a great sacrifice in overall constitution, and the breeding powers of their family are impaired, so much so, that practically every backyard breeder that is not familiar with proper inbreeding, will cast it aside as a viable method for breeding.

(2) The use of crossbreds enables many new cockers and backyard breeders to participate in this hobby, who would otherwise be prohibited from competition, due to the comparative scarcity of purebreds and to the high prices that are demanded for them.

(3) Crossing, where it increases vigor, improves reproductive abilities. The vigorous of broodcocks and productiveness of broodhens always have good vitality. Reproduction requires a high expenditure of energy, and to maintain this level of reproduction, the fowl must have stamina. While the loss of vigor may not be apparent in the form or outward appearance of the fowl, it will show in their ability to reproduce. Vigor is not so essential in breeding for conformation of body or color of plumage or for show qualities, but it is very essential in breeding and reproduction.

I am not saying that purebred fowl are necessarily poor in the area of reproduction. It is not impossible for the breeder to breed purebred fowl, and at the same time, maintain the vitality necessary for good reproduction, but close breeding for either form or function will not insure you will get good future broodfowl, any more than the same kind of breeding with mongrels will produce great performers.

(4) New breeds and varieties are produced by crossing. Most of our modern American Games are the result of crossbreeding. Crossing induces variation and it is in taking advantage of these variations that new breeds and varieties arise. Some crosses, or hybrids, possessing desired characteristics breed true, and the type, or conformation of body, at once becomes fixed. On the other hand, the great majority will not breed true, and years of careful selection will be necessary to fix the type. The Plymouth Rock, Wyandotte, Rhode Island Red, and other domestic breeds are all the result of crossing, and the American Games are no different. In fact, the American Game resulted from crossing many breeds. They have in their ancestry the blood of the Old English Games, Irish Games, Spanish Games, and Aseels.

Breeders are just beginning to learn what may be accomplished by crossing, and it is not unreasonable to expect great improvement in the performance qualities of American Gamefowl when breeders master the science and art of crossing. Often great progress can be made in a single successful cross or hybridization as in a dozen or even a hundred generations of purebred selections.

There is a fascinating field for developing new breeds, varieties and strains by crossing old breeds, varieties and strains of fowls where great performance is the principal purpose sought after, but it should only be undertaken by those who have the skill, experience, and patience.

The first cross will give offspring of one or two kinds: either they will resemble in one or more characteristics of one of the parents exclusively, or they will show resemblance to both. Certain characteristics blend while others do not. Where the offspring resemble one parent, and the males and females of that cross are bred together, some of the second generation will resemble the other parent, and when these are bred together they will breed true, the offspring will all resemble their parents.

This was proven by a friend of mine, and master breeder. He bred Doms to White American Games. The first generation was all white, taking after one parent. When these crosses were bred together, there was reversion to the Dom parent, some of them being barred, and in mating these barred crosses together they bred true and produced only barred offspring.

Another test was in crossing a straight (*single*) comb American Game with that of a pea-comb American Game; the offspring lead practically all pea-combs. Breeding the crosses together, the offspring reverted to the one side of the breeding, some of them showing straight (*single*) combs. Breeding this straight (*single*) comb offspring together, they bred true to the character straight (*single*) comb. Pea-comb is a dominant characteristic, straight (*single*) recessive, and recessives breed true, while the dominants do not (when a recessive has been introduced). Knowledge of these facts is very important for they will often prove useful to the modern cocker and backyard breeder.

> *"It has always been a matter of surprise to me, to see the wonderful avidity, even in experienced breeders, in expressing a wish of obtaining a single cock from a day's fight, that has exhibited something out of the common routine of play, in order to breed from, when I have been sensible of the impropriety of the cross he was destined to make, in fact, with hens that were as dissimilar in feather and other necessary similarities, as possible. If uniformity in their general appearance is absolutely necessary in forming a regular breed, I cannot help expressing my wonder at well-informed men running into an error so fatal to the welfare of judicious breeding; and which must convince a reflecting mind, that from such unnatural or at least incompatible crosses we are indebted to the public for such a strange medley of colours as we see in every main, when a few years' attention would exhibit cocks of a very different stamp."*
>
> W. Sketchley

<u>DISADVANTAGES OF CROSSING</u>: In the paragraphs mentioned above, the advantages of crossing have been recognized. If the discussion were to stop here it might be thought that the modern cocker and backyard breeder must necessarily cross his fowl. But there are certain disadvantages, some of which will now be considered:

1) First, before there can be any crossing, there must be breeds to cross. Therefore, it is obvious that a purebred American Gamefowl must be maintained of each of the

parental breeds used to make the cross. This is inconvenient, as it requires that stock of the varieties crossed be kept pure in order to have the individuals for making the cross. In other words, the modern cocker and backyard breeder would have to maintain two purebred flocks and provide room for the hybric progeny.

2) Crossbreeding tends to lower the breeding value of the hybrid progeny by making the progeny more heterozygous and by making selection among the progeny less effective.

3) The hybrid progeny, resulting from crossbreeding, should not be used for breeding purposes.

4) Maintaining two separate breeding flocks constitutes a distinct handicap for the individual breeder in his breeding operations because fewer progeny could be raised from each purebred family and because there would be less chance for selection than if only one purebred family of fowl was maintained and crossbreeding was not practiced.

5) There is no need for crossing if proper methods have been followed in breeding. If vigor and fertility is to be restored through crossing, other characteristics may be lost, it will be up to the breeder to decide whether the gain is equal to the loss. For example, let's say you are breeding a Black-Breasted Silver Duckwing (Grey) American Games and they have lost vigor and fertility; a cross with Black-Breasted Red American Games will restore their vigor and fertility, but you will lose the perfection in the Grey color, and it will take several years to eradicate this trait. If color, or any other trait, is very important to you, more important than the points gained, and there is a chance it may be lost by crossing, then you should hesitate to make the cross, and depend rather upon the introduction of birds from other lines of the same family or strain to improve vigor and fertility.

6) The two alternatives are crossing and outcrossing. The theoretical objection to crossing is that it disturbs the bloodline, and the influence of ancestry is lost. In other words, "while it may improve the breed, it spoils the blood." While crossing often results in improved strains that excel their parents, causing a tendency upward, it is also true that crossing sometimes reverses the engine of evolution and throws backward. This usually happens when it is continued beyond the first generation. Breeding crossbreds with crossbreds will start the engine going backward. In other words, reversion will happen, and the result is likely to be mongrels, or even a type resembling in some characteristics of the wild ancestor. Indiscriminate or haphazard crossing will lead to degeneracy just as surely as will indiscriminate inbreeding. The first cross will give vigor, possibly as much as a dozen crosses.

While the benefits of crossing cannot be ignored, it must be remembered that the mongrel condition of many American Games that we see today are due to indiscriminate crossing.

"I know of no system in breeding so big with error, as that of the general propensity of crossing. Nor do I think it warrantable, unless your present brood of fowls is wanting in some required excellence which cannot be deduced from themselves..."

W. Sketchley

The result of crossbreeding: The crossing of two superior animals of different breeds usually results in:

- Improved fertilization (An efficiency of fertile eggs).
- Improved Hatchability (A better percentage of chicks hatched).
- Improved vitality (An increased in vigor and stamina).
- Improved longevity (A longer more productive lifespan).
- Improved viability and livability (A much lower chick mortality).
- For meat production, an increased growth rate.
- And in commercial egg laying breeds, improved egg production, especially in the pullet year.
- And in sport breeds, an improvement in ability and performance.

The results of these hybrid offspring are usually better than either of the two original breeds from which they were produced.

Experienced cockers and backyard breeders have long known that the crossing of two breeds of rather extreme characteristics also results in increased vigor and stamina. This is otherwise known as "hybrid vigor," which produces gamefowl that are bigger, better, faster, stronger, smarter, and more powerful than either of their parents. Nevertheless, there is a downside. Crossbreeding is one of the most definite and specific means of producing variability in a family of fowl than any other method of breeding. In other words, crossbreeding is sure to increase the potential for variation in any yard. As a result, it will produce offspring that are very unpredictable in all their characteristics and traits. So, if you are breeding for uniformity, crossbreeding is not the way to go.

"The act of crossing often leads to the reappearance or reversion of long-lost characters; and in most cases it would be impossible to distinguish between the reappearance of ancient characters and the first appearance of absolutely new characters."

Charles Darwin

THE CONSEQUENCES OF CROSSBREEDING: For every cocker or backyard breeder there is always a temptation to crossbreed. Although there is a strong desire to improve certain qualities, in most instances the crossing of two breeds, which are pure but very different, is a mistake. The appearance alone of a flock of crossbred fowls, when compared with the pure breeds from which they originated, should convince anyone that this is a bad plan.

Here are three examples of crossbreeding that can produce very likeable and favorable results, initially, but in the end, the results and consequences are always the same, unpredictability in all future progeny.

Example one: This is when birds of opposite or unlike characters are mated together. The first cross is often very good due to hybrid vigor. However, in this example, the mixing together of both parents makes for a combination of unpredictability. In this case there is a definite split of characters between the offspring, showing traits of both parents. There is no uniformity. All the brothers and sisters look different.

Example two: This is when the broodcock and broodhen carries traits that are dominant over the other, or are the result of sex-linkage. In this case, the results of the offspring are not what the breeder expected or hoped to achieve. When the trait you are hoping to perpetuate is recessive but you are breeding to a bird that carries a dominate trait, that trait negates the recessive. In this case, the results you wish to see will come, partially in the second generation, but not the first. You must be familiar with dominant and recessive traits, as well as, sex-linked traits.

Example three: This is when the birds, which possess similar characteristics, are mated together. Since many of the characters will blend very nicely, the progeny of the first cross are often fantastic. They will usually show an even greater improvement in their average appearance and performance, in the first generation, than seen in the first example. In this instance, the mixing together of both parents makes for an excellent combination, and comes together in one neat package, the offspring.

Although these examples show the importance of selecting fowl that complement each other very well, as you can see, the first cross is not so bad. As a rule, occasionally they possess some slight advantages in their form and function, and will show a fair degree of uniformity with regard to the desired traits. Consequently many aces are produced. However, the breeding value of future offspring from hybrids is greatly reduced.

In the examples of one and three, the offspring of second crosses are always inferior to the original purebred birds. As a result, the outcomes are always varied and often disappointing. This is when the characters of the original birds (the grandparents) begin to break up, as it is called, and reappear randomly and indiscriminately within the offspring. Uniformity and consistency is gone forever!

Further breeding of these crossbred, or hybrid progeny, will always result in a great variety of types and variations in the characteristics of the offspring. Therefore, they should not be mated in any way, either among themselves or back to their parents. A good rule is to avoid crossbreeding wherever possible, and to resort to it only as the last extreme toward a definite aim or purpose.

THE INFAMOUS THREE AND FOUR WAY CROSS: Sometimes it is beneficial to introduce another breed to further the blending, or to introduce still other characteristic or trait that may be desired in the new breed, or to introduce yet another trait to enhance the hybrid qualities. By simply breeding a third family onto the original cross, let's say a bird that is the result of a hatch and sweater cross and another bird that is a pure Aseel, you are performing what is called a three way cross.

A four way cross is a little different. By breeding two birds that originated from a two way cross, let's say one bird is the result of a cross between a hatch and a sweater, and the other bird is the result of a cross between a lacy roundhead and an Aseel, if you were to breed them together you would have a bird that is the result of a four way cross.

Personally I don't think this is always the best way to go. Some people think by crossing a family known for speed over a family known for power, then over a family known for cutting, and eventually over a family known for gameness, that they will produce the perfect bird, a complete bird, and one that can compete against the best in competition. Sorry, it just doesn't work this way, unless you're the luckiest person in the world! If you ask me, a four way cross is four times the problem too. Whether or not this works for the production of a battlecross still remains to be seen. There are so many characteristic and traits to consider. Therefore, the more bloodlines you enter into the mix, the more complicated it becomes. This makes it impossible to predict, with any accuracy, to what degree which traits they will inherit and which traits they will not.

Always be goal oriented when using the three or four way cross: Whenever you decide to use a three or four way cross always have a goal in mind, especially when selecting the specimens for breeding. Make sure you are breeding towards very specific results, and never as an attitude of "let's see what happens if" type of breeding.

The concept of three and four way crossing is interesting and on paper it looks good, but the truth is it can be very problematic. In most cases, the result is the production of mongrels. The offspring are different in their characteristics. Some are large, some are small. Some are high stationed and tall, some are short and stalky.

RECIPROCAL CROSSES: This is the alternate crossing of a cock and hen of two different breeds or varieties. The effects and outcomes of reciprocal crossing in the breeding of American Games is an interesting phenomenon. When two birds of the same general type and character are crossed, the

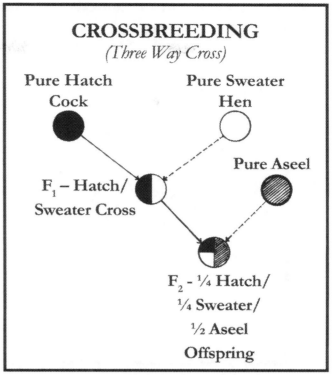

An example of a three way cross.

progeny are similar, no matter which type was used as the father. If, however, the parents are widely different, the resulting progeny will vary with the varying size of the parents. For example, if one parent is a bantam and the other is a large bird, the size of the egg, and therefore, the size of the chick, will be like that of the mother. If the mother is a bantam the chicks will be small. If the mother is of full size, the chicks also will be full size. There are many other features which give similar results, but in general, the progeny will always resemble each other regardless the differentiation of characteristics of the parents.

MAKE SURE THEY NICK: Many new hybrid combinations are continually tried by breeders, but as we well know, when crossbreeding, the matings do not always "nick."

As the superiority of first-generation hybrids over so-called pure breeds results from the circumstance that the variability and deficiencies of one breed are hidden by the fact that the second breed happens to be pure for those points, it follows that the closer two breeds are related, the better the chance that hybrids between them will not be particularly good.

In the production of first-class first-generation hybrids, the quality of the hybrids depends on the "nicking" of the two breeds. It is important that the cock be homozygous for all the important genes in regards to the hens which may be impure (and vice versa). But as we need only comparatively few cocks, it is of greater importance, and certainly more promising, to select a strain of cocks especially for this particular purpose. This should be done as follows: in a family of American Games, selected for quality in performance and conformation of body, a number of cocks should not only be mated to hens of their own family, but equally well to hens of the family for which they will be crossed with. This will give us data about the greater or lesser suitability of those cocks for

290

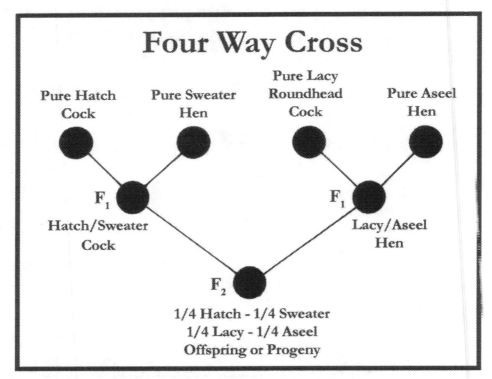

An example of a four way cross.

this particular purpose. The most successful cocks should then be bred to their own purebred close relatives, and such test matings should again be made with their sons, and so on.

CROSSBREEDING AND THE PERPETUATION OF QUANTITATIVE TRAITS When we are dealing with traits such as speed, power, cutting and gameness, we are dealing with traits that are governed by what is known as quantitative traits. These are genes that will only express themselves through birds that carry those traits in high quantities. Once these birds are crossed with another they will only be expressed if the other bird carries the same gene, and with the same or better intensity. Quantitative Traits must be bred over and over, generation after generation, until it is highly concentrated in the blood. For instance, "Gameness" didn't come overnight; it was produced as a result of breeding to birds that were known to carry that trait more intensely than the rest.

Traits that are quantitative in nature must be homozygously matched. Only through the matching of characters is a cross successful.

If a person understood the mechanics of crossbreeding he could stand a better chance of producing some fairly decent battlefowl. What should he know and understand?

- He should know which breeds cross best with his fowl.
- He should know the right way to practice and make use of this type of crossing.
- He should understand the right sequence in which to match up the characters and traits that are important to his ultimate goal.
- And he should understand the effects of dominant and recessive traits, as well as sex-linked traits.

CROSSBREEDING TO IMPROVE SHOW QUALITIES: In breeding for show purposes, it is considered bad practice to cross different strains of the same breed. The first cross often produces good birds, but the next generation is likely to break up and fragment their characteristics within the offspring to the point that they are no longer uniform.

> *"When two species or races are crossed, the offspring of the first generation are generally uniform, but those subsequently produced display an almost infinite diversity of character."*
>
> *Charles Darwin*

THE CONTINUED PRACTICE OF CROSSBREEDING: Through the years, the results of this type of breeding have shown great advantages in overall form, function, and beauty, especially in first generation crosses. They tend to be better in most of their characteristics and traits than either of their parents. For American Gamefowl breeders, who are interested in the production of hybrid battlefowl, this fact has not gone unnoticed. It is for this reason that the crossbreeding of American Games has become the most popular method of breeding for the majority of cockers.

When crossbreeding is practiced, the usual hope by the breeder, whether consciously or unconsciously, is to increase the strength, power and performance abilities of his fowl. This is accomplished by increasing vigor through the production of hybrids crosses. This is known as "Heterosis," appropriately termed "Hybrid Vigor."

Whether these breeders understand it or not, they do believe that the mating of fowls of different breeds, varieties or strains, and consequently those which are absolutely unrelated, tends to produce offspring which are unusually strong and vigorous, more so, in fact, than when crossing does not occur. There seems to be considerable foundation for such a belief, that crossing is therefore used for the production and purpose of hybrid battlefowl. Inadvertently, they also increase vigor or vitality, which contributes to the birds overall strength and ability. However, this hybrid vigor is only sustained for the first generation cross.

Occasionally there is a cross that nicks so well, the offspring are exceptional in every way. The offspring possess some desired quality in high degree that it is necessary to make the same cross whenever offspring are desired. Therefore, to continue crossbreeding it is necessary to maintain two distinct pure breeds year after year, and to destroy the hybrids as soon as they cease to be of use or have a definite purpose.

Requirements of such a breeding system: Although crosses are more common than purebreds, especially for breeders of American Games, it is important for the breeder to understand that it is the parents that are used in the cross that are of the greatest importance. This requires many separate pens, houses and yards, for the sexes of each pure breed, and for the crosses. Whenever this is done, it is usually inconvenient and difficult, as it requires that families of the varieties crossed be kept pure in order to have the individuals for making the cross. This is a practice that is both expensive and troublesome.

A departure of uniformity: I'd like to point out that progeny that are uniform are produced only when the parents are fixed in their particular type, and breed true. It is only when they are from separate and different but distinct lines of descent that decidedly beneficial result from crossing can be expected.

It must be clearly understood by anyone who contemplates crossbreeding, that while the offspring directly resulting from the cross are often quite uniform in color, conformation of body (type) and size, when these latter individuals are mated, their offspring usually vary in color, type and size, and the variation may be all the way from individuals resembling one of the original parents of the cross in one or more particulars through many gradations and combinations to individuals resembling the other parent, to something quite mutant. Uniformity is very largely destroyed and can only be regained by the selection in successive generations of individuals embodying the desired characters. This is a long, slow process, and for this reason the crossing of varieties or breeds should be left in the hands of the expert breeder who has some definite and good reason for making the cross.

Success depends on the replication of certain breeding combinations: For the experienced cocker who understands the value of an occasional cross, he only resorts to this when it is obvious that the offspring will possess some desired quality in high degree, such as certain performance abilities or special show qualities. He also knows, in order to attain the same outcome, it is necessary to make the same exact cross. In other words, success depends on the breeder repeating the same breeding combination of cock and hen in order to achieve the same results. As soon as the original cock and hen are gone, so is the success. That's the problem with crosses, the success is only temporary.

THE BENEFITS OF HYBRID VIGOR: Much has been written about "hybrid vigor," and many different theories have been proposed to give an explanation of the phenomenon. We touched on this subject in preceding paragraphs. It is my hope that it will become much clearer in the following paragraphs. Let us examine the facts first.

The mechanics of hybrid vigor: When we compare the results of three separate groups of chicks, each from parents of various degrees of variability, such as purebreds, multi-crosses, and first hybrid crosses, we find that there are huge variations in the chicks between the three groups. The proportion of bad ones is lower in the first crossbred generation, and the highest in the multiple cross offspring, and the purebred chick were somewhere in the middle.

By combining the germ-cells of two pure and distinct breeds, such as a "Hatch" with that of an "Aseel," we hide the fact that many of those germ-cells in both breeds may be genetically poor in quality. For illustration purposes, let's assume that X and Y are genes, which are very important (with hundreds of other genes) in order for a good hereditary makeup. If we state this in terms of a genetic formula, the "Hatch" breed may be pure for gene X (XX), while in respect to gene Y it may be unpredictable, so that in this breed we find many heterozygotes, XXYy, and even some that are lacking Y (XXyy). On the other hand, let's say that all the birds in the "Aseel" breed are pure for Y (YY), but some are lacking gene X (XxYY or xxYY).

Now, if we cross the two breeds, the "Hatch" and the "Aseel," all the hybrids will have both X and Y at least once, and there will be no chicks lacking either X or Y among them. In other words, the purity of one breed for some genes covers up the fact that within the other breed there exist inherited weak points, impurities in respect to valuable genes, and vice versa, of course. We call this the "Blanket Effect," where the qualities of one breed cover up the qualities of the other. Whether this works in our favor or not is a question of great debate.

It would seem that if this is how hybrid vigor functions, it would be possible, by careful work, to bring up the quality of any family with the infusion of one hybrid bird, to a level of that of the best hybrids. I am sorry to inform you that hybrid vigor will only function in the first generation cross. After that the results are very mutant like. The only way to improve a family is to start with first-class foundation stock, and by breeding and selection methods that will allow us to get the group homozygous in respect of all the necessary genes.

Hybrid vigor can give you a false perception: The visible phenomenon of hybrid vigor can, at times, overshadow the benefits of purity of breeding. However, on the other hand, indiscriminate breeding of crossbred or hybrid fowl may also result in degradation of quality.

Crossbred gamefowl have the reputation of being better than purebred ones. However, the crossing of distinct breeds is so often done by inexperienced breeders, who have no idea why they are crossing their fowl. They have no idea that it's to achieve and attain hybrid vigor, and that hybrid vigor is responsible for the improved characteristics and traits, and not so much of the "inheritance" of those characteristics and traits. Ancestry certainly plays a role, and hybrid vigor can make up for many faults, but the improvements are very temporary. Although hybrid vigor benefits the individual of the original cross, it cannot be passed from one generation to the next. That is a false perception.

A great difference between the breeding of American Games for exhibition (the poultry show) and American Games for sport, has been in the way in which they breed their fowl. One practices inbreeding, line-breeding and outcrossing for maintaining strong family foundations (purity of blood) and uniformity, while the other practices crossbreeding for better performance capabilities. One has a future, the other is short-lived.

Special note of interest: Do not confuse hybrid vigor with superior genes or with proper inheritance, they are not the same! Hybrid vigor cannot be passed from parent to offspring or generation to generation.

Hybrid vigor can be disappointing: It is certainly not true that the abundance and vigor and vitality of hybrids are a universal rule in living nature. Both in plants and in animals some hybrids are very feeble and weak. Some hybrids, like most goat x sheep hybrids and turkey x chicken hybrids, are not even born alive. Many species hybrids are highly sterile, both in plants and in animals, and there may be some connection between the complete sterility of some hybrids and their overflowing of abundance in qualities.

In hybrids between gamefowl and domestic chicken breeds I have never seen or heard of first-generation hybrids that were sterile, although sterility and very low fertility among descendants of crosses are quite common.

If we examine the quality of crosses, and compare this quality with that of the pure breeds crossed, we generally find the following fact: the next generation hybrid crosses are usually stronger and more vigorous than the best individuals of the two breeds crossed.

The advantage, if there is an advantage, lies in the fact that the unpredictability in quality in the hybrid group is very much higher than in the two original breeds. In other words, when within the two breeds crossed, there are a certain proportion of outstanding, first class fowl, a proportion of second-raters, and a certain proportion of culls. This enables you, the breeder, to eliminate the heritably substandard or weak specimens, and keep only the very best. The problem with hybrid crosses is that you will have to cull more.

Hybrid vigor and the effects on hatching eggs: Back in the days when I breed pure Colonel Givens and pure Bruce Barnett Sweaters, I noticed that when I crossed them, the eggs of the two pure breeds and the eggs of the hybrid crosses of both breeds, when hatched side by side in the same incubator, the hybrid chicks always hatch early and all together, while the purebred chicks hatched over a longer number of hours. I have also been informed by other breeders that this was true for them as well. I thought that you would find this interesting. If this should happen to you, now you will know why.

THE SELLING OF CROSSBRED FOWL:

There is one aspect of crossbreeding that should be discussed here, namely, the advantage for some breeders to sell hybrid offspring (known as battlefowl) to his customers. Until recently, a breeder, selecting his birds by the old method of choosing the best individuals, could sell his choice birds to others without much fear of creating competition within the market, his strains were so very impure anyhow that it really didn't matter.

The breeder of today, who specializes in purity of blood, believes that it is best to sell crossbred birds, not his purebred fowl. For him, to give his customer broodfowl that are highly homozygous, would be like selling the goose that lays the golden eggs. He is very protective of his bloodline and is not willing to share them with others. He wants to take advantage of their great popularity by selling fowl but not the actual blood. Today, the usual system of buying somebody else's cocks to make up broodpens (crossbreeding between families) makes most breeders sell material from which their customers could, only with great trouble and patience, breed up first-class strains.

Author Kenny Troiano, and his mentor and friend Tony Saville - February 8th 2009.

Recently much has been written on a comparison between poultry-breeding and the breeding of corn. In corn, where the natural increase is enormously great, and crossbreeding much easier than enforced self-fertilization, the commercial methods of seed production mostly consisted of keeping two pure strains separate and of crossing them to get seed for a commercial crop. The seed merchants, for reasons of personal profit, are propagating a double cross, the crossing of a hybrid with a hybrid. Harvests from double crosses are generally not as good as from single crosses, but as seed production is much cheaper, profits for the seed-merchants are greater. Where good uniformity is important, as in sweet corn for canning, the firms are still selling first cross seed.

Some American firms have started something similar in poultry. The method of issuing hybrids between inbred strains to different egg suppliers, and buying back their hatching eggs, is highly suited to enterprising individuals who hate risking the possibility that somebody else may profit from their efforts. Blind inbreeding is the first step, and the next is to try out combinations of those inbred strains to find suitable hybrid combinations to lay the eggs that will have to be fertilized by males of still another hybrid. Just as in corn, both theoretically and practically, a single or a triple cross should always be superior to that of a double cross. The advantage lies entirely in the possibility for the originator of such methods to build up a big business monopoly.

THE PRACTICE OF INFUSION
The introduction of new blood in order to improve the family

Every strain, regardless of its greatness, may have one or more weak points. Some strains have many. Even though you are careful in your breeding practices, as in inbreeding or line-breeding, not to mention carrying out a strict selection criterion that includes ruthless culling, you may still experience a number of characteristic that will need to be selectively bred out and eliminated. When this happens, do not despair, as there are other techniques which you can use to overcome this problem.

In order to correct, or at least modify, these weaknesses or undesirable characteristics, there are times when you will need to add new blood. By adding characteristics and traits of another bloodline, ones that is stronger in the areas of your strain's weaknesses, some families can actually be improved, especially if done in a moderate degree. This technique is called "Infusion."

There are many ways to introduce new blood into your fowl. The most common are "OutCrossing," otherwise known as Outbreeding, and "Grading-up." (Notice that I didn't say Crossbreeding) Simple infusion, however, is accomplished a bit differently. I will explain in just a moment.

HOW TO INFUSE NEW BLOOD: In introducing new blood, it is a good idea not to infuse it haphazardly. It is beneficial to determine how well the new blood will blend or "nick" with the blood of your birds before going full force with the infusion.

For instance, let's say you have purchased a cock, which you believe will improve your fowl. He should first be mated to three or four selected hens as an experiment or trial mating. The quality of the offspring from this mating should be carefully observed and evaluated. If the results are good, you can most likely integrate the blood of that cock into the rest of the family. However, I would recommend using the offspring from the first mating or infusion to further the infusion process instead of the original cock (original source of outside blood). This will not only give you an opportunity to test out the fitness of the new blood for use, but by using the offspring of the "trial" mating, it will cut down the percentage of new blood introduced on the family as a whole, thereby

Every family is a product of infusion of some sort.

lessening its disturbing influence, while at the same time, securing in some measure benefits accumulated from the use of new blood.

Although we used the cock to illustrate the infusion of new blood, you may prefer to purchase one or two hens instead. In this case, you can mate these hens with a selected broodcock from your own family of fowl, and if the results of these trial matings are good, you can use the offspring, stags or cocks, for the further introduction of the new blood.

THE 1/16th INFUSION METHOD: This is a method that is just the reverse of grading-up. The 1/16th infusion method is the introduction of a strain into an already established strain, for the purpose of improving its characteristics and traits in small, but

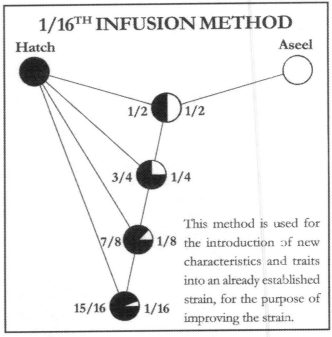

This method is used for the introduction of new characteristics and traits into an already established strain, for the purpose of improving the strain.

A systematic method used for the introduction of new characteristics and traits into an already established family.

significant, increments. It is not used to completely change the strain. It is also used for refreshing the bloodline. This is why it is so important to be careful of what you introduce into the family, for it can destroy the quality and uniformity of your strain forever. The idea is to breed a special individual (new genetic pool) into your family that will compliment or improve your family. For example, in a family, such as a Hatch, the idea is to introduce blood, such as Aseel, and then breeding back to the Hatch bloodline until you are at 15/16th's of the Hatch blood and 1/16th of the Aseel blood. Once you reach this point, line-breed to the Hatch side and discard the Aseel blood entirely. What you are left with is a family of fowl that is a little better is some areas of its makeup.

THE NEW COCK SYNDROME: Through fear of "Family Degeneration" many cockers and backyard breeders consider it absolutely necessary to bring in new broodcocks each year. Very often they make a practice of exchanging cocks with another breeder. In fact, this has become the trend among most cockers. Sandy Hatch and Walter Kelso were fanatical about this. This is inspired by the right idea, but it is likely to be accompanied by trouble. If it is your desire to introduce new blood, the rule should be to do so, not just because it is new blood, but because it is far superior to your own in many of their attributes. It must appear to be a win-win situation.

GUESSWORK AND SPECULATION: It is very difficult to raise standard-bred, high-quality American Games if new blood is added to the family each year. You may buy a purebred broodcock to mate with your purebred hens, and later find that the two strains failed to nick properly. That is, the mating may throw offspring with defective traits, such as a disproportioned conformation of body, or poor color, not to mention, poor performance abilities and gameness. These are traits that will take several generations of special breeding to eliminate or fix. In short, the introduction of new blood, in most cases, is a matter of guesswork and speculation, not good breeding practice.

TAKE YOUR TIME: A better way to introduce new blood is to take three years to do it, and experiment with the individuals produced before going at it full force. Purchase a few hens of the desired strain and mate them to your best cocks, or secure a couple of good cocks and mate them to your best hens. Then study their offspring for a couple of years, and if they are satisfactory, in every way, mate the new blood to the rest of the family.

BE VERY CAREFUL AND KNOW THE RISKS: Although many cockers and backyard breeders tend to infuse new blood into their fowl by adding outside blood, you have to be very careful you don't ruin the originality of your blood. If it becomes necessary to infuse blood into your family of fowl from an outside source, be very careful about the blood that you add and how intensely you add it in. This is a time when the marking of the chicks is critical, and I mean critical. Meticulously mark all the offspring.

I personally would not infuse new blood, from an outside source, into my family of fowl. However, if there came a time that I found it necessary to do so, I would infuse the new blood into a small group of my birds first, and make a separate family out of them. If in time the infusion look to be beneficial and did not bring in new weaknesses or faults, I would then begin to integrate it into the rest of the family. I would do it slowly though, in fact, I would do it one line at a time, starting with the worst line, and working my way to the top.

INFUSING BLOOD FROM ANOTHER LINE OF THE SAME FAMILY: Infusing one line into the other, but from the same family is by far the best method of infusion. There are fewer risks and many more benefits. If I should experience a number of characteristic that I will need to eliminate or breed out, such as a change in conformation of body, a undesirable throwback to their color of plumage, a reduction in overall size, low station, poor health, or worse, a lack of gameness, I will breed a cock or hen from one of my other lines that is especially strong in those areas, into the line in question (infusion), then breed it back out by line-breeding back to the original line that was having all the problems with.

At this point, it is important to select progeny that are free of the problem. If it is Line "A" that is having all the problems, I will infuse blood from Line "B", and then breed Line "B" back out, leaving the good qualities of Line "A" and replacing the undesirable qualities of Line "A" with the attributes of Line "B". This takes a long time, but it's a much safer way to go.

IT'S IMPORTANT NOT TO INTRODUCE UNDESIRABLE CHARACTERS OR DISEASES: With the introduction of new blood into an established family of fowl, it is very important not to introduce undesirable inherited characteristics or diseases. The idea is to strengthen the family, not weaken it.

As a precaution against disease, it is always safer to bring in hatching eggs from a desirable outside source. Hatching eggs should always come from a flock that has proven healthy, vigorous and have all the attributes that you desire. Chicks from these outside eggs should be brooded and reared with chicks from your fowl. This gives you a direct comparison in regards to growth rate and development, rate of maturity, special attributes, as well as physical defects. It also gives you great insight as to their general health and wellbeing, in short, their constitutional vigor and overall vitality and viability.

THE DANGER OF INTRODUCING NEW BLOOD: I've touched on this subject a bit throughout the chapter, but I wanted to reiterate the importance and dangers of introducing new blood. In any well-bred family, especially one that is well established, the danger of deterioration through the introduction of new blood is very much more real than any danger of deterioration through lack of new blood, especially in fowl that are bred with outstanding attention to essential and substantial characteristics and traits.

While this point can be hard to demonstrate, I do believe that a blending of bloodlines, long separated, tends to bring out latent or dormant ancestral characters (more especially, the most troublesome faults of a variety). Therefore, before making extensive use of a bird of a different breed, variety or strain, or fowl of unknown breeding, an experienced breeder will try the new blood in special matings, for a number of years, in order to find out how it will "nick" with his family of fowl. A breeder may try a bird in this way a number of times with different mates without getting the results he wants.

There are breeders who are always trying to produce something which does not already exist. Some, who are interested in producing a new breed and others who are trying to improve an existing breed. Even after a good deal of experience, they are still prepared to take chances on a new bird that has caught their attention, and will quickly infuse it into their general matings, usually by adventurous crossbreeding. Often with the result that faults, requiring years of careful breeding to eliminate these faults, and which will crop-out all through the progeny.

The experienced breeder never relies on a new bird until he has fully tested it. He will maintain the family in its original form until breeding tests proves the new infusion has been successful.

Special note about the introduction of new blood: Where a breeder has developed a strain of fowls of especially fine quality and ability, he should hesitate a long time before he introduces new blood. If he decides to do so, he should use caution as to the method by which he does it.

THE PRACTICE OF OUTCROSSING
A much better alternative to crossbreeding

Focusing on the best individual broodfowl allows a breeder to introduce exceptional genes into his flock. When a breeder is able to successfully mate a great broodcock to a great broodhen, he will undoubtedly create a good number of high quality offspring. Although it is the principles and practice of breeding that will take him to the highest levels of competition. There are two general methods of breeding that are used in the production of gamefowl: "Inbreeding" and "Crossbreeding." Any one or a combination of methods can be used, depending upon what kind of progeny you are looking for. In using any of these methods, remember that the broodcock and the broodhen each contributes fifty percent to the genetic makeup of the progeny.

So far we have discussed "Inbreeding, Line-Breeding, and Crossbreeding." In this chapter we will discuss "Outcrossing." Without outcrossing, inbreeding and line-breeding are nothing more than dysfunctional breeding methods. Outcrossing is the link that makes the whole thing doable.

As most of us well know, great broodfowl are difficult to find, as there are very few that are considered exceptional. Only a small number of breeders have the good fortune to possess even one great broodcock or broodhen during their lifetime. Although, some have had the great fortune to inherit or come into possession of great broodfowl, for most breeders, they must create their strain through a painstaking process of breeding their best individuals over many generations.

Even the fortunate breeders who have outstanding broodfowl do not limit their matings to only one line, as this can be extremely dangerous. Even the best lines can breakdown at some point. If you are only working with one line, it is a given that it will, in time, breakdown. Often this happens because of poor selection and faulty breeding practices, such as intensive inbreeding, or line-breeding for too many generations, beyond the well-known "Dead End Zone."

You cannot line-breed forever without running into problems. There will be a time when you will need to add or infuse new blood. It is better to do that with a distantly related line than to bring in outside, unknown blood by crossbreeding. When new genes, especially defective genes, are introduced into the bloodline by crossbreeding, it reduces the influence of the original genes, or lineage. Crossing inevitably waters down the genes which created the original bloodline (or ancestry) and causes a rapid deterioration in the qualities that makes this bloodline special and unique from others.

As you can see, despite the most careful breeding practices, a great bloodline can still break down for no apparent reason. This has led some breeders to speculate that there is a tendency in nature towards mediocrity, which works to pull down, over time, exceptional strains to average or second-rate levels.

To guard against the eventual deterioration of their strain most breeders maintain a number of lines, distantly related, but all belonging to one principal bloodline. They draw on these other lines, from time to time, to infuse with their most exceptional line. This improves vigor and helps to replace traits that might have been lost due to improper selection or defective breeding practices or in the extreme case, where the principle line has completely fallen apart. This is where outcrossing comes into play; it enables the breeder to fall back on their other lines instead of adding blood from outside sources.

In the following paragraphs, I will help you to understand the benefits of outcrossing and how it works. I will try to show you the comparison of its use, what it means for commercial breeders and what it means for American Gamefowl breeders. You will see that they couldn't be more different.

WHAT IS OUTCROSSING? Outcrossing, otherwise known as "Outbreeding," is probably the most misunderstood form of breeding. Yet, it is the easiest and safest method of breeding in producing high quality competitive fowl. Today there are two versions of outcrossing. One method works fine for commercial poultrymen and backyard breeders, and the other method is used mostly by American Gamefowl breeders. There are some who think both ways are satisfactory. Wrong! Here's why!

In the following paragraphs is an explanation of the two methods and who should use them.

What "Outcrossing" means to commercial poultrymen and backyard breeders: Outcrossing is a term used by most commercial poultrymen, for the production of eggs and meat, and backyard breeders, who mostly raise general-purpose type breeds. For these breeders, outcrossing usually signifies the introduction of "outside blood" of some other strain, or some other family of fowl than that with which the breeder is working on, but always of the same breed and variety as his own.

For these breeders, the object in outcrossing is to improve the family or strain in some point or character, which it may be lacking, and by introducing blood from another strain, which is stronger in the characteristics and traits the other lacks, they will improve the strain.

A good example of this would be the breeding of a White Leghorn Rooster from one breeder to a White Leghorn Hen of another breeder. They are of the same breed and variety, but from a completely different strain.

For the modern cocker, who breeds American Gamefowl, it would seem that their method of outcrossing is synonymous with crossbreeding. Not really. They are able to breed this way because they don't infuse blood of different breeds into their fowl. For instance, if they are breeding Rhode Island Reds, they only infuse Rhode Island Reds. And most breeders of high quality Rhode Island Reds do not experiment by crossing to other breeds like American Gamefowl breeders do. In most cases, Rhode Island Reds come from Rhode Island Reds. You will not find an infusion of Plymouth Rock in them.

What "Outcrossing" means to breeders of American Gamefowl: For the American Gamefowl breeder, however, the function of "outcrossing" is used a little bit differently. In fact, breeding to blood, outside the immediate family, is understood to be nothing more than the crossing of breeds, such as Hatch to Aseel, or the crossing of strains, such as Hatch to Sweater. When it comes to the breeding of American Games, the term "outcrossing" actually means something entirely different.

In effect, outcrossing is the introduction of new blood, but blood that comes from a different "line" within the same family or strain of fowl, which have been inbred or line-bred for a number of generations. It means the use of cocks from lines different from those of the hens, but belonging to the same breed, variety and strain. It is breeding within family lines, but not within breed lines. Simply put, it is the mating of fowl that are related, but distantly related.

For these breeders, the object of outcrossing is to:

- Improve the characteristics and traits of one line of the family, or strain, which it may be lacking, by introducing blood from another line of the same family or strain, which is stronger in the characteristics and traits the other lacks.
- Hold the good characteristics and traits already established in the one line, and to capture the good ones from the other line.
- Attempt to get rid of the undesirable traits in one line and obtain only the good ones from another line.

Outcrossing American Games does not mean the introduction of blood of a different breed, variety or strain as used by commercial and backyard poultrymen, or the introduction of blood from some other source that the breeder knows nothing about, such as often seen in crossbreeding.

If a careful system of inbreeding, line-breeding and outcrossing is practiced, crossbreeding to improve stamina (vigor and vitality) of the strain will probably seldom be necessary. This is the main purpose of outcrossing.

I can hear the question buzzing in my ear. *"But, what if they carry the same name, such as Hatch?"* The problem with this is that not all Hatch fowl are the same. Outcrossing is, indeed, an attempt to improve the quality of your fowl by the use of blood from birds which you, the breeder, believe to be superior, but it is not recommended that you use birds from other breeders to do this, even if they carry the same name. Do not get carried away with the "Name Game" that goes on every day in this hobby. I will talk more about this in a moment.

"What if the other fowl look and act completely the same as mine?" If a person took two completely different families of fowl, even though they seem very similar is all their attributes, such as comb types, color of plumage, leg color, etc., just because these two families look alike, act alike, and perform alike, when bred, the offspring couldn't be more different. This is not outcrossing, this is crossbreeding. That's right; they are nothing more than a hybrid battlecross. Even though they are built alike and look something alike, they still come from totally different strains.

Just understand this - Outcrossing consists of mating birds of the same strain but of different lines. It's the mating of pure individuals that are "related" to each other, but "not closely related." In other words, they are distantly related but still within the same tight, inbred bloodline. Outcrossing is occasionally resorted to when the breeder desires to introduce new blood for a specific result.

IT IS IMPORTANT TO KEEP A CLOSED YARD: You may ask why? Well, when it comes to American Gamefowl, the various varieties and strains within the breed are quite diversified, and the introduction of any other bird, despite their variety, strain or bloodline, even though they carry the same name, is nothing more than a cross. For instance, a Hatch bird in one man's yard can be, and in most cases is, quite a different bird from another man's yard, even though they're also Hatch. They are different in both their genotypical characters and phonotypical characters, and the results from such a breeding would not be what the breeder would expect, especially in the second generation progeny.

WHY IS IT NECESSARY TO OUTCROSS? Outcrossing is an important function of the breeding process, for this is a family, which the breeder is working on to achieve a specific purpose or function. He will inbreed, line-breed, and eventually outcross, all in the effort to perpetuate the line, fix or set their traits within the line, and refresh and rejuvenate the blood for future success. This is a valuable strategy for maintaining a bloodline, and has minimal effects from inbreeding depression.

There are many reasons to outcross; however, it is usually done with three objects or goals in mind:

(1) To develop greater vigor in the progeny and improve general health in the flock - vigor and vitality are likely to be increased, especially in the first generation as a result of outcrossing.
(2) To improve fertility and hatchability.
(3) When there is a lack of improvement in your present breeding program, which indicates that a particular line is simply lacking or has lost the right genes.
(4) To correct some defect which it is apparently impossible to correct within the line.
(5) To introduce some desirable feature, which the established line does not possess.
(6) To avoid the dreaded "dead end zone," known to occur with line-breeding to one individual for far too long.

The real purpose of outcrossing, however, is not only to develop greater health and vigor in the progeny, or to correct some troublesome defect within the family, but to provide for the combination of desirable qualities from two distinct lines, both of the same principle bloodline. For American Gamefowl breeders, probably the most common reason to outcross is to produce "battlecocks" without the indiscriminate use of crossbreeding.

CAREFUL SELECTION IS A MUST: It is important to remember that very little is to be gained by this method if the individuals have not been carefully selected. If careful selection has been made in line-breeding, it is doubtful if outcrossing should be resorted to except for one of the reasons mentioned above. Even under these conditions, outcrossing should be cautiously done, for fear that the variations, which are produced, follow a different line or direction from that which is desired.

I want to point out that uniform progeny are produced only when the broodfowl are fixed in their particular type, and breed true, and it is only when they are from separate but distinct lines that particularly beneficial results from outcrossing can be expected.

The most outstanding advantage gained in outcrossing is in respect to the constitutional vigor of the progeny. In the F_1 generation the effects of inbreeding may not be very noticeable, but in outcrossing they are usually quite noticeable.

INFUSING NEW BLOOD WITHOUT CHANGING GENETIC INTEGRITY: Remember, the primary reason for outcrossing, especially that of American Games, is to infuse new blood, but without changing the genetic integrity of the strain. When it comes to gamefowl, this can be a most impossible or even dangerous. Although this is a system that is generally spoken of as adding new blood, when it comes to American Games, where many desirable characteristics are well established, the adding of new blood should be done with caution, if at all.

Many good gamefowl have been ruined because of this practice. The breeder should introduce new blood in such a manner as not to involve the entire family. Single-mate the new blood, then test the offspring before adding the new blood on a large scale.

The addition of new blood has a tendency, as a rule, to increase the average performance of the individuals in the next generation. Thus, the breeder thinks he has made a big improvement. However, if the truth were known, he has lessened their chances of being able to carry their good characteristics to the next generation.

If the outcrossing is used to produce hybrid battlefowl, this type of breeding is all right, however, none of the cocks or hens should be used as broodfowl. In other words, eat the pullets and use the stags and cocks for competition, but never use them in the broodpen.

For myself, since I raise the Colonel Givens Hatch, I have two possible routes that I can take to refresh the blood of my family. I can get another cock or hen direct from Mr. Givens, that's if he has maintained the same exact blood as when I first received them. Or I can go to one of my other established lines within the same family or strain. If I get another Colonel Givens Hatch cock or hen, from another breeder, I have to hope that they have not changed the structure of the family too much in comparison to mine. This is a huge risk!

The way that I breed them now, I can keep my fowl going strong and true for many years without introducing any outside blood. From my original Colonel Givens family, I have four lines that are good solid lines. I will outcross within these lines, breeding one line over the other every five or six years to refresh and rejuvenate the blood. Then I can continue my line-breeding programs.

OUTCROSSING IS GREAT FOR IMPROVING VIGOR: For most breeders, the purpose and function of outcrossing is used to improve vigor and vitality, and still maintain its original blood, rather than introducing outside blood from another breeder. Here is an explanation of this function.

As we all know well, the effects of "inbreeding" have been understood in terms of the homozygous condition of genes for desirable and undesirable characters, homozygosity of the genes for desirable characters, constituting the advantages of inbreeding, and homozygosity of the genes for undesirable characters constituting the disadvantages of inbreeding.

The effects of "outcrossing," on the other hand, are understood in terms of the heterozygous condition of genes for desirable characters introduced from each of the lines crossed. The situation is further discussed in the chapter on "Crossbreeding" and "Hybrid vigor," also known as "Heterosis."

If we examine Mendelian's theory of genetics, it suggests very strongly that the characters, morphological and physiological, result from the action of the genes residing on the chromosomes. That in the production of each character more than one gene is concerned. No one individual possesses all the favorable characteristics and traits. Each is a random sample of good and bad. Usually, "normality" is dominant over "abnormality." This being so, the F_1 individuals must contain the maximum number of different genes. Heterosis is related to heterozygous.

The most plausible explanation of hybrid vigor (or heterosis) resulting from outcrossing is presented here. One of the parents possesses dominant genes in a homozygous condition, which produce a certain amount of vigor, while the other parent possesses another group of dominant genes in a homozygous condition, which produce the same amount of vigor as in the other parent.

Each parent, of course, carries the recessive genes of the dominant ones carried by the other parent. When the two parents are crossed, the F₁ progeny carry a dominant gene from each of the parents, and therefore, have twice as many dominant genes as each of the parents. The dominant genes, however, are each in a heterozygous condition, and I would assume that they are as effective in producing vigor when in a heterozygous condition as when in a homozygous condition.

THIS IS A STRATEGY THAT REQUIRES THE MAINTENANCE OF TWO OR MORE LINES WITHIN A BLOODLINE: An outcross is extremely important if you're looking to improve body type, since conformation cannot be improved by crossbreeding. This is just another reason to establish more than one line of the same family. You can maintain that same family indefinitely by infusing blood from one of the other lines every five or six years or so.

The desirability of outcrossing will depend upon the probability of an improvement from such a procedure, and upon the necessity for introducing new blood for the purpose of keeping up vigor and vitality of a family of fowl, and/or, in some cases, in an attempt to improve the quality of the fowl by the use of blood from fowl which the breeder believes to be superior to his own. But for the American and Old English Gamefowl breeder, he must keep a number of well established lines in order to take advantage of outcrossing. I will talk more about establishing and maintaining lines latter, but for right now my aim here is to differentiate between crossing and outcrossing, also, to show you the pros and cons of both.

WHEN TO OUTCROSS: In an inbreeding or line-breeding program, there are red flags that indicate that it's time to outcross. These include: unexpected appearance of an undesirable trait; lack of improvement in your present breeding program, which indicates that your birds simply do not carry the right genes. Other signs include: a rapid or drastic reduction in fertility, hatchability, and chick survivability, or generally poor health throughout the yard.

THE PITFALLS OF OUTCROSSING: Outcrossing can be an advantage, as well as, a disadvantage. Although outcrossing can improve health, appearance, etc. it can also bring in new weaknesses that you did not know were even there.

You must always remember that outcrossing has a tendency to destroy the uniformity of the strain, though, in some respects may have the exact effects you were looking for. Although, there may be problems in introducing new blood in this manner, it will be to a much lesser degree than seen by crossbreeding with a different breed or variety of gamefowl all together. The desirability of outcrossing will depend upon the probability of an improvement and upon the necessity for introducing new blood to improve conformation and ability, or in keeping up vigor.

When you bring in new blood, you may not see the changes you desire until the second or third generation. So until then, you are taking that risk of bringing in new weaknesses. This is a good reason to establish more the one line within a family of fowl. When it is time to outcross, select a bird from Line "A" and breed it to Line "B." That way you are not introducing outside blood that you know nothing about.

To further reduce the risks of outcrossing, select birds that are not deficient in any of the characteristics you have been working on. Also make sure they have been properly inbred. An inbred father or mother is likely to be proponent, which means they are able to pass on their attributes to the majority of their offspring. Prepotency can only result from homozygosity.

Other points to take into consideration are:
- Continual outcrossing is to be discouraged, as much may be lost and little gained.
- It is usually better to avoid mixing the bloodlines of several strains.
- Only outcross to one line at a time.
- To reduce any of the risk related to outcrossing, be sure to select birds from those lines that are not deficient in any of the properties you have been working on.

OUTCROSSING IN COMPARISON TO INBREEDING: When inbreeding, there are two or more common ancestors, depending upon the amount of inbreeding. The closer the amount of inbreeding, the more common ancestors there are. For commercial poultrymen and the average backyard breeder, the term "outcrossing or outbreeding" is used in contradistinction to "inbreeding." In their method of outcrossing there are practically no common ancestors. Whereas in outcrossing of American Games they are distantly related, but they are of the same ancestry. In this way, they are improved but not affected by outside influences.

OUTCROSSING TO STRENGTHEN AN INBRED FAMILY: Since you cannot line-breed forever, there will be a time when you will need to add new blood, or you will eventually hit, what is called, "The Dead End Zone." What happens is - when you line-breed, to let's say a special cock, the idea is to achieve a more or less clone of that cock by breeding him to his direct descendants, generation after generation. If everything goes well, you will reach 7/8th to 15/16th of his blood. It is at that time you will need to add new blood or you could reap the effects of "inbreeding depression." This is where outcrossing comes into play, but not from outside sources, rather from another line within the same family.

A practical test to determine whether inbreeding is producing undesirable effects in the strain is to outcross. If a noticeable improvement in fertility, hatchability, chick viability and adult viability result from outcrossing, there is very good evidence that the flock may be too closely inbred. Outcrossing will strengthen and refresh the family without destroying everything you have been working towards. Why go to all the trouble of line-breeding only to undo everything in one crossbreeding.

Care should be taken in selecting broodfowl for the outcross, and it should be done in a limited way. In this case, it is always better to add blood that is related, but not closely related.

After the progeny from tested outcrosses have proven themselves to be superior to the original blood, more extensive outcrossing may be undertaken. From the genetic standpoint, it would be safer also to restrict the outcross to but one line of the strain at a time.

OUTCROSS TO MAINTAIN UNIFORMITY: It is a great mistake to use cocks of different bloodlines and especially of different varieties or breeds in the introduction of new blood, as it can only result in securing a specimen which lacks uniformity, and consequently suffers in its overall value and quality.

For the modern cocker, where the main purpose of breeding is the production of battlefowl, and where he cares very little for the uniformity of his fowl, from the show room point of view, it is common practice to crossbreed every year by purchasing and using new cocks from other breeders. It must be kept in mind, however, that in making such a step, such as crossbreeding, it has a tendency to destroy the uniformity of the flock. But for the breeder who cares very much for the uniformity and consistency of his fowl, outcrossing is the way to go.

WHAT ABOUT BIRDS THAT DIFFER IN THEIR CHARACTERS? Commercial Breeders use outcrossing for the purpose of determining the inheritance of certain characteristics. For instance, they will cross Single-comb White Leghorns with Single-comb Black Leghorns for the purpose of determining the inheritance of white and black. Genes for white are outbred with genes for black. Commercial Breeders also use outcrossing for the purpose of determining the manner in which the two kinds of genes are transmitted from generation to generation, such as crossing a Single-comb with Rose-comb, in which case genes for single comb are outbred with genes for rose comb.

This is significant for American Cockers for the reason that (as breeders of American Gamefowl) we can carry out a similar practice to achieve comparable results. Although it is our goal to always improve uniformity, it's a good idea to know what characteristics our fowl are carrying within their blood, so that we can either perpetuate them or eliminate them.

Note of interest: I'm not saying to infuse outside blood, but to perform a test, one that is separate from the original family, a side breeding of sort. It is important to always discard the contaminated individuals before they make their way into the family or strain.

OUTCROSSING AND HYBRID VIGOR: As long as the breeder uses cocks from the same family line, and takes pains to select vigorous, healthy stock, this plan of breeding has many great advantages. In some respects, outcrossing may have the same effects, although in lesser degree that would follow crossing with a different variety or breed. This is referred to as hybrid vigor, and is what's responsible for the production of most battlefowl today.

Cockers and backyard breeders don't realize that outcrossing does a good job of achieving hybrid vigor without the use of outside blood. If you maintain a number of good inbred lines, within the same family or strain, and you maintain a certain separation over time, such as a good five or six years of separation, when you finally carry out the outcross, hybrid vigor is the result. The best part is that you can use the outcrossed progeny as broodfowl if they should be exceptional.

OUTCROSSING AND THE PRODUCTION OF BATTLEFOWL: In the preceding paragraph, we discussed, briefly the possibility of attaining hybrid vigor through outcrossing. Although, crossbreeding is normally practiced by cockers for the production of battlefowl, great progress can be obtained by the use of this method. Battlefowl are frequently made by crossing say a Hatch with a Roundhead, as well as, other breeds and combinations. Should outcrossing, for the purposes of producing battlefowl, be encouraged? I say of course it should. You can get the same hybrid vigor breeding one line to another related line, as you can by breeding one family to another unrelated family. If the lines are distant enough, say at least five years of separation, it is likely you will see the effects of hybrid vigor.

The breeding together of distant cousins has many advantages: By outcrossing a family for the production of battlefowl, you gain the benefits of both purity of blood and hybrid vigor, without losing the deterioration of genes through mutations and mongrelism. If they prove to be good, they can be used as broodfowl later down the road. You cannot say that when it comes to crosses.

OUTCROSSING EFFECTS ON HATCHABILITY: The gain in constitutional vigor, as a result of outcrossing, has been demonstrated many times, both in plants and animals. Every time I outcross my family of Hatch, I notice an increase in hatchability in both lines.

A FINAL WORD: A word of advice, be very selective when choosing broodfowl, and know the person you're buying your fowl from. Whenever a breeder has developed a strain of gamefowl of especially fine quality, or where he has developed a strain of birds with extraordinary performance capabilities, he should hesitate and think long and hard before he introduces new blood. If he decides to do so, he should use caution as to which method he decides to use.

THE PRACTICE OF GRADING-UP
Improving mongrels through the use of a superior cock

"When two varieties are allowed to cross freely, and one is much more numerous than the other, the former will ultimately absorb the latter. Should both varieties exist in nearly equal numbers, it is probable that a considerable period would elapse before the acquirement of a uniform character; and the character ultimately acquired would largely depend on prepotency of transmission and on the conditions of life; for the nature of these conditions would generally favour one variety more than another, so that a kind of Natural Selection would come into play."

Charles Darwin

WHAT IS GRADING-UP? This is a process most generally used by breeders to improve or modify the qualities and characteristics of "mongrel" fowl, or fowl that are mediocre or mixed, such as seen in multiple crosses. This is achieved by mating inferior hens, repeatedly, to pure or standard-bred broodcocks of superior quality, from another breed, variety, or strain, for successive generations.

Although, this is a process known for changing one breed to another, or a mixed group of fowl into a "purebred" strain, the majority of cockers and backyard breeders would characterize this as a process of "grading by crossing." While crossing is involved, grading-up is more a process of deliberate introgression, which is intended to change the genotype of a breed, variety or strain. With a little patience an existing flock may be improved or changed completely, and for the better or worse, depending on your aim and ability as a breeder.

Grading-up is most commonly practiced in the commercial poultry industry for improving production farm flocks, but does offer excellent value for the modern cocker and backyard breeder in the breeding of American and Old English Gamefowl. It involves the use of high-quality cocks in flocks of average-quality hens. Most cockers and backyard breeders, who buy good cocks and put them with average-quality hens for the purpose of improving the qualities of their fowl are unconsciously grading. The only reason they are not successful is their lack of knowledge of the grading process.

It is also a valuable tool for the exhibitionists that are interested in reviving and saving some of our endangered varieties of fowl as well, such as the Black-Breasted Black-Red American Games, or Gingers, otherwise known as Red Quills. These are fowl that are disappearing fast.

Grading-up may even be applied in an attempt to multiply the numbers of broodfowl rapidly, or to counteract problems due to inbreeding depression, but more often it is an attempt to introduce new characters, which are perceived to be highly desirable. American Games, like many other breeds of poultry, have a high rate of reproduction, and from a small group we can, in a few generations, build up flocks of good size.

The practice of buying broodcocks to bring up the quality of a flock is quite common, and we shall see that, provided we can establish strains of very high quality and purity, the trading and distribution of cocks can be used to bring up the overall quality of all American Games in a very rapid and efficient manner.

THIS IS NOT A NEW IDEA, BUT AN OLD ONE: This is an old system long used by professionals in cattle, horses, swine, sheep, goats, dogs and other farm stock. This practice is an acceptable practice because of its ease of use and relatively low cost. As one of my mentors once told me - *"when it comes to the principles of breeding, the failure to make the most of "grading," is the largest single mistake of all backyard breeders."* The same thing is true in breeding American Games, the failure to make the most of "grading," by the use of purebred broodcocks is the cocker's greatest single mistake. There are many flocks of American Games which can benefit from such a system. Instead, they continue to practice indiscriminate crossbreeding. Every breeding season they buy new cocks from different sources to cross with, never establishing anything special, and most of all, not really benefiting from hybrid vigor, which is the reason for crossing in the first place.

Through the years, the value of grading has been well demonstrated. Its improvement of certain characteristics and traits, such as conformation of body and certain performance capabilities, not to mention color, has shown that it has significant possibilities in improving many gamefowl strains. In four or five generations, by the use of purebred broodcocks, a multicolored mongrel-looking lot of chickens may be bred up to a uniform type, resembling closely the breed to which the broodcock belongs, and having all the attributes of that breed.

HOW IS GRADING-UP USED? As you can plainly see, results such as these demonstrate quite clearly the possibility of thousands of flocks throughout the country being improved through the use of well-bred broodcocks. Grading-up is achieved by an initial cross or outcross to another breed, variety, strain or line, followed by backcrossing to the required percentage of purity. By crossing and backcrossing to purebred cocks of a desired bloodline, in successive generations with hens of a mixed flock, you can achieve ninety-nine percent purity. Traditionally, it takes eight generations to replace ninety-nine percent of the original bloodline. However, I have seen great success in only five or six generations of grading-up.

Although the selection of the cock is extremely important, the pullets or hens should be selected with great care.

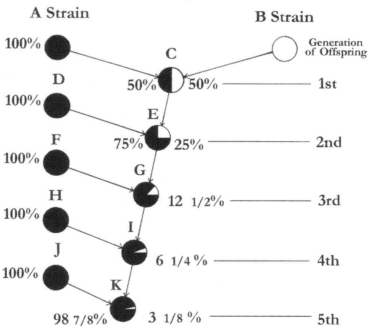

Grading Chart

A Strain   **B Strain**

100%   C   Generation of Offspring

D   50%   50% ——— 1st
100%

E   75%   25% ——— 2nd
F
100%

G   12 1/2% ——— 3rd
H
100%

I   6 1/4 % ——— 4th
J
100%

K
100%   98 7/8%   3 1/8 % ——— 5th

Grading-Up Chart: Improvement is made by the use of improved cocks. In this case strain "A" is a pure bred cock, while strain "B" is a mongrel hen.

Once the initial cross is made, the pullets or hens that are produced should be selected, in each generation, which most nearly resemble hens of the desired bloodline, or the desired breed and variety of the broodcock used, and in turn bred back to another broodcock from the same breed and variety. This is important for this process to be successful. Remember, you are attempting to change the characteristics of the mongrel flock into the ones that are present in the cocks of the desired bloodline.

Repeating this practice for several generations, will increase the proportion of genes of the original purebred cock in its progeny, significantly, and will lead to rapid improvement. In seven or eight years, the fowl can be brought to a point where, for all practical purposes, it is purebred. In fact, the flock will reach a point that it is nearly as good as a purebred one.

As a result, the progeny produced in latter generations will look much like a purebred of the desired bloodline, both in genotype and phenotype. For instance, a breeder may want to change his yard of mixed and crossed-up fowl into a pure "Hatch type bloodline." To achieve this he must have enough pure Hatch type broodcocks to enable him to upgrade his mixed fowl without worrying about inbreeding. Since these Hatch type cocks will be bred with the offspring pullets for several generations, it is important not to breed them to close.

Let's put this into perspective. Let's say you have a flock of hens, no hen is exactly alike. In fact, let's say the hens are all of different strains of American Games. Some are Sweaters, some are Roundheads, and some are Kelso's, and there are some hens that are Aseels. Let's say "Hatch" is the strain of choice, so you purchase the best Hatch cocks you can find. The first breeding with a purebred "Hatch" cock will result in offspring that will carry one-half pure Hatch blood. In succeeding generations this becomes three-quarters, seven-eighths, fifteen-sixteenths, etc. It is easy to see why improvement is so rapid. With each new generation, the proportion of genes of the existing bloodline decreases by half the proportion present in the preceding generation. However, gene replacement slows down with each generation. It takes at least five generations with the desired bloodline to replace ninety-nine percent of the original blood, and, for all practical purposes this will make the upgraded birds a purebred Hatch.

<u>Grade-cocks should never be used for breeding until well established and fixed</u>: During this process all the progeny produced from "Grading-up" are called "Grades." Since they are the result of purebred and mixed breeding, grade-cocks should never be used for breeding until the uniformity of the fowl has been well established and fixed. Nor should cocks of different breeds or varieties be used, as this will destroy all the uniformity obtained, and quickly degrade the fowl once again into mongrel type fowl.

<u>It is important to obtain new blood by returning to the original line</u>: This can also be a form of "topcrossing." Topcrossing is a breeding system whereby the breeder returns to the original line when adding new genetic material. For instance, a three-quarter Hatch/one quarter Sweater cross is a result of topcrossing a Hatch-Sweater crossed hen with another pure Hatch cock. In upgrading, it takes at least four or five, and as many as eight topcrosses with the desired bloodline to consider the upgraded bird as pure. Again, the purity of the cocks must be emphasized to ensure success in the grading-up process.

<u>The important thing in "grading" is to begin with an ideal and stick to it</u>: If the result sought is uniformity of excellence in conformation of body and color of plumage, the breeder should select a strain that is especially good in those areas. Under no condition should this purpose be departed from. If performance is desired, the object will be quickly secured by the use of a broodcock that has a good pedigree in that respect each year.

However, if the broodcock is chosen, as he naturally will be, from a strain of winners, the cocker will have the satisfaction and pleasure of not only achieving greater success as a result of his effort and patience, but also in learning a lesson in the breeding of supreme interest through the gradual realization of his ideals, both in the broodcocks increased performance and in the gradual unfolding of a distinct conformation of body (type) and color of plumage.

THE MECHANICS OF GRADING-UP: Here is a simple explanation of what takes place when we breed high-quality purebred broodcocks to hens of mediocre quality. First we must assume that the cocks we are using are all alike, and that they are pure, homozygous, in respect to the factors that we desire and need. Second, we must also assume that they do not have, and for this reason cannot pass on, any genes that are undesirable.

If we use a cock pure for a particular trait, referenced as (AA), on hens that are lacking in this gene, referenced as (aa), the offspring will all have the trait, but they will be heterozygous (Aa). If this trait is a desirable factor, this will mean an improvement. If we use the same or another purebred cock again, the mating of the pure cock (AA) to impure hens (Aa) will give us fifty percent pures (AA) and fifty percent impures (Aa).

Now, let's see what happens in the next generation. Here there will be two kinds of matings, (AA) x (Aa), which will again give fifty percent pures, and matings of (AA) with (AA), in which all offspring will be pure in respect to this trait, like the father. This means that in a series of repeated matings, with cocks homozygous for a desirable gene, the proportion of birds that are still not pure in respect to that particular factor will be halved.

We must also calculate the same thing in respect to the absence of an undesirable gene. If the hens, which are mated to our good cock, carry it, their chicks will be heterozygous (bb) x (BB) gives (Bb). In the next mating (bb) x (Bb) fifty percent of the offspring will already be pure (bb) like the pure father, and exactly as in the case of a desirable dominant, the proportion of individuals who differ from the constitution of the purebred males will be halved in every subsequent generation.

In other words, repeated matings of cocks of high purity, even when starting with hens that are quite different, will rapidly transform the whole group into a purebred group of the same constitution as that to which those cocks belonged.

WHAT ARE THE REQUIREMENTS OF GRADING-UP? Grading-up can only be accomplished if the bloodline that is to be used will breed true to type. That is, the bloodline must be genetically pure and prepotent, at least as far as the characteristics for which it was developed are concerned, so that when it is bred, its characters are more or less the same characters that appear in its progeny.

The object is not to restore lost vigor or other lost characteristics, nor to establish new breeds, but to improve the flock by means of the sire only. This brings up a good point. Grading nearly always involves the use of purebred broodcocks of high quality on mediocre, mongrel, or a mixed flock of hens. In all actuality, the mating may be made either way, to a purebred hen or a purebred cock, but the cock is generally used for the purebred parent, since he represents half the "flock," as far as progeny are concerned. In other words, a hen can only produce a limited number of eggs in a breeding season, but one purebred cock can fertilize a large number hens. By this method it is possible to raise a practically pure flock from mongrels in just a short time or within a certain number of generations.

In general, a broodcock used for grading should be of the same breed and variety as the hens: In no case should cocks of different breeds or varieties be used in the following years, as such a step will destroy all the uniformity obtained and quickly degrade the fowl again into one of mongrels. Nor should the male offspring (grade-cocks) be used for breeding until the uniformity of the flock has been well fixed.

HOW LONG DOES IT TAKE? In my experience, it only takes a few generations of the right kind of mating to make a very respectable family of fowl. I have found that fowl with exceptional uniformity, with regard to conformation (type) and color of plumage, may be secured from a mongrel flock of mixed types and colors by the use of standard-bred American Game cocks for at least five, and as many as eight successive generations.

For all practical purposes, eight cycles yield pure stock. Most large stock breeders with open registries grant pure status after six generations. In cases where one variety is being graded to another or one strain of a variety or breed is being upgraded by an addition from another strain, far fewer cycles are usually required before all of the offspring can be returned to the regular mating system.

Grading is sometimes criticized as changing the character of a breed. If done properly and carried to at least the fifth generation, the breed's purity is preserved. For some breeders, the process of grading-up a flock is too slow. By securing a few purebred birds, or hatching eggs from purebred birds, the desired end may be attained much more quickly.

A combination of rolling matings and grading can also be used to develop new breeds or varieties by mating half or three-quarter-blood brother to sister, and selecting once birds start to show the desired traits. A combination of these techniques can fix the desirable traits and build up the population.

THE DISADVANTAGES AND DANGERS OF GRADING-UP: The great disadvantage of grading-up is the fact that it is not likely to be closely or continuously followed. Changing the breed or type of broodcock each year will get you nowhere. The weakness of grading, as a practice, lies in its success as a method. For most breeders, once a certain degree of perfection has been reached, grading will most likely be discontinued. This occurs largely for the reason that, in the second or third generation, cocks are produced, which very closely approach standard birds in appearance, the temptation is to use them for breeding purposes. In other words, the failure to make the most of "grading" is due to the occasional or frequent use of "grade-cocks." As soon as the breeder uses a "grade-cock," improvement will cease and retrogression will begin. At any rate, all the ground gained is at least partially lost. The situation is the same in principle where grading is practiced in a purebred flock.

Remember that "grade-cocks" are nothing more than the progeny produced from "grading-up." Since they are the result of purebred and mixed breeding, they should never be used for breeding, as this will destroy all the uniformity obtained, and quickly degrade the fowl once again into mongrel type fowl. Let me emphasize my point, for this is very important to understand. As I mentioned before, a "grade-cock" may have, apparently, all the characteristics of the purebred. He may look so attractive that the breeder is tempted to take a chance and use him for breeding, with the result that improvement is likely to go backward. The "grade-cock" may himself have all the characteristics, but he lacks the ancestry or bloodline necessary to insure the transmission of those qualities, and instead of grading-up, the process is liable to become mongrelizing.

It should also be clearly understood that the broodcock should not only be purebred, but he should have that purity of breeding that extends to all the attributes that are important to American Games. In other words, he should be from a strain that is known to consist of good conformation of body, color of plumage, good temperament, and outstanding performance qualities, not to mention, gameness.

The Black Pearls are a product of Grading.

The object of grading is improvement. The cocks used for grading should be selected from families whose qualities of attributes are higher than that of the flock which is being graded.

What dangers are there to the genetic integrity of the breed? I have been asked this question many times. It is true, grading-up can be dangerous, and for some an unnecessary exercise. The introduction of new alleles risks the loss of the unique and integrated allelic interactions of the breed. This can very well be the outcome if the purpose of grading-up is achieved. If this is the result, it must be recognized that the integrated genome of the breed has been contaminated, and that the changed type represents new allelic combinations. In practice, a new breed will have been created, but at the expense of the original breed. This can be good or bad depending on your goal.

Grading-up has been known to overcome problems that tend to occur due to inbreeding, however, there are times when grading-up will cause the very problems you are trying to avoid. The requirement of backcrossing for eight consecutive generations has the possibility of reestablishing a level of inbreeding almost as high as previously, and the breed will continue to face the same problems. Are the problems real? Experience has shown that many numerically small breeds do not suffer as a result of their genetic bottleneck. The priority must be to prevent introgression from any source.

GRADING-UP IS NOT FOR EVERYONE: It must be clearly understood that "Grading-up" is not recommended for the average cocker, especially the beginner. Grading-up should only be practiced when it is impossible to purchase or keep purebreds of that particular variety.

Also, the availability of hatching eggs (from the top breeders here in the United States) makes it easy to simply replace the entire flock of mongrels with chicks from high quality fowl.

<u>GRADING-UP IS ONLY USED AS A LAST RESORT</u>: It must be clearly understood that grading-up is not a practice that is recommended in preference to purchasing or keeping purebred fowl. The use of certain inbreeding and line-breeding courses is by all means preferable.

Grading-up should only be practiced when it is impossible to obtain or to make the necessary investment for purebred fowl in the improvement of your fowl. In the breeding and raising of American Games, the cost of birds, which are purebred and true to type is relatively small when compared with their superiority over mixed stock. As a rule, it is more reasonable and economical to begin with purebred birds, and if need be, to start with a small number of fowl.

<u>CONCLUSION</u>: The whole system of improving American Games, by introducing cocks of outside sources, stands or falls with the purity and quality of the strain from which the cocks derive. When a breeder succeeds in producing a highly pure, highly competitive strain of gamefowl, he is most likely practicing proper methods of breeding, such as inbreeding, line-breeding, and outcrossing, combined with proper selection and culling. In this case you could bet that practically all undesirable impurities (genetic variability) are bred out. When you have broodfowl such as this, the improvement of families of other breeders can be accomplished through the process of grading.

THE PRACTICE OF BREEDING
BY MEANS OF COMPENSATION
A method of offsetting the weak by strengthening it with the other

The practice of offsetting the weak points of one sex by strengthening it with the other is a common one. This is called "Breeding through Compensation of Characteristics." This practice has been highly studied, and has become a well established and accepted system of breeding. Today it is recognized and used by the commercial poultry industry, and with master breeders all over the world. I feel it is a practice we can all benefit from.

HOW DOES THIS WORK? If you are breeding your family, and after a number of generations you are still not seeing the attributes that you desire, there is a good chance that they are simply not in or apart of their genetic pool. It is at that time that you will need to consider practicing the "breeding through compensation of characteristic" method.

The idea is to select and breed fowl that have certain contrasting characteristics and traits, ones that are missing in one family but exist and are beneficial in another. For instance, let's say that you are working to create a family of Black-Breasted Black-Reds. They have many good attributes, but they lack the conformation of body and seem to be shorter in station than you would like. So you get a cock from another family, such as a Black-Breasted Red, one that has some very good attributes and has the desired conformation of body and is extremely high in station. You breed them. What you will normally get is a portion of the offspring that are low stationed, a portion that are high station and a portion that are of the station that you are looking for. With this type of breeding you will also get a variety of colors as well. Out of those, you select the ones that are the closest to the attributes that you are looking for; breed to those and cull the rest. You will have to select and cull in favor of certain attributes, but this will bring you closer to your goal. You should see favorable results in about five generations.

Contrary to the example I have just given you, try to make sure both birds share as many trait as possible, like a black-breasted black-red with another properly colored black-breasted black-red. Try not to select fowl that will change too many characteristics at one time. Sometimes you may have no choice, such as the example I just gave you. The proper colors may not be available. Or they may have the proper color of plumage but carry with them too many faults.

As long as you are familiar with the laws of genetics, the breeding of fowl that have contrasting characteristics are very beneficial. They can also be used in a beneficial way.

There is one thing to keep in mind and that is, when breeding through the "Compensation of Characteristics" it is the hen that will have the greatest influence on her offspring, especially the stags. She will determine more than ever the quality of her entire family, for she is the strain. Therefore, more defects and faults can be improved on, or eliminated by selecting the proper hen.

Here are just some of the reasons for using this method:
- Used for introducing new traits when creating a family.
- Used for improving characteristics within a family by increasing the number of homozygous traits in a family.
- The benefits of increasing the number of homozygous traits when creating a family by infusions of outside blood carrying the same homozygous trait.

Here are some key points to consider when using this method:
- Make sure the contrasting traits are extreme enough, such as a low station with that of an extremely high station.
- Be mindful of recessives and dominant traits.
- Consider sex-linked traits.

FAILURE TO STRENGTHEN WEAKNESS MAY RESULT IN THE INTENSIFICATION OF THAT WEAKNESS: Once you have selected broodfowl that are as free from defects as possible, it is time to evaluate where they may still be weak. In the "Breeding through Compensation of Characteristics" individuals of the opposite sex should represent, as much as possible, the strength in those areas where weakness are known in their companions. In other words, if one individual or family is known to produce offspring with wry-tails, use an individual or family that is known to have good, strong tails. Failure to do so, may, and usually does, result in the intensification of that weakness, or whatever weakness they may have, and may finally result in the presence of a weakness or defect which becomes quite permanent throughout the entire family of fowl. Once this point has been reached, it can be almost impossible to eliminate the weakness or specific defect.

SOMETIMES IT'S BEST TO REPLACE OR ELIMINATE THE QUESTIONABLE SPECIMEN: If for some reason it is not possible to properly balance the mating, or a particular breeding with a stronger more ideal individual, or select characteristics that will work more in your favor, it is sometimes best to use another mating instead, which will be stronger and more beneficial to the future of the family.

Actually, the best action to take is to eliminate the weakness altogether. By culling individuals that are known to carry a particular weakness or defect you eliminate the problem. Unfortunately, most breeders are not willing to do that. They have an emotional attachment to a particular bird, and their desire is to produce more like them, even though they may have a serious fault or two. Don't fall into this trap! You are better off to cull that bird and find something else, something with no apparent defects, than to continue with something that is less than ideal. The idea is to improve or offset that particular weakness, not to perpetuate it.

SELECTION AND COMPENSATION IN BREEDING: Progressive selection can apply in practice to only a few of the more important characteristics and traits. It is in effect selection for the elimination of faults, which the breeder regards as intolerable. When birds with such faults have been eliminated, what remain will always show considerable variation, and this will be most noticeable in superficial characters.

The practice of continued, careful breeding reduces differences, but due to the fact that it develops the breeder's ability to distinguish slight differences, the proportion of what he considers good broodfowl in his family may not be significantly changed. There is usually a tendency, partly in his fowl and partly in the breeder's selection, to develop a family in the direction of its strongest points. The most effective measure of success in this area is the written standard, competition, and the difficulty or ease of selling future offspring, which are unquestionably weak in any superficial character.

Having eliminated the most "unlike" individuals by progressive selection, the breeder proceeds to make appropriate matings of those he has reserved. Not simply of individual characters, but characters of the pair (cock and hen). His objective is to secure in both sexes, as much as possible, "likeness" to the "type" to be produced (sexual differences of conformation of body and color of plumage, etc.). When the bird of one sex varies from the typical in any character, in order to secure in the other sex the opposite variation in that character, nearly all variations must be small. As a rule, this balancing of opposite tendencies in variation is of little use when the characters considered represent wide variations, for the result of the combination of such characters is likely to give many intermediate grades of blending of characters and only a very few of any desired grade.

The mating of individuals "differing widely" in any character is good practice only when the desired character cannot be secured by breeding together of "like" individuals. The object of the "compensation method" in mating is not to enable the breeder to use for breeding purposes a large proportion of his stock as possible, but to enable him to equalize the tendencies toward variations in the individuals nearest the proper type. A skilled breeder never uses, in his regular matings of an established variety, birds varying noticeably from the type which produces the standard type.

Experience shows that, when the object is to produce uniformity of conformation of body and a high performance average, the most reliable breeders are those individuals with the fewest faults. The "good all-round bird" is almost invariably more valuable as a breeder than the bird that is noticeable for a special excellence of one or a few characters.

THE BLANKET EFFECT: To consistently produce above average fowl, it requires birds that have a good foundation. These are fowl that have been bred tight. They come from bloodlines that are so fixed or locked genetically that they all look, act and perform the same. This is accomplished by the practice of inbreeding and line-breeding. These types of fowl come from breeders that practice "Closed Yard" breeding. In other words, they never introduce outside blood of any kind, especially ones they know nothing about.

For beginners, many times they are forced to buy fowl that are nothing more than hybrid crosses. These are usually battlefowl that someone has sold as pure broodstock. These are fowl that will not produce great offspring, especially after the second or third breeding season. To combat this situation, there are many breeders who practice what is called, "The Blanket Effect." In theory, it works something like this:

1. Bird number one - is from a tightly bred family with a lot of good traits, but has a few minor weaknesses (much like a blanket with a few holes in it).

2. Bird number two - is also from a tightly bred family with a lot of good traits, and also has a few minor weaknesses (like another blanket with a few holes), but they are different than bird number ones.

3. Both birds - are very similar in many in their characteristics and traits, however, one bird is stronger in one or two areas than the other.

4. Here is how it works - one blanket, used by itself, doesn't do a real good job of keeping out the cold, but when you lay the second blanket on top of the first, like the crossing of two distinct but separate families, the strengths of one blanket completes the other, and vice-versa. Or in other words, the desirable trait of one covers the undesirable traits in the other, and vice-versa.

Although this theory appears sound, it is speculation at best. There is much to debate on its practicality and apparent legitimacy, especially when you consider all the variables, such as dominant and recessive traits, traits that are incomplete or partially dominant, sex-linked traits, sex-limited traits, complimentary traits, and quantitative traits, not to mention random genes, additive genes, interacting genes, modifying genes and lethal genes. Some defects are dominant while others are recessive, by mistake, you could very well be perpetuating the very trait you were hoping to eliminate.

If you decide to practice the "Blanket Effect," make sure that you take all of these possibilities into consideration. The idea is to predict, with great certainty, the result or outcome of your offspring, and not by guesswork or speculation.

EPILOGUE

"The road to happiness lies in two simple principles: find what it is that interests you and that you can do well, and when you find it put your whole soul into it, every bit of energy and ambition and natural ability you have."
John D. Rockefeller

START RIGHT NOW: Through this book, I have done my best to give you the principles and the tools that you need to create or maintain a strain of high quality American Games, and to preserve them for future generations. They have worked for me and for countless others, and they can work for you as well. But this is where the information, motivation, and inspiration ends and the perspiration begin. You and you alone are responsible for taking the actions needed to create the fowl of your dreams. Nobody else can do it for you.

You have all of the ability and the resources you need, within the pages of this book, to start right now and eventually create the fowl that you want. I know you can do it. You know you can do it. So go out there and do it! It's a lot of hard work, but a lot of fun as well. And remember to enjoy the journey!

THE GREATEST GIFT IS THE GIFT OF KNOWLEDGE: Most master breeders did not learn these principles in F.F.A., 4-H, or at the shows, and only a few of them learned them at home from their fathers and grandfathers. These are principles that have been passed down from person to person by mentors, friends and acquaintances, and more recently, in books and seminars. Now you have the core of those principles in your hands.

I want to encourage you to read this book over and over several times. Underline the things that are most important to you and reread what you have underlined. You will discover that with each rereading, you will not only reinforce what you already know but you will also discover something new, some principle or law that perhaps didn't register during the first time through. It takes a while to absorb and assimilate all of these principles of breeding. Make sure to give yourself that time.

The greatest gift you can give is the gift of knowledge: What could be more helpful than to free a person from their limited beliefs and old wives tales, and help them to create the fowl that they truly desire from what they already have in their yard. You'll be amazed at how thoroughly you can change someone's thinking and their way of doing things, simply by providing the essential facts, which all master breeders know and practice.

So many cockers and backyard breeders currently live in a state of objectionable acceptance or hopelessness in relation to their limited beliefs and what they can expect from their fowl. It is time to turn that around. We all have the power within us to create the fowl we want. It must be earned through hard work, and part of that work is first learning, and then putting what we have learned into practice using time-tested principles that are guaranteed to bring about our desired results.

HOW WE LEARN: One of the most fascinating and mysterious properties we humans have is the capacity to learn. We have the ability to change in response to experience and to retain that knowledge throughout our lifetime. In fact, the ability to learn and to establish new memories is fundamental to our very existence; we rely on memory to engage in effective actions, to understand the words we read, to recognize the objects we see, to decode the auditory signals representing speech, and even to provide us with a personal identity and sense of self.

However, people learn in different ways. And no one has a better learning style than anyone else. Some expert's say there are many different learning styles, such as **Listening learners**, **Seeing learners**, and **touch or experience learners**.

It's simple really. Think about one of life's earliest lessons, often taught by our mothers: "**The Stove Can Burn You.**" Listening learners heard their mother, they believed the information she gave them, and never touched a stove. Seeing learners watched their mother touch the stove, noticed what happened and never touched it. And experience learners touched the stove; but only once!

Studies have shown that we learn by a multiple of ways, such as reading, hearing, seeing, discussing, and by experience. Learning also occurs in situations, activities; it is social and reflective as well.

Here are the percentages of how we learn:
- 10% of what we **READ**
- 20% of what we **HEAR**
- 30% of what we **SEE**
- 50% of what we **SEE** and **HEAR**
- 70% of what is **DISCUSSED** with **OTHERS**
- 80% of what is **EXPERIENCED PERSONALLY**
- 95% of what we **TEACH TO SOMEONE ELSE**

Notice, the best way to learn is to teach others. As they say: "Tell me, I forget. Show me, I remember. Involve me, I understand.

TEACHING THESE PRINCIPLES TO OTHERS: One of the most powerful ways to learn anything is to teach it to others. It forces you to make clear of your ideas, face inconsistencies in your own thinking, simplify and organize what you have learned, and more significantly, it forces you to walk your talk. But most importantly, it requires you to read, study, and speak about the information over and over again. The resulting repetition reinforces your own learning.

One of the great benefits to me, in researching and teaching these principles of breeding is that I am constantly reminding myself about the principles, and how important it is to use them in the perpetuation of high quality fowl.

Think about whom you might teach these principles to: Could you teach a seminar at your local club? Offer a class at the local feed store? You don't have to be a master of these principles to lead a discussion group. You just have to be willing to initiate a discussion of the principles. This book will teach you everything you need to know to lead a productive discussion, and help others in putting these principles into practice.

Imagine if everyone practiced these principles when breeding their fowl. The results would be extraordinary. And you could be the person who makes that happen. If not you, then who? If not now, then when? I am always available to help my readers succeed, and I will perform seminars whenever asked, but it takes everyone to participate, in some way, for all of us to see desirable results.

WHEN YOU LIFT UP OTHERS, THEY WILL LIFT UP YOU: And here's another major benefit, the more you help others succeed in life, the more they will want to help you. You might wonder why mentors are so successful. It's because they have helped so many people get what they want. People naturally support those who have supported them. The same will be true for you.

One of my mentors once taught me - "to be a student to those above me, a teacher to those below me, and a fellow traveler and helpmate to those on the same level." That's good advice for all of us.

WE NEAR THE END OF OUR JOURNEY: Our journey together is about to end. You must travel the remainder of the distance alone. If you have followed the information I have given you, success is certain, for you are in possession of the great Master-Key to breeding. This Master-Key will unlock the gate to creating the greatest fowl the world has ever seen.

Congratulations! You now have the knowledge to perpetuate high quality American Games that can compete with the best and that can stand the rigors of time. And remember, if you share with others what you have learned, then this book will not be an ending, it will be the beginning of a new era, both for you and for American Games.

A FINAL WORD

I would like to thank you for reading my articles and books. It is my sincere hope that this material will help you in breeding higher quality fowl. For those who have purchased my books and eBooks, the support has been truly wonderful. It has inspired me to continue my writing and to produce more books and articles of the finest quality.

I would like to end this book by sharing the following thought with you:

In a time when our future as American Cockers is uncertain, one thing remains the same, American Gamefowl must endure the test of time. They must survive the hardships of life's trials and tribulations, passing on their proud heritage and legacy for the benefit of all Americans and future generations of cockers. We must not allow these birds to follow the fate of the dinosaurs.

As I have said many times, "American Games are our past, our present and our future. If we lose them, we lose a big part of ourselves." We cease to be American Cockers!

As far as I'm concerned, the survival of American Games is more important than the sport itself. The love for the bird must exceed our desire of the fight. Without a commitment of excellence, an essential and historical breed of fowl is doomed. Can you imagine a world without gamefowl in it? It will be a sad day, not only for us, but for the entire world.

Remember, once they are gone, they are gone forever! Extinction is not an option!

Hope you enjoyed the book, and thanks again for reading it.
Yours truly, Kenny Troiano
Fellow Cocker and Gamefowl Enthusiast
www.maximustroypublications.com

BIBLIOGRAPHY
AND RECOMMENDED READING

1. A Study of "Old English Game", by David Holden 2010
2. ABC's of Poultry Genetics, by Dr. W.F. Hollander, Ph.D. 1989"
3. ABC's of Poultry Raising, by J. H. Florea 1977
4. All Breeds of Poultry, by Frank L. Platt 1925
5. American Poultry Culture, by R.B. Sando 1912
6. American Standard of Perfection 2001 Edition
7. American Standard of Perfection, 1905 Edition
8. American Standard of Perfection, 1927 Edition
9. American Standard of Perfection, 1938 Edition
10. American Standard of Perfection, 1942 Edition
11. Animal Scam – The Beastly Abuse of Human Rights, by Kathleen Marquardt 1993
12. Approved Practices in Poultry Production, by Biddle and Juergenson 1963
13. Backyard Poultry Keeping, by John C. Taylor 1944
14. Backyard Poultry Raising, by John F. Adams 1977
15. Baldwin's Book of Modern Game Bantams, by John P. Baldwin 1936, 1988
16. Biology, by Raven, Johnson, Losos, Mason and Singer 2008
17. Biology, by Sylvia S. Mader 2004
18. British Gamecocks and Cockers of the 18th & 19th Centuries, by John Palmer
19. British Poultry Standard, by C. G. May 1971
20. Charles Darwin – On Evolution, by Glick and Kohn
21. Charles Darwin – on Natural Selection 1809-1882
22. Charles Darwin – On the Origin of Species, by Charles Darwin
23. Charles Darwin – The Concise Story of an Extraordinary Man, by Tim M. Berra
24. Charles Darwin – the Power of Place, by Janet Browne 2002
25. Charles Darwin – The Voyage of the Beagle
26. Charles Darwin – Voyaging, by Janet Browne 1995
27. Chicken Raising Made Easy, by Paul W. Chapman 1943
28. Chicken Tractor, by Andy Lee and Pat Foreman 1994, 2002
29. Cock Fighting All Over the World, by C. A. Finsterbusch 1929
30. Cockfighting and Game Fowl, by Herbert Atkinson 1938
31. Cocking Science, by Old Family 1939
32. Commercial Poultry Farming, by Charles and Stuart 1950
33. Commercial Poultry Raising, by H. Armstrong Roberts 1918 and 1920
34. Darwin – discovering the tree of life, by Niles Eldredge 2005
35. Darwin's Century – Evolution and the Men Who Discovered it, by Loren Eiseley 1958
36. Disease and Enemies of Poultry, by Pearson 1897
37. Disease and Parasites of Poultry, by Barger, Card and Pomeroy 1958
38. Disease of Poultry, by Biester and Schwarte 1948
39. Disease of Poultry, by Calnek and Barnes 1991
40. Disease of Poultry, by Leonard Pearson 1897
41. Egg Farming, by Willard C. Thompson 1936
42. Evolution – The Triumph of an Idea, by Carl Zimmer 2001
43. Evolution 101, by Randy Moore and Janice Moore 2006
44. Exhibiting Poultry for Pleasure and Profit, by Loyl Stromberg 1978, 1999
45. Eyewitness Evolution, by Linda Gamlin 1993 and 2009
46. Farm Poultry Production, by Card and Henderson 1948
47. Feeding Poultry, by Gustave F. Heuser 1955
48. First Lessons in Poultry Keeping, by John H. Robinson 1907
49. Free-Range Poultry, by Katie Their 1990

50. Game Fowls - Their Origins and History, by J. W. Cooper, M.D. 1869
51. Game Strains Illustrated, by Tim Johnson 1997
52. Genetics and Animal Breeding, by Oliver and Boyd 1968
53. Genetics and Evolution of the Domestic Fowl, by Lewis Stevens 1991
54. Genetics of the Fowl, by F.B. Hutt 1949
55. Glorified Dinosaurs – The origin and Evolution of Birds, by Luis M. Chiappe 2007
56. Glover's Breeders' and Cockers' Guide, by F. R. Glover
57. Gregor Mendel - And the Roots of Genetics, by Edward Edelson 1999
58. Gregor Mendel - Planting the Seed of Genetics, by Simon Mawer 2006
59. Gregor Mendel - Father of the Science of Genetics, by Harry Sootin 1959
60. H. Flock's Revised Breeder's and Cockers' Guide 1904
61. H. Flock's Revised Breeder's and Cockers' Guide 1924
62. Handbook of Bird Biology, by Cornell Lab of Ornithology – Editors: Podulka, Rohrbaugh, and Bonney
63. Handbook of Poultry Nutrition, by W. Ray Ewing 1941
64. Handling and Nursing the Game Cock, by A.C. Dingwall
65. Harrison Weirs - Game Fowl 1988
66. Histories of Game Strains, by Grit and Steel 1940
67. Histories of Game Strains, by Grit and Steel 1955
68. History of Cockfighting, by George Ryley Scott 1983
69. History of Game Strains, by W. T. Johnson and Frank Holcomb 1984
70. How to Build a Dinosaur – the new science of reverse evolution, by Jack Horner 2009
71. How to Read Darwin, by Mark Ridley 2005
72. How to Run a One-Man Poultry Farm, by Haydn S. Pearson 1947
73. Johnson's Breeders' and Cockers' Guide, by W. T. Johnson
74. Judging Poultry for Production, by Rice, Hall and Marble 1930
75. Kasco Poultry Guide 1943
76. Lewis Wright & His Poultry, by Dr. Joseph Batty 2001
77. Livestock and Poultry Production, by Bundy, Diggins and Christensen 1954
78. Manual of Ornithology – Avian Structure and Function, by Noble S. Proctor and Patrick J. Lynch 1993
79. Merck Veterinary Manual 1998
80. Modern Biology, by Holt, Rinehart and Winston 2002
81. Modern Breeding of Game Fowl, by Narragansett 1982
82. Modern Poultry Farming, by Louis M. Hurd 1944
83. Old English Game Colour Guide, by Dr. J. Batty 2000
84. Old Poultry Breeds, by Fred Hams 2004
85. Oriental Gamefowl, by Horst W. Schmudde 2005
86. Ornithology, by Frank B. Gill 2007
87. Poultry Behavior and Welfare, by Appleby, Mench, and Hughes 2004
88. Poultry Breeding – Genetics and Systems of Breeding, by G.E. Mann, M.A. London 1960
89. Poultry Breeding – Theory and Practice, by Hagedoorn and Sykes 1953
90. Poultry Breeding and Genetics – Edited by R.D. Crawford 1990
91. Poultry Breeding and Management, by James Dryden 1943
92. Poultry Breeding and Management, by William W. Broomhead
93. Poultry Breeding Applied, by Hays and Klein 1952
94. Poultry Breeding, by Morley A. Jull 1940
95. Poultry Colour Guide, by Dr. J Batty and Charles Francis 1979
96. Poultry Craft, by John H. Robinson 1911
97. Poultry Culture – Sanitation and Hygiene, by B.F. Kaupp
98. Poultry Culture, by Dr. Hess and Clark 1930
99. Poultry Enterprises Revised, by Dickinson and Lewis 1946
100. Poultry for Home and Market, by James B. Cooper 1944
101. Poultry Genetics, Breeding and Biotechnology – Edited by Muir and Aggrey 2003

102. Poultry Guide Post, by Philip R. Park 1912
103. Poultry Handbook, by Rudolph Seiden 1947, 1949
104. Poultry Health Handbook, by L. Dwight Schwartz, D.V.M. 1977
105. Poultry Husbandry, by Morley A. Jull 1938
106. Poultry Keeping Today, by Walter Brett
107. Poultry Management, by Heuser, Hall and Bruckner 1952
108. Poultry Oddities - History, Folklore, by Loyl Stomberg 1992
109. Poultry Production in the South, by King and Chesnutt 1948
110. Poultry Production, by Bundy and Diggins 1960
111. Poultry Production, by Card and Nesheim 1972
112. Poultry Production, by Leslie E. Card, Ph.D. 1952, 1953, 1956
113. Poultry Production, by Lippincott and Card 1946
114. Poultry Science and Practice, by Roy H. Waite 1929
115. Poultry Science and Practice, by Winter and Funk 1956
116. Poultry Science, by Ensminger 2004
117. Poultry Shows and Showing, by Dr. Joseph Batty 1999
118. Practical Poultry Breeding, by Don C. Warren 1953
119. Practical Poultry Keeping, by Dr. Joseph Batty 2000
120. Practical Poultry Management, by Rice and Botsford 1949
121. Practical Poultry Production, by Lamon and Kinghorne 1920
122. Principles and Practice of Poultry Culture, by John H. Robinson 1912
123. Productive Poultry Husbandry, by Harry R. Lewis 1913, 1914
124. Profitable Poultry Production, by M.G. Kains 1910
125. Raising Poultry Successfully, by Will Graves 1985
126. Raising Poultry the Modern Way, by Leonard S. Mercia 1990
127. Raising Stags for Sport and Pleasure, by John Batty
128. Rare Poultry of Ashe, by Rex Woods 1976
129. Roberts Commercial Poultry Raising, by H. Armstrong Roberts 1947
130. Sport in the Olden Time, by Sir Walter Gilbey, Bart. 1975
131. Starting Poultry Keeping, by The staff at Poultry World
132. Starting Right with Poultry, by G. T. Klein 1972
133. Storey's Guide to Raising Chickens, by Gail Damerow 2010
134. Storey's Guide to Raising Poultry, by Leonard S. Mercia 2001
135. Success with Hens, by Robert Joos 1914, 1928
136. Successful Poultry Management, by Morley A. Jull 1943
137. Taking Wing, by Pat Shipman, 1998
138. The American Game Fowl Standards, by Anthony Saville 2006
139. The Art of Cockfighting, by Arch Ruport 1949
140. The Art of Faking Exhibition Poultry, by R Scott, George 1934
141. The Autobiography of Charles Darwin, 1809 - 1882
142. The Back Yard Flock, by Mike Strecker 1993
143. The Behavior of the Domestic Fowl, by D.G.M. Wood-Gush 1971
144. The Best of "Fulldrop", by E.T. Piper 1989
145. The Best of Narragansett 1985
146. The Breeding and Management of Fighting Cocks, by Everard Simpson 1781
147. The Business Hen, by H. W. Collingwood 1892
148. The Call of the Hen, by American Poultry School 1925
149. The Chicken Book, by Smith and Daniel 1975
150. The Chicken Health Handbook, by Gail Damerow 1994
151. The Cocker, by Sketchley 1814
152. The Cockers Handbook, by Marshall Beard 1998
153. The Complete Book of Poultry-Keeping, by Stuart Banks 1979
154. The Descent of Man, by Charles Darwin
155. The Evolution of Darwinism, by Timothy Shanahan

156. The Family Poultry Flock, by Lee Schwanz 1987
157. The Game Cock - From the shell to the pit, by George. W. Means 1922, 1929
158. The Game Fowl, by P. Proud 1814
159. The Greatest Show on Earth, by Richard Dawkins 2009
160. The History of Cockfighting, by George Ryley Scott 1975
161. The King of Fowls, by Mark Marshall 1988
162. The Mating and Breeding of Poultry, by Lamon and Slocum 1927
163. The Mistaken Extinction – Dinosaur Evolution and the Origin of Birds, by Dingus and Rowe, 1998
164. The Modern Cocker - Books #1, 2, and 3, by Roy "String King" Bingham
165. The Monk in the Garden "Gregor Mendel", by Robin Marantz Henig 2000
166. The Old English Game Fowl, by Herbert Atkinson 1924
167. The Origins and Evolutions of Birds, by Alan Feduccia, 1999
168. The Poultry Book, by Harrison Weir 1912
169. The Poultry Guide, by Kaupp and Surface 1940
170. The Poultry Profit Guide, by John P. Weeks 1952
171. The Rise of Birds, by Sankar Chatterjee 1997
172. The Royal Pastime of Cockfighting, by R. H. 1709
173. The Scientific Breeding of Gamefowl, by Floyd Gurley 1992
174. The Scientific Feeding of Chickens, by Harry W. Titus Ph.D. 1949
175. The Theory and Practice of Breeding to Type, by C.J. Davies
176. The Variation of Animals and Plants Under Domestication – Volume One, by Charles Darwin 1868
177. The Variation of Animals and Plants Under Domestication – Volume Two, by Charles Darwin 1868
178. Understanding Modern Game, by Dr. J. Batty and James P. Bleazard 1988
179. Understanding Old English Game, by Joseph Batty 1976
180. What Darwin Didn't Know, by Geoffrey Simmons, M.D. 2004
181. Who Was Charles Darwin? by Deborah Hopkinson 2005

GAMEFOWL BREEDERS MANUAL AND COCKERS GUIDE

Chronicles of Kenny Troiano

Volume One

A Practical Dissertation of American Gamefowl and their History

A GREAT BOOK FOR THE PROGRESSIVE COCKER

This "Limited Edition" book is a collection of articles written by Kenny Troiano, for Magazines such as "The Gamecock," the "Grit & Steel, and the Poultry Press," a project that has spanned over five years. This book has 326 pages of good information, ranging from Selection to Breeding to Culling. It also covers subjects such as Natural Incubation, Chick Care, Health Care, Showing, and of their incredible History. Not only is this book perfect for the beginner, but enlightening for the veteran cockers as well.

This book is well illustrated with more than 150 black/white and color pictures, many drawn by artist Diane Jacky. Diane is one of the world's foremost living artists of poultry and pigeon standards. We feel she has out done herself with her work on American Games.

EDITOR OF THE GAMECOCK MAGAZINE
J.C. Griffiths

We received a copy of "The Gamefowl Breeders Manual And Cockers Guide" by Kenny Troiano, and find it has many topics on some of the problems facing the Cockers of today with a full explanation and drawings showing how to do many of the things discussed in the book. He not only tells you how but includes many excellent drawings showing you how. We believe the drawings and pictures to be superior to anything we have seen in the past. We believe this book contains something for everyone regardless of whether a beginner or a pro. We would definitely recommend this book to every cocker. This is the first book to come along in several years that definitely has the cocker at heart in the articles contained in it, and most important, it is from a cocker today who faces the problems of today with some very definite answers.

PRESIDENT OF THE AMERICAN GAME FOWL SOCIETY
Mr. Anthony Saville

The excellent detailed information Kenny Troiano has been able to create, in the form of his book, is the opportunity for all lovers of American Game Fowl to glean further knowledge to advance the breed into the next generation. If anybody is going to be involved with American Game Fowl, this book will ensure that the very best information advances their aspirations to keep the "Very Best Specimens," saving individuals invaluable time and effort. This book is the result of Kenny's many years of "Hands On" education of breeding, feeding, conditioning and raising American Game Fowl. If I was starting out with American Game Fowl today I would have loved to have the opportunity to learn all the information from this fine book. My copy of this book will be one of my most treasured possessions. Without any fear of contradiction, I believe that this book is the finest book on American Game Fowl ever written.

If you have a passion for gamefowl, or know someone who does, this book is for you. The subject matter is the same used by many of the greatest cockers, and used to create the best bloodlines.

Order Your Copy Today!

P.O. Box 2727

Ramona, CA. 92065

www.maximustroypublications.com

ALSO AVAILABLE IN EBOOK VERSION